FROM A SQUARE TO A CIRCLE

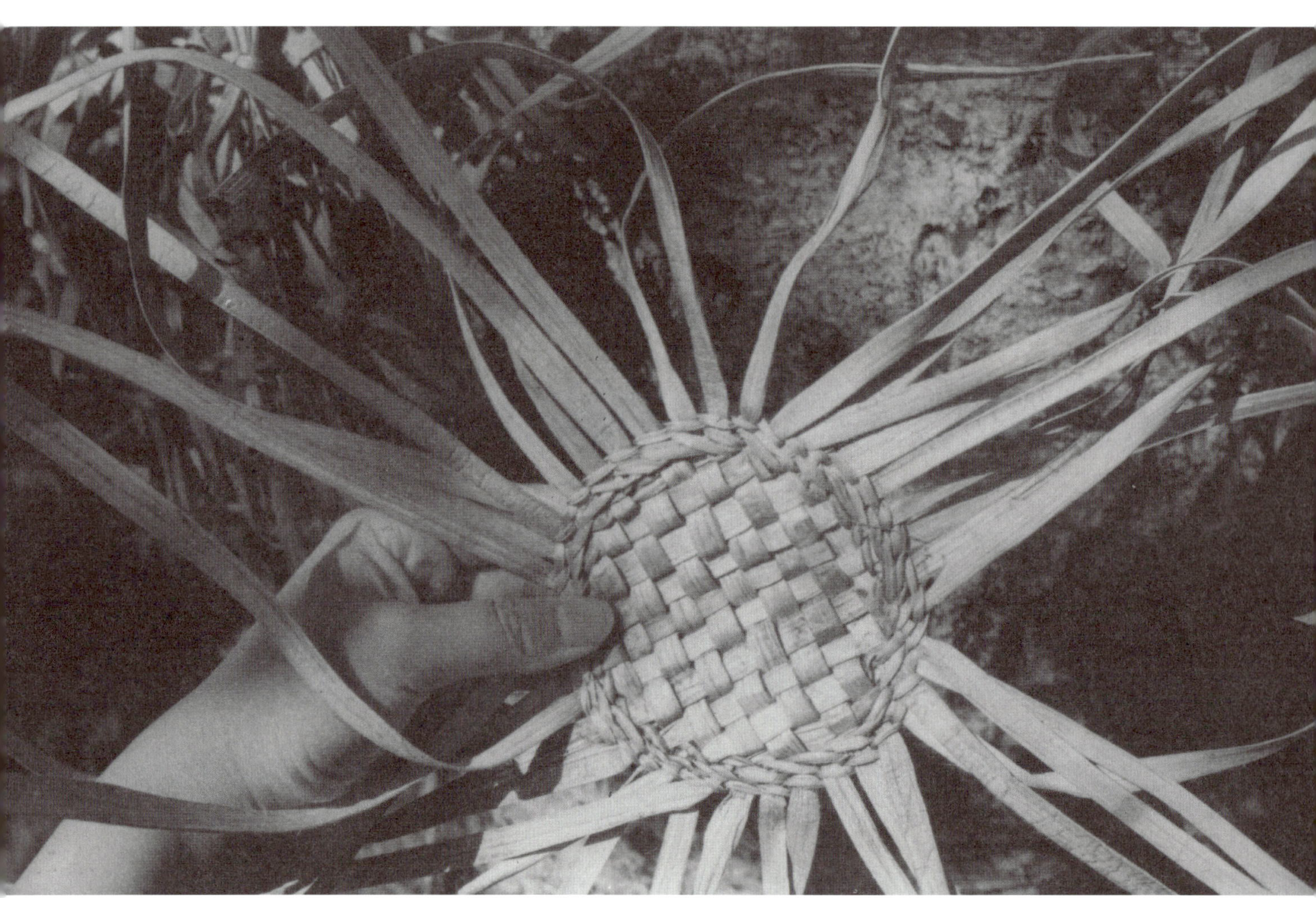

From a Square to a Circle

Haida Basketry—Delores Churchill's Memories of Learning to Weave

Delores Churchill

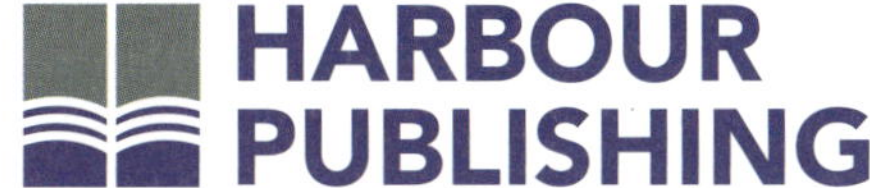

2 3 4 5 — 28 27 26 25

Harbour Publishing Co. Ltd.
P.O. Box 219, Madeira Park, BC, V0N 2H0
www.harbourpublishing.com

Cover and text design by Libris Simas Ferraz / Onça Publishing
Front cover photo by Hulleah J. Tsinhnahjinnie
Printed and bound in South Korea

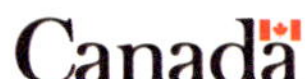

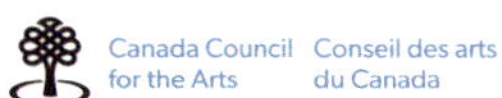

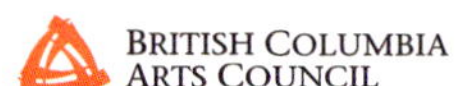

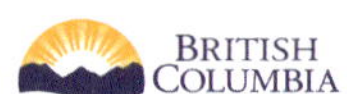

Harbour Publishing acknowledges the support of the Canada Council for the Arts, the Government of Canada, and the Province of British Columbia through the BC Arts Council.

Library and Archives Canada Cataloguing in Publication

Title: From a square to a circle : Haida basketry / Delores Churchill.
Names: Churchill, Delores, author.
Description: Includes bibliographical references.
Identifiers: Canadiana (print) 20240416945 | Canadiana (ebook) 20240416988 | ISBN 9781990776854 (softcover) | ISBN 9781990776861 (EPUB)
Subjects: LCSH: Haida baskets. | LCSH: Basket making—British Columbia. | LCSH: Churchill, Delores. | LCSH: Haida artists—British Columbia—Biography. | LCGFT: Autobiographies.
Classification: LCC E99.H2 C48 2024 | DDC 746.41/208997280711—dc23

In memory of my mother, Ilst'ayaa (Selina Victoria Harris Adams Peratrovich G̱aw Git'ans); my grandmothers, Kuujuuhl (Edith George); Ilskyalee (Jane Harris Davis); and Naanii Skujuus (Elizabeth Coode); and to the true Masters—our ancestral weavers.

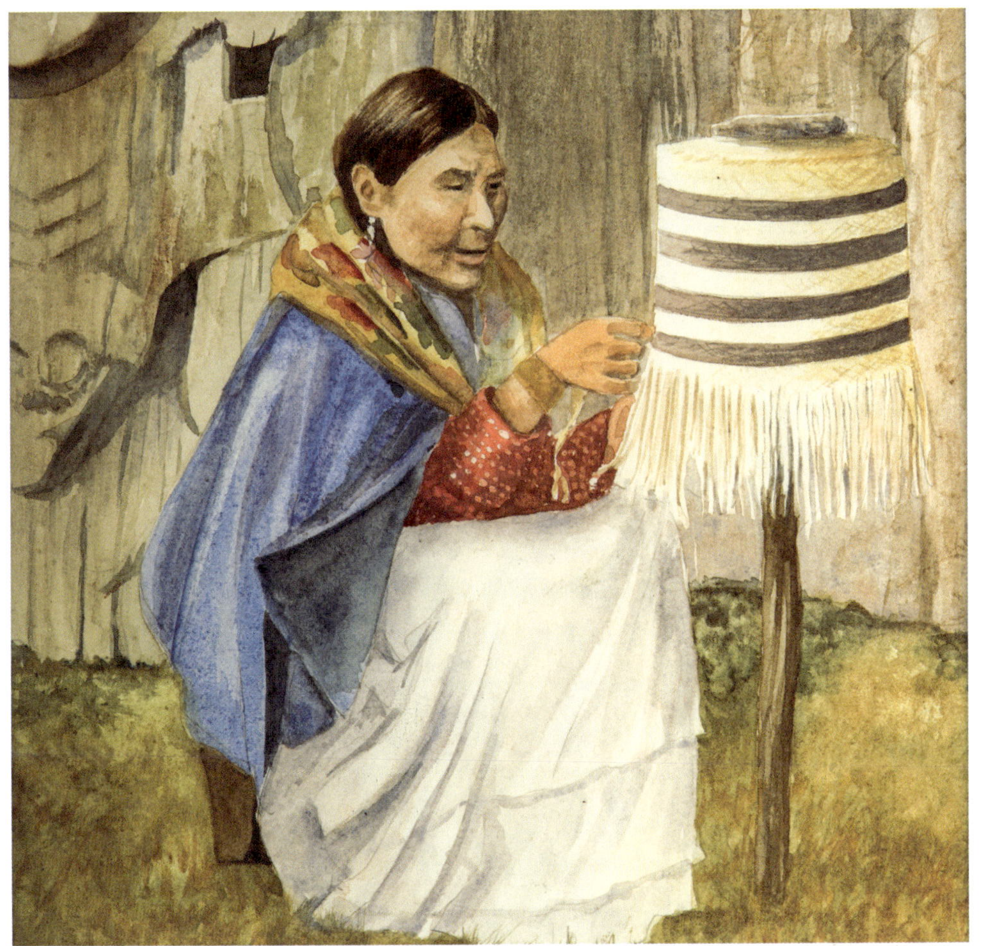

This is Delores's cousin, Haida artist Freda Diesing's grandmother, from Masset, weaving a spruce root Potlatch Ring basket in 1897. Freda inherited the gold bracelet shown. Watercolour painting based on photo taken by Edward P. Allen in 1897. *Evelyn Vanderhoop*

> "Basket weaving is the most prized heritage that we receive from our ancestors. These ancient ones continue to teach us for the trees, fire, water, animals, land and ourselves… Listen! Do you feel their spirit? It is in the air around us."

—DELORES CHURCHILL, First Peoples Fund, 2003 Community Spirit Award

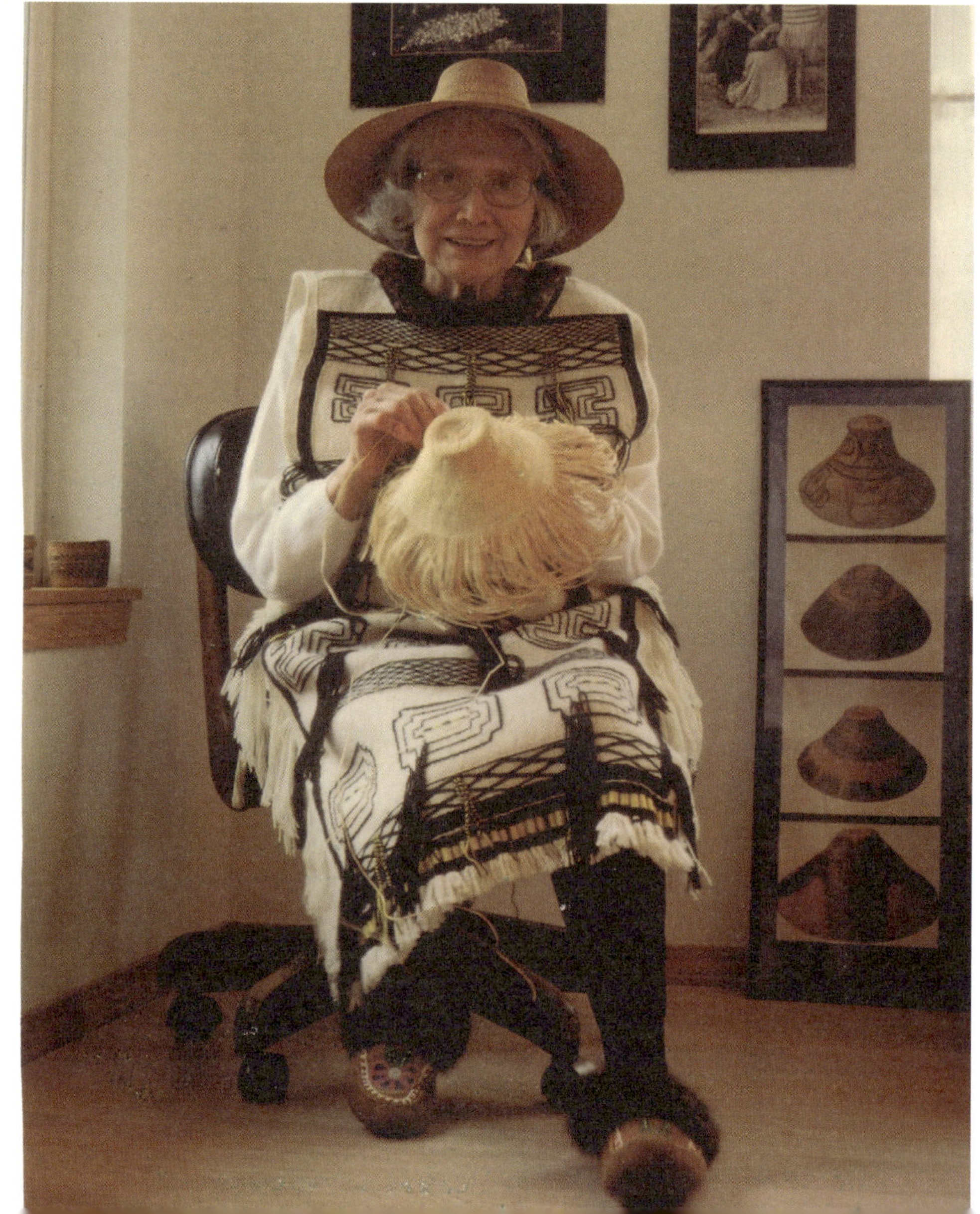

Delores's spruce root hat made by her sister-in-law Primrose Adams, in payment for teaching her how to weave and attach the potlatch rings to a spruce root hat. The Ravenstail tunic she is wearing is the first made by Delores for her grandson Justin Burns. Delores works on a "Long Ago Person Found" dajangee (hat) replication in progress. *Hulleah J. Tsinhnahjinnie*

Table of Contents

Watercolour portrait of Delores Churchill, the artist's mother, as a gift on her eightieth birthday. *Evelyn Vanderhoop*

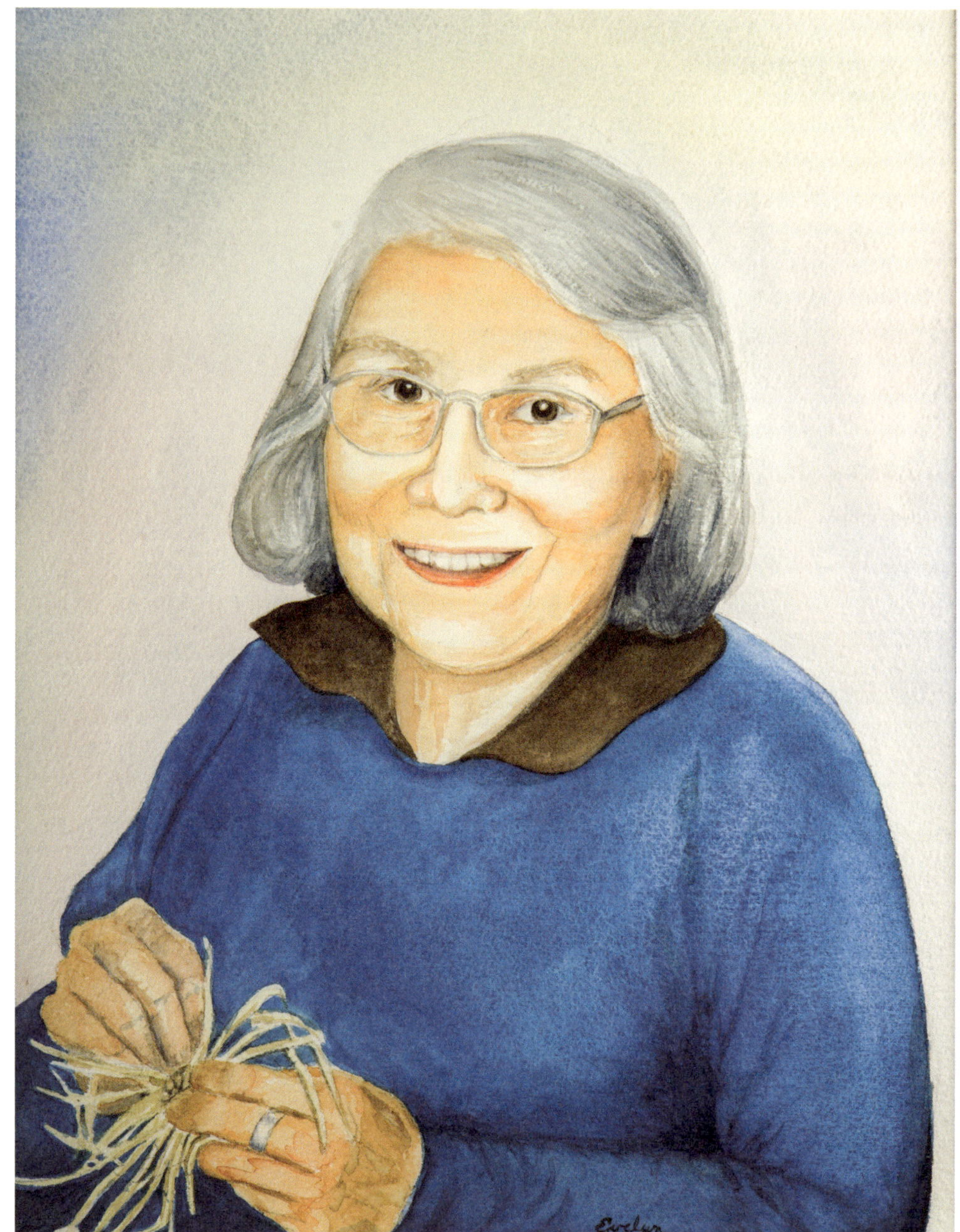

“I was a bookkeeper for years, then I became momentarily insane and became an artist.”

DELORES CHURCHILL

Foreword

Iskyalas, Delores Churchill, was born October 23, 1929, in G̱utaawaas (Old Massett), Haida Gwaii, to Selina Victoria Harris Adams Peratrovich G̱aw Git'ans (Ilst'ayaa), of the G̱aw Git'ans Gitanee Eagle Clan, and Alfred Adams (Skilgyaans), of the Kyanuusalii Raven Clan.

Delores's life has gone through great change. Like her mother, she did not attend residential school. She grew up having the privilege of speaking the beautiful language of X̱aad Kíl (Haida language) and following the Haida annual harvesting cycle. Her early experiences provided her knowledge of Haida history and lifeways and gave her an understanding of the Haida relationship to the land, to others and to our place within the universe.

During her childhood, a few utilitarian weavings were still in use. However, after the Second World War, the majority of Haida children were sent to boarding schools where Indigenous activities and language were frowned upon. They no longer had the opportunity to learn from the elders. Younger women came home and were not interested in learning to weave. Delores's mother wove but Delores took no interest in weaving until she was an adult.

After raising a family and building a career as the Ketchikan General Hospital assistant to the controller, Delores retired at the age of

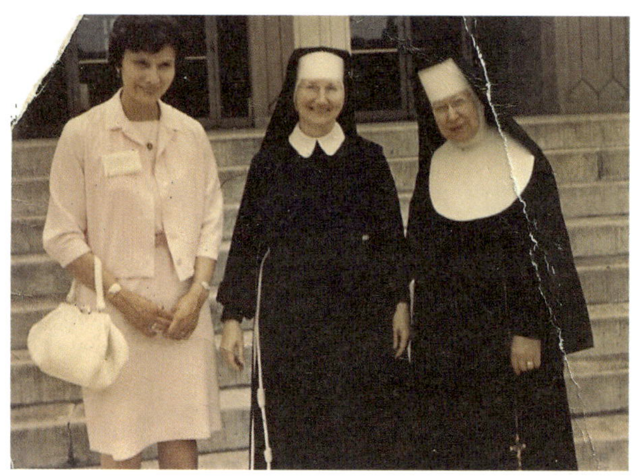

Delores (left) attended the University of Chicago at 36, where she completed courses in hospital accounting. Here, she is standing with the Catholic Sisters of Peace. *Churchill family*

forty-five to assist her mother in the teaching of Haida basketry. With a mischievous twinkle in her eyes, Delores explains, "I was a bookkeeper for years. Then I became momentarily insane and became an artist."

After Selina passed away in 1984, Delores took on her mother's responsibilities as the weaving teacher. Since that time Delores has carried on Selina's legacy and taught hundreds of people how to weave.

At the time Selina began to teach, the Tlingit basketry art form was also at the same risk of loss as Haida weaving. This knowledge drove Delores to learn from Tlingit and Tsimshian elder weavers as well.

Delores honours her weaving teachers by passing this knowledge on to the next generation. The Sealaska Heritage Foundation, a regional Native non-profit organization founded to support the culture and arts of the Haida, Tlingit and Tsimshian people of Southeast Alaska, sponsored a weaving workshop from 2004–06 in Hoonah, Alaska, with financial support from the Administration for Native Americans. This workshop provided Delores with the opportunity to give back Tlingit weaving knowledge to the Hoonah people.

The first wool weaving instructions that Delores and her second daughter Evelyn Vanderhoop took were with Cheryl Samuel. Cheryl spent years researching textile weaving of the Northwest Coast and published her findings in *The Chilkat Dancing Blanket* (1982) and *The Raven's Tail* (1987). At a time when young people were not learning textile weaving, Cheryl had the desire and wherewithal to study in museums and to work with the last of the elder weavers, including one of Delores's Tlingit teachers, the late Jenny Thlunaut.

Delores's passion for this form of weaving is best described in her own words: "When I began learning to weave wool from Cheryl, I became obsessed. I breathlessly said to Cheryl, 'I can't eat. I can't sleep. It is like I am in love!'"

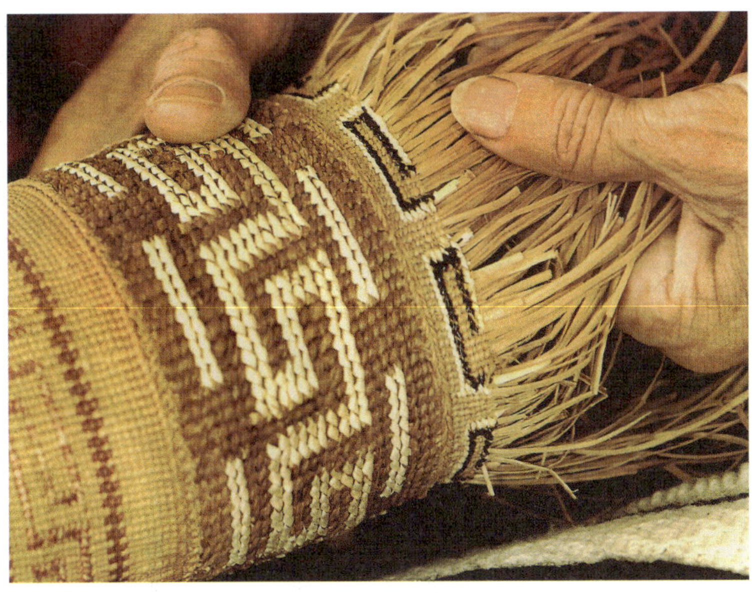

Delores is weaving a sample of Haida, Tsimshian and Tlingit basketry for use in her classes. *Tom Pich*

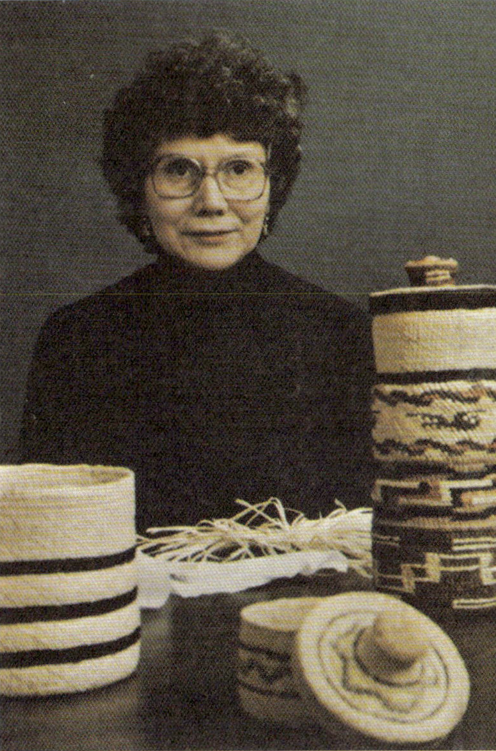

Delores is photographed here with her baskets. The baskets on the left and centre include the Haida Potlatch Ring Band. The tall basket is a sample of four Nations' weaving styles. *Larry McNeil*

Delores spearheaded the weaving of the Ravenstail *Mother Robe* that travelled to Hoonah, Juneau, Whitehorse and Ketchikan to be woven on by weavers in those communities. It was presented to the Alaska Native Brotherhood Grand Camp, Ketchikan. This robe is currently housed at Totem Heritage Center with the condition that all local dance groups may use the robe for ceremonial events.

Delores and her daughter Evelyn wove a Ravenstail robe in the village of Old Massett that is believed to be the first to be woven there in over 150 years. The robe is held in a private collection. Today, Delores and Evelyn weave and teach both Ravenstail and Naaxiin (Chilkat) robes.

In 1991, Delores and Evelyn wove a cedar bark robe with Ravenstail trim for Ketchikan High School that is the first one woven in about two hundred years. Holly Churchill, Delores's youngest daughter, taught Delores and Evelyn the traditional method of pounding the

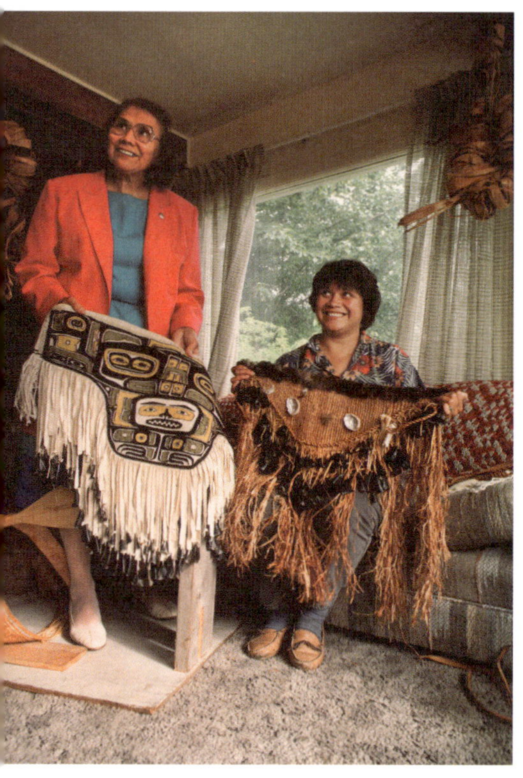

Delores is holding her first Naaxiin apron and her daughter Holly Churchill is holding her cedar dance apron. *Hall Anderson*

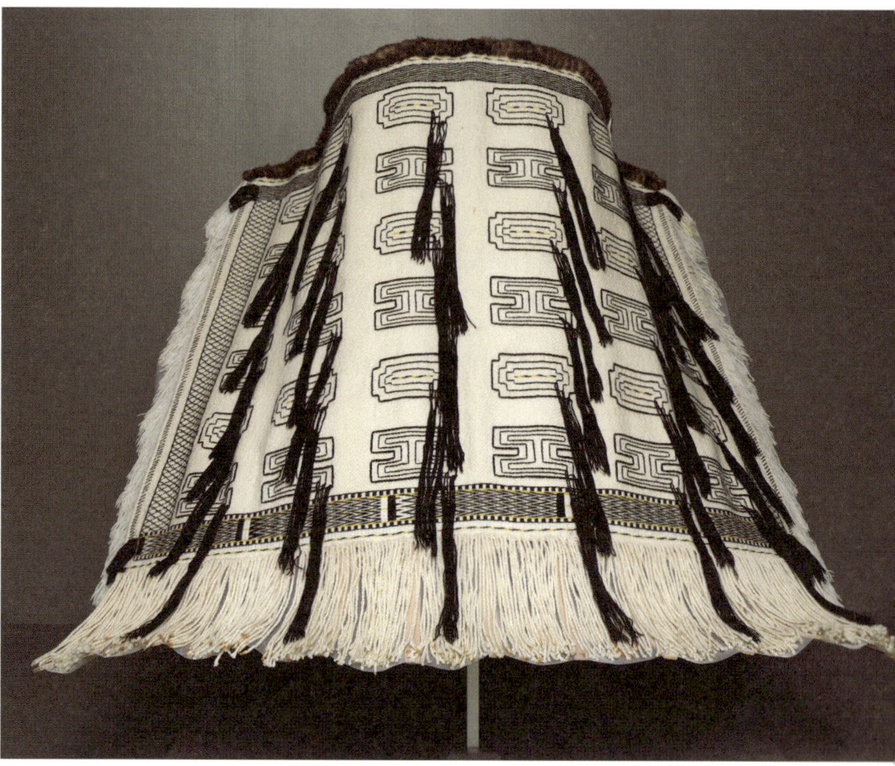

This Ravenstail robe was woven on Haida Gwaii and belongs to Delores and Evelyn Vanderhoop, one of her daughters. *Alaska State Museum*

material that Bill Holm, former director of the Burke Museum, had learned in his archival research and had shared with her when she began to weave the ancient cedar garments.

Delores emphatically states, "I will never create another cedar garment due to the difficulty of working with the material, the lengthy time it takes to prepare and weave, and the hardship on the hands." Holly, however, continues to weave magnificently beautiful cedar bark garments.

The desire to learn as much as possible about weaving enticed Delores to study the ancient weaving collections in major museums. Through her studies, she has brought back techniques to today's weavers that were no longer in use.

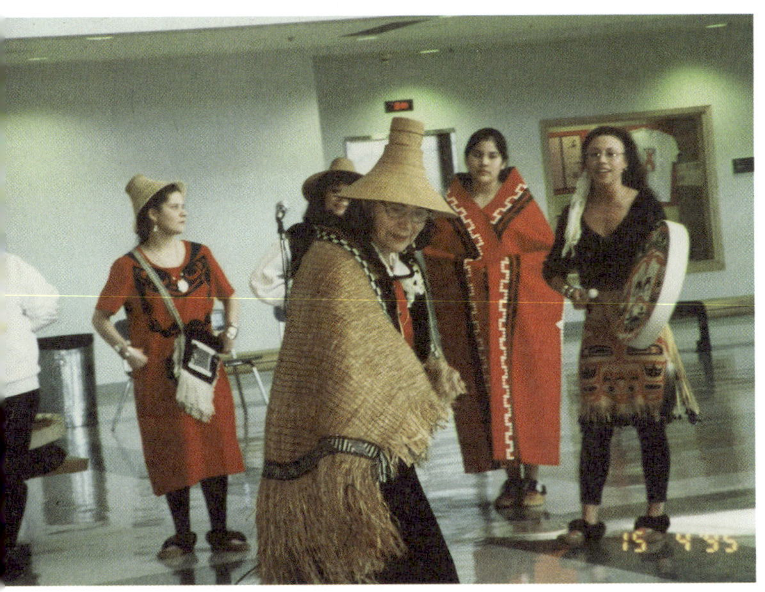

Delores is in the centre of the photograph, dancing in her pounded red cedar bark robe and surrounded by singers Gloria Burns, April Churchill, Cara Wallace and Teresa Varnell. *Ward Serrill*

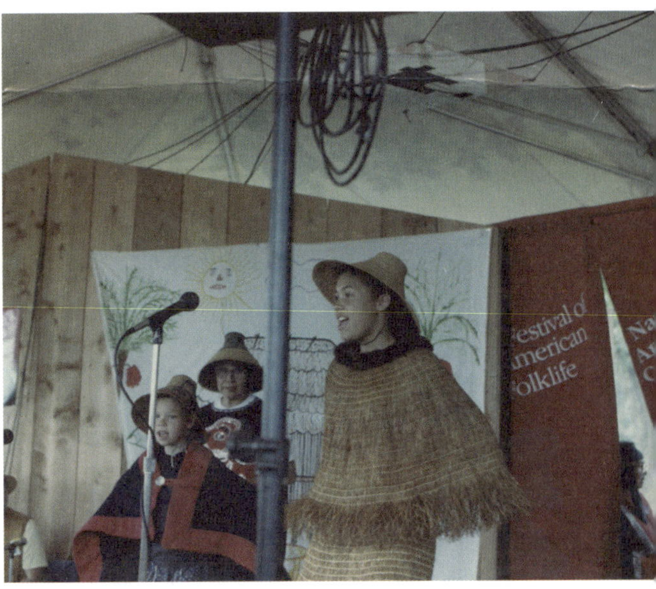

Delores stands in the background between her granddaughters Tiffany and Carrie Anne Vanderhoop as they appear at the 25th anniversary of the Smithsonian Institution's Folklife Festival. Carrie wears a cedar bark rain cape, dance apron and hat woven by Delores's daughter Holly Churchill. *Churchill family*

Delores has had the great privilege of studying baskets that have been discovered at archaeological sites. This includes the woven items found at the Thorne River Estuary in the Tongass National Forest and the spruce hat of the Long Ago Person Found in northern Canada.

When lecturing about basketry, Delores highlights the significant impact that individuals have had on the revival of ancient Northwest Coast art forms. Such artists include Robert Davidson who, in 1969, raised and potlatched the first totem pole in Old Massett village in nearly one hundred years; and Freda Diesing and Nathan Jackson, who taught at the Ketchikan Museum's Totem Heritage Center, Ketchikan, Alaska, in the early 1970s. Delores also admires her brother Victor Adams, who was a carver and had carved a canoe in the 1960s when canoe carving was no longer being done. She acknowledges all of those from the Haida, Tlingit, Tsimshian and all

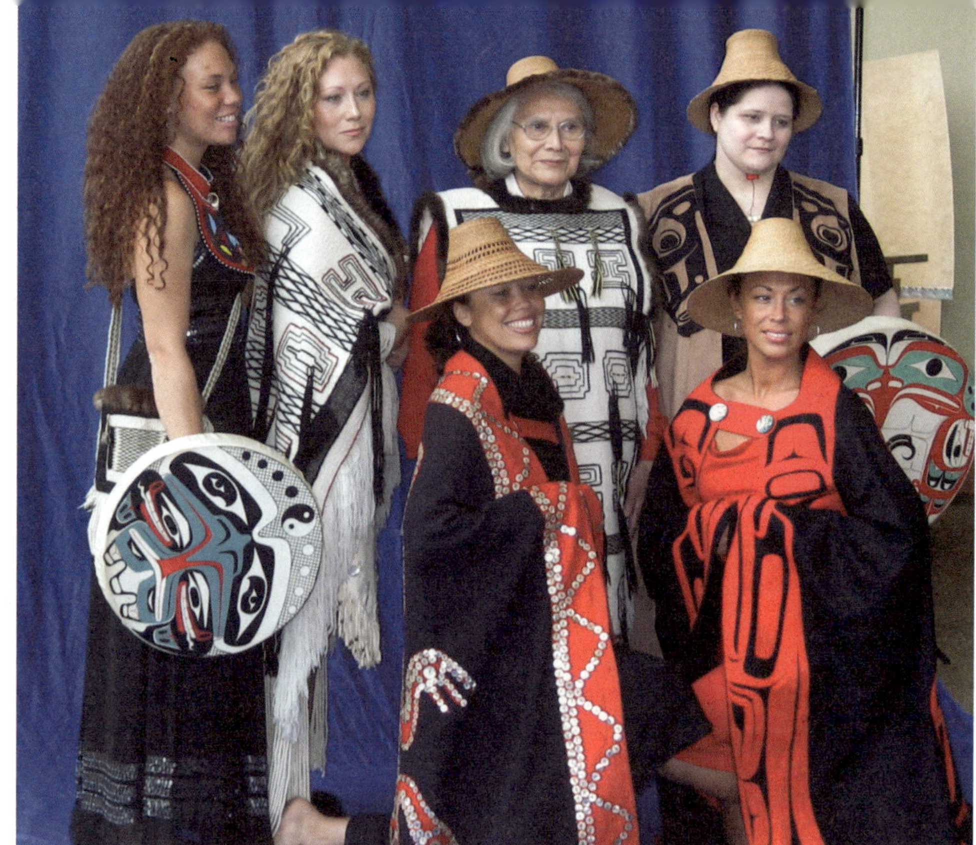

Delores in Washington, DC, with all her granddaughters to receive the US National Endowment for the Arts Lifetime Achievement Award in 2008. Back row, left to right: Tiffany Vanderhoop, Paula Varnell, Delores and Gloria Burns. Front row: Carrie Anne Vanderhoop and Teresa Varnell. *Churchill family*

Indigenous Nations that quietly kept the knowledge and skills of these ancient art forms alive.

Among Delores's many honours are the Rasmuson Foundation Distinguished Artist Award, the Alaska Governor's Award for the Arts, an honorary Doctorate of Humane Letters from the University of Alaska, an Alaska State Legislative Award, several First Peoples Fund Awards, and the National Endowment for the Arts Lifetime Achievement Award for her contribution to keeping the art of weaving alive and elevating it from a craft to an internationally recognized art form.

Many call Delores a master weaver. She, however, never calls herself that and instead draws our attention to the true masters and their works, stating categorically, "Each time I view the weavings of our ancestors, I am overwhelmed by the beauty and spirit of each. The works of our ancestors often move me to tears of admiration and gratitude. These are the masters and I am their student."

After learning and mastering the traditional methods of weaving, Delores began to explore the more modernistic approaches, finding, as she says, "Pure pleasure in weaving pieces that express my stories, emotions, and perceptions."

Delores encourages creativity and adaptation of weaving techniques through the use of nontraditional materials and colours; combinations of weaving techniques; sculpturing; and invention of design, as many represent the understanding and the technology and new knowledge of the time of the weaving artist. However, Delores stresses that each of the coastal First Nations' weaving styles are unique. She advises her students that innovative pieces will retain their Nation's identities when the rules are intimately known: "To break the rules, one must know the rules."

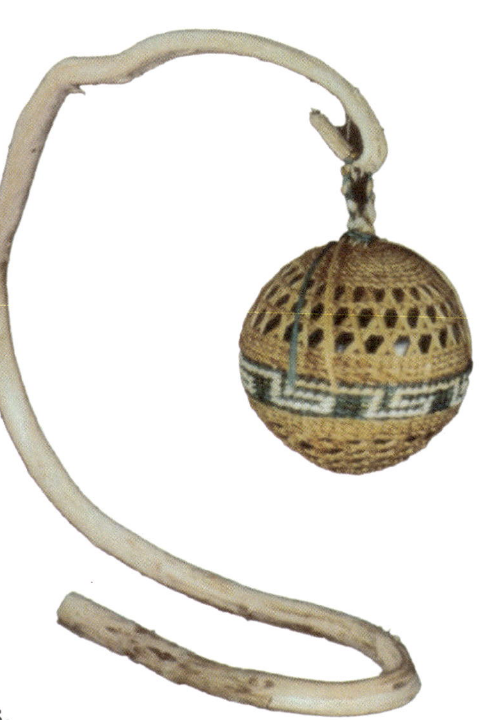

This Haida Gwaii driftwood and glass ball piece features spruce-root weavings by Delores. *Churchill family*

All three of Delores's daughters are weaving artists and teachers. Each of her grandchildren weaves. Two of her grandsons are also Haida artists. Delores's grandchildren and great-grandchildren are also Haida singers, dancers and learners of Xaad Kíl.

Among her siblings' children and grandchildren there are many weavers, artists, carvers, creators of regalia, singers and dancers. The art of weaving, carving, storytelling, singing and dancing within her family is an unbroken line, having never been forgotten even through the socially and economically disruptive times after Western contact.

Delores has added teaching Xaad Kíl to her life's work. "The Haida language is important to my understanding our ways of being and doing because it is descriptive in a way that English is not and makes it possible to express myself from my cultural perspective. My language connects me to everything—the forest, ocean and the spirit beings. When I pray, I pray in my language so that my requests and appreciation are fully understood."

Selina, Delores and her daughters have taught hundreds of people to weave. Many of those students have achieved recognition for their artistic works. Some have become teachers of weaving and

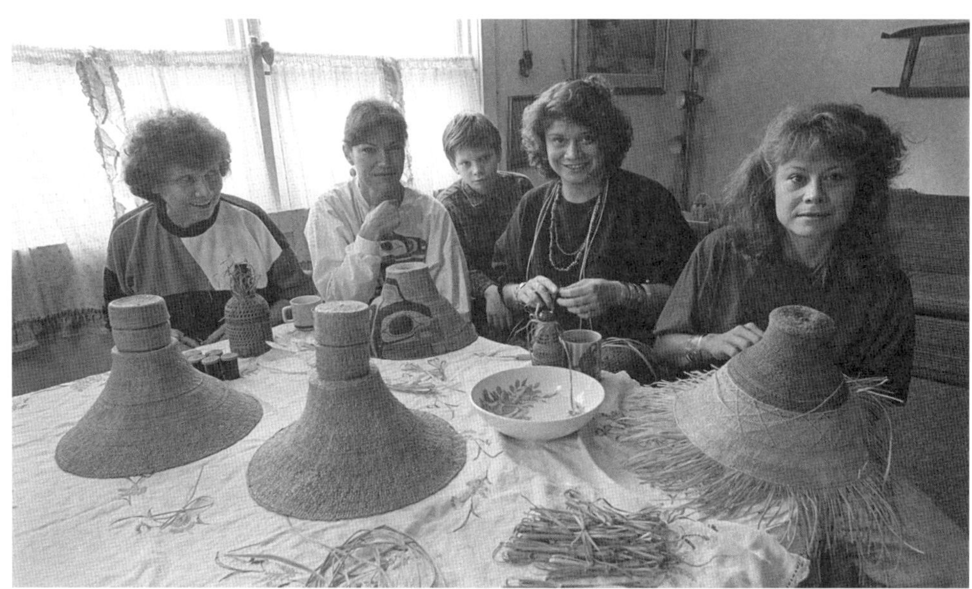

Delores and her daughters prepare for a family show at Scanlon Gallery, in Ketchikan, Alaska. Left to right: Delores, Evelyn, Holly's son Aaron, Holly and April. *Hall Anderson*

are enlarging the circle. Delores is an avid learner and her life reveals that she understands that we are gifted with knowledge and skills but these are of little use if they are not shared. She often states, "If knowledge and skills are not shared, they will eventually die away."

Delores's commitment to sharing everything she knows about weaving comes from the modelling of her mother and Delores's own observation and concern: "As long as our art is seen only in museums, we will be considered people of the past."

At the time of writing this book Delores is ninety-four. She continues to pass on traditional weaving knowledge and teaching Xaad Kíl.

Delores has led a life that contributes to the beauty, richness and depth of the Earth's humanities. In the writing of this book, she has expressed her hope that the children, grandchildren and great-great-great-great-grandchildren never forget the traditional Haida weaving and culture, which is based in our responsibilities and relationships to the Earth and to each other as the members of the Haida Nation and of Earth's broader family.

—April Churchill, Evelyn Vanderhoop, Holly Churchill and Michael Nicoll Yahgulanaas

Preface

The weaving arts are thousands of years old. Yet they still live and continue to teach us the way to be in this world. My vision is that with the passing on of the intellectual property with which I have been entrusted, the beautiful Haida weaving arts will support the continued growth of the Haida culture. My hope is that the teachings of my mother's traditional Haida style of harvesting and weaving, and my life's learning, will carry on through the work of the weavers of today and into the future. My dream is that others will find the peace, connection and sheer joy that filled my life with the many gifts the weaving arts have to offer.

The technique that is used today, to take a plaited square base to a circle, is an adaptation that my mother, Selina Victoria Harris Adams Peratrovich (Ilst'ayaa), added to the continuation and growth of Haida weaving. Before she figured out how to manipulate the corners of a plaited square to set the circle directly at the turning edge, the technique was to gradually compact twine in a circle on the base around a plaited square centre. Her adaptation of technique produces plaited baskets and hats whose transformation from square to circle is not only easier to execute but it is aesthetically beautiful. This method is uniquely Haida. It applies Haida plaiting and twining techniques to the weaving of our traditional cedar weaving material; and

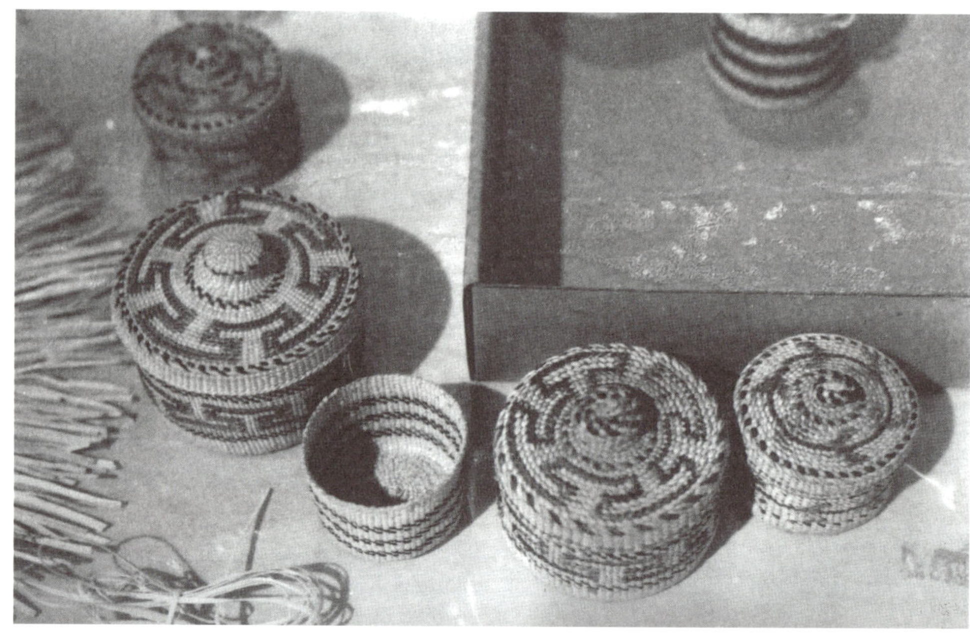

The rattle-lid spruce storage baskets made by Selina, Delores's mother, were her most popular design. *Churchill family*

the Haida weaving identifiers are still obvious (Chapter 5). Other First Nations weavers who have taken up my mother's method apply their unique tribal techniques, and the weaving identifiers of their Nations remain evident. This sharing of knowledge and method is part of our histories, revealed by the baskets that we weave.

A traditional plaited cedar bark hat begins as a square, transforms into a circle, widens to a gently sloping crown, and evolves to a wide brim. The hat's warp holds the hat's shape, while the spiral weaving technique allows no breach on the walls. From square to circle, the hat remains uniquely Haida.

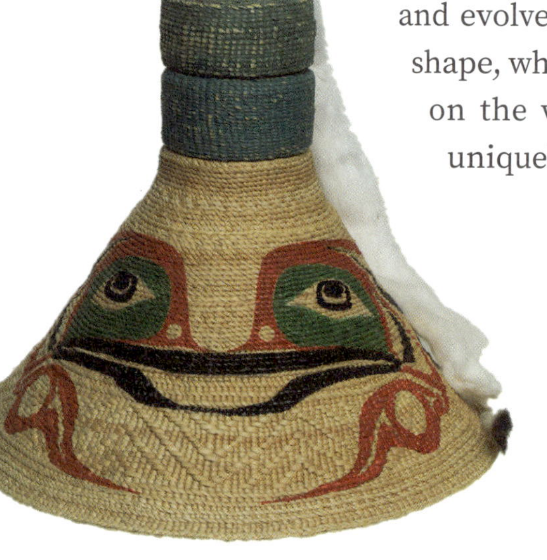

This *All the Relatives* spruce root hat was woven by Delores and Holly Churchill. Delores's grandson Donald Varnell painted the hat with a family crest design of the frog. Other family members harvested roots: April Churchill, Paula Varnell, Evelyn Vanderhoop, Carrie Anne Vanderhoop, Rosalie Bellis, Holly Churchill and Delores's mother, Selina Peratrovich, in addition to friends Mary Lou King and Janice Criswell. *Alaska State Museum*

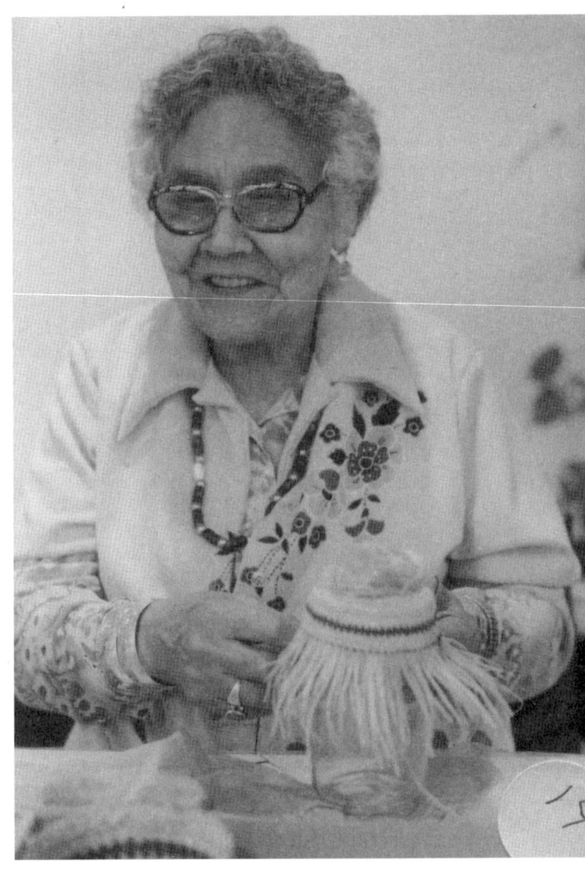

Selina Peratrovich weaving a spruce root basket. *Tony Pope*

Like the cedar work hat, my mother's life and my life went through many transformations. Since the time our ancestors made first contact with Europeans, many things were done to essentially change Indigenous people from "squares" into "circles"—to take the "Indian" out of us. However, through many adaptations and transformations, the Haida remain a unique people whose culture continues to be based in our connection to the land, sea and sky. The ability to adapt quickly allows us to hold on to the foundations of our culture and continue as a vibrant people. The traditional Haida weaving arts teach us how to stay connected and how to continue as Haida.

At the time my mother taught her first weaving class in 1964 at the Alaska State Museum in Juneau, there were a handful of elder Haida weavers I knew of, including Lydia Charles, Julia Davis, Amanda Edgars, Lucy Frank, Louisa Peele, Carrie Weir, Emily Thompson, Grace Wilson, Florence Davidson, Agnes Yeltatzie, Eliza Abrahams, Lucy Young and Hannah Parnell. Some were my mother's students while others had taught her their way of weaving. Those few weavers left were weaving primarily for sale in the craft/tourism markets. There was little interest from the younger generation, including myself, to learn this art form.

When my mother began to teach weaving, potlatching, feasting, dancing and singing, these arts were just coming out of hiding. They were then being revealed to the younger generations that had been subjected to the social disruption of missionaries, government, and the harshness of the reserve, and residential and public schools. There have always been those that carried the strand that binds us to the past. The practice of cultural activities may not have been seen outside of our society but there have always been those who refused to let go of our ways of being and knowing. My mother was one of those tradition bearers.

Haida basket weaving has always been a part of my life. When I was a child, my mother wove our baskets for harvesting potatoes, picking berries, collecting bird eggs and harvesting clams, seaweed and mussels. Her goat horn and soapberry spoons were held in her woven spoon baskets. Woven cedar work hats protected us from the sun. She and others also wove baskets that were sold in Port Essington, Vancouver, Prince Rupert and Victoria to the curio and collector trade. Although I grew up in the presence of my mother weaving, helping with the harvesting of bark and roots, I did not think about weaving being a major part of my life. As a child I would not sit and watch her weave—the first step to becoming a weaver.

My reproof of weaving came when I was quite young. My mother had taught a basketry unit to my class at Massett Day School. She told me to undo my weaving and to make a cylindrical basket instead of the flared one I was weaving. I acted like I did not hear her and just kept weaving.

At the end of the unit, the teacher decided to enter the student baskets into an art show in Victoria. My mother, who was not happy with the shape of my basket or the way I was behaving, told the teacher not to enter my basket. The teacher insisted that all baskets would be entered. As it turns out, I won a first-place blue ribbon and a prize of five dollars. When the prize arrived, my mother called me to the front of the class and gave me the ribbon. She then called up another student to receive my five-dollar prize. In a fury of hurt feelings, I threw the ribbon on the floor and vowed, "I won't ever weave again!"

At every turn I spurned my mother's urgings to learn to weave. I wanted something different. I wanted an education and career. After going to college, I became the Ketchikan General Hospital assistant to the controller. Because I loved math and numbers, and the money was good, I thought that I would be a bookkeeper all of my life.

In 1972 my mother received a letter from a collector who had purchased a basket from Ida Benzell, a Siltnzlet weaver who was ninety-two years old. The collector wrote that he was sad knowing that when Ida was gone, the weaving art form would die, because no one was learning. (I have since learned that her descendants are carrying on that weaving tradition.)

When I told my husband about the letter, he said, "It's true. You should sign up to take a weaving class from your mother." I enrolled in her Ketchikan Community College class. "What you doing here? You go home," my mother gruffly said to me when I arrived for class. Ron Inouye, the coordinator of the class, walked over to my mother, put his arm over her shoulder and gently said, "Selina, Delores has paid and we need her registration to have enough students to offer the class. We need her to stay." At last my mother gave in. If it had not been for Ron intervening on my behalf I may never have learned to weave.

Serving as my mother's apprentice, assistant, and later continuing her legacy as a teacher, has gifted me many times over. Learning from my mother was difficult at times. She was a perfectionist and expected the best from her children. She burned my first baskets, saying, "People will know you learned from me. Your baskets need to be good." As my weaving improved, I was glad she burned those first baskets. I would not want those to represent my work.

It takes years of weaving before a basket can be created like those woven by the masters and housed in museums. It is like ballet. When my daughter took ballet, she was not allowed to get into toe shoes until she had spent years mastering the techniques and building her strength. It is the same with basketry. There are years of learning to prepare material, which is the most important part of quality weaving. When I was asked by the University of Alaska to teach a class, my mother said, "You are not ready." For the next two years, it seemed that all I did was prepare material.

Even before learning to weave, I was overcome with the desire to learn all I could about my peoples' art forms and ancient ways of being. While I was still a bookkeeper for the Ketchikan General Hospital, I took a leave of absence to visit the Royal British Columbia

Museum in Victoria. Upon entering the museum, I was enthralled with the totem poles, designs and weaving.

I had little interest in our art forms before learning about governmental laws that were intended to take our culture from us. In fact, when I was a child, I was afraid of the poles that were still standing. I had thought that the elders that I had seen crying when they passed remnants of these poles were afraid as well. I did not know, at that time, that they were crying for all the people who had died from the diseases that had hit our people after contact, and most recently for them, the devastating flu of 1918.

I am grateful to have come to my senses before it was too late. I learned to weave from my mother in the traditional way, which begins with the forest visit to pull up spruce roots or to accept the cedar trees' gifts of long strips of cedar bark.

I was also extremely fortunate to learn to weave from other traditional Haida, Tlingit and Tsimshian weavers. Because they shared their intellectual property with me, I have been able to pass these skills and information on to the next generations of their people. The knowledge of my teachers stretches back thousands of years. The five-thousand-year-old basket that was found in the Thorne River Estuary and several baskets (four thousand years old) that were found at south Baranof are proof that our earliest ancestors practiced basketry.

Through my study of weavings that are stored in Europe, Canada and the United States, our ancestors have been able to pass to us the techniques that were being used by the Haida, Tlingit and Tsimshian at the time of contact.

A grant from the Alaska State Council of the Arts gave me an opportunity to study the weavings at the British Museum in London. The British Museum collection is remarkable. My mother and I had met Jonathan C.H. King, then the assistant keeper with the Department of Ethnography at the Museum of Mankind at the British Museum, when we had worked at the *Sacred Circles Exhibition* at the Nelson Gallery in Kansas City. While we were at the British Museum, Jonathan gave us full access to any object we wanted to examine. He introduced us to all the museum directors and treated us with utmost respect and regard. My mother enjoyed Jonathan's company and held him in very high esteem.

The study at the British Museum revealed techniques that were no longer in use. In fact, if I hadn't learned a six-strand ending from the frayed edge of a hat in the collection, I would not have known how the weaver had ended the spruce root hat that was found in the glacier with the three-hundred- to five-hundred-year-old man found in the Tatshenshini-Alsek Park in northern British Columbia in 1999.

During my studies at the British Museum, my mother's assistance was invaluable. She was able to explain and identify people in photographs and to describe the uses of old baskets and the meanings of hats and other objects.

My mother upheld the Haida principle of humility. She stressed this with her children and rarely gave us compliments. When we were blessed with one of her compliments, we knew we had done well. When I showed her how the six-strand ending was done on the museum hat, I was thrilled when she said, "Hmm, you're smart alright."

As access to new technology increases it will be possible to more fully understand the construction of these beautiful works of art. New archaeological sites will be discovered. Places of origin and uses will likely be easier to pinpoint. The research and science of the past and today will be built upon. Some of it, including mine, may even be corrected. This is the nature of research. Research and science are proving our ancient knowledge and stories to be true. It is through the science of mitochondrial DNA, which is inherited exclusively from the mother, that I learned more about my ancestry. Dr. Brian Kemp, a molecular anthropologist at Washington State University Pullman, informed me that I was related to the ancient hunter who had been discovered in 1999 in the Tatshenshini-Alsek Park glacier. This hunter is known to the Champagne and Aishihik First Nations as the "Long Ago Person Found" in the Southern Tutchone language. The hemlock pollen found on his squirrel garment revealed that the young hunter had walked a long way from the coast.

Even before Dr. Kemp told me that the "Long Ago Man Found" and I were connected through DNA, I had felt a strong connection when I learned that his spruce root hat was the first artifact that the archaeologists saw. It had blown up into the air when their helicopter was landing at the site. The Sealaska Heritage Foundation provided the funds and the Champagne and Aishihik First Nation graciously allowed me to study the dajangee (hat) of the Long Ago Man Found. The late Sarah Gaunt, the lead anthropologist, shared photos of the hat from all different angles, which was vital to my full understanding of the construction of his spruce root hat. This discovery of Long Ago Man Found reveals and supports our stories: that in ancient times we were people who travelled from the coast well into the interior.

Since 1972, when the Totem Heritage Center in Ketchikan began offering weaving classes, there have been many, many students. Yet, there are less than ten that I know of who have dedicated their lives to a weaving career. In the cash economy of today it takes a strong personal commitment to dedicate one's life to weaving because there is very little financial pay-off. The real payment received is the joy that comes when accepting the gifts from the forest and through the weaving of this wonderful art form.

It is heartening, however, to see the many weavings at potlatches, feasts and celebrations that have emerged over the last twenty years as more and more of our people are weaving. The challenge for weavers is to stretch beyond what has been learned and to aim for the perfection of the weaving works of the masters, which are housed within museums around the world.

Weaving connects us to the past, and teaching passes the art of weaving on to the future. Each generation of weavers will contribute their interpretations and artistic expressions to the growth of this vibrant art form. My mother's students, my students and then their students will keep this art alive long after our names are forgotten.

The Haida oral history tradition of passing history and knowledge to younger generations has kept our history, culture and traditions alive through many hardships. Although the Haida are quick to adapt to new technology and situations, the core of the culture is intact because our elders diligently told our stories and modelled over and over again the way Haida believe and do things. I can only speak to what I have been told by my elders and what I have seen, done and learned. *From a Square to a Circle* begins here, in the old-fashioned way of starting a story. "This is what I was told and how I know it to be."

Chapter 1 describes those people who were important to my learning. Chapter 2 provides a glimpse into the lifeways of our people and a context for the Haida weaving arts. Chapter 3 shares stories about harvesting with baskets that were still in use when I was a child. Chapter 4 explains my family's harvesting techniques. Chapter 5 shares Haida weaving techniques and provides basket-weaving instructions for the featured baskets.

This book is intended to support Haida instructors who have many years of weaving experience. Through my research and sharing with weavers from other cultures, I have learned that the weaving techniques are actually common to weaving worldwide. The materials and the way these techniques are executed by the Haida are unique and it is our intellectual property. In my classes and my mother's classes, we respectfully asked non-Haida students not to sell or teach the weaving of Haida-style baskets. Copyright laws do not properly protect Indigenous property rights. We own intellectual property in the collective through maternal inheritance. Our tangible and intangible properties are evidence of our legal rights. Copyright laws do not protect our collective rights and cultural laws into perpetuity, as is required to uphold our laws of inheritance. Nor do they recognize our form of identifying and making our legal claims through cultural ceremony. It is only through the respect of those who have come to understand and respect the importance of these precious rights that we are able to protect them.

Acknowledgements

The knowledge that all cultures have ancient weaving traditions, which were likely to have been in use before pottery or carved containers were made, represents for me one of the concepts of yah'guudang (respect)—that all things are connected. Weaving belongs to all of us. Weaving connects us to all other cultures and people.

Nothing of significance is achieved without the contribution of a great many people. The shared weaving knowledge spans over four decades of my learning and teaching, all of which was possible because of the many organizations and people whose visions and passion helped keep the Northwest Coast weaving arts thriving and growing. Their contributions over these many years made it possible to write this book.

Acknowledging all those who have contributed of themselves is impossible. There are so many who provide housing and care for instructors; find funds; donate time; implement workshops, classes, and lectures; exercise influence; and, of course, there are the students who have grown into fine weavers and teachers. These people leave footprints that last beyond lifetimes. Most of these people work in the background and are rarely noticed, but without them, the world would be less rich and diverse.

I would first like to thank the Rasmuson Foundation and the National Endowment for the Arts for the financial support that provided the time to write this book. Through this kind of financial support, artists are able to engage in projects that otherwise could not be done.

The arts and humanities are alive and well, in large part, because of the universities, museums, organizations and agencies that provide funds and opportunities for artists to achieve artistic excellence. These have contributed, over many years, to my ability to research, teach and create, for which I am immensely grateful. I would especially like to thank the following organizations: The First Peoples Fund, the Alaska State Council on the Arts, the State of Alaska Percent for Public Art, the Tongass Historical Museum (Ketchikan), the Totem Heritage Center (Ketchikan), the Alaska State Museum (Juneau), the US National Park Service (Sitka), the Institute for Alaska Native Arts, the Sealaska Heritage Foundation, the Ketchikan Area Arts and Humanities Council, the Anchorage Museum and the Yupiit Piciryarait Cultural Center (Bethel).

Support from the Alaska State Council on the Arts, the Sealaska Heritage Foundation and the National Endowment for the Arts provided me with opportunities over many years to conduct research in museums in Europe, Canada and the United States, including the British Museum (London); the National Museum of Natural History, Smithsonian Institute (Washington, DC); the National Museum of Civilization (Hull, Quebec); the Field Museum of Natural History (Chicago); the Völkerkunde Museum (Hamburg, Germany); the Linden Museum (Stuttgart, Germany); the Museo de América (Madrid, Spain); the Museum of Mankind, the Royal British Columbia Museum (Victoria); the University of British Columbia Museum of Anthropology (Vancouver); the Canadian Museum of History (Gatineau, Quebec); the Anchorage Museum and Alaska State Museum (Juneau); Burke Museum (Seattle); Pitt Rivers Museum (Oxford, England); Museum of Anthropology and

Archaeology, University of Cambridge (England); and World Museum (Liverpool, England).

Each of the following individuals went well over what was expected to help me with museum studies, for which I am very grateful: the late Dr. George McDonald, Director, and Dr. Andrea Laforet, Head of Ethnography, Canadian Museum of Civilization; Jonathan C.H. King, Assistant Keeper at the British Museum; and Steve Henrikson, Curator of Collections, Alaska State Museum.

Learning from ancient finds at archaeological sites was invaluable to confirm, for those outside of our society, that our weaving arts have existed for thousands of years. The assistance from the many that helped during my research include Sarah Gaunt, Steve Henrikson and Terry Fiffield.

My greatest respect and gratitude go to the many people whose work in the background over many years has contributed significantly to the revival and growth of the Northwest Coast peoples' arts, including the weaving arts. These people worked with my mother and me to bring the weaving arts to the forefront: Virginia McGillvray, Roxanne Adams, Peter Corey, Bill Trudeau, Jackie Crabb, Ron Inouye, Victoria Lord, Gertrude Johnson, Mary and Willard Jones, Nathan Jackson, Freda Diesing, Dennis Demmert, Jane Pollard-Demmert, Ellen Lang, Hall Anderson, John Harrington, Chris Hansen, Marian Blankenship, Esther Littlefield, Dr. Rosita Worl, Norma Jean Dunn, Dr. Simpson, Dr. Menzi, Pricilla Shulte, Alice Tersteeg, Virginia Byrd, Linda Halfon, James Autry, Denise Blankenship, Suzie Jones, Jan Steinbright, Pat Wolfe, Edna Lambole, Debbie Krause and Christine Metsner.

My heartfelt thanks to the many, many individuals who have consistently supported bringing weaving classes to their communities, who hosted the instructors and who played key roles in the resurgence of the weaving arts. Among these are James and Mary Lou King (Juneau); Mike, Edna and Dawn Jackson (Kake); Marg Peterson (Hoonah); Christine and Gordon Greenwald (Hoonah); Carol Williams (Hoonah); Chris Tolson (Hydaburg); Virginia Demmert (Craig);

Irene Peratrovich and her daughter, Tiny (Klawock); Lani Hotch (Klukwan); Mona and Tommy Jackson; Janell Privet (Wrangell); Ruth Demmert, Pauline Duncan and Gerry Kennedy (Sitka); Pearle Pearson (Skidegate); and Leslie Williams (Massett).

Deciding to write a book was easy, but actually writing the book was not as simple as imagined. Without the help of my children and grandchildren, this book may never have been finished. Their many varied contributions have filled me with overwhelming appreciation for their commitment to the weaving arts. A very special thank you to my daughter April Churchill for her guidance in organizing and writing my memories and stories.

The late Peter Corey, whose lifetime of work has been so important to the preservation and perpetuation of Southeast Alaska Native Arts, brought extensive knowledge to the editing of the material. His work in developing comprehensive basketry terminology has been most useful in the writing of this book. My mother would be pleased to know that Peter agreed to serve as the book's editor. It was with deep sadness that Peter passed away before the writing was completed.

I thank Karen Hofstad for her contributions—both for her relentless support and for her financial help. She saw the need for a copy editor and designer and moved this book forward. Many thanks to Patty Fiorella and Sarah Asper-Smith for their work. Thanks, also, to Dr. Launette Rieb for a careful and thoughtful review of the book.

A very special thank you to Chris Hopkins, Dave Rubin, Michael Nicoll Yahgulanaas and my daughter Evelyn Vanderhoop, widely recognized visual artists, who so kindly contributed paintings to this book.

Thanks also go out to Hall Anderson, Jack Littrel, Hulleah Tsinhnahjinnie, Ward Serrill, Tom Sadowski, Felix Wong and others for their photographic contributions; and of course, to the museums who shared their archival photos.

The Council of the Haida Nation and Terri-Lynn Williams Davidson gave me the opportunity to document my life. The memories that came to consciousness during interviews, some good and some not so good, all added to my understandings of why I do what I do, and why I have come to know what I know. Some of these memories are shared in this book.

Thank you to all of the young people who helped with this book in many varied ways. It gives me hope that through their dedication, our traditions and culture will go on and on into the future.

My sincere appreciation is extended to those who understand the importance of Haida weavings to the world of art and who, through their practice of collecting, make it possible for weavers to dedicate time to the creation of weavings and the continuation of this ancient art form. Dr. Robert White, Robert Davidson, Terri-Lynn Williams Davidson, Reggie Davidson and Joe and Nancy Kovalak, to name a few, have supported many artists and weavers. The Alaska State Percent for Art Program has contributed immensely to public art collections throughout Alaska as well, and the museums that access new works for their collections all assist in elevating our weaving creations. All of these deserve the highest respect for supporting the arts.

Those art galleries that have invested in gaining the knowledge about the weaving arts and helped to bring this art and knowledge to the world are vital to its growth.

Thank you to all the weavers and students who will carry on. This fine art form will live on because of your commitment to weaving and to gaining cultural knowledge. Without the cultural knowledge and connection to the land, the art of weaving has little meaning and is reduced to a craft.

CHAPTER ONE

My Teachers

My Teacher and Mentor—My Mother

My mother, Selina (Ilst'ayaa), was born April 1, 1889, in G̲utaawaas (Old Massett, Haida Gwaii) to Jane Harris Davis (Ilskyalee), of the G̲aw Git'ans Gitanee Eagle Clan, and to George Harris (Waahlankinas), the eldest nephew of Chief Siigee of the Skidaaw K'aaw Raven Clan. She left this Earth on December 23, 1984.

My mother was born and raised in a time when the canoe was still a major mode of transportation, the puberty house and ceremonies were still in use, marriages were being arranged by the uncles, tribal slaves still lived in the village and children were beginning to go to residential schools. She lived through the great flu epidemic of 1918–19, watching with horror and despair as this terrible disease virtually wiped out her immediate family.

She was of the generation that had just followed the incursion of the strange culture onto Haida Gwaii. The Anglican mission had only been in Massett for thirteen years prior to her birth. Although Canada began to survey Haida Gwaii in 1875, Indian Affairs had not established an office in Massett until 1910, twenty-one years after her birth.

My mother only reached the third grade. Her maternal grandmother, Edith George (Kujuuhl), told my mother that she could not

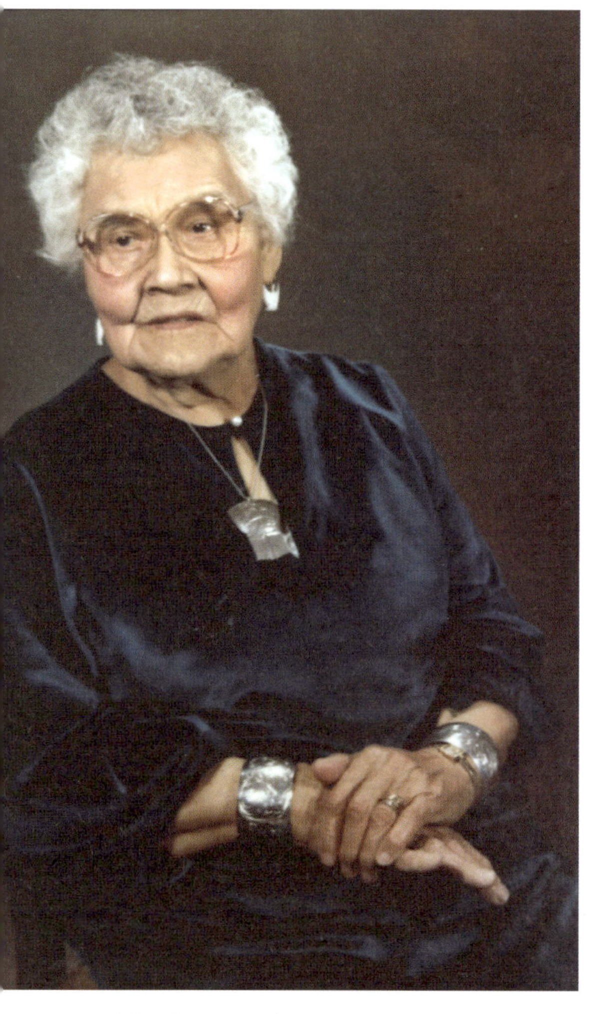

Selina Peratrovich.
Churchill family

go to residential school because those children came back not wanting to speak Haida and were not interested in the ways that helped the village. Instead, Selina would stay with her grandmother and learn the ways of the Haida. My mother related time and again, even into old age, that she had really wanted to go to school and remembered, with deep regret, sitting on the beach by the dock and sobbing as the boat left with the village children.

It was not until my mother was married that she learned to read English from her husband, my father, Alfred Adams. He taught her to read from the Bible. She read the Bible everyday of her life. She loved Jesus and was able to bring together Haida spiritual understandings and the teaching of Jesus without compromise to either. Along with telling Haida oral stories and teaching lessons of old, she loved to recite English nursery rhymes and sing nursery songs to her children.

Although my mother could read from the Bible, her English was very broken and she primarily spoke X̱aad Kíl. Because of her limited use of English, my siblings and I communicated with her in X̱aad Kíl, which is one of the reasons that we retained our fluency of this wonderfully expressive language. Much of my work with her in the classroom was as a translator.

After my father passed away from bone marrow cancer in 1945, my mother married a Tlingit widower, George Peratrovich, and moved to Ketchikan. My older sister Jane (Kujuuhl), younger sister Mae (T'aayhlwaad) and I moved to Ketchikan with her. I was sixteen years old. My older brother Victor (Stast), a fisherman, also came along with us but returned to Massett after the fishing season.

While in Ketchikan my mother continued the traditional lifestyle of harvesting, weaving and putting up food and medicine. She had always been a shrewd businesswoman who was good with money and continued her business activities of trading seaweed for ooligan grease and bringing cash in through the sale of dried halibut, shell art and weavings. She was a woman who was "good with her hands," (the way the Haida reference an artist) and was always able to provide what was needed. Without patterns she would sew, knit, embroider and crochet clothing, regalia, quilts and other household linens.

Strong, brave, enterprising, demanding, loving and an artist—my mother Selina was all of these and more. She always had a quick smile and a glorious sense of humour.

She was also incredibly stubborn and strong-minded. When she was eighty-five years old, my siblings and I gathered to say goodbye to her at the hospital in Seattle. My siblings were extremely upset with me when I walked into the hospital room and said, "Mother, you cannot die right now. You signed a contract with the Totem Heritage Center to teach. They are expecting you."

The next day when we went to visit her, we were amazed to find her packing her little suitcase to go home and to get ready to teach her weaving class. She lived and worked for another ten years, supporting herself through her weaving until the year she died.

My mother's home was always filled with splendid smells. Spruce pitch for healing cuts and bruises and Hudson Bay tea to clean the blood and heal colds were always warming on the stovetop. During the harvesting season the house was heavy with the sweet smell of cedar and devil's club. In later years these smells were intermingled with the smell of the menthol that she used to ease her arthritis pain, about which none of us ever heard her complain.

The smell of bread rising, baking or frying seemed to draw many visitors. Anyone, at any time, who came to visit was served a hearty, delicious meal or pie with tea. Guests were always treated like royalty and subject to her affection and fantastic sense of humour.

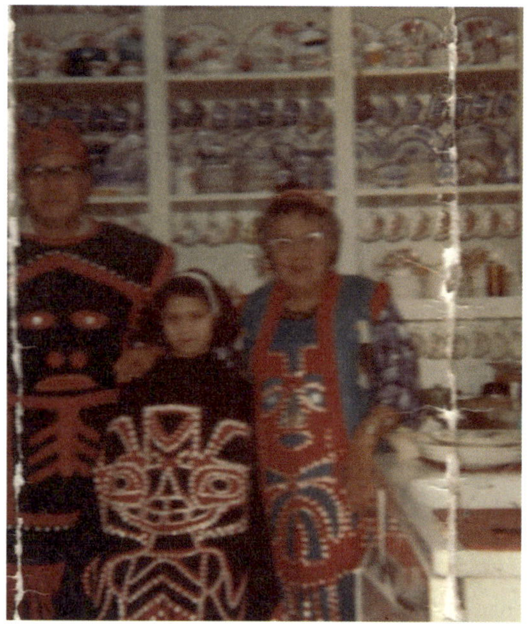

Selina with her second husband, George Peratrovich, and Delores's daughter, Holly, standing in front of one of Selina's dish cabinets. *Churchill family*

The elderly who came to visit would affectionately greet each other and then sit quietly together for about ten minutes before starting up conversation. The guests could be a mixture of Haida, Tlingit and Tsimshian, each speaking their own language with the occasional English word. Yet they understood each other. Visitors in her home created great peals of laughter.

My mother always upheld the Haida tradition of rising in the early hours of the morning. After her ceremonies of gratitude, she cleaned her home, set her bread and had a large pot of stew or seafood chowder on the stove. By the time the rest of us rose she was ready to work on her weaving and other projects or to go out to harvest or do other chores. She made use of every moment of the day, making hard work look like lots of fun. At the end of the day, when it came time to rest, she would puff sharply from her chest, "huu huu, huu, huuuu," a Haida way of saying, "I'm tired but it is good. I am done."

My mother loved china dishes, silver, crystal and fine linen, as all Haida women did. Her cupboards were filled with many sets of dishes, which were used regularly at her table. She was often seen elegantly walking down the street in a fur coat, with a fashionable hat and stately cane. As she walked, she cordially bowed her head slightly in acknowledgement of people passing by. She liked to go on car rides. She kept up with the new appliances, always saving and paying cash for everything she had.

She was an active member of the Alaska Native Sisterhood. She respected and admired the Queens of England, Victoria and Elizabeth. On one of her adventures, she and her best friend Florence met Queen Elizabeth, who visited Haida Gwaii in 1971.

My mother always faced matters head on. When the Episcopalian (Anglican) Church closed the Native-built "Indian Church" (St.

Elizabeth in Ketchikan), they required that the Ketchikan congregation integrate at St. John's church. She insisted that she and her children would go to the "white people" church even though many of the Native and non-Native members were dropping out because of the integration.

At that time Natives still sat on the left-hand side of the church as a matter of habit. She, however, would march down the aisle to the front rows of the church with her grandchildren trailing behind. She would seat herself and the children on the right-hand side of the church. When people started to talk against the church, she would not join the conversation. She held strongly to the Haida principle not to speak badly about others or focus attention on bad things. She told all of us that thinking or talking mean would bring bad things to us. Over the years, through her respectful and accepting nature, she built loving and long-lasting relationships with the non-Native congregation and Ketchikan community members.

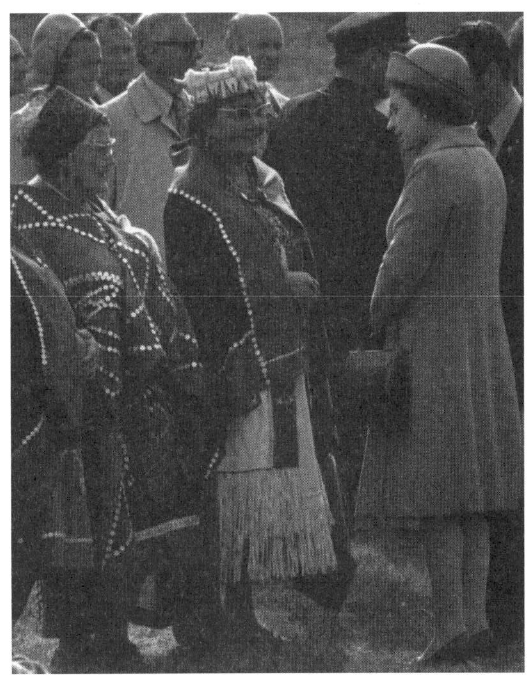

Selina and Florence Davidson meet Queen Elizabeth in 1971 in Sandspit, Haida Gwaii. *Ulli Seltzer*

My mother adapted easily to new things and bent easily with the winds of change. However, culture was really important to her. Over and over again she told my children about their Haida family, history and stories. She taught them to sing and dance when they were very young. And when they had children, she taught her great-grandchildren to sing and dance. She had the wisdom to make sure that my children went to Haida Gwaii each year so they would know their family and the ways of being Haida.

As the Haida moved into the changing world, Western education was identified by our leadership as an important part of surviving as a people. The elders emphasized getting an education so that we could take good care of our families. Things had changed and my mother wanted her children and grandchildren to do well in this new world.

Weaving was seen as time consuming and even those who wove for sale saw that the time it took to weave a basket, and the prices people were willing to pay, would not support a family in the cash economy.

In 1971 my eldest daughter, April, asked Selina to teach her to weave. Along with my other daughters, Evelyn and Holly, she had spent her childhood and youth helping my mother harvest bark, grass and roots.

"No, no, my dear," my mother said. "You'll neglect your housework and your children if you start weaving. It does not make enough money to help you. No, you shouldn't do that."

While visiting my mother, April would watch her weave. One day April came in with a small bumpy basket and put it in front of my mother, who covered her mouth in the way of the old people laughing and started to chuckle, asking, "Who made that nice basket?" April said, "I made it. I took some of your scraps and learned by watching you.

Seeing that April was not going to give up, my mother at last gave in and said, "You come every day and I will teach you to weave." April spent the next year visiting my mother and learning to weave in the old style, just as she had learned to knit, crochet, sew and bake from my mother. The Haida way of learning is to watch, try, undo, watch, try, undo...until the skill is mastered. Selina taught April to measure by finger widths and with her hand and arm lengths. I use a tape measure. My mother used to say to me, "Just see what you want to do and do that." I couldn't do that. I need to lay out and plan my basket.

After teaching April, my mother taught Isabelle Rorick, my brother Victor's daughter, and then Isabelle's mother, Primrose Adams.

Baskets in my mother's early days, and in her mother's, grandmothers' and great-grandmothers' time, were made by most women for actual use, and the young women who did not go to residential school were all still learning. Only after the Second World War did Haida weaving of baskets become purposefully and primarily for sale and the young women had no interest in learning.

My mother made baskets both for use and for sale. As a young woman she sold her baskets to museums and shops in British Columbia, including Port Essington, Vancouver, Victoria and Prince Rupert. She told me that my father, Alfred Adams, and Charles Edenshaw also sold hers and other women's weavings to museums and shops when they travelled for business or for the Native Brotherhood. In her later years, my mother sold her work to museums such as the Smithsonian Institution, the Alaska State Museum, the Ketchikan Museum, the British Museum, to major collectors and to the new collectors that had resulted from her classes.

My mother had learned as a child to harvest bark and spruce roots from her maternal grandmother, Edith George (Kujuuhl), and her mother, Jane Harris Davis (Ilskyalee), while helping them. When she was in her early twenties, she learned to prepare and to weave spruce roots from her mother-in-law Elizabeth Adams (Kode/Code/Kude), of the Kyanuusalii Raven Clan. My mother related years later that when she was learning to prepare and weave with roots, she would try and try and sometimes go off and cry because it was so difficult for her to get it just right.

When my mother was first learning to weave spruce roots, a blind woman, Mrs. Mark Ingram, was paid to help her split spruce roots. My mother learned to weave cedar bark hats from Hannah Parnell, who was also known for her cedar bark twine and rope making.

My mother wove mostly in spruce root until she was teaching classes. Flora Dundas, a Tsimshian weaver from Metlakatla, offered her red cedar bark. "That's okay, I weave with spruce roots," my mother replied.

"What's the matter with you? I'm giving you money," Flora playfully chided. My mother accepted the gift and started using this material to teach beginning students.

Later, my mother added yellow cedar to her weaving when I mistakenly took bark from a yellow cedar tree and we found it to be soft, supple and suitable as weft (see Chapter 5).

Traditionally, family members teach family members how to weave. However, because of the changing times, people were not teaching or learning weaving. In 1964, Jane Pollard Demmert invited my mother to teach a weaving class at the Alaska State Museum in Juneau. This was the first formal class that my mother taught.

In 1972, my mother announced to me that she had a job teaching at Ketchikan Community College. I was stunned and asked how it happened. She explained, "I went to Dr. Simpson at the college and told him that Haida basketry was going to die out if he did not hire me to teach."

My mother was eighty-three years old at that time. The thought of her going to the college and telling Dr. Simpson, in her extremely broken English, that he had to hire her was, and still is, amazing to me. At that time, there were only three weavers on the Alaska side of the border weaving Haida style, and many of those few that were still weaving in Old Masset, on Haida Gwaii, had learned from my mother.

She told me that when Dr. Simpson had asked how much she would charge, one of the professors was walking by and she said, "How much you pay him? You pay me what you pay him." They agreed and she began her teaching career at the age of eighty-three.

Because the college was a public institution, she was required to teach all people who registered, not just Haida or Native. The first classes did not include Native students but one of the outcomes of these early classes was to begin the long climb of elevating Haida weaving from a "craft" to a recognized fine art form. Before this, her baskets and other weavers' baskets were being sold for the same prices as those sold in craft stores or home furnishing shops.

My mother did not raise her prices on her baskets. It was her students—who became collectors—who raised the prices. The first was a basket of the size that she had been selling for $35. When she quoted this price to one of her students, the student refused to pay that price. Instead she insisted that the basket was worth no less than $350 and promptly purchased the basket at ten times the asking price.

After gaining an appreciation for the hard work, the artistic expression and uniqueness of the weaving and the materials, the non-Native students, who subsequently became collectors, increased the purchase of baskets to their actual value. Galleries and shops began selling the weavings as fine art.

When her classes began to be taught at the Totem Heritage Center in Ketchikan, and through the Institute of Alaska Native Arts, they began to fill with Native students.

My mother became known for her weaving artistry. She travelled widely, researching in England, and teaching in Old Massett, Haida Gwaii; in Kansas City, Chicago, Boston, Hawaii, Washington, DC, and Seattle; and in Alaska: Ketchikan, Juneau, Sitka, Anchorage, Fairbanks, Craig, Klawock, Bethel and Yakutat.

Museums sought her work and collectors helped her to elevate Haida weaving from a craft to a recognized fine art form.

During the summer of 1982, when she was ninety-three years old, my mother and I were in London and Washington, DC, teaching and lecturing on basketry. When she was ninety-four years old, she taught in Anchorage. She even taught as far north as Bethel, Alaska, where she easily made friends with many of the Yupik people.

My mother was honoured by the Governor of Alaska and had she lived long enough would have received the National Endowment for the Arts Lifetime Achievement Award. The award is given only to living recipients. She had been selected but did not live long enough to receive the award at the ceremony in Washington, DC.

My mother made many friends and had many adventures after starting to teach weaving. Among these was our lifelong friend Mary Lou King, who had taken a weaving class with us at the Alaska State Museum in Juneau. When that first Juneau class was over and we were saying our goodbyes, Mary Lou offered to house us the next time we were in town.

In the early days of teaching for the University of Alaska, per diem and housing were not provided. When we got to Juneau to teach another class, we found that we did not have a place to stay and could not get a hold of anyone that we knew.

My mother said, "Call Mary Lou King. She invited us to stay with her." Exasperated by the situation, I said, "Mother, when strangers offer something like that, they don't really mean it. It's like saying, 'How are you today?' They are just being polite." My mother responded firmly, "Call her."

Mary Lou took us in without hesitation and from then on, we always stayed with her when we taught in Juneau.

The summer before my mother died, when she was ninety-four years old, she and I had walked two miles into the woods to collect spruce roots in Juneau with Mary Lou. While digging roots, the weather had turned on us and my mother said, "We won't be able to build a fire here to cook the roots." Mary Lou boasted, "Oh no, I can build a fire in the rain with wet wood."

My mother sat patiently as Mary Lou and I tried to build the fire. Mary Lou finally gave in to the fact that a fire was not possible. She was concerned about my mother walking back to the road through the muddy trail and under the rain.

There was a small rowboat on the opposite bank of the river that belonged to the director of the Boy Scout Camp, who was working on our side of the river. Mary Lou had hip waders and suggested to him that she bring the boat over to him and he paddle my mother to the road. He agreed.

Mary Lou ran ahead on the trail and when my mother arrived at the road, Mary Lou had recovered her fire building reputation by having a blazing fire waiting. However, the weather had gotten worse and my mother suggested that the roots be cooked at Mary Lou's house. We packed up and continued our fun at Mary Lou's.

Throughout the adventure we all had a good laugh at ourselves. My mother loved adventures and laughed easily when things did not go exactly as planned. When I look back on that day, I am completely impressed with my ninety-four-year-old mother hiking two miles

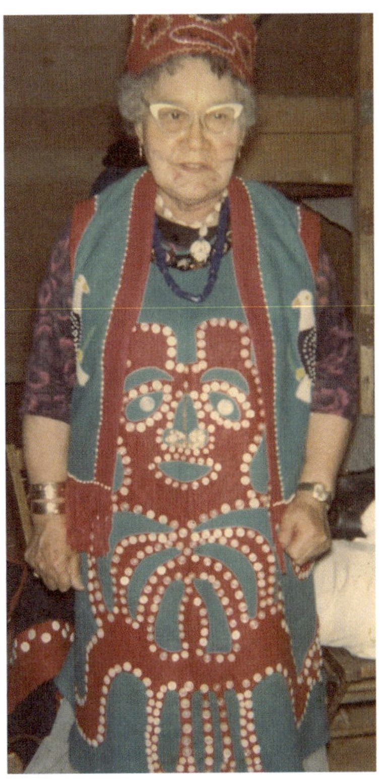

Selina made her own regalia and used her own crest designs. Here, she is wearing regalia made with cloth appliqué with shell buttons. *Churchill family*

into the woods the year before her death, and her lively approach to doing things when she knew that she did not have long to live.

After the passing of my mother, Mary Lou's husband James shared with me, "When Selina stayed with us, I always felt like royalty was with us." James and Mary Lou maintain the Selina Peratrovich Art Scholarship with the University of Alaska.

After being told by the doctors that she had less than a year to live, my mother travelled to communities where her family members lived to give her most valuable belongings to the people she wanted to inherit them. The tunic pictured on this page was made by my mother. I gifted it to Jenny Cross's daughter Shayla because it is an important physical reminder that we are related.

During her last year, my mother made calls to people who were important in her life. Chief Cumshua (Charley Wesley) often related the last call she made to him, in which she shared with him her pride in his work of carrying on the traditions, culture and history. The call meant a great deal to him.

Ever the optimist, two weeks before she passed on, my mother was making plans to attend a Chilkat weavers' gathering in Haines, Alaska. She did not live long enough to attend that gathering.

Mother passed away peacefully at home, surrounded by her family, on December 23, 1984. When weakness had finally overcome her and she lay on the sofa, she instructed me to put up a Christmas tree. The day before she died, she told me to put a large deer meat stew on the stove, telling me exactly what she wanted in the stew. Like so many Haida women of her generation, her face was virtually unwrinkled at the time of her death.

Words cannot describe all that my mother was—creative, ingenious, humble, a loving, caring mother, gracious and beautiful. She would share anything that she had with others. She was always there for her children, grandchildren and great-grandchildren. Through all the hardships she suffered and all the joys she experienced, she always put her faith in God. Her last breath was to model for us the way to let go of our spirit and let it move gently out of body to the next place of our spiritual journey. She looked forward to seeing all her friends and relations on the other side.

My Other Teachers

The time spent with my teachers, the last of the weavers in my mother's generation, was so valuable to my learning. It was not just learning to weave but also learning about their lives, their hopes, their dreams, and the reinforcement they gave to my childhood learnings about yah'guudang (respect for all things and all things are connected). All of my Haida, Tlingit and Tsimshian weaving teachers have left this Earth. I often get very lonely for them and that generation's gracious way of being.

Lydia Charles, a Haida weaver, had a gentle and joyful way. During the time I was Ketchikan General Hospital's bookkeeper, there were no social service programs for patients. The Catholic Sisters of Peace, who were administering the hospital, required that the administration do volunteer work for patients. I spent my time with the elderly. Lydia was in long-term care. I looked forward to my visits with her when she and I would weave together. She taught me her way of weaving Haida style, and because she wove slowly and meticulously, it was easy to learn from her. She was so happy that someone wanted to learn to weave.

Flora Mather, a New Metlakatla Tsimshian, enrolled in one of my mother's early classes. During class she was weaving her basket with the warps standing right side up and clockwise rather than in the Haida style of weaving with the warps hanging down and moving counterclockwise. Flora wove beautifully and the way she was weaving was easier for me to understand at the time. We agreed that

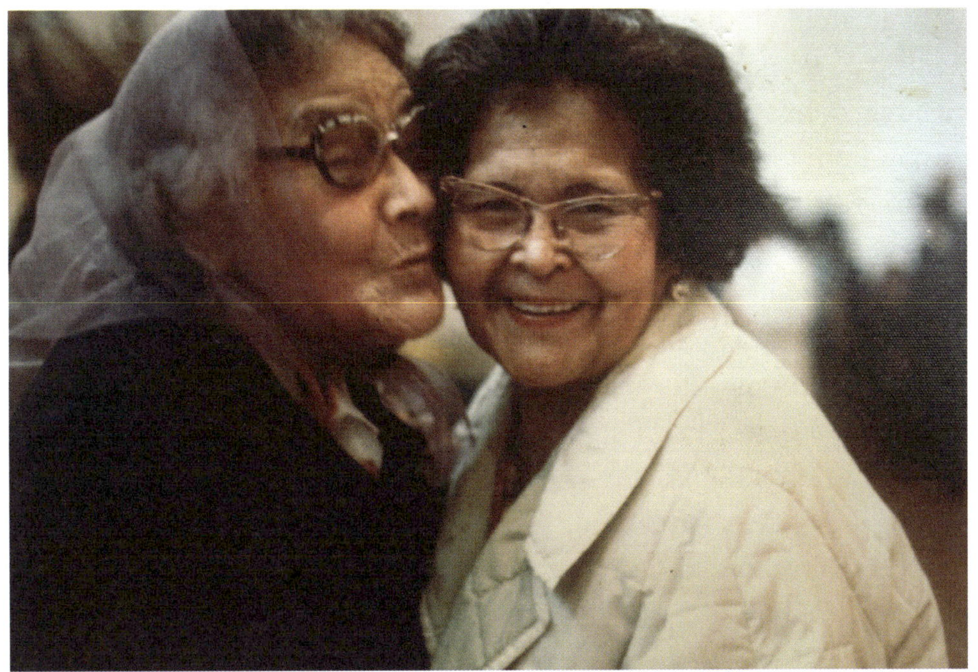

Selina kissing Flora Mather, a fellow weaver living in Ketchikan. *Churchill family*

I would help her get bark and she would teach me to weave in the Tsimshian style.

Dora Bolton, a New Metlakatla Tsimshian weaver, could understand English but did not speak it very well. She was the last one in Alaska at that time doing the Tsimshian lightning false embroidery design. Dora wove red cedar using wide material, but the weaving was woven evenly, her material preparation was superb and her baskets were exquisite. The evenness of her weaving is particularly important because using red cedar as weft, as meticulously as she did, is very difficult.

Brenda White from New Metlakatla taught me the Tsimshian style of plaiting when I was teaching a unit on Haida mat weaving on a loom. She had such an old-fashioned dry humour that she would leave me laughing at her hilarious comments.

Lydia Pawsey, a Tsimshian from New Metlakatla who lived in Ketchikan, was not one of my teachers, but she needs to be remembered for her contribution to keeping the Tsimshian weaving arts always present in Ketchikan throughout her life. She was a prolific weaver and sold her works in the Cape Fox Village of Saxman. Her selling of Tsimshian baskets in the Tlingit village, where she did not reside, reveals how Haida, Tlingit and Tsimshian held each other up, respecting and caring for each other. We all saw ourselves as one people who needed each other if we were to survive and grow through those times.

Esther Littlefield, a Tlingit weaver and elder, was the first weaver to get me interested in teaching Tlingit weaving. She was taking a class from my mother and had a dream from her grandmother telling her to weave Tlingit style, not Haida. My mother nodded toward me and said, "Ask her. She has been learning to weave with the warp standing up from Tsimshian."

I suggested that during her dream, Esther should ask her grandmother to show her how to weave in Tlingit style because I was learning Tsimshian and had not yet learned the Tlingit weaving. Sure enough, she came to class and was able to weave in the Tlingit style. She wove this style in her own unique way and taught me to weave the way her grandmother had taught her in the dream.

Esther worked at the US National Park Service in Sitka, Alaska, where we taught classes. A young girl who was conducting a tour said to her group, "We used to have big wars with the Haida."

After the tour group left, Esther called the young lady over and said, "My dear, these are my Haida friends." She gently went on, saying, "It was before my time, but my grandparents told me that the Haida would tow big canoes full of potatoes to sell to us. After they sold us the potatoes, they would sell us the big canoes. The Haida and Sitka Tlingit were close trade partners. They are our friends."

Esther upheld the knowledge that together we would stand strong but separately we would surely fall. She spoke this truth openly, respectfully and with power anytime the principles of respect and care for each other needed to be brought forward.

Esther brought this truth home to all of us who were attending a Ravenstail workshop in Sitka when she interjected into a hot debate about the origins of Ravenstail. "Look at the forest. There are cedar, spruce, hemlock and alder growing together. Their roots are intertwined. If one of the trees falls over, all of them are weakened. Is it so important to argue about where Ravenstail originated? Or is it more important to be thankful that so many are again doing Ravenstail?" She ended by reinforcing, "Together we are strong." The debate did not continue.

Learning from my elder weavers went beyond the learning of weaving techniques. One day, after my mother had passed away and I was in Sitka teaching a class, Esther asked me to visit her. The previous time I had been in Sitka I had found a greyberry bush and had hastily picked the berries into a garbage bag and dropped them off with Esther before leaving Sitka. I had not had time to visit with her then and looked forward to spending time with her on this trip.

She greeted me in her usual joyful and kind way. After serving me tea and a short salutary conversation, she quietly said, "Your momma is gone now, so I need to teach you to give your best. Don't give gifts in garbage bags. Clean your gifts and put them in nice containers. I am not mad at you. I just want to make sure you don't do that to someone else and make your people look 'eeshaan.'" (This is the Tlingit equivalent of "kaa.ngaa," the English equivalent of "poor, silly person.")

Esther always told the truth, even when it was hard for her, and she always said what she had to say in the most respectful, loving way—the old-fashioned proper way. I really miss her and her counsel. Esther was a 1991 recipient of the National Endowment for the Arts Heritage Fellowship Award for her regalia making.

Annie Lawrence, a lovely Tlingit weaver, was in long-term care at the Sitka hospital. When I was teaching in Sitka, I went to visit her and found her despondent, just staring into space. I had brought her some spruce roots to weave and offered them to her. "No," she said. "My eyes are too weak. I can't weave anymore."

Before I left I leaned over and whispered, "I am going to leave the roots under your pillow and then you can dream about the times you went harvesting and were weaving."

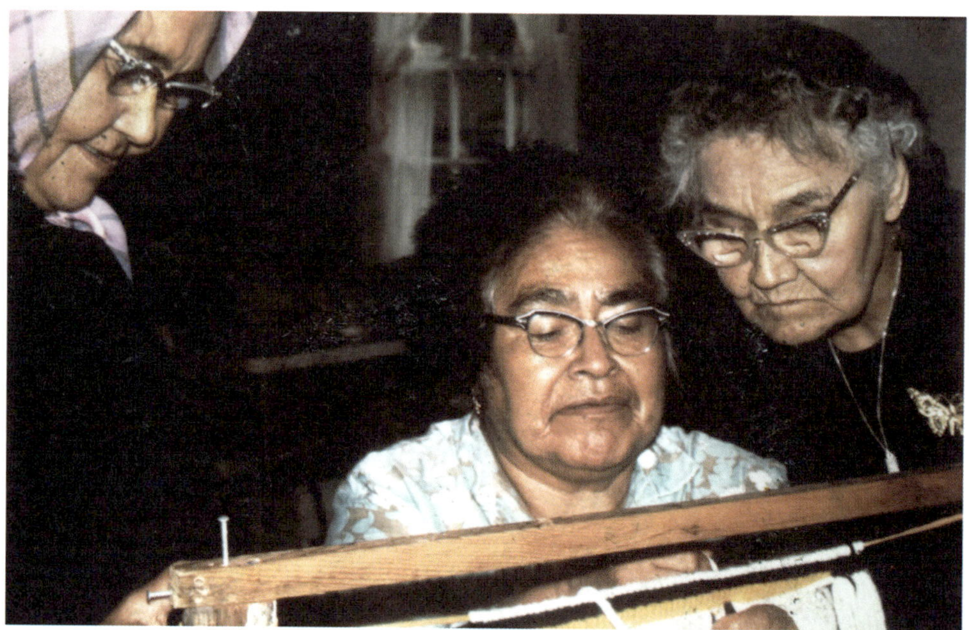

Florence Davidson and Selina watch Annie Lawrence weave. *Churchill family*

When I went back to visit her she was happy, sitting up and weaving the roots I had left. The first thing she said was, "Can you bring me more roots?"

I sat with her and asked if she would teach me to weave her Tlingit style. She was really happy I had asked, sharing with me that her daughters and granddaughters were not interested in learning—just as I had not been interested in my youth when my mother wanted me to weave.

I felt such humility when, years later, Annie's granddaughter took my class and I was able to give her the gift from her grandmother that had been left with me. I cared for it until she was ready to receive it.

Ida Kadashan, a Tlingit weaver who lived in Hoonah but was originally from Klukwan, was always so sweet to me. Each time I taught in Juneau she would come to demonstrate Tlingit weaving and to show her support for my teaching Tlingit style weaving. The University of Alaska videotaped her style of weaving so that it would not be lost. Ida expressed many times how important it was to teach and to learn to weave.

Bell Deacon, an Athabascan weaver, taught me willow root weaving. However, she said, "I am teaching you but you are not to teach anyone as long as my daughter is weaving and teaching."

I have never taught and will never teach this style of weaving because Bell's daughter and granddaughter, as well as other Athabascan weavers, are carrying on this tradition. Bell was such a beautiful spirit. My mother really enjoyed being with her and showing her how we prepared spruce roots. Bell was a 1992 recipient of the National Endowment for the Arts Heritage Fellowship Award for her basketry.

Jenny Thlunaut, a Chilkat wool weaver and a Tlingit basket weaver from Klukwan, was a true Christian woman that upheld the Tlingit ways and expressions of respect. She was kind, loving, appreciative and accepting of everyone. She started teaching in the last part of her life and expressed regret that she had not started teaching earlier.

Jenny amazed me when I watched her weave baskets. She would apply her designs without counting. She wove her baskets so quickly it was hard to see what she was doing. When I asked her to slow down, she would try but would soon be weaving quickly again. Weaving was second nature to her and she simply could not slow down.

I had asked her about an archival photo I had seen where an old Tlingit woman was lying on the floor in a fetal position weaving a basket. Jenny explained that in her grandmother's time, the Tlingit women wove on the floor with their knees up to their chest and wove on the other side of their legs. I tried this position but it was too uncomfortable for me.

Jenny was an exceptional teacher, explaining complex techniques so they were easy to understand. After working with her I went back to Ketchikan to finish my Naaxiin (Chilkat) piece. I became confused on a braid and called her on the phone for help. She told me, "If you can think backwards, it is easy."

She went on to explain, "Okay, when the pattern is over two and under one on the front side then the back is under two and over one. Just think backwards."

Jenny was a 1986 recipient of the National Endowment for the Arts Heritage Fellowship Award for her blanket weaving.

Cheryl Samuel, the author of *The Chilkat Dancing Blanket* and *Raven's Tail*, was also one of Jenny's Chilkat weaving students. Jenny asked all of those that she had taught to weave to teach others what she had taught us. She was so grateful that Cheryl had spent so much of her life researching wool weaving, writing books and teaching weaving.

I, too, am very grateful to Cheryl. She received an internal call and passionately started giving her life over to researching, writing and learning all she could about the wool textile weaving of Ravenstail and Naaxiin (Chilkat). Her work spans a time when people were not teaching or learning this magnificent art form. She studied robes and weavings that had been carefully stored in museums around the world. She understood that time was not on her side. The wool weavers were very elderly and she proceeded to work with the last of the weavers. Her work and love for weaving and the people of this weaving will live on, and this textile weaving knowledge will grow for years to come.

There are others who have taught me through their research, including Wilson Duff, George Emmons, Erna Gunther and, of course, Bill Holm, who fell in love with our art forms and spent years researching at a time when Indigenous people had no financial or political abilities or the access needed to make these studies. His work with the eldest of our peoples during that time has allowed their knowledge to contribute to the resurgence of the coastal arts.

Northwest Coast Indian Art: An Analysis of Form by Bill Holm, published in 1965, represents about twenty years of research that started in the early 1940s. The sharing of his research gave upcoming artists, who had no access to these wonderful pieces, an opportunity to learn from the work of our ancestral masters and the information of the eldest living at that time. Bill never hesitated to share the knowledge he gained.

Early on, Bill Reid, Robert and Reg Davidson, Pat McGuire, Guujaaw and Jim Hart, renowned Haida artists, followed the same path of diligently researching the oldest pieces of our ancestral masters to bring back into view the magnificent power of our design and carving art forms. These people, too, have become my teachers.

The Haida law of yah'guudang is represented in appreciation for the gifts that the universe brings to us no matter through what path those gifts come. Those who have laid foundations, and those who have built on the foundation to bring us new knowledge about ancient ways, deserve my humble respect and gratitude. Haw'aa.

CHAPTER TWO

My Beginnings

My Homeland — Haida Gwaii

Haida Gwaii is an archipelago located off the coast of British Columbia about one hundred kilometres east across Hecate Strait. Graham and Moresby Islands are the largest of about 150 other islands.

The Haida territories extend over Haida Gwaii, across the American border to the middle of Prince of Wales Island, including the surrounding waters.

The written word and our oral histories document the moving of some Haida from the area around Langara Island, on the northernmost tip of Haida Gwaii, to the territories on Prince of Wales Island about two hundred years ago. However, our ancient story documents some Seegaay relocating to this area, travelling on seal bladders across what is today known as Dixon Entrance, before the first trees came to Haida Gwaii.

Our stories tell of the time we lived through the ice age on the mountaintops of Haida Gwaii. As they were told to me, our stories reveal that we have been in our territories from time immemorial. The elders repeated time and again that we were placed on these islands where everything we needed for our well-being is provided, and that we are responsible to care for all life forms within our homeland. This is the very foundation of Haida culture.

Our ancient stories tell of Raven finding the people in a clamshell at Naikun. They tell of the origins of the Raven and Eagle people. They tell of the origins of our poles and weaving. They tell of how to care for our homeland and also reveal the consequences of misusing the life forms and gifts from our homeland.

Haida Gwaii has always provided people with an abundance of everything needed to live a good life, that is shelter, transportation, utensils, clothing and food. The tree of life—the cedar tree—grows in abundance and to great heights. The spruce and hemlock trees and the forest foliage provide food, medicine and weaving materials. The ocean and beaches provide salmon, halibut, octopus, seal, sea lion, clams, abalone, scallops, seaweed and an abundance of other seafoods. We are a people of the land and sea. Our culture arises from our relationship with all living things on Haida Gwaii.

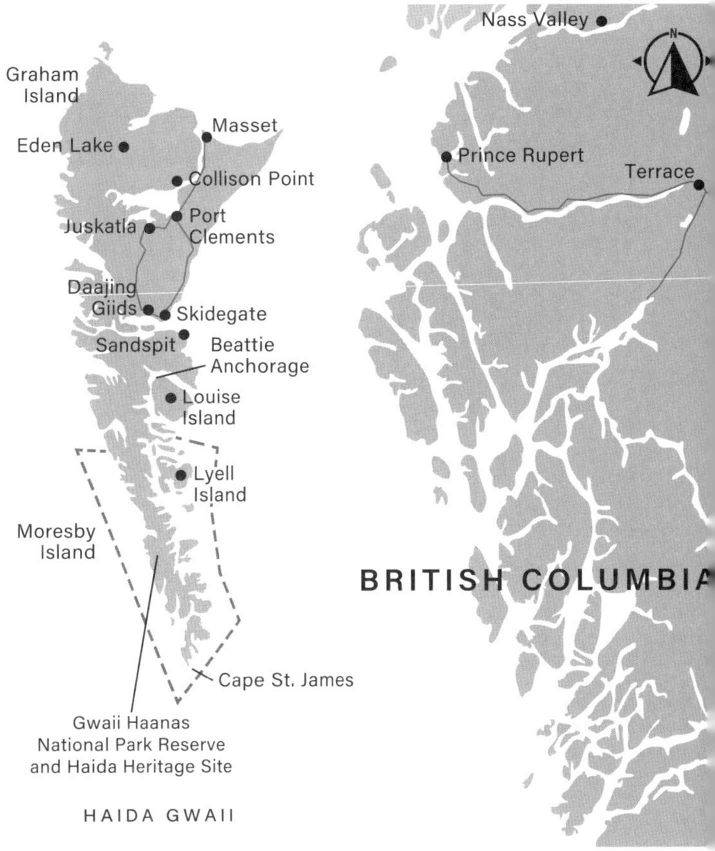

Map of Haida Gwaii and the west coast of British Columbia.

There was a time when the ocean level was so low that it was virtually dry land where Hecate Straits now exists. Glaciers melting after the ice age are thought to have contributed to the flooding spoken of in our ancient flood stories, which are proving archaeological and geological findings. We know through our stories that there are many villages underwater.

We have a saying, "The world is as sharp as a knife," and our territorial seas and the Pacific Ocean weather remind us often that we (humans) are not the beginning and the end of all things but simply a piece of the greater cosmos. Hecate Straits and Dixon Entrance can be formidable. They remind us that we must be respectful or the supernatural and life forces will provide consequence.

The village of Old Massett, where I was born and received my early training, is located on the northern end of Graham Island. Before moving into the village, which had previously been a food harvesting area, my clan lived up the Masset Inlet and cared for the Aayan G̱andlee (Ain River). Our clan also owned a house in the village of Howkan, on Prince of Wales Island, before the missionaries and government closed the village and the villagers were relocated into the new village of Hydaburg in Alaska.

Graham Island, where I gained my harvesting and cultural knowledge, provides an abundance of food in areas in which I was able to participate in the annual harvests, including Yakun Point, Tow Hill, North Beach, Yan, Shag Rock, Seven Mile, Wiah Point, Naden Harbour and River, Langara Island, Masset Inlet; and the Yakoun, Ain, Awun, Denan and Jaalan rivers and watersheds.

Along the sandy beaches and the shoreline, spruce trees provide spruce roots. The moss-covered forests provide cedar bark. The marsh and cliffs provide plants for food, medicine and basketry embellishment.

Our territorial seas are the home to many fish species. Seals, sea lions and whales, including killer whales, abound. The beach ecosystems provide an array of shellfish and ocean plant foods.

Haida Gwaii is a magnificent place that is full of life. The power can be overwhelming. Her beauty is breathtaking. Words cannot adequately describe what must be felt, heard and experienced to truly understand.

Haida Traditional Social Order

Our social structure is really very complex, with each person within the society having specific responsibilities and rights. Many of our published stories appear to be simplistic, but this could not be further from the truth. The stories are told with the assumption that the social and cultural information is known. This brief summary is provided to add context to weaving in relationship to our social order. There are many fine books that are easily accessible for those who would like to explore this area in greater detail.

Although research for those writings most often includes interviews with Haida elders and experts, the people who are from outside the Haida society are the primary authors. Because they do not have the intimate knowledge that is known within our Nation, they are not able to provide the "whole story." The information that they provide is limited to what they are told by a few or written by observers that first came to our islands. The other problem with these types of writings is the authors make conjectures that fall within the context of their own culture's understandings, personal biases and life experiences. Many times their conclusions are not accurate. When gleaning new information from these writings, including this one, which is written from my clan's and my personal perspective, always go to a variety of recognized tradition bearers to verify accuracy and to get further information that will provide greater understanding.

"How do you know, and who told you this?" are questions I was asked once. Some of my knowledge I can pinpoint to a specific person, place, time and context. But this question is like asking, "How do you know and who told you how to turn on a light?" So much of what I know is from living in the culture and hearing the stories from many people. For my generation and the generations before me, all of this was just a part of us. We learned by living it, through the Haida method of teaching by modelling and hearing things over and over.

Haida citizens belong either to the Eagle or Raven Moiety. I belong to the Eagle side, G̱aw Git'ans Gitanee Clan of the Dougwaa lineage. We originate from one of the four daughters of Labret Woman, whose family was located on the east coast of Graham Island.

Inheritance is matrilineal. All tangible and intangible properties are inherited from our mothers, including the side into which we are born. The rights and responsibilities of my clan have been passed to me through my mother's line and the rights of my children through me. My grandsons cannot pass their clan rights to their children. When a child is born of a male clan member and the mother is not Haida, the ancient tradition of adoption is implemented and, within our clan, the child is adopted into a traditional marriage family.

From ancient times we have married with other coastal Nations. Our tradition of adoption ensured that the children born of a Haida man and a woman from another Nation would have full rights as a Haida person, even if their mothers were not Haida. We have continued that ancient tradition. I have adopted the grandchildren and great-grandchildren of my brothers Victor and Oliver, whose sons did not marry Haida. These children are full members of our clan and have full access to inherited clan rights. The rights of our adopted females continue to travel through their female line of descent. When this was done for children born of non-Haida mothers, it did not take away the child's right within their mother's Nation. The children would be Haida in Haida territory and retained their clans and rights of their Nations of origin. These adoptions are honourable. Our names, crests, songs and stories we may use, and the areas of Haida Gwaii from where we come, that we share and that we are responsible for protecting, are passed to us from our mother.

Crests identify which moiety, tribe and clan we belong to. Each person may only use the crests owned by their clan. Even though the G̱aw Git'ans Gitanee Xaadee belong to the Dougwaa Git'ans lineage and share common crests, each of the individual clans within the lineage have obtained additional crests. The common crests that identify us as one lineage include the Guud (Eagle) crest, which identifies our clan's moiety, as well as Ts'ang (Beaver), Hlk'yan K'uustaan (Frog) and K'aal (Sculpin). The crest that is exclusive to the clan I belong to is Ilsjaadee, the Aayan watershed lucky forest fairy. Many of our female names begin with "Ils" and come from the Aayan watershed. My name, Ilskyalas, means "looks like the forest fairy."

The Sculpin is a spiritual crest used by our clan for personal protection. It is used as a tattoo crest, as well as for other spiritual reasons, because it has great powers.

The Beaver crest originated with the Tsimshian. My mother said that before contact, our tribe's iitlaagaada (Chief) Daayang and the Tshimshian Chief, Laagee.aak, exchanged robes and headpieces as a symbol of respect and to document a trading agreement that included sharing Hecate Straits. The crest that Laagee.aak gave to Daayang was the Beaver crest. Daayang gave Laagee.aak a headpiece that was embellished with a yellow woven circle. This exchange of robes, headpieces and crests made us as close as bloodline family.

We have no rights from our father other than those given by treaties or agreements that have been passed down to us from generation to generation. But one can receive some rights from one's father's side if one is known to be a xants (a reincarnation) of a person on an opposite side. I carry a Kyanuusalii name from my father's side because I am xants of his sister's child, who died when she was very young. I may use this name but when I pass from this world my clan has no right to pass this name on because it belongs to the Kyanuusalii. Just because I have a Kyanuusalii name does not mean I have any other Kyanuusalii Clan rights.

Like the Eagles, Ravens share a mother of origin and are related to each other in similar kinds of clan groupings. We refer to Ravens as opposite-side family members. These opposite-side blood relatives are important family members who play a large role in our social, ceremonial, educational and economic lives.

The traditional marriage law was that Eagles and Ravens would marry each other and those in the same moiety could not marry because they are considered immediate family. All Eagle women in my generation are my sisters and the men are my brothers. As well, all the Eagle women in my mother's generation were my mother's sisters. The aunties on the opposite side are known as skaan and when speaking they are referred to as kaanii (auntie).

Among our clan's traditional marriage families are the Raven Clans of Skidaaw K'aaw, Kyanuusalii and the Yaku 'laanas/janaas. Yaku 'laanas represents the male side and janaas represents the female side of a single clan, styled as Yaku 'laaanas/janaas. My maternal grandfather was George Harris of the Raven Skidaaw K'aaw Clan and my paternal grandfather was Adam Kude of the Stastas Eagle Clan. My father was Kyanuusalii, and my brothers Ivan, Victor and Oliver married into the Yaku 'laanas.

The relationships between the sides are maintained through careful expressions of respect, payback and acknowledgement of how important these blood relatives are to us. These obligations to each other keep us close and contribute to the sharing of wealth, which continues today. Whenever anyone from the opposite side does something for us, we have to pay them something. When we have feasts or potlatches we "hire" the opposite-side family to do the work and pay them and acknowledge them in public, just like when I received my name, Ilskyalas.

My uncle John Marks (Stastas Clan) was not happy when he heard my siblings and I were still being called by our childhood names. After the related High Women were consulted and the names selected, my Eagle uncles hosted a dinner at Uncle John's house, which included opposite-side relatives to serve as witnesses. He paid his wife, Charlotte Marks from the Raven Kun 'laanas/janaas Clan, to "put" the names on us. Eagles do not give Raven names and vice versa. Instead, the opposite-side person is paid to "put" the name onto an individual. This payment to the opposite side is used when new regalia comes into our clan as well.

Traditional Governance

I was told that one of the meanings for "Chief" is "servant of the people." Chiefs are not the same as a king. Chiefs are humble, hardworking and make certain that all clan members are well cared for. I watched Chief Wiah (Willie Matthews) live in that way. In our tribe and clan, Chiefs don't own anything but rather hold the clan properties in trust for the present and next generation. The level of tribal and clan support and contributions are a public gauge of a Chief's wealth and prestige. Chiefs inherit the treaties and agreements of the previous Chief. In my opinion, this is one of the reasons we have maintained continuity in culture and in the Nation's political objectives. Unlike Western government, which elects parties that may change direction and objectives after an election, the Haida continue forward as directed by the ancestors. The power of the Chief comes from the High Woman of his clan. Recently, people have been calling these women "matriarchs." I never heard this term when I was growing up or until the last few years. It is an example of trying to apply English words to Haida concepts. When people say matriarch, it does not mean that these women are Chiefs. Women can and have become Chiefs because of unique circumstance or earned respect, but we are matrilineal in inheritance and patriarchal in governance, with the male serving as the Chief. Men primarily serve as Chiefs but it is the women who are the power behind the Chief. The High Women are the power because they are trained to know the history and laws, and because as mothers and aunties they know what the people need. High Women know their clans inside and out and the people trust them.

Within our tribe, one of the key responsibilities of the High Woman (the eldest, most knowledgeable and wisest woman) is with the potlatching of a Chief. When the Chief passes away it is up to the High Woman to make certain that the next Chief is selected in co-operation with the High Women of the other related clan. The High Woman helps the Chief name the next person who will step into his position when his life here ends. She is known as "The Woman Who Holds the Chief's Name." She does what needs to be done for the previous Chief's memorial headstone moving from the residence to the mortuary place and ensures that all parts of the Chief's investiture are done properly, including making sure that the proper people are doing their part during the preparation and at the potlatch.

My mother was the High Woman of our tribe and I helped her follow through on her responsibility of potlatching my brother, Chief Gaalaa (Oliver Adams). After he passed to the other side, my mother, as the High Woman of the Tribe, made certain that the next village Chief, Chief Iljuwaas, was potlatched. This work is not done in isolation. High Women from other clans, including relations from the opposite side, work together so that all issues that may exist may be dealt with before the investiture potlatch. The High Women from each of the clans that play a public role at the potlatch are verifying the agreement of their clans.

When my mother passed away, my sister Jane (Kujuuhl) became the High Woman of our tribe. When Chief Iljuwaas was alive, he acknowledged Jane to be the High Woman of our tribe and consulted with her regularly. My sister May and I had the duty to advise Jane, who then gave him guidance. He took this seriously and kept us well informed.

When my sister left this life, her position and responsibilities passed to me as the oldest, culturally knowledgeable woman. A woman must be past her moon (menstrual cycle) to serve as one of the High Women and be recognized for her knowledge and wisdom. This balance between the High Woman and the Chief as expressed in the Haida language means the Chief stands at the front of the canoe and the High Woman gives him the power to move forward.

Haida Potlatches and Feasts

Legal business is taken care of and reaffirmed at feasts and potlatches. While the law against potlatching existed, legal business in Haida Gwaii was taken care of at smaller “family” dinners. To protect what was happening, witness and work payments of traditional goods became money payments in envelopes. These things might have been outlawed by the governments of Canada and the US, but our people knew they were important and had to be done.

Our potlatches and feasts are formal and highly structured. Who speaks, who dances, what is said, who is paid, in what order these things are done, and who accepts witness payments are all significant and affirm our legal and social positions within our Nation. When we had to hide and adapt what we were doing, this internal structure was still observed. Now that we are not "criminals" for having potlatches and feasts, we openly do these things and are grateful that the structure came to us with so much intact.

Originally Old Massett was a Raven village until Chief Siigee of the Skidaw K'aaw Raven Clan passed the position to his son Wiah, of the Sgaajuugaahl Git'ans Gitanee Eagle Clan, of the Dougwaa Git'ans lineage. Chief Wiah built a large clan house, Nee 'iiwaans (big house, more commonly known as the Monster House) and potlatched the house where he made payment for the work. The building of this house showed everyone that Chief Wiah deserved to be the village Chief even though he was Eagle and not Raven. The building of this house proved him to be honourable, a strong leader, a hard worker and wealthy enough to be a village Chief.

Yah'guudang — The Foundation of Haida Culture

Yah'guudang can be translated to "respect." But it has a much bigger meaning than "respect." It means to respect everything, and that all things are connected to all other things and the well-being of everything depends on the well-being of everything else. Yah'guudang encompasses everything that we think and do. It is the very essence of Haida culture.

It is not respectful to speak highly about oneself or one's clan. To do so brings down one's level of status. Instead, a clan expounds upon how great the opposite side is in comparison to how lowly one's own clan is. Even today when someone starts acting like what we call "too big for himself," people lose respect for him or her and the clan. This comes into conflict with the Western way of doing things. Writing a resumé is embarrassing and hard to do because it is all about expounding on how great we are. Even the writing of this book has been difficult since I am relating information about myself, my clan and my people.

When I was young, people were careful not to talk disrespectfully to others because the offending clan would have to have a dinner and make payment. People were careful about how they talked to others because of this rule. There are lots of similar rules.

Another rule that is still strong today and that helps to regulate inter-clan relations: If an Eagle falls down and a Raven helps the person who fell down, the Eagle must make payment and vice versa. Likewise, if I say three times that I like or touch something belonging to a Raven, that person has to give it to me but then I have to give back something of greater value and then the Raven has to give me something of even greater value and this goes on and on. It is expensive to get into this circle of payback. In my time everyone was careful about this.

Another custom observed today is if someone from the opposite side loans us something, payment has to be made. If a knife is loaned, a payment of something metal must be made. If someone from the other side compliments me at a function, a small payment needs to be made. We are reciprocal people and these rules help us to always recognize the opposite side (moiety).

There are many ancient rules that govern how we relate to each other, including when someone needs help. We are told, "Don't ask if someone needs help. Instead, just step in and help." Respect and esteem are obtained by proving to be a hard worker and a giving and respectful spirit.

When our population was decimated from somewhere between 10,000 and 15,000 people to about five hundred, it became necessary to come together in order to survive. The southern villages moved to

Skidegate and the northern villages moved to Old Massett. Each of these was a clan-owned village and the Chief of each at that time had to give permission for anyone to move into the village. The story is the same at both villages. Anyone moving into the village had to agree not to interfere in the village Chief's authority and that everyone was to stay out of the business of individual clans and to work any problems out in the old way of negotiation between clans. The agreement to share everything is based upon the traditional sharing of everything through the marriage system. In Skidegate and in Massett, the same phraseology is used to describe this agreement. As the old people said, "They agreed to 'throw their lot together.'" When I was young, the way we shared areas revealed how everyone was welcome to harvest in all areas of Haida Gwaii.

Our Place in the Universe

The Haida spiritual beliefs are complex as well. The fire pit, which was the centre of the big house, was the intersection of all things spiritual and is a simple description of our spiritual view. The powers and supernatural beings of the sky, the Earth beneath, the forest and the ocean, come together within the centre of the house. We do not worship supernaturals but take guidance and learn from the consequences they bestow. They are with us at all times. We know that each living thing is endowed with spirit and that they live within their own social structures. Our spirituality is about living every day respectful to all things. It is not about worshipping anything but living a respectful life and being grateful. My mother told me that men would vision quest using the steam house but women were born with vision, which came during the monthly cycle.

It is too bad that the missionaries did not take time to fully understand our spiritual understandings. Maybe the poles and crests that were burned, sold or stolen would still be with us.

When the Anglican Church came to Massett to teach the message of Christ, the Haida spiritual beliefs were similar to the main doctrine of the church, although the language was different. The Haida believe in one Creator, as do Christians. Haida say "mind" while Christians say "heart." Haida say "respect" while Christians say "love." Haida believe in an afterlife in which the actions of this life determine the next life. Christians believe in an afterlife as well. My mother modelled being a strong Christian who observed the spiritual understanding of the Haida without compromise to her interpretation of Christian spiritual beliefs.

Sometimes I wonder how it is I was so lucky to live in a time when love and respect for each other was extremely strong. I wonder why I was so lucky not to have to go to residential school and to live in a time when the villagers did not commonly use alcohol. I wonder why I was blessed to have so many tradition bearers in my life. I don't know what I did in my last life to deserve so many blessings, but I am thoroughly thankful for all my gifts during this life.

In My Mother's Time

To put my mother Selina's time into context it must be remembered that the first contact that the Haida had with those from the European continent was in the year 1774 when Juan Perez anchored outside of Kiusta. Although ships came to trade and a trading post had been established in Massett in 1869, twenty years before my mother was born, the traders had little impact on the lifeways of the Haida. Claims of political assertion over Haida Gwaii did not happen until after British Columbia's confederation with Canada in 1871. It was only about seven years before my mother's birth that the Canadian government claimed our land and seas of Haida Gwaii, leaving only some small reserves at a few old villages and at some of the harvesting campsites. These, too, the Canadian government claimed jurisdiction over and still do to this day, although we know that we, the Haida, own all of our territories, including reserves.

At the time of my mother's birth, the Haida depended upon the traditional way of life and the cash economy was making its entry into the culture. The international border between Canada and Alaska, laid down in 1903 without consultation with the Haida, divided families. The border had little meaning to the Haida who travelled freely back and forth within the territories of Haida Gwaii and the southern end of Prince of Wales Island, as had been done for thousands of years. This situation remains a problem. The Indian agent's office was opened in 1910, twenty-one years after my mother was born.

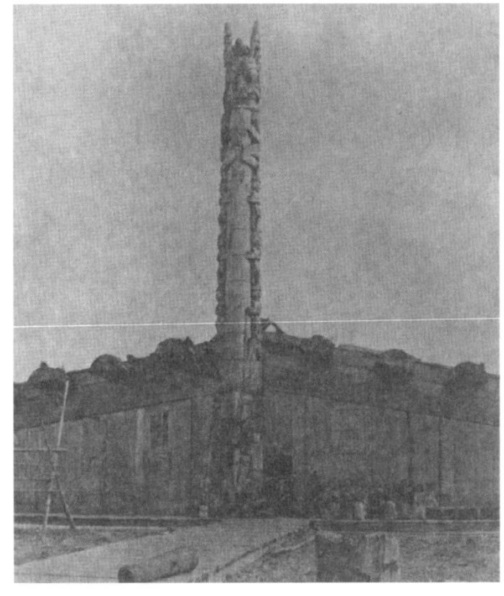

Exterior of Nee 'iiwaans, the house of Chief Harry Wiah, in Massett. *Royal BC Museum, B. Buxton, 1882*

Nee 'iiwaans (the monstrous house) of Chief Harry Wiah, in Massett, was still standing when Selina was born. She told me that her elders had told her that in long ago days, the house had been home to many people. She said that by the time she was born, the only residents were Chief Wiah; two of her aunties; Wiah's two nephews (including the next Chief Wiah); William Matthews and a couple of slaves. It was still the custom for the sons of the Chiefs' eldest sisters to live with their uncles so that they could be trained by the Chiefs and be ready to someday take on the responsibilities of the Chief positions.

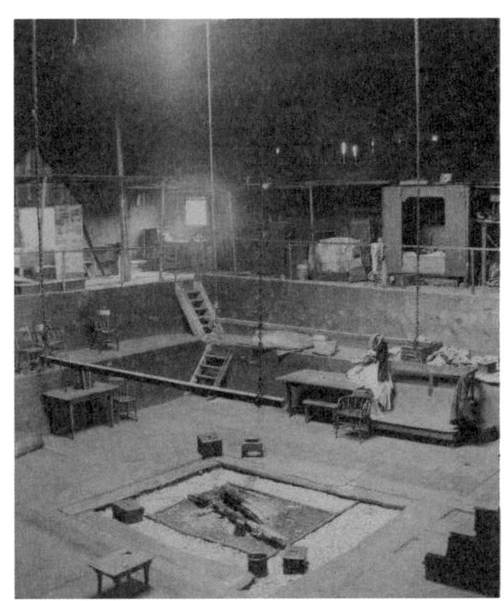

A photograph of the inside of Chief Harry Wiah's house, Nee 'iiwaans, taken before it was torn down. *Royal BC Museum, Richard Maynard, 1884*

Nee 'iiwaans, the great house of my mother's uncle, was torn down during her early teen years. The great poles had been cut down, sold or burned, and the household items had been removed. The grand clan house was replaced with a smaller "white-man's" nuclear family-style house.

When Selina saw the old photo of the interior of Nee 'iiwaans, she told me that as a toddler she had fallen into the central fire pit. An old woman pulled her out of the fire and bathed her in cold water. My mother had been severely burned but as an adult she only had a few scars on her scalp and her neck. The old woman told my mother that she would live a long life. As noted earlier, this prophecy came to pass and my mother lived to the age of ninety-five and she was still supporting herself with her weaving through the year that she passed away.

By the time of my mother's birth, the Haida population had been severely diminished from introduced diseases. Through permission of Massett Village Chief Wiah, the Haida from outlying villages had moved into Massett in order to help each other survive.

Reverend William Collison opened the Anglican mission in Old Massett in 1876, only twenty-two years before Selina was born. My mother was told that Reverend Collison cried when he saw the people. This was important because a Haida prophet had warned that when the people with a new religion came to the village, the people were to accept only those that were humble and to send the others away if they were proud. The tears of Reverend Collison revealed his humility and he was accepted.

My father's uncle, Dr. Kode, was a spiritual and healing doctor and would even be called by the church to help with sick people. He was also a canoe builder. My mother said she was scared of him because when he walked he growled a deep puffy grunt with each step.

My mother told me that long ago, when our clan was going to build its first house at Massett, a prophet warned our people that he had dreamed three times that the ocean wanted the spot where the house was to be built and would knock the house and poles down if they built it there. Our clan ignored the prophet's warning and built the house there. Sure enough, the ocean took the land and knocked the house down. Our poles were floating in the ocean and our clan lost its status in the eyes of the villagers. We regained status when we potlatched the sea and burnt the poles as gifts to the ocean. We then built the Gawgiit house at a higher elevation. The ocean did take that piece of land, which is no longer visible from shore.

My mother's father, George Harris of the Kyanuusalii Ravens, went whaling on the *Mascott* schooner at the age of twenty-five. Before he left he sang a goodbye song that he had composed for Selina, who was five years old, and her older sister Louisa. My mother told me this story and sang the song as she and I flew into Hawaii on our way to teach a weaving course in the 1970s. Sadly, I have never been musically inclined and do not remember the song.

In April 1894, Selina's father did not return home, lost at sea. Later, her uncles heard rumours that George was stranded in Japan and they got jobs on a schooner to search for him, but they did not find him. They did, however, find another relative that the Haida had thought dead, Samuel Girard Davis. He was living in Japan with a Japanese woman.

When the uncles suggested to Sam that he come back to Haida Gwaii, he told them that he liked his life in Japan and did not want to leave. The uncles were worried about him and after getting him intoxicated they took him on the schooner that was returning home.

By the time Sam sobered up, they were at sea. He was sad that they had taken him from Japan. A few years later, the uncles arranged a marriage between Sam and my mother's widowed mother, Jane Harris. They married at the Anglican Church in Old Massett on January 17, 1897, when Sam was thirty-two years old and Jane was twenty-seven.

My mother was eight years old when her mother married Sam and she stayed in Massett with her grandmother Edith George (Kujuuhl) when Sam and Jane moved to Howkan on the Alaska side of the border. When Selina became lonesome for her mother, she and her grandmother went to live in the house that Kujuuhl owned in Howkan. My mother's half-brother Kenneth was born to Sam and Jane.

In 1904, when my mother was fifteen, her uncles travelled to Howkan from Massett to announce that they had arranged a marriage for her. Kujuuhl said, "No. She is too young. Wait a few years. She

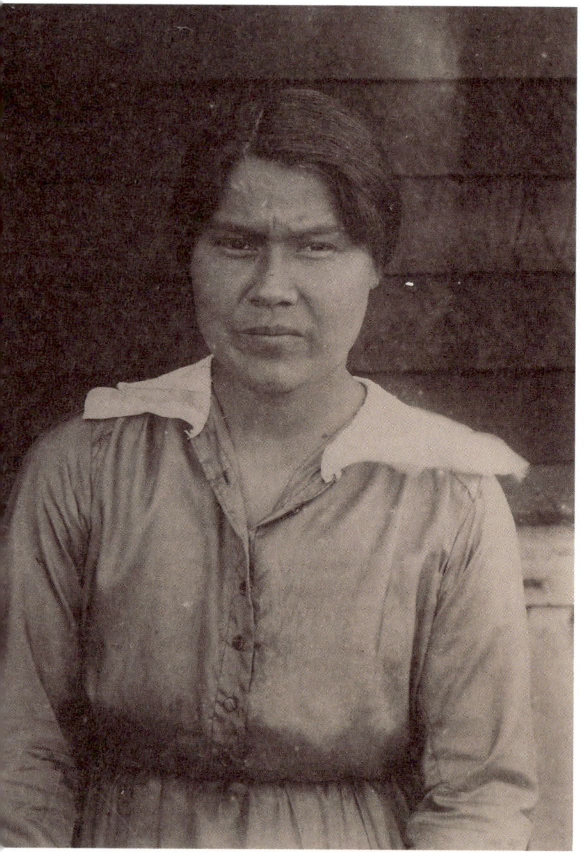

Young Selina, Delores's mother. *Churchill family*

does not know how to be a wife and take care of a house or family. They will just send her back to us."

Four years later, her uncles returned to Howkan to bring my mother back to Massett to marry. Her grandmother insisted that Selina was still not ready. The uncles were prepared for her argument and said, "That's alright. We found a rich man who can hire people to help her."

The uncles returned to Massett with my mother. Kujuuhl refused to return to Massett to see her precious granddaughter marry the old man that the uncles had selected.

A few days after my mother arrived in Massett, she went to the boathouse where she had heard her betrothed was building a canoe with his uncles. She had been told that Alfred was old and was a widower whose children from that earlier marriage had all passed away.

She walked to the boathouse and peered through a hole in the wall to sneak a peek at the man to whom she was promised. Upon seeing Alfred, she gasped aloud, "He is an old man! I don't want to marry an old man!"

When she told the story, she would stop and chuckle, saying, "He looked up and saw me. I think he was thinking, 'She is not as pretty as my sister, Louisa.'"

My relative, Augustus Wilson's father, was planning to travel to Howkan the next day. She asked him to take her back to her grandmother in Howk̲an. He agreed and told her to meet him on the beach before it got light. She went down to the beach when everyone was sleeping and was picked up by the canoe party.

The canoe headed out on the usual route that went to Port Simpson on the mainland, and then across Hecate Straits, to trade goods. After travelling for some time, an old woman in the boat shouted, "I'm getting wet!"

The pounding of the canoe had cracked the bow and water was trickling in. They tried to patch it using spruce pitch and tried to hold the bow together with cedar rope, but the crack kept getting wider and water began gushing into the canoe. They began to sing their death chants. As daybreak came upon them they saw land. The old woman, who was bailing, said, "Stop chanting. We will bail while you paddle as hard as you can toward that island."

They bailed and paddled as fast as they could but the canoe finally split. My mother was known to be a good swimmer. The old woman threw Augustus to her, saying, "Maybe the two of you will be strong enough to reach land."

Four-year-old Augustus was holding a toy canoe, which made swimming and pulling him along nearly impossible. My mother grabbed the little carved canoe and threw it out into the ocean. Even as an old man, when Augustus told the story, he was still heartbroken over her throwing away the little canoe that his uncle had carved for him.

As my mother and Augustus went into the water she promised the Creator that she would marry that "old man" if everyone made it to shore alive. Her prayer was answered and everyone lived.

The village had sent a search party at daylight when they found Selina missing and learned that she had left on the canoe back to Howkan. The search party picked up the cold and wet castaways and brought them to Port Simpson.

As soon as Alfred, my mother's betrothed, heard of her departure, he boarded a steamboat that just so happened to be docked in Massett and whose next stop was Port Simpson. In his rush to catch up to her, he had forgotten the wedding ring. He bought two wide gold bracelets from John Marks of the Stastas Eagles, who at the time was carving in Port Simpson. These bracelets were used in place of the wedding ring when my mother and Alfred married at the Anglican Church in Port Simpson, on August 31, 1908. Her maternal aunt Emily George and Alfred's brother-in-law Daniel Stanley witnessed the marriage.

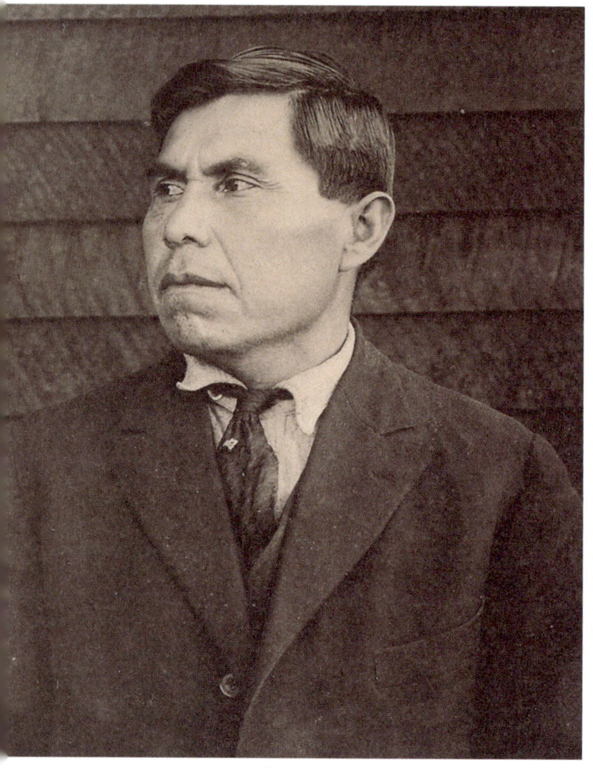

Young Alfred Adams, Delores's father. *Churchill family*

My father, Alfred, was born in 1876 to Adam Kudee (Adams) of the Stastas Eagles and Elizabeth Kudee (Adams) of the Kyanuusallii Ravens. His Haida name, Skilgyaans, means "Standing Chief" (Skil means "wealth" and gyans means "standing") and he was acknowledged as the Kyanuusalii Chief. Henry Alexander, my father's nephew, was acknowledged as taking that place after my father died. The Kyanuusallii originated at Hippa Island located on the west side of Haida Gwaii.

Alfred was sent to the Industrial School for Boys (the Ridley Home for Boys) in Metlakatla, BC, and returned to Massett after graduating when he was about seventeen years old. He had learned to read music and to play the organ at school, which amazed everyone in the village. Some of the old ones thought it was magic. I only heard him play classical music and hymns on the piano.

The missionaries had sent band instruments to Massett but no one knew how to play them. My father took the instruments home one by one and taught himself to play each of them. When he had command of all the instruments he taught the men in the village to read music and to play. This was how the Massett Brass Band was born. He was the band leader.

Skidegate, Hydaburg and other villages along the coast also had brass bands. The bands would travel to each other's villages for band competitions. Some of the old Skidegates loved to tell the story of when the Massett Band woke up the village as they marched through the village in the early morning hours, wearing their uniforms and playing their brass band music with great enthusiasm.

The tradition of arranged marriages continued for some in the next generation. My father was Ida Smith's tribal uncle and he arranged her marriage to Jeffery Smith. Jeffery was a short man with

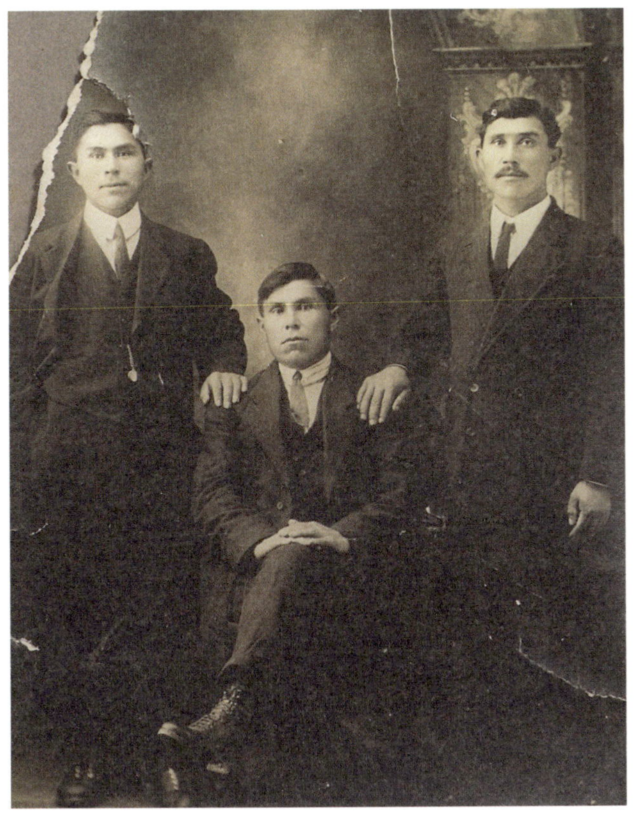

Chief Willie Matthews, Alfred Adams and Henry White. *Churchill family*

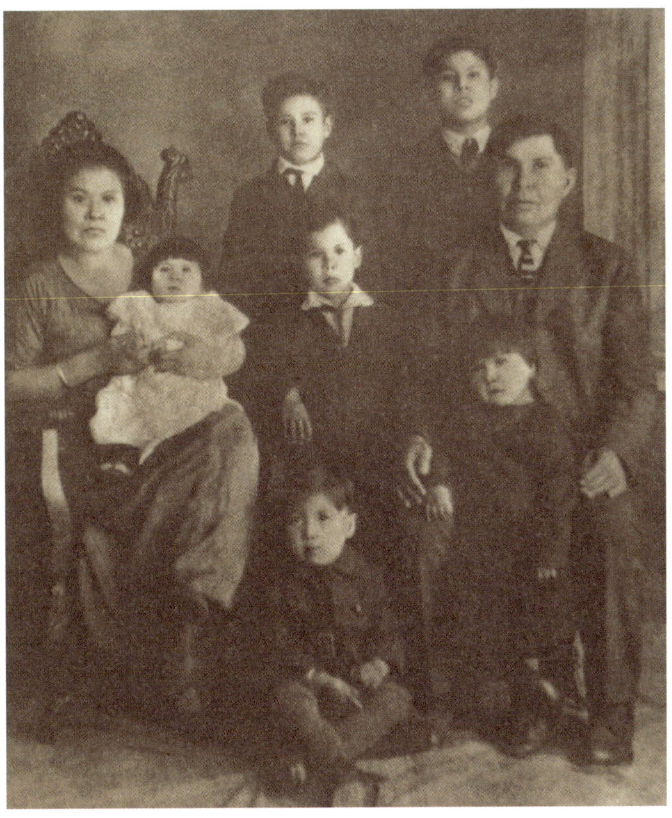

Selina and Alfred sitting with Selina's first six children (out of ten children total). Selina holds Baby Victor. Back: Oliver, Ivan. Middle: Livingston, Alfred. Front: Lorne and Julia. *Churchill family*

the deepest and most beautiful baritone voice I have ever heard. He became the Massett Brass Band leader and a member of the Massett Choir.

My father served as the lay preacher at the Old Massett Anglican Church, St. John's, and as the Massett Day School grades 4–5 teacher.

My mother told me about how hard he and Henry White worked on behalf of the church and the village with no pay. In those days people worked hard for each other without expectation of pay. This was one of the things we were all taught when we were growing up.

My father and Henry helped to translate the Bible, the prayer book and hymns. My father could translate the Bible into X̱aad Kíl as he read aloud from the English Bible. During a time that "Indians" could not gather in groups of more than three except for church, and could not gather to discuss land and rights issues, his sermons were always about forgiveness, love and respect and were related in some way to matters of land and rights.

My mother had a beautiful soprano voice and sang in the church choir. Ethel Jones, of the Kun Janaas Ravens, and Grace Wilson-Dewitt, of the Duugwaa Stl'ang Janaas Ravens and wife of Augustus Wilson of the G̱aw Git'ans Gitanee, often spoke with great tenderness and pride about the "old days" when the church choir prepared for months to sing the "Hallelujah Chorus" on Christmas.

My mother and father had ten children. The firstborn, Nancy, died while still an infant. The older children attended residential school. My father believed that if we were going to be able to regain recognition of our title and rights, all of his children needed to get an education. By the time I was born, only my sister Jane and brother Victor were at home.

There was no running water or electricity and everything that needed to be done was through manual labour. Water was carried from a stream before bathing and before washing dishes, clothes and diapers. Wood was chopped for heat. Most food had to be harvested and put up. Clothing had to be sewed. A clean home was one of the values that raised esteem. This was a lot of work, particularly when there were so many children, even though children were expected to fully contribute to the family. My father hired his sister Emma Alexander (Kaanii Xuuhliiyang) to help my mother care for the children.

My parents were the owners of the Adams and Sons General Store Ltd. in Old Massett, which was located on the piece of property that they had purchased together. Because the Haida traditional inheritance laws require that property returns to the deceased man's clan, the name of the store ensured that the property, store and the family properties would instead pass to my mother's family.

Shortly after my mother and father wed, Kujuuhl died. There were two old women who had lived with Kujuuhl and my mother moved them into her home. One day my father's sister Emma (Kaanii

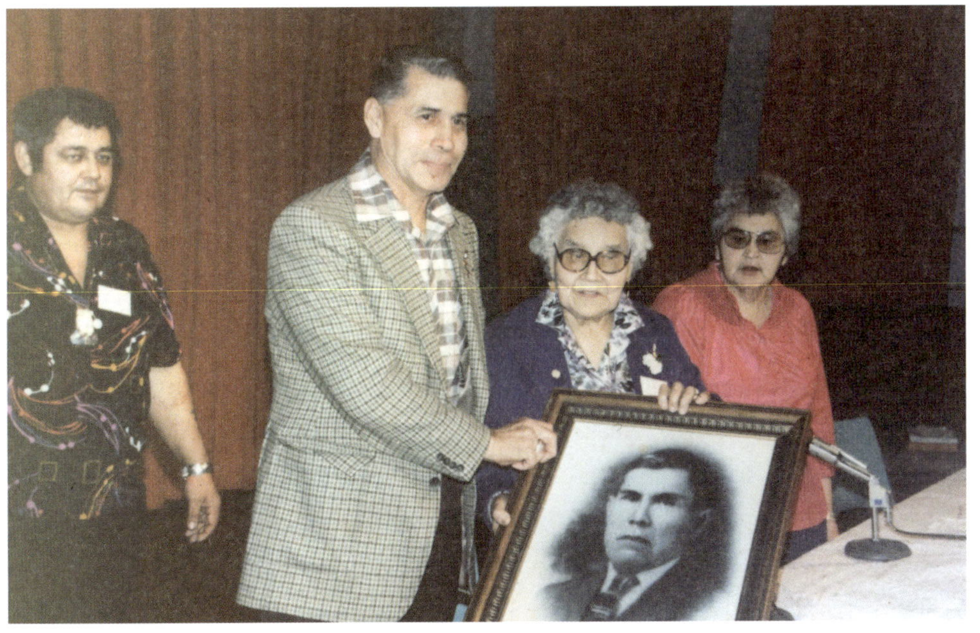

Ed Newman of Bella Bella, presenting a portrait of Alfred to Selina at the 25th anniversary of the Native Brotherhood. Selina's friend Mary Williams of Massett, Haida Gwaii looks on. *Prince Rupert Daily News*

Xuuhliiyang) walked into my mother's house and said, "Why are you taking care of those old slaves?"

My mother was astonished and said nothing. Her grandmother had always treated these two old women with respect and my mother thought they were her aunties. After Emma left, my mother asked the women if they were really slaves. They said it was true that they had been captured by the Haida as children. The missionaries had sent them back to their village as older women but they didn't understand their own language. They had been treated badly by their own people when they had gone home, so they returned to Haida Gwaii. By then Chief Wiah, who was their master, had already died, so his sister had taken them into her home.

The slaves of the high families were treated with great respect and often as family members. In fact, a grave marker that is at the foot of Wiah's grave has no name. It only states, "Servant of Chief Wiah, who wished to be buried at his master's feet."

My father Alfred was highly respected by everyone up and down the coast. He was the first President of the Native Brotherhood and much of his personal money went to supporting the work on title and rights. He had modelled the Native Brotherhood after the Alaska Native Brotherhood (ANB). My mother's stepfather, Sam Davis, had worked with the ANB and helped Alfred put together the British Columbia Native Brotherhood Constitution.

My father travelled up and down the coast working for Indigenous Peoples' rights. The Native Brotherhood had been the only Indigenous Peoples' organization that did not take any money from the government. The women in all the villages made baskets and shell art for the tourist market to support the work of the Native Brotherhood.

The Native Brotherhood worked for retention of title and rights, no taxation without representation, and equal social benefits and rights, including the right to pre-empt land, to vote, to end control of day schools and residential schools by religious bodies, and for the right to provide for family through full participation in the economy. Because of my father and others in his generation who worked steadily for the people through the Native Brotherhood, the "Indians" were given the right to the family allowance that all other Canadian families receive. Peter Kelly, of Skidegate, worked both with the Native Brotherhood and the Allied Tribes for the same objectives. The work that these leaders of that generation started is still in progress today.

My father, along with other Haida, gave testimony to the 1913 Royal Commission (the McKenna-McBride Commission on title and rights). The response to that testimony came in 1927 and further took away rights through laws that disallowed talking to lawyers and accountants, forbade gathering in groups or raising money to address title and rights and limited educational opportunities.

In 1918, the Spanish flu devastated the village. My mother became really sick with it and did not know that nearly her whole family had been wiped out from the sickness. When she woke, the only ones left were her sister's children, Eva, Ronald and Rita. My father and mother formally adopted these children. Years later, when she told the story and counted on her fingers all who had died, she would again be overcome with a silent grief.

In Massett it was widely known that during my mother's marriage to my father, she was the one who harvested food, owned cows and kept a big garden. She even did the hunting and slaughtering! My mother rowed her small skiff along the beach to gather driftwood and cut it up, just like a man!

My mother may not have learned the many things that a good wife should know, as her grandmother claimed, but she quickly put into action all that she had learned through the modelling of her elders. Some of it was learned through trial and error.

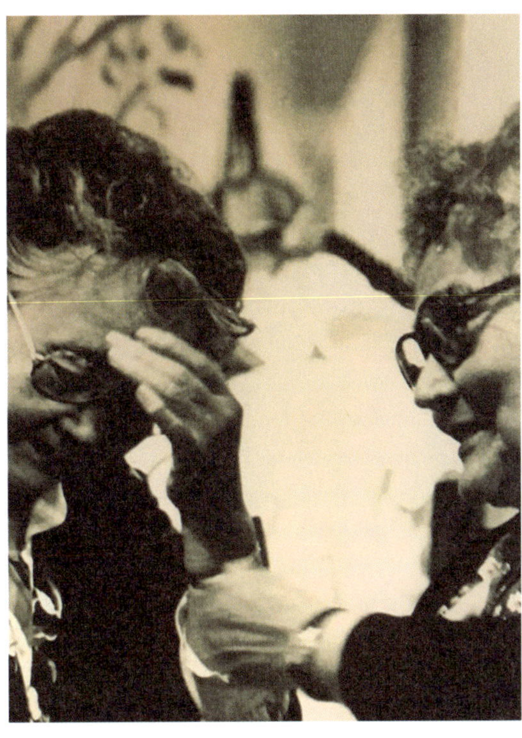

Florence Davidson, one of Selina's closest friends, shown here with Selina. *Ulli Seltzer*

Florence Davidson, of the Yaku Janaas Ravens, and my mother loved to tell the story about their first experience of smoking fish by themselves. They sliced up the fish, they built the fire in the smoke house and they took turns hanging the fish just as they thought they had seen others do. However, each time they went into the smokehouse to hang the fish, they came staggering out gasping for air, with their eyes scrunched closed and tears running down their faces.

An old woman walked by them, shaking her head, and chided, "Hey, what is the matter with you two? Don't you know that you hang the fish first, then build the fire?" After the old woman had left, the two young women looked at each other and began to roll on the ground laughing until their sides were aching. They both loved to tell this story and always laughed as if it was just happening again.

Both Mother and Florence, as well as others in that generation, loved to tell stories that made fun of themselves. They were all good at "telling on themselves." Their escapades, as they told the stories, were hilarious. I loved listening to them visit, as it was always filled with roaring laughter.

Florence Davidson liked to retell the story about the high bush cranberries in Aayan. My mother was the Woman of Aayan. As the Woman of Aayan, she was responsible for going to Aayan to pick the high bush cranberries. After my mother and her clan sisters did the first pick, my mother would come back to the village, pick the best ones out of the harvest and place them into small, square, wooden boxes that she brought to Florence Davidson's husband, Robert Davidson Senior. When this was done, the rest of the village went up to get their cranberries and brought the best of their pick to my mother, also in small wooden boxes. Selina then preserved these to be used at community dinners and to share with others in the village. In those days everything was shared with everyone in the village, but it was important to respect the ceremony of harvesting in places that were the responsibility of other tribes and clans.

My strongest memory is that everyone loved and cared for each other. That no one said, "This is mine or that area is mine." No, instead everyone worked together and everyone shared what they had. It saddens me to hear a few people haughtily declare, "This is our territory. This is ours." My generation never heard those words until recently by a few. Instead, the generation before mine modelled what it is to be Haida—gracious, kind and sharing, recognizing that we are all connected and everyone's well-being depends upon the well-being of everyone and all other things.

My Childhood

My mother lived in a period of extreme change. By the time I was born in 1929, my mother and other villagers were ordering goods from catalogues and the houses were all built in the nuclear family style. We still did not have running water or electricity and most of the domestic work was done manually.

My mother collected and displayed china and silver in her home. Putting up food included drying, salting, jarring and canning. We kept food cool with outdoor cabinets and root cellars. In the summer we used ice blocks that we got from the canneries. When the ice block refrigerator came to Haida Gwaii, in X̱aad Kíl it was called "the place food is put before it is thrown away."

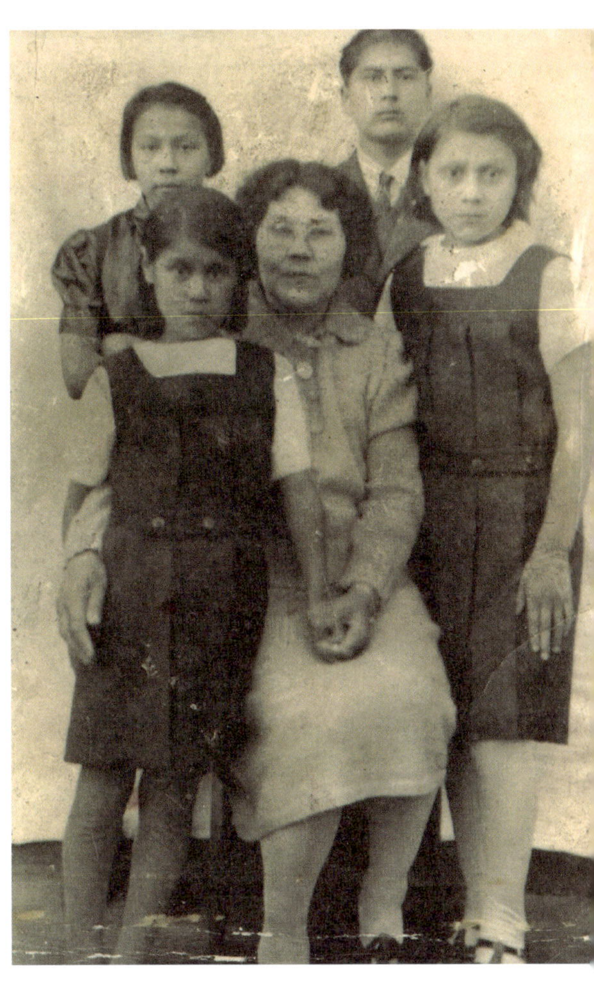

Selina with her younger children circa 1939. Front: Mae (T'aayhlwaad); Back: Jane (Kujuuhl), Victor (Stast) and Delores (Ilskyalas). Mae and Delores are scared of the photographer. *Churchill family*

Our home had traditional woven and carved items. My mother's goat horn spoons, wood soapberry spoons and soup ladles were kept in woven spoon baskets. Our potatoes were stored in woven potato baskets. Our woven work hats sat ready for the summer harvesting season. Some of my mother's projects were stored in woven women's workbaskets and her jewellery was kept in covered baskets. She kept her harvesting baskets stacked in a box when the season ended and the baskets had been wet down and folded flat. Reuben James Harris, known as "Jimmy," my grandfather George Harris's younger brother, had a large copper shield on his wall. Others had the odd carving. I often wonder what happened to all the goat horn spoons, weavings and carvings that I saw in village homes when I was growing up.

Just after I was born, my mother was poisoned from eating crabs. She told us she actually died for a time. While she was in the death state, she said that she had left her body, saw everyone in the room and floated over the village. She found herself in a house that was being built and a man came up to her and said, "What are you doing here? Your house is not ready yet. You have to go back." She woke up to the singing of the death chant. In those days family members did not cry in public over death. Instead, people from the opposite side cried and sang death chants. Because of the poisoning she could not breastfeed me. Alice Parnell became my wet nurse.

I had five natural-born brothers and four sisters. Their names are Nancy, Ivan, Oliver, Livingston, Lorne, Julia, Victor, Jane and Mae. I also had the three other siblings—Eva, Ronald and Rita—who my mother had adopted when her sister Louisa died during the Spanish Flu epidemic. My three stepsiblings, George, Rosa and Clara Peratrovich, joined the family when my mother married George Peratrovich.

Of my natural-born siblings, Nancy died a year after she was born. Livingston died from tuberculosis before he married. Ivan was married to Connie Jones (Yahkw Janáas) and had two children: Margret and Ivan Junior. Lorne married a Tsimshian woman, Irma Dundas, who was from New Metlakatla, in Alaska, and had three children: Margret, Sylvia and Lorne Junior. Oliver Adams married Dora White (Yahkw Janáas) and had four children: Babs, Tommy, Carol and Sandra. Julia married Bill Yants (Yaats' Xaadee) and had one boy, William. Victor married Primrose Davidson (Yahkw Janáas) and had seven children: Victor Junior, Joyce, Isabelle, Merle, Alice, Alfred and Errol. Mae married Frank Jones and Don Tracy (Yaats' Xaadee) and had five children: Ernestine, Roslyn, Frank, Alfred Jones and Montell Tracy. Jane married Ralph Bennett, Nick Kristovich and Judson Brown and had five children: Victor, Ralph, Pearl, Lisa and Nick. When Jane passed in 2022, she left me the only living child of my mother.

One day after Jane went to residential school, a young woman came walking toward Mae and me. We ran and hid behind the cow pile. The woman shouted, "Don't be afraid. I am your sister, Julia." Mae looked up at me and said, "Tell her we don't need another sister. We have enough sisters." Julia had been away at residential school and we did not know her. When we recalled the story to Julia, Mae and I would laugh and laugh. Julia, our ever-so-serious sister, would look at us with no expression. I think she thought Mae and I were silly.

My memories are full of my mother helping old people by bringing them firewood and food. She also took old people in and cared for them. Chief Gaalaa, who belonged to the Ts'iits' Git'ans Gitanee, was one of the elders she cared for in our home. He had part of his nose bitten off during a fight. He would pay me to get brown paper bags that he would mix with flour paste. He put this mixture on the hole in his nose so it looked like he had a full nose. I think he did this because a traditional Haida spiritual belief is that if a body part is missing we cannot go to "Haida Heaven." That was the term used during my time for the place that the Haida go before returning to earthly life as xants. Before he passed away, he gave his name, Gaalaa, to my mother, as his way of thanking her for taking care of him. Her brother Alec carried this name, which was later taken as my brother Oliver Adams Chief's name.

My older sister Jane stayed at home in her early years, but like my older siblings she then went to residential school. She is two years older and when she was in the village she spent most of her time with friends her own age. The late Adelia Jones-Adams (Yahkw Janáas) was her best friend. Adelia enjoyed reminiscing about all the fun and crazy things that she and Jane did as children.

Breakfast and lunch were fairly informal but suppertime was very formal, with my father sitting at the head of the table. All meals began with prayer. Mother's china and linens were used at each meal. Adults carried on conversation during the meal while the children sat eating quietly and listening. When we came to the table, the men and boys would stand and help push the chairs in for the women. Even for the female children. When we left the table, we excused ourselves.

We spoke Haida in our home because my mother spoke broken English. In one sentence with few words, using the proper emphasis and tone, a story can be told that would have required paragraphs of English. It is also the best way to relate funny stories because the language is so descriptive. When I was growing up, there were many funny sayings that were commonly used by everyone.

Like my father, I loved reading and his extensive library of books provided me with all the reading material that I needed. In the evenings, the family would often sit in the living room singing or listening to my mother sing as my father played the piano.

My youngest sibling, Mae, was born premature. She was so tiny she fit into my father's hand. When I first saw her I thought she was a rat and screamed my head off. My mother kept Mae alive by placing her in the cooler of two warming ovens on the back of the wood stove. She fed Mae with cheesecloth soaked in cow's milk. Mae was sickly throughout her life, spending many years in a body cast in hospitals. She eventually died from cancer, a disease that is rampant in our family. But she was my best pal. We had so much fun playing with each other. Her two daughters, Ernestine and Roslyn, and her sons, Alfred and Frankie, inherited her quirky view of the world and unique sense of humour.

My father hired Josie Bell to help take care of their children, and others to help with the cooking and cleaning. This allowed my mother to do her many other chores and projects, including weaving, harvesting, sewing, hunting, tending to her garden and cows, and helping with the Anglican Church Women's group and the Native Brotherhood.

St. John's Anglican Church in Massett was central to the activities of the village at that time. Church holidays were observed. There seemed to always be choir practice. Women carried a cedar bark woven "missionary" bag that held their Bibles, prayer books and hymnals. At the end of the harvest season in the fall, the congregation brought part of their harvest in a basket as an offering. When service was over, the baskets were auctioned off to fundraise for the church.

My father led the church services and gave the sermons. He always preached the love of Christ and the importance of forgiveness. Children attended service and Sunday school and we all knew to sit quietly and to listen.

When there was death in the village, the church bell would ring a death toll. My father would go immediately to comfort the family. The Haida believe that the spirit of a person is huge and stays with us until the body is buried. Because of this there are many rules around death. Everything stopped in the village. No meetings were held. Radios were turned off and everyone spoke softly and limited conversation. The family wore black armbands and covered their windows and mirrors with cloth. The clan members of the person who died did not cry in public. Just before my mother took her last breath, she told me not to cry and to be strong. She said, "There will be plenty of time to cry after the funeral."

In my time everyone seemed to have prepared for his or her death. Death was recognized as part of life. Some had their coffins stored under their houses. The opposite side took care of the funeral and the family, including keeping the family fed and comforted, dressing the body, lining the coffin, digging the grave and putting on the funeral feast.

The clan members could not dance until the headstone was moved to its final resting place, about a year later—or when everyone was through grieving and ready to let the person's spirit leave. At the memorial feast, which the clan members of the dead person would host, the people who took care of the funeral were paid. In my time money was put into an envelope because potlatch gifting was illegal. Today, goods are given out at the feasts. My mother told me that the headstone moving is what took the place of raising memorial poles and posts, after these could no longer be raised.

Whenever we went to visit others or were at public events, the children were required to sit quietly, sometimes for hours. Even adults did not talk when someone else was talking. The old rule—requiring payment if you walked in front of an opposite-side person three times in a public setting—was still observed.

When we went to Captain Andrew Brown's house for dinner, I would never get dessert because he would do and say all kinds of funny things behind my father's back. I could never keep myself from hysterically laughing, which looked to my father as if I was being rude. My father did not know Andrew Brown was making me laugh and my dessert would go to Andrew. He really was a very funny man and could tell the greatest stories.

My Naanii Skuujuus and Kaanii Xuuhliiyang wanted me to live with them because I was xants in their clan. I already went everywhere with them, so my mother finally gave in and I stayed with them for a couple of years. These are the years that I learned the bulk of what I know about food harvesting and preparation.

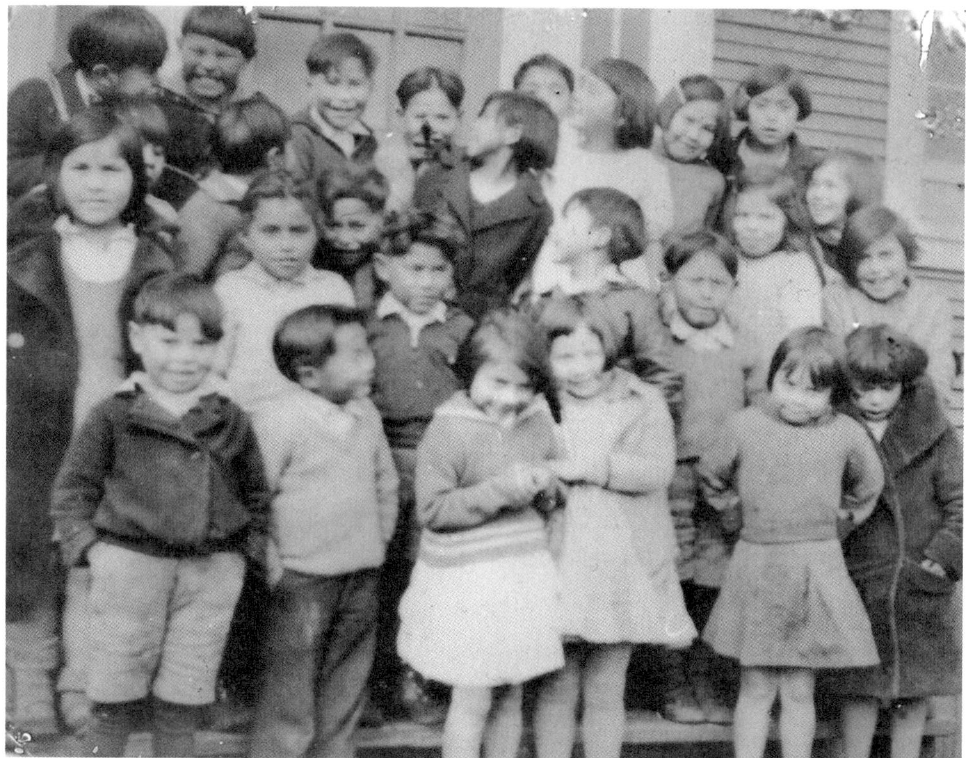

An Old Massett Day School class photo with Delores in the centre of the front row. *Churchill family*

I attended Old Massett Day School and although I understood English a bit, I did not speak English. That first day, when the teacher called "Delores Adams" I did not know that was my name since I was called by my clan child's name, Gubaadaslee. I sat there until my sister Mae poked me and said, "They're calling your name. Say 'present.'" I replied, "I will not say 'present.' I don't want a present. I don't even know that lady."

I went to Old Massett Day School in the village from primer to grade 3 when my family had to move to Prince Rupert, BC, to care for my brother Livingston, who was dying from tuberculosis, and to help care for my sister Mae, who was in a cast and needed to be hospitalized.

I went to Prince Rupert public school, which allowed only a certain number of "Indian" kids to attend because the law did not let large numbers of Indians gather in a public space. Indian agents did not come to the school to send us to residential school.

I was lonesome for my home and family and would spend hour after hour going over and over the things I had done at home. I think that is one of the reasons so much of my childhood can be remembered as if it were yesterday.

It was not easy going to an integrated school. Some of the non-Indigenous children could be cruel and would gang up and kick and punch us. I still have scars on my shinbones from those beatings.

I did make a best friend, Eleanor Fitzgerald, who was Irish. She lived in the basement of the Prince Rupert courthouse because her father was the gardener. She and her family were very kind. Eleanor died from influenza right after World War II.

At that time the restaurants had signs that said, "No Dogs or Indians Allowed." The first time we went to a restaurant that allowed Indians we were seated in a booth and a curtain was drawn in front of us. I asked my father why they did this. "It's because we pray and they don't want other people to stare at us," he replied.

Smile's restaurant was the only restaurant that fully welcomed Indians. I think it was because the restaurant served fishermen and Indians who were in the industry. Smile's is still in the same spot at the Prince Rupert harbour in Cow Bay and it is still my favourite restaurant in Rupert.

When we lived in Prince Rupert, the Anglican bishop wanted to learn to speak Haida, so I taught him. This probably contributed to my retention of my first language.

I remember the terrible fear and hiding under the concrete bridge at the Rupert courthouse when the World War II bomb drill sirens blasted. My brother Ivan was serving in the war and we were always worried about him. He came back a war hero with a chest full of medals.

We moved back to Massett after Livingston died and Mae was released from the hospital. "Indian" children could not go past Grade 8 in public schools and I would not be able to return to school in Rupert. My father wanted me to continue my education, which could be done at Massett Day School. I had skipped Grade 5 when I was at the Rupert school.

When we moved home, the New Massett parents wanted a local school for their children but did not have enough enrolment to receive provincial school funding. They invited four others and me from the village to enrol into their school. The stipulation was we would have to disenfranchise as Indians. When I asked my father what "disenfranchise" meant, he told me I would have to quit being "Indian" and could not live on the reserve. The five of us told the organizers that we did not want to quit being "Indian" and we would not be disenfranchised. They wanted the school so badly that they agreed that we could go to the school without disenfranchising, but when school officials came for visits, we would have to stay home. We attended the school and officials never did visit the school. I was a strong student, particularly in math. I was able to attend this school for Grades 9 and 10.

When my brother Ivan came back from the war, he could not live in the village any longer because Indians had to disenfranchise to join the military. He was no longer an "Indian" and could not live on the reserve. Although a war hero, he and his family had to move to Prince Rupert, which was hard on him. He had horrible war memories but had no family members in Rupert to help him through the psychological wounds. He led the Prince Rupert Canada Day parade each year wearing the many medals he had received.

My father died in 1945 from cancer. After he died, my brother Lorne put in a pool hall where the family general store had stood. When my mother moved to Ketchikan to marry my stepfather, George Peratrovich, an Alaskan Tlingit, she rented the family home out to a relative with all furnishings, books and personal items stored in the house.

Jane, Mae and I moved to Ketchikan with our mother in 1946. Our brother Victor came with us but went back to Massett after the fishing season was over.

Our family home in Old Massett burned to the ground while we were in Ketchikan, along with all the historical information that my father had collected. It was sad when it happened and even sadder when I became fully aware of the value of the historical documents that had burned.

I graduated from Ketchikan High School. In my opinion, the Canadian public school system was better than the American system because it was easy to be an A student on the American side of the border, except in history class. Canada and the United States have different interpretations of the American Revolution. The teacher asked, "Who was John Paul Jones?" I quickly raised my hand and replied, "Oh, he was the American pirate who sacked the coast of Britain." That is the wrong answer because in the United States, John Paul Jones is an American hero. As well, General Custer, the great "Indian" killer, was considered an American hero at that time. But I knew the truth and let my children know that he was actually a madman.

I really liked going to Main School in Ketchikan. Because of a Haida woman, Nettie Jones, and her Tlingit attorney, William Paul, fighting for her children's rights to attend public school, Ketchikan schools were integrated in 1929. Also, before we moved to Ketchikan, the first civil rights laws in the United States had been passed in Alaska in 1945 because of the courage and work of Tlingit woman Elizabeth Peratrovich. Ketchikan was a fishing town and the Norwegians, Japanese, Filipino and the "Indians" mixed easily.

When we moved to Ketchikan there were few Haida living there. Martha Shields, from the Saxman Cape Fox Tlingit Tribe, took my mother as a sister when she saw the Beaver crest bracelet my mother was wearing. That Tlingit family took this adoption seriously and we were invited and included in everything they did.

There were many smoke houses on the beach located at the south edge of Ketchikan. These belonged to the Tsimshian. They very generously shared a smokehouse with my mother. No one bothered the smoke houses. No fish were stolen and nothing was vandalized.

The Alaska Native Brotherhood and its counterpart, the Alaska Native Sisterhood, were really strong at that time and the membership

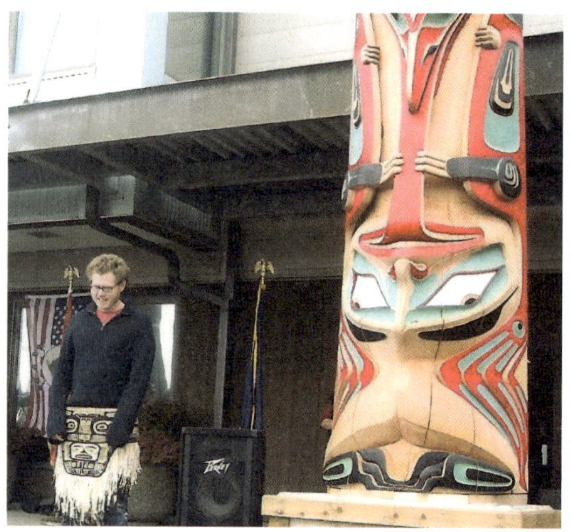

Donald Varnell, Delores's grandson, carved the pole pictured. The pole was commissioned by the Ketchikan Indian Corporation in 2004. He is wearing a Naaxiin dancing apron woven by Delores. *Dana Rivers*

was large. My mother joined the Sisterhood and, like the other women, worked hard to support that work.

The "Indian" fishermen brought in herring eggs, eulachon, halibut and salmon and shared it at the dock. Some had cash to help with gas but if someone came with a bucket and had no money they were not turned away. This doesn't happen any longer. Today, sharing like this is illegal in Alaska. Thankfully, in Haida Gwaii the Haida worked for and retained the right to access resources for cultural reasons and food.

The Ketchikan Tsimshian, Tlingit and Haida got together and would go for picnics together at China Town. Everyone shared everything and helped each other. It did not matter what tribe or clan people came from. We knew if we were going to move forward we all needed each other. My children grew up in "Indian Town" and had the great privilege of having Haida, Tlingit, Tsimshian and people from many nationalities and cultures as friends.

The unity of the Ketchikan "Indians" continues through the Ketchikan Indian Community (KIC), the Alaska Native Brotherhood and Alaska Native Sisterhood, whose members include Tlingit, Haida and Tsimshian. The pole that my grandson Donnie Varnell carved stands in front of the KIC Tribal Health Clinic along with the Tshimshian pole by David Boxley, and Tlingit carver Israel Shotridge's pole. These poles represent this unity.

People living in "Indian Town," as our area of town was referred to, fully participated in the St. Elizabeth Episcopal Church, which was built and supported by the congregation through fundraising of Tsimshian preacher Father Paul Mather and the building skills of the "Indian" people. The church was a place where all three tribes joined together for social and spiritual reasons. The men cooked pancake breakfasts and the congregation held bazaars, fairs and events around the church calendar. The youth climbed mountains, went to camps and belonged to the youth group. The choir was large and we had our own organ player. There was a lot of love for each other.

After I graduated from high school, I married Allen Churchill in Ketchikan in 1949, when I was nineteen years old. We had three natural-born children: April Victoria Churchill (X̱iihlii Kingang), Evelyn Dee Vanderhoop (Kujuuhl) and Holly Churchill (Dlaa K'uunaa). I also have two stepsons, Mike and Gary Edwards. At the time of this writing, I am the naan (grandmother) to nine grandchildren and the naan k'aayaa (great-grandmother) to nine great-granddaughters and three great-grandsons. I also have eight traditionally adopted children, who are the grandchildren and great-grandchildren of my brothers Victor and Oliver.

When I was twenty-nine years old, my husband lost his legs when a drunk driver hit his car. I became the sole breadwinner for a number of years. While I worked, I also went to Ketchikan Community College, took correspondence courses and won a Blue Cross Summer Scholarship at the University of Chicago. All of this was possible because the community of Ketchikan, the Sisters of Peace and the Native community were behind our family. Don Newman, a Kaigani Haida, and his wife Millie, a Tsimshian from New Metlakatla, were so important to helping me with the children through this time. I often think about how lucky I was to be a Native woman in the '50s, to have a husband who encouraged and supported me in every way.

In 1982, my mother, my brother Victor, my sister-in-law Primrose Adams, Nathan Jackson and his sister Nora and I were in Chicago to demonstrate at a Northwest Coast exhibit in the Field Museum. We were walking down a sidewalk together when Victor suddenly stopped and asked, "Delores, does this remind you of anything?" as he looked at the low clouds. I looked up and immediately knew what he was talking about.

Skilee Aaw, Dorothy Bell's grandmother, from the Ts'iits' Git'ans Gitanee Clan, had told us an ancient prophecy that predicted there would come a time when buildings would be so high that the tops

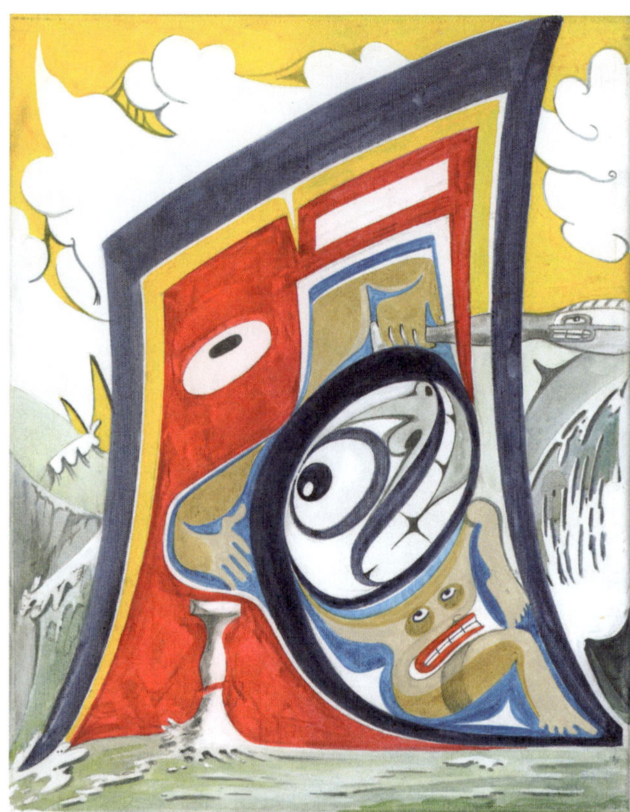
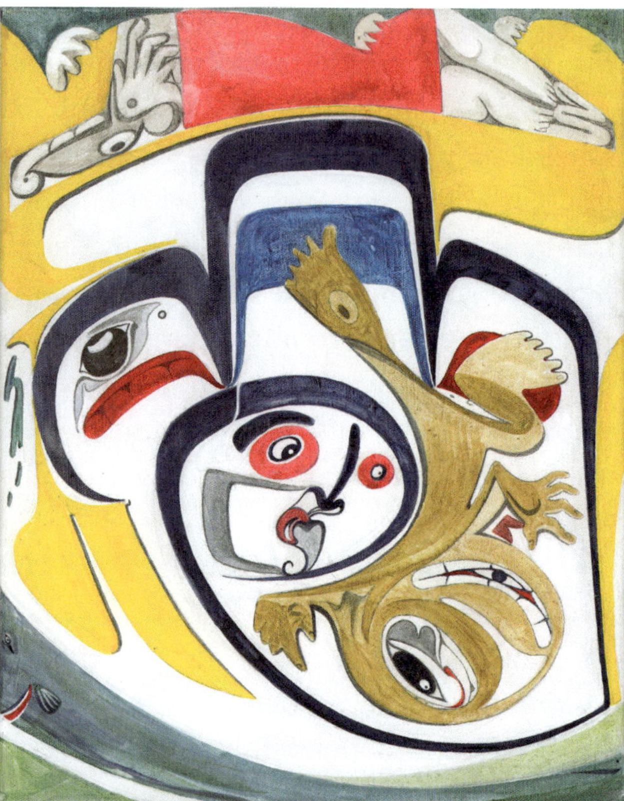

could not be seen, and here we were looking at buildings whose tops were hidden in the clouds. It was eerie to see that the ancient prophecy was fulfilled.

My mother lived through huge changes, from travelling by canoe to travelling the world on a jet. She and I lived through the time that the village as a whole moved to harvesting camps to days that harvesting was done by immediate families. We lived in the time that X̱aad Kíl was nearly the exclusive language spoken to a time that X̱aad Kíl is spoken only by a few, and the younger generations are working hard to recover the use of the language.

The ancient prophecy that Skilee Aaw had told us included a warning that the day was coming when people would not be speaking X̱aad Kíl. People laughed at this prophecy because everyone was speaking Haida and no one could imagine people not speaking the language. Yet here we are today at the brink of the prophecy coming true.

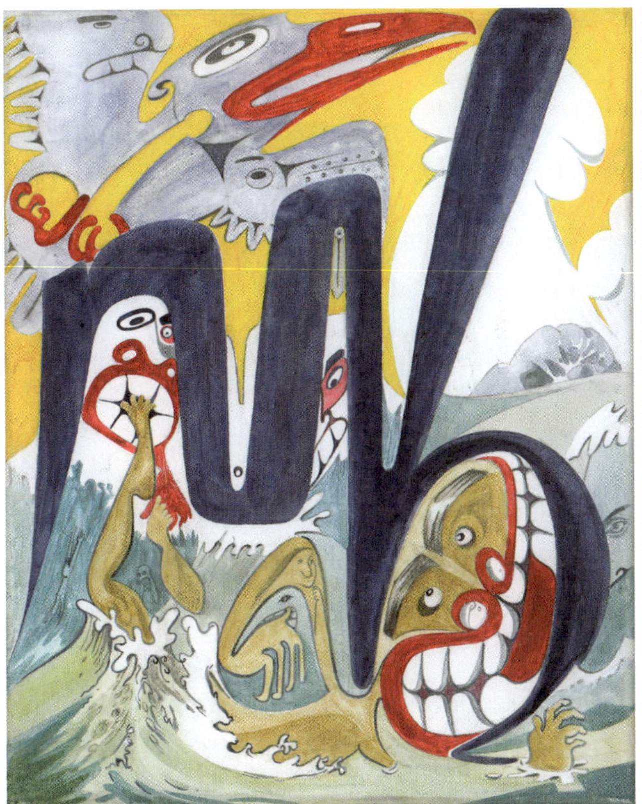
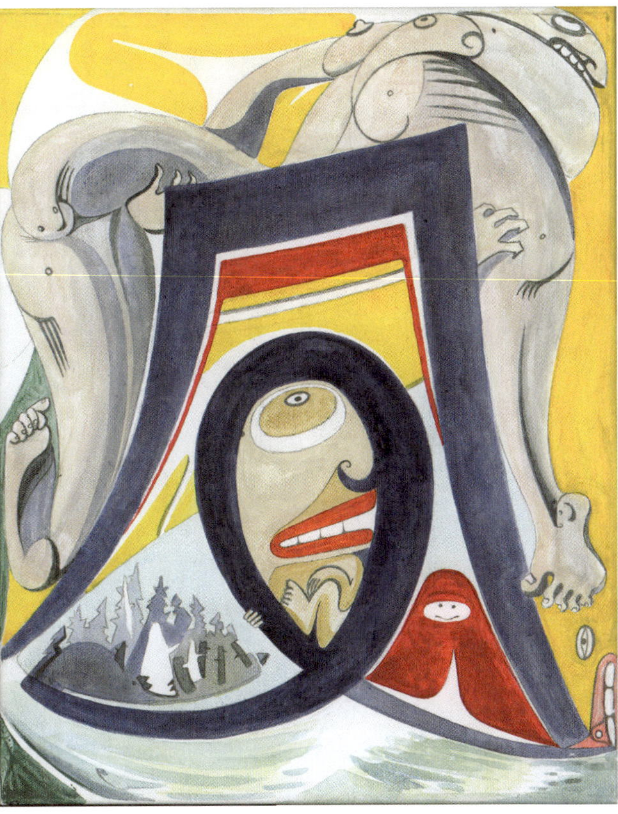

Remember, 2008.
Michael Nicoll Yahgulanaas

Prophecy is given to warn us. It does not have to come true if we change our ways. I am optimistic that this prophecy will not come true because so many of our young people are learning the language. Like the weaving arts and ceremonies, we can save this expressive, rich language and make certain that it is used within our homes, in our schools, at our meetings and at our feasts and potlatches. In my opinion, the language is really the only thing that makes us uniquely Haida. It explains everything we need to keep our culture living and growing. It explains our relationship to land, sea, supernaturals and all living things.

I am thankful that the Creator gave me this time in history to live. I know that I am fortunate to have been able to be immersed in the Haida culture, with Haida Gwaii, and with very knowledgeable and loving people. I am thankful that I learned to weave and have lived long enough to see the beauty of the Haida culture revealed to the world.

CHAPTER THREE

Haida Calendar

Harvesting Times

My harvesting memories provide context to the descriptions of the baskets that were still in use when I was young, in relationship to the Haida way of life and worldview. For greater detail about harvesting cycles, *The Haida Gwaii Marine Traditional Knowledge Study* is available through the Council of the Haida Nation. Nancy Turner's *Plants of Haida Gwaii*, from 2004, is also an excellent resource.

When I was a child, we followed the harvesting calendar and the whole village began to travel in February to different places to harvest foods. The spring through fall harvesting season continued until the end of October, followed by the beach harvest, trapping and hunting through the fall and winter months. Where and when we travelled depended on what was in season. When foods became ready at the same time, but at different places, some would go to harvest in one area while others would go to another. Throughout the season, when we finished harvesting in one area, we would return to Massett to store the food, work the gardens and ready ourselves to go to the next area. When we returned in the fall, everyone shared the season's bounty. This communal sharing ensured that everyone had what was needed to make it through the winter. In the fall, through a communal effort, the village houses were repaired, new ones built and the village cleaned.

There were not many people in the village when I was a child because so many had died from smallpox, tuberculosis, the flu and other introduced diseases. Everyone was protective of each other and shared everything freely. I only heard people saying good things about others. Because everyone had lost so many in their families to diseases, they were thankful for those who had lived. Also, as my mother did throughout her life, people still held to the spiritual understanding that thinking or talking bad about others would bring bad luck. If a person was found to be negatively criticizing another person, the offended clan could call for a "Making It Right" feast, which could be costly.

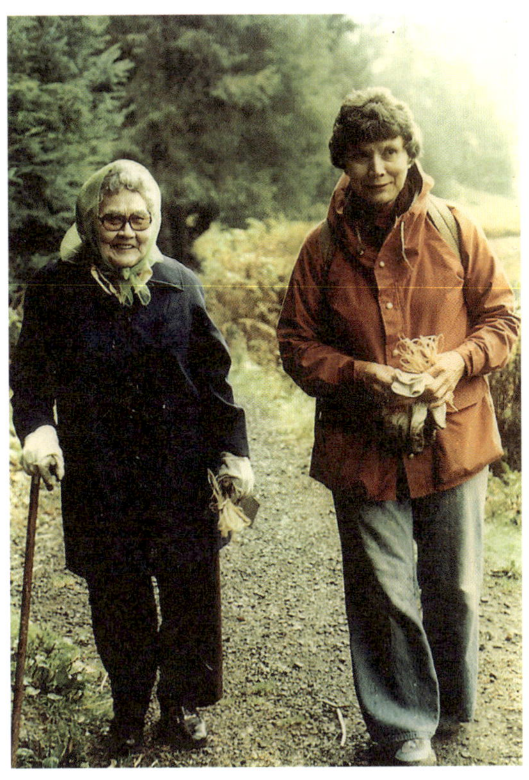

Selina and Delores returning from a harvest. *Tom Sadowski*

I don't remember any canoes being used when I was a child. Instead, villagers had wooden rowboats and skiffs. Very few of the skiffs had gas motors. Most would load the little boats and row from Massett Inlet to the harvesting areas, including Langara Island, Seven Mile, Wiah Point and Shag Rock. When the villagers went up the inlet to the rivers, including the Yakoun, Aayan, Awan, Deenan and the Jaalan, they would row up the tidal eddy along the shoreline or put up a sail in the centre of the little rowboats. Haida men were historically known as great canoe builders and quickly adapted that knowledge to building the largest fleet of fishing boats on the coast, until changes to governmental licensing pushed the Indigenous people out of the industry.

No matter where we went to harvest there were things that were similar about each camp. Every family had a little shack at each place. Shacks were simple and used for shelter, sleeping, cooking and nightly visiting. There were beds, a table and chairs, and a little potbelly stove in each. The things that were left in the shacks the previous season were never stolen or vandalized because the Haida value of respect for self, clan, tribe and Nation was strong. We all knew that if one person did things that hurt others or was shameful then the whole clan was looked down on until the wrong was righted. This responsibility to others was strongly stressed by the elders, our parents and our aunts and uncles.

During the workday, older children would care for babies and smaller children while the adults worked. Wherever we went there was a cradle in the corner of the one room shack. All the cradles were made the same with the wrapped blankets and ropes intersecting in the middle, where the ropes that hung from the ceiling were attached.

When a baby or toddler could not be soothed, the child was tied to the back of one of the women with a blanket. The child was rocked and hummed to sleep as the work continued. Well into old age, my mother continued the practice of walking her grandchildren and great-grandchildren to sleep on her back, humming, "mmm m, mmm m, mmm m..."

At dawn the women rose and made breakfast for everyone. Anyone who missed breakfast had to wait until the evening meal after the work was finished. There were no late risers. Everyone, including each child, had tasks to do during harvesting and preparation. Adults harvested and prepared food. Children were not allowed to prepare food until we became teenagers, but we were learning as we carried out our duties during the day through the Haida modelling method of teaching. Children would carry wood and water, fetch and clean, and do whatever the adults needed done to keep the work running smoothly.

Cleanliness was stressed from very early childhood. The camp and our living spaces were cleaned thoroughly and everything put in its place at the end of each day. Most of the day we worked at camp but the adults made work seem like a lot of fun and no one complained. We would make contests out of our duties and work hard at being the fastest, the best or the strongest.

Songs and prayers of thankfulness always started the harvest. Everyone paid careful attention to what was being worked on. While harvesting and preparing food, the adults did not engage in casual conversation. We had all been trained from childhood to respect the life of those things that gave freely of themselves so we could live. Children knew that loud and unruly behaviour when the harvesting and preparation was going on was disrespectful and would bring quick correction from any adult in earshot. Everyone knew stories about what bad things could happen when we behaved disrespectfully.

After the day's work was done, the area cleaned and made ready for the next day, we gathered to visit by campfire light or coal oil lamps. The evening was filled with laughter, happiness and a warm, comfortable sense of safety and belonging. I particularly loved the nights when the storytellers would share old stories with us.

In those days, stories were told word for word. If a storyteller missed a word or forgot to tell the story properly, someone would clear his or her throat and the next storyteller would pick up the story and finish telling it.

I wish I had learned how to do the finger string actions for some of the stories. One such story that I really loved was about Raven travelling. The storytellers would make a little stick "walk" across the stretched-out finger string whenever Raven was travelling.

Another thing that I really miss about the storytellers is the sign language and the great drama. There were actions for paddling, harpooning, shooting, walking along, surprise, fear and for most every action in the story. The drama of the story was created by the use of over-exaggerated facial expressions and language pitch, tone and tempo. What can be said as tragic in Xaad Kíl can also be said hilariously, it just depends on how the words are said.

The late Wesley Bell was so good at using the old sign language and dramatic emphasis that even though he was speaking Haida to non-speakers, the story was easily understood.

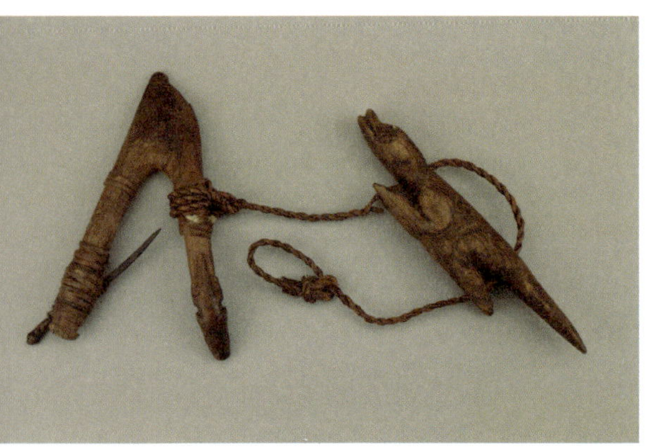

Haida halibut hook with cedar cordage. *Canadian Museum of History*

The Haida say, "When the tide is out, the table is set." In the fall, winter and early spring months we harvested and put up beach foods including butter and razor clams, geoduck, cockles, gooseneck barnacles, chiton, mussels, urchins, china caps, lady slippers, abalone, sea cucumbers, crab, cod eggs, scallops and octopus.

In March and April, the herring eggs, clams, crabs, halibut, black cod and other cod were harvested. The spring salmon harvest also began as the fish travel through Haida Gwaii waters to their home rivers along the mainland coast.

In mid-March, after harvesting razor clams, we would return to Massett and the women and children would prepare the garden beds to plant potatoes, turnips, rutabaga, onions and carrots in April. Everyone had a garden in the village and many had gardens across the inlet, including my mother.

In April and May, fiddlehead ferns, sprouts and black seaweed were harvested. The precious sockeye began to come home to provide us with food.

We picked our elderberries in Massett in May and June. We had to be at North Island (Langara Island) by early June to harvest ancient murrelet. On our way we stopped at a bare rock to collect seagull eggs.

In June, the salmonberries and wild strawberries were ready for harvest. A delicacy that was served regularly in our homes was a bowl of mixed berries including jarred elderberry, smothered with eulachon grease and a sprinkling of sugar.

In July, blueberries and huckleberries were picked. At the end of August and September, salal berry stands were visited. In October, dog salmon, high-bush cranberries and Hudson Bay Tea for medicine were ready to be harvested. Crabapples, ground cranberries, lingonberries and many root medicines were harvested in the fall as well.

In addition to following our traditional harvesting cycle, many, including myself, were involved in the commercial harvests. When

I got older, I went to work at the cannery in Inverness on the mainland. My mother was involved in the traditional trade economy and through her weavings and the family store income, she contributed cash to the family.

In those days there was no time for ceremonial events during the harvesting season. As was the ancient custom, these were held in the winter and were disguised as family dinners or church-sanctioned holidays because of the Canadian government's efforts to ban these events and church disapproval.

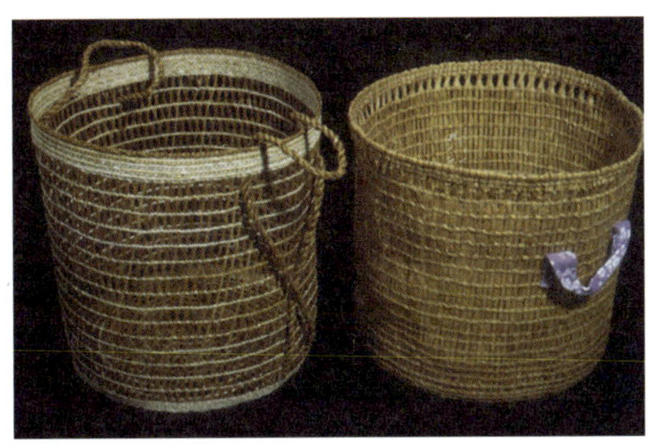

This red and yellow cedar clam harvest basket (left) has rope tab handles threaded through the basket wall, and a bail handle attached to the side tabs. Right: Seaweed basket. *Alaska State Museum*

By the time I was harvesting, few people were still using the harvest baskets. I was fortunate to see the baskets that were still being used. The late Ernie Collison, a Haida Nation leader from the Eagle Ts'iits Git'ans Gitanee Clan, wanted to see the baskets come back into use in our homes and daily life. He lived long enough to experience the resurgence of ceremonial weavings. It is also my hope that our utilitarian baskets return to their rightful place in our harvesting cycle and homes.

Tow Hill — Razor Clam Harvest

Tow Hill is located on Graham Island to the north of Massett, at the mouth of the Hiellen River. Tow Hill is a spiritual and magnificent place that is full of life, power and beauty. At the base of the hill, in the volcanic-formed rocks, there is a blowhole that spews a pillar of ocean spray as the tide rises. On a clear day, the Haida territories on the Alaska side of the border can be seen from the hill and the beach.

Tow Hill has a brother, Towustasin, who lives near Juskatla. The faces of both these hills are near mirror images of each other. Ga waahl ga gwii, (long ago, so long ago no one lives today who saw it) Tow and Towustasin were constantly arguing until Tow decided he could not stand arguing with his brother any longer. He tore himself

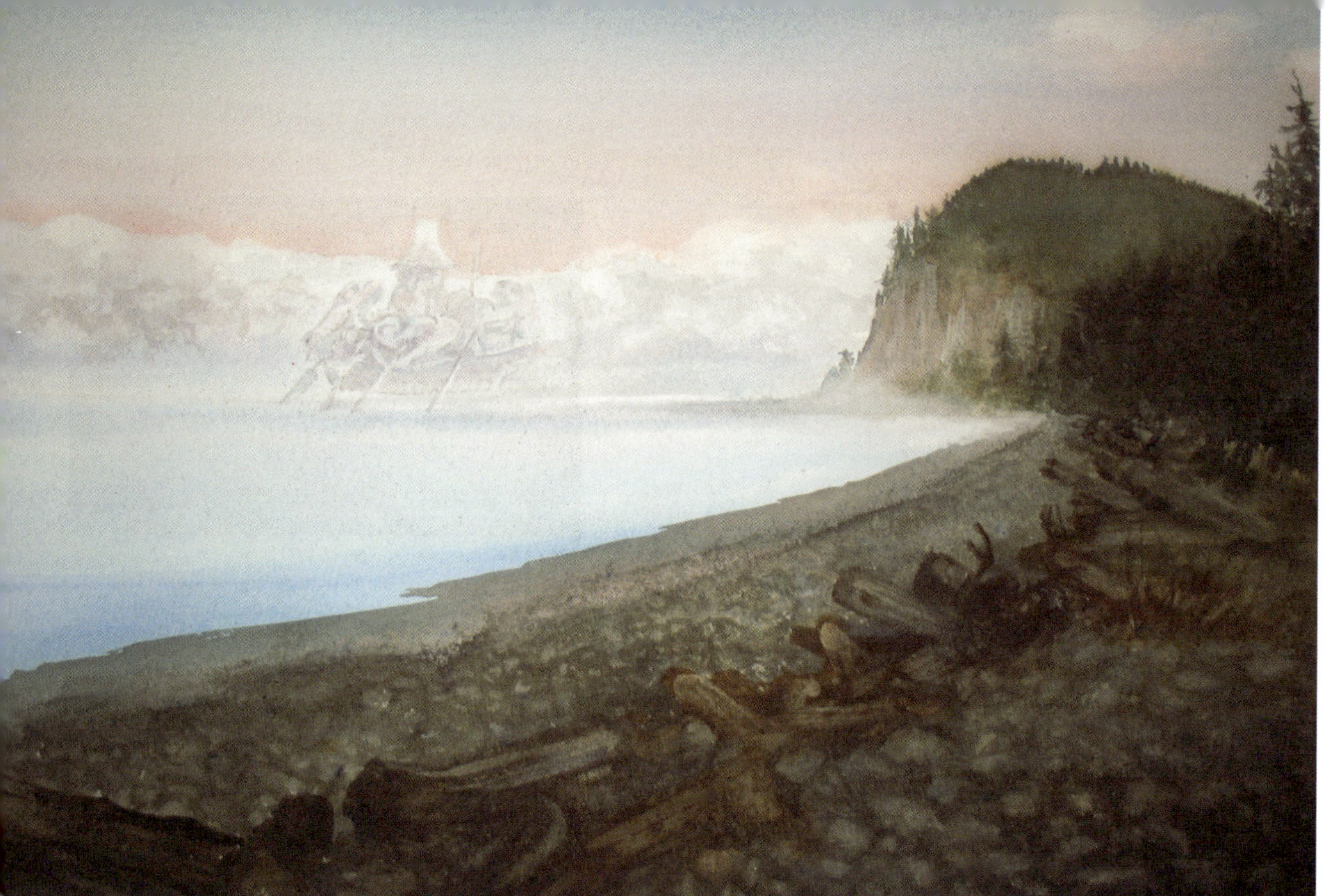

Tow Hill, a watercolour landscape painted by Delores's daughter Evelyn Vanderhoop. *Evelyn Vanderhoop*

from his brother and dragged himself down to the mouth of the Hiellen River, settling where he stands now, next to the Hiellen River. In his move he created Massett Inlet and Delkatla Slough. Rocks can be seen all along the inlet that fell from Tow when he moved to just north of Yakun Point.

When I was a child, Tow Hill was called Taaw Hill, conceptually meaning "a place with lots of food." Berries and forest foods, crabs, razor clams, cockles, scallops, horse clams, gooseneck barnacles, seals, deer, cod eggs and even chiton, a type of mollusc, and seaweed can be found at and around Tow Hill. In the winter, after the northwesterly wind blows and creates deep surges within the ocean, cockles and scallops are thrown onto North Beach, just north of Hiellen. When I was young the river was called híilaang (thunder). It is a place that gifts us an abundance of food.

In February, the villagers went to the Hiellen River on a cordwood trail from Masset to dig clams for personal use. The clams were cleaned, soaked in salt water, boiled, skewered together and then hung in the smokehouse. The smoked clams are chewy and tasty. Razor clams, salt, pepper, potatoes, onions and eulachon grease with a sprinkling of seaweed makes the tastiest chowder. When we had finished digging, we went back to Massett and the garden plots were prepared with seaweed, cow manure, starfish and fish heads.

In March, when the tides were really low, we returned to Hiellen for the first commercial razor clam dig of the year. Because my mother and father owned the store in Massett, they did not go out for the commercial razor clam dig. Instead, they stayed behind to make sure everyone got their seasonal harvesting equipment and supplies. My father's mother, Naanii Skuujuus, and his sister Kaanii Xuuhliiyang brought me out to the commercial dig. We travelled out to Hiellen on the backs of rickety old cannery trucks. Like every place we moved to do harvesting, each family had a little shack. We did not bring frying pans with us because cooking was done right on the cooktop of the potbelly wood stove or on the open beach fire. We did have pots and a kettle for making the stews, soups and tea. Once a week, a supply truck brought us staples like flour, salt, lard, yeast and baking powder. If the digging happened during the season of Lent, the bread that was made was unleavened.

The teacher moved out to Hiellen with us and held school between the tides. She lived in a "clam shack" like the rest of us and ate the same food that we ate.

We all worked as one unit for the benefit of everyone. The work was divided between adults, teenagers and even the younger children. Adults and teenagers dug the clams. The bigger children ran the buckets or the clam baskets down to the surf to rinse the sand from the clams, then they would run these up to the younger children, who separated the broken and small ones from the larger clams and graded them the way the clam buyers had instructed. The clam basket was easier to use than buckets because the water and sand ran out quickly, it was smaller and lighter than the bucket, and it was easy to wash the clams in the surf by just dipping and swishing the sieve-style basket, clams and all, into an oncoming wave.

If the clamshells were cracked or too small, they would not get top prices. Children would bury the little ones back into the beach. The women prepared those with broken shells for our meals or smoked them. The clams that were suitable for the commercial market were carefully laid into rectangular wooden boxes that had a metal tag attached on the inside. These boxes of clams were stacked on the truck and brought to the Massett cannery.

The pay went to the adults and was used to help support the family. In the old days this is how it was done. Everyone worked together for the well-being of everyone. Children were expected to do their part for no pay. We all thought this was the greatest fun and had contests to see who could get the most, run the fastest, and have the least broken shells. When the tides quit being really low, we returned to Massett and the gardens were seeded.

In early April, we returned to Tow Hill again to commercially dig clams, which are closer to the surface at that time of year and easier to harvest. Some of those clams were sent to Kaasan on the Alaska side of the border for processing.

Those times spent working and playing together still live on in my mind as if it were yesterday. Little did I know that soon clam baskets would no longer be used during harvest; that the village as a whole would quit going out together to dig; and the school would quit sending the teacher out to teach between the tides. It is amazing to me how much I took for granted and how truly blessed I had been. It is my hope that these wonderful baskets again take their place in the harvesting of clams, and the circle from forest to sea is again complete.

There are many examples of the style of basket I saw and used during clam harvesting that are stored in museum collections. The baskets in the right-aligned photo on page 3 include a stylized expression of the Haida Potlatch Ring Band. The Haida identifying "jog" to the right can be seen on the rim and design.

Shag Rock, Halibut Fishing with Cedar Twine and Rope

In the month of April, we would go to Shag Rock to fish for halibut. Before we got to the halibut banks, we would hunt octopus (nuu) for both food and halibut bait. My mother showed us the octopus homes in rocky crevices or in a hole under a rock. The octopus is a good housekeeper, which makes it easy to find. Clamshells, crab shells and other debris left from their feasting are thrown out around their homes.

My mother would take a stick with a hook on the end and she would tell us not to move at all and to be quiet, then she would sit very still and gently move the shells around outside the octopus's den. Slowly the octopus would begin to emerge. One tentacle would come out and she would stir the shells, another tentacle and she would stir the shells. When at least four tentacles had appeared, my mother would suddenly grab the devilfish and jerk it out of the den. If we were going to eat the octopus, she would kill it and use sand in her hands to pull the outer flesh off. If it was going to be used for halibut bait it was killed and put into gunnysacks to be cut up for bait when the fishing started.

Shag Rock was an area of responsibility for my father's people, the Kyanuusalii Raven Clan. We only went to Shag Rock with a member of my father's clan, which was usually my k`aagii (uncle) Lolie (Lawerence Stanley) and Kaanii Xuuhliiyang. One year, after my brother Victor had just returned from residential school and he was feeling pretty smart, Kaanii Xuuhliiyang gave us the usual speech that welcomed us to harvest from this area but reminded us that we could only come to Shag Rock when someone from their clan was with us. She turned to get off the skiff as Victor, under his breath, said, "Who wants to come to this old pile of rocks anyway?"

Kaanii Xuuhliiyang whipped around and pointed her finger directly at him, quietly and firmly stating, "Look here. We fought you people for this old pile of rocks and we won. You will not come here without one of us."

First of all, Haida are trained not to point at anyone. It is a sign of complete contempt. An auntie from the opposite side, especially one who we loved so much, speaking so harshly and pointing her finger at any of us was shocking and unthinkable. Victor later confessed how ashamed he felt for his smart remark.

Kaanii Xuuhliiyang was referring to a war between our clans hundreds of years ago, when a male of our clan married the woman who was holding the Kyanuusalii Chief's name until a new Chief would be selected and potlatched. Our clan male helped her care for their areas of responsibility and soon began acting as if our clan owned these. The members of the Kyanuusalii became insulted and the two clans went to war. My father's people were the victors and one of the conditions for our clan to harvest in any of their areas was that a member of the Kyanuusalii had to be with us.

The importance of this story is that although we had warred and our clan had lost that war, we continued to carry on the traditional marriages between our tribes and clans, and continued to share the resources from our areas of responsibility.

The Kyanuusalii are responsible to ocean and beach areas, while my clan is responsible to the Aayan river, watershed, forests and lakes. The marriages ensured that both clans had access to everything that was needed to thrive.

When we got to Shag Rock, the first halibut caught would be cleaned and then hung for a few days. When it was cooking it had a terrible odour but it was unbelievably delicious.

When we were children, my Kyanuusalii cousin Betty (Swanson) Thompson and I went out with k`aagii Lolie to jig for halibut. He pulled a halibut aboard and it was flopping around. She and I started giggling at the halibut. Lolie turned to us and instead of his usual beaming smile, he glared sternly. He did not say anything but dropped us off on the beach. We had not eaten and Betty said, "But what about our lunches?" He did not answer and went back out to fish. We ran to my mother and told her how mean Lolie had been. She asked us to tell her what happened. When we told her about the halibut and the two of us laughing, she said, "We have to respect everything that is living. We don't laugh at things that are dying. The halibut was giving its life for us. It deserves respect." Then she sent us to bed without any dinner.

Years later I overheard my mother telling my daughters not to play with the crab she was getting ready to cook. "If you don't respect them, the ocean will take you and we won't have luck getting food. You go home now."

The halibut that was caught was filleted and weights were put on top of the fillets until the excess liquid had drained off and the fillets felt grainy. A crow was shot and hung near the fish drying racks. This kept the crows away as the halibut was dried. The fillets would then be hung on cedar drying racks. The blowflies hadn't hatched yet and the hanging fish was not bothered by flies. As soon as the fillets quit dripping and the surface felt dry to the touch, they were hung on wood drying racks and turned as they dried in the sun.

The racks were brought in at night or when it rained and hung from the ceiling. Everyone wore scarves or hats in the house because the halibut continued to drip and we were told that worms would fall from the drying halibut. After the fillets dried, they would be stacked in tin containers and kept in a dry place until we returned to our village.

The halibut heads were salted for later use. The cooked intestines were chewed by an adult and then fed to the babies and small children. My mother continued the practice of chewing food and feeding it to babies. My eldest daughter remembers grinding her teeth to keep from saying anything when my mother would feed chewed food to her babies.

As a child I saw the traditional halibut hooks hanging in homes but did not see them in use. The hooks I saw used to fish halibut when I was a girl were metal hooks. There are many examples of the unique wood halibut hooks that make use of cedar in the collections

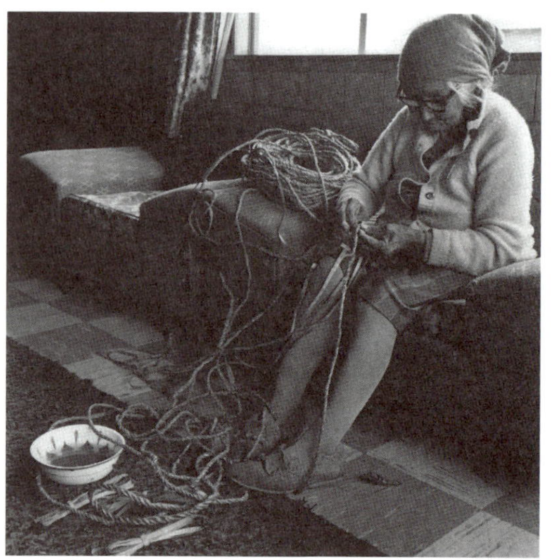

Hannah Parnell making twine. *Ulli Seltzer*

of museums. The halibut hooks of long ago used cedar twine, cordage and rope.

Cordage is often used as handles for baskets. It is an important technique to weaving cedar garments. Because a single strand of weft is not strong enough for the twined rows of a garment, the wefts, particularly if the garment is to be used, need to be spun into cordage.

My auntie Hannah Parnell was a weaver who made twine and rope. She was one of the important Massett Haida tradition bearers, who helped to keep song and dance alive. June Russ, Massett Village Chief Iljuuwas's wife, who grew up with Hannah, loved to tell stories about the secret dance practices held in Naanii Hannah's home.

Seaweed Harvesting Baskets

After putting up the halibut at Shag Rock, we returned to Massett and prepared to go to Seven Mile or Wiah Point, on the northern tip of Haida Gwaii, to harvest black seaweed with Naanii Skujuus, Kaanii Xuuhliiyang, my mother and Uncle Lolie.

Seaweed is nutritious and a staple Haida food. It can be eaten much the way chips are eaten or sprinkled into seafood chowders. Seaweed, dog salmon eggs and eulachon grease is an absolutely tasty soup. Warning: seaweed is also a laxative and should be eaten in moderation.

Black seaweed grows where there is ocean surf hitting the rocks. When I was young, only teenagers and adults collected it. I have since learned that this type of seaweed is an ancient plant and if it is not picked properly it will not come back the next year.

While adults harvested seaweed, children collected black mussels, little green urchins and black chitons that would be eaten for

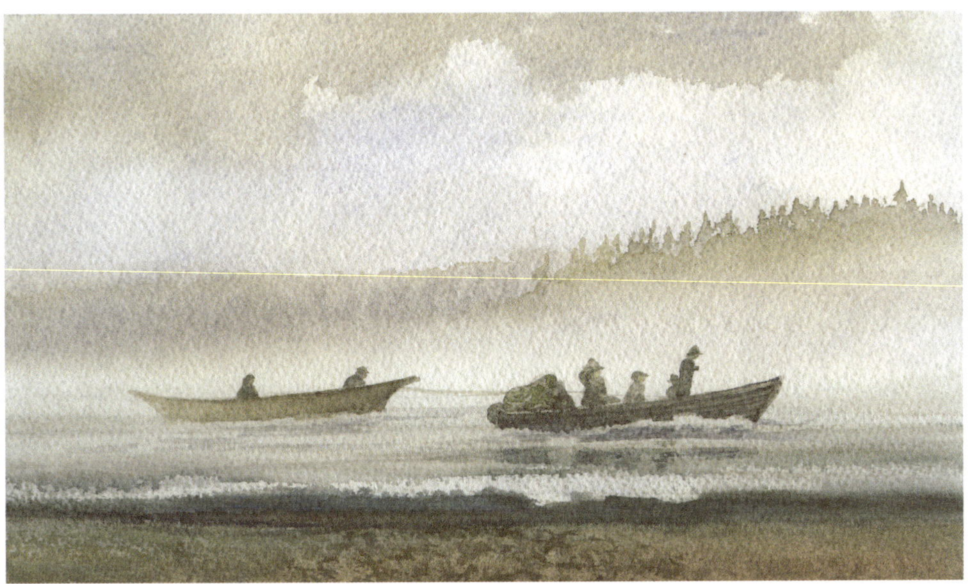

Harvest Grounds, another painting by Evelyn Vanderhoop, Delores's daughter. *Evelyn Vanderhoop*

lunch or supper. The shellfish were either put into a pot with no water and steamed in their own juice or were cooked right on top of an open fire. If chitons are cooked too long they become rubbery and hard to eat. The urchins are cracked open without cooking and the orange sections are eaten raw. These are sweeter than the large purple urchins. It is the only food source I know of where the pieces that are not used are disposed of on the beach where the urchins do not live. If the waste is deposited where the urchins make their homes, we were told that the urchins would move away.

Sieved spruce root baskets and gunnysacks were used to harvest seaweed. After it was picked and put into the basket, we would rinse it in the ocean while shaking little shells and ocean twigs out through the open-weaved basket. The rinsed and drained seaweed went into a burlap gunnysack.

The preparation done then was exactly as it is done now. The first step is to rinse the seaweed in salt water and shake out tiny shells and any other debris. The seaweed basket makes it easy to clean the seaweed since the tiny shells and sticks go right through the sieve walls.

Next, the seaweed is placed on vertical racks that are covered with a clean bed sheet or, if the weather is just right, the seaweed

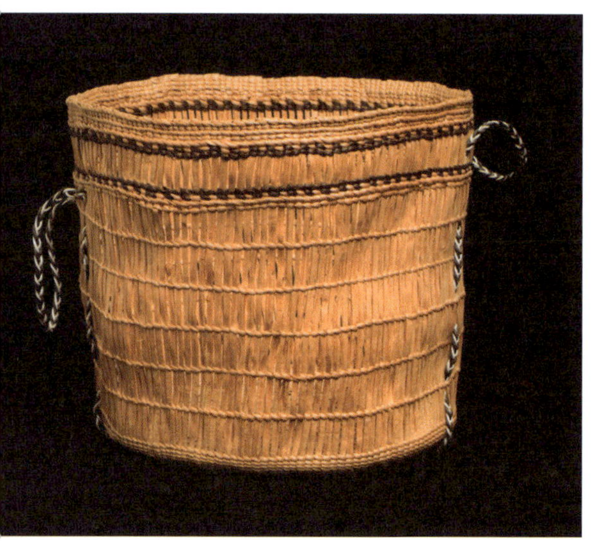

Spruce root seaweed harvest basket. *Private collection*

can be dried on warm beach rocks. When I was a child, the racks were made of cedar. Cooled clam, mussel or chiton broth can be poured over the seaweed before drying. The broth-soaked seaweed is beyond delicious.

The little pads of seaweed are turned and sun-dried until they are semi-dry. If the sun is shining the seaweed is dried in the wind and sun. Because we all had woodstoves, we brought the rack into the house in the evening or when it was raining to continue drying near the stove. Today, many use electric dehydrators or do a final toast in a low-temperature oven. In my time some of the old people would not chop the seaweed. Instead, they cut it into squares and layered the dried squares into wood boxes. The layers were about two inches thick.

My mother harvested seaweed and halibut to trade with the Nish'ga for Nass River smoked eulachon and eulachon grease. Eulachon is an oily fish much the same as smelt, only much oilier. In February, when the eulachon boat came to Massett, we had our first taste of spring. Fresh fried eulachon is eaten head, bones, guts and all and is scrumptious.

Haida Gwaii does not provide eulachon any longer. I was told that long ago the eulachon came to Haida Gwaii but because we showed disrespect for them, they did not return to our island. This story reinforces the need to be respectful to all living things.

Most everyone was still using seaweed harvesting baskets when I was young. However, the gunnysack was used to carry the heavy load to the drying racks. Today, large onion bags have replaced both basket and gunnysack.

The seaweed-style basket discovered at the Thorne River Estuary in the Tongass National Forest on Prince of Wales, Alaska, in July 1994, reveals that on the coast we have been using this style of weaving for at least 5,600 years. I was able to study the basket fragments

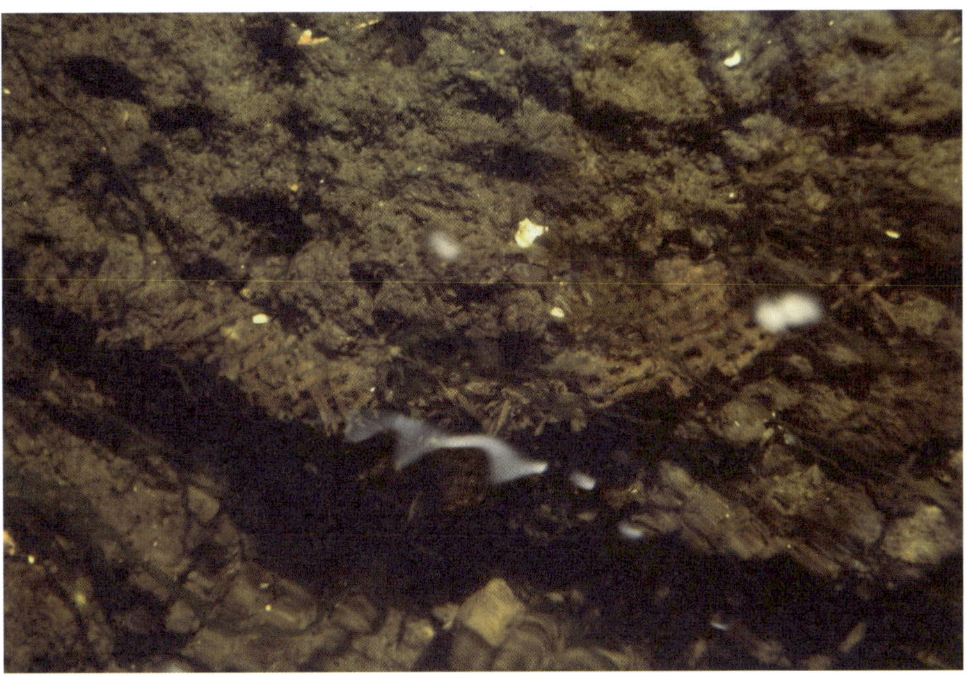

Thorne River basket as found in the mud. *Alaska State Museum*

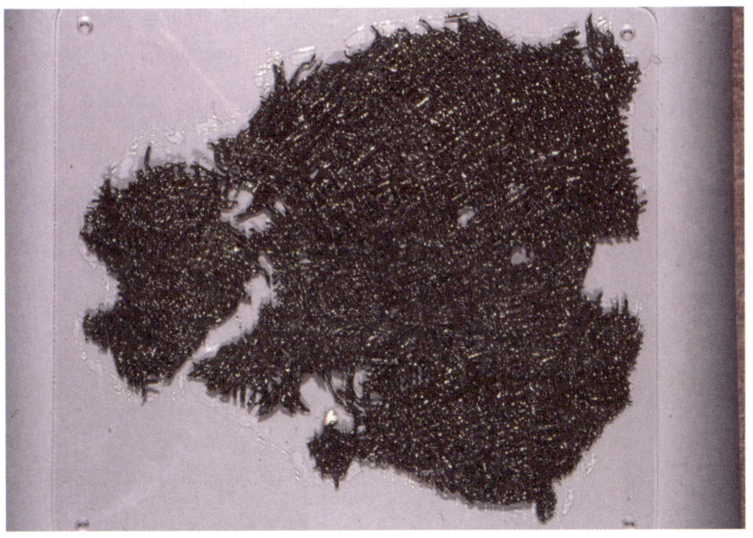

Museum workers clean fragments of the Thorne River basket. *Alaska State Museum*

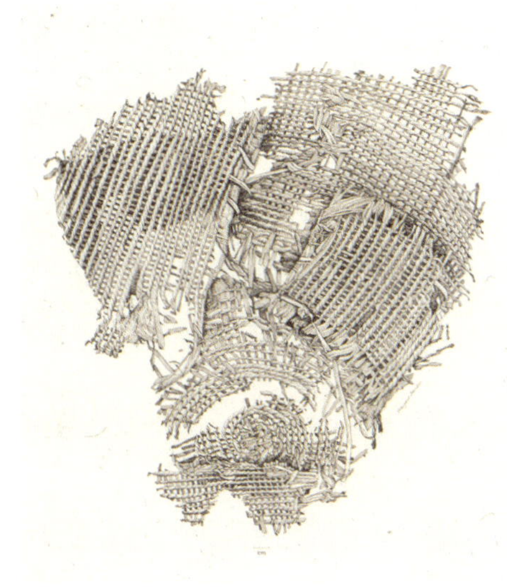

Technical drawing of the Thorne River basket. *Margaret Davidson*

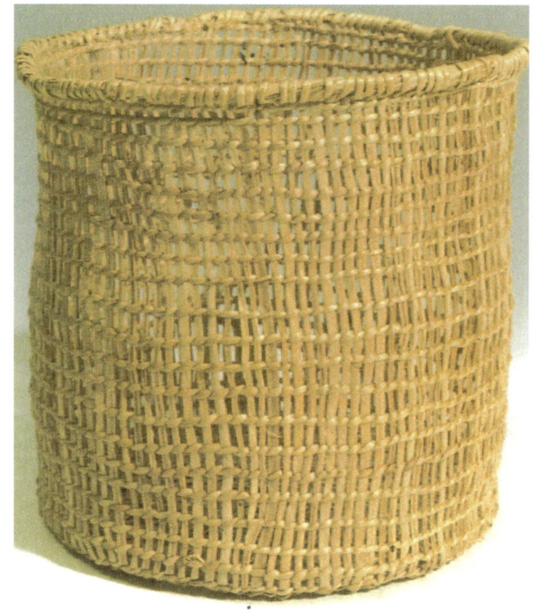

Replication of the spruce Thorne River basket by Delores Churchill. *Alaska State Museum*

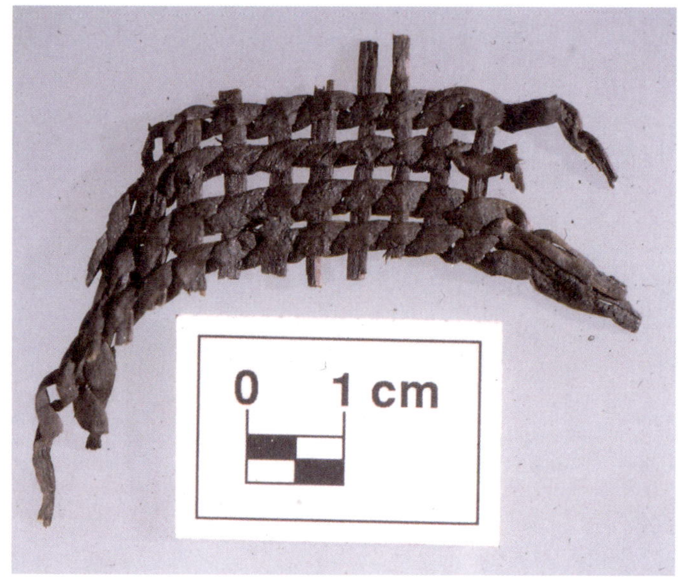

The starting swatch. *Alaska State Museum*

and replicated what appears to be a weaving student's small basket. The Thorne River basket is preserved at the Alaska State Museum. Steve Henrikson, Curator of Collections, has always made this spectacular find available for anyone who is interested in studying ancient weavings.

The seaweed harvesting basket would be a great basket to weave as a start to a utilitarian basket collection that is actually used.

Bird Egg Collecting Baskets

At the end of May or first of June, we jumped into k`aagii Lolie's little gas boat and headed out to the west coast to Langara Island. On our way to Langara Island for our annual ancient murrelet harvests, we stopped at a small island of rocks with no trees to harvest the seagull colony's eggs.

The seagull nests were on rocks and made up of dried grasses. Each nest had two to four eggs. We only took one or two from each nest. When we were collecting the eggs, the seagulls would fly overhead screeching, pooping on our heads and a few brave ones would dive toward us. The eggs are larger than duck eggs and have a deep orange yolk.

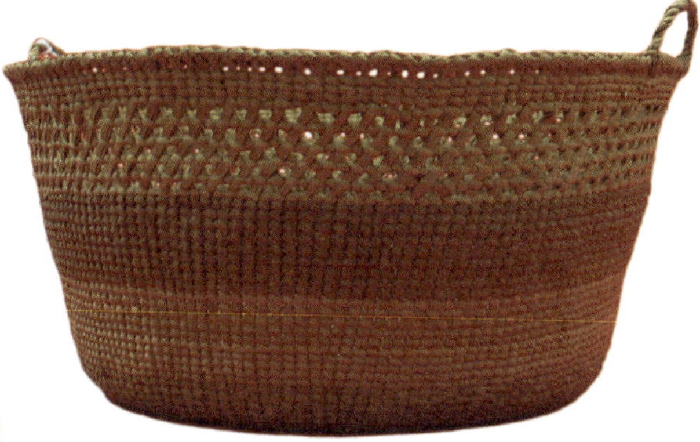

Basket used for gathering seabird eggs. *Canadian Museum of History*

We only took enough eggs to be eaten while they were fresh. The small size of the baskets we were given also helped us not to take too much. When we got to Langara, we put the eggs into a bucket of salt water and those that did not sink had an embryo. Those that did not sink were boiled and given to the old people to eat. No one else was allowed to eat those eggs, but the rest of us feasted on the delicious boiled seagull eggs that had sunk in the salt water. Eggs were also fried, scrambled and used in baking. I have not had seagull eggs in years until recently when a relative brought me eggs. Each spring I start wishing for them. I have never eaten the embryo eggs.

We had to be at Langara between the last week of May and first week in June to harvest the ancient murrelet. When they flew in, there appeared to be thousands. The sky would get dark there were so many. They nested under the old spruce trees where they burrowed holes for their nests. The male and female murrelets took turns caring for the nest.

At the end of each harvest, before we left Langara, k`aagii Lolie would make a horizontal cut at the base of a spruce tree and a vertical cut through the bark as high as he could reach. The tree pitch would run like bleeding through the bark. Over the winter this piece of bark would become saturated with the pitch and form a board-like stick. As soon as we returned the next season, Lolie would peel this pitchy bark board from the tree. When the birds came in at night, he would light the pitchy bark and hold it up in front of the cliffs. The birds would fly toward the sputtering light and knock themselves out against the cliffs. We would run around picking up the stunned birds, wringing their necks. The adults plucked, cleaned and salted the birds down. These were stored in a barrel to be eaten later.

The murrelet eggs were harvested by reaching into their burrows under the trees. There were one or two eggs about the size of a bantam chicken egg in each nest. We would not take an egg from a nest with only one egg and we only took one from the nest with two eggs. This is the way we helped them to come back each year.

I liked the murrelet eggs but I really loved the taste of the murrelets. There are no longer enough murrelets to use as a food source. I don't believe there is anyone in my children's generation who has eaten murrelets or their eggs. The sport fish lodges built over the nesting grounds introduced rats and logging contributed to the demise of this lovely bird. It saddens me that the Haida no longer have this as a food source but it saddens me more that the population of these seabirds has been reduced so drastically that they could disappear from the Earth.

In the museums I have visited, I have seen many baskets of the size and style that Kaanii Xuuhliiyang gave to us to harvest the eggs.

Fish Carrying Baskets

Pollution, acidification, climate change, irresponsible logging practices and over-fishing, both locally and high seas, have diminished the salmon stocks. Many of the rivers that I knew to have salmon no longer have runs. The Yakoun River, which was very close to losing its stock, came back because the Haida closed the river to fishing until the stocks built up again.

Salmon is a staple food for Haida people. In the old days, we first harvested the oiliest fish—sockeye—in May and June. The less oily salmon, coho and pinks, came in June and July. The most important salmon, chum or dog salmon, started arriving in the latter part of September through October. Dog salmon was important because it had so little fat and when dried, it lasted through the whole winter. The oilier salmon may become rancid after a time and they freezer-burn sooner. Some of the salmon was salted or smoked and then canned.

I only went to the inlet river fishing at the Yakoun once. I think it was because we were still at Langara Island putting up food during the sockeye run when I was very young. When I became old enough to work in the cannery at Inverness, on the mainland, I was not on Haida Gwaii for the dog salmon run.

We went up the inlet with other people from the village to fish for sockeye. We all used rowboats that had a sail pole hole in the centre seat. When we rowed we travelled along the shore in the tidal eddy. When the wind and tide were just right, the sail would go up and we skimmed along Massett Inlet. When the current was running fast it felt like we were flying. The canvas sail made a hypnotic sound as it moved back and forth and would put all of us to sleep. If we were awoken because we had gotten beached, no matter the time of day, we would have a picnic lunch at that spot.

When we got to the Yakoun River, the first child that spotted a sockeye and hollered "Aayo" was treated special and given a gift. The old people sang a welcome song to the salmon. Today the Massett Haida hold a "Welcome Home" ceremony at the mouth of the Yakoun. Robert Davidson Junior brought this ceremony back.

Seals are right behind the sockeye at the mouth of the rivers. To keep them from stealing the fish and tearing up our river gillnet, a seal was killed and hung near the mouth of the river. The dead seal did not stop the bears who came at night and sometimes took their share of the fish we had caught.

Like every other place that we harvested, everyone had a little shack. Everyone shared the large smokehouse. If we did not get up early enough to eat breakfast, we did not eat until all the fish of the day was processed. In my time they only took enough fish that could be worked on and finished that day.

The fish were caught in river gillnets and brought to the preparation area by older children. When I was young most people used gunnysacks, large enamel bowls and buckets to carry the fish from the river. A few were still using the fish basket. I have not seen anyone use the fish basket in this way since that time.

The salmon were filleted and then hung to drain the excess fluid and to dry the surface in the wind. These were then put into the smokehouses. The heads, tips and tails were salted and put into barrels for winter use. Nothing was wasted. The bones and eggs were even smoked. The entrails were placed back into the river with a prayer of gratitude to ensure that the salmon would return the next season.

Children could not kill or work on fish meant for humans. But if we had pets, we were given the blemished fish to prepare for our pets. In this way we were able to practice what we had learned while watching the adults cut fish.

Seal was also hunted at that time. The Haida do not eat blood so the seal was rinsed and rinsed until the water ran clear. The oil was cooked out of the meat, then cooled and skimmed off the top. The cooked meat was stored in barrels of the seal oil. The seal liver was cooked and eaten right away. Few Haida eat seal or sea lion any longer. It may be that when the Haida started keeping cows and deer were introduced, these meats replaced seal meat. Seal has a strong distinctive taste, which I love, but acknowledge it may be an acquired taste for others.

My mother was surprised when I stuffed cooked seal fat into a seal's cleaned intestines and hung it in the smokehouse. "How did you know how to do this?" she asked. "Kaanii Xuuhliiyang showed me how to prepare seal." Kaanii Xuuhliiyang was my main teacher for harvesting and putting up food. She was patient with me. The memory of this time is joyful and full of a child's wonder and excitement.

Weaving was traditionally a woman's art except for weaving of nets, traps and weirs or any other tool or equipment that a man used to hunt or fish. Fish baskets were woven by women and used to move fish from weir, net, trap or harpoon.

Berry Picking Baskets

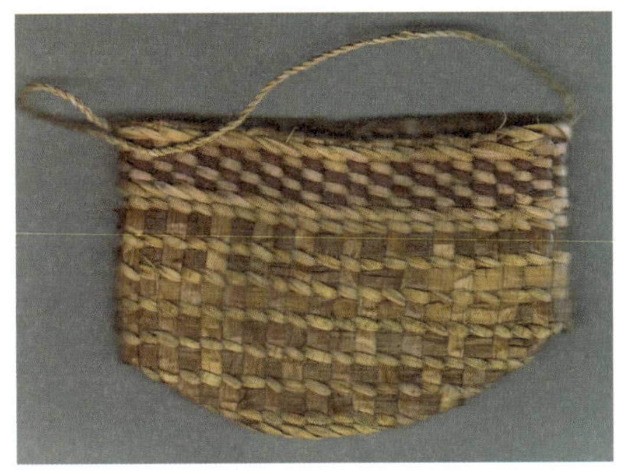

A toddler's berry basket woven for Nina, April Churchill's granddaughter. *Churchill family*

Berry picking began in early spring and continued through early fall. Berries were the Haida fruit requirement of a healthy diet. Even when apples and oranges first became available, they were expensive and scarce. Today, when seated at a potlatch or feast, guests will find an apple and orange at the place setting. This is carried forward from the days when having an abundance of this fruit indicated wealth.

Berries come into season at different times and in different areas. We picked berries in and around Massett at some of the harvesting campsites and around canneries where we were working.

Berry baskets are primarily made from spruce root and come in many different styles and sizes. The smaller berry baskets were still in use when I was young. My mother told me that in the days before buckets, there were three sizes of baskets. The small basket hung on the front of the chest, the medium one hung on the back and the large one was where all the berries were placed.

In the days before contact with those from Europe, the berries were mashed and dried in blocks or stored in bentwood boxes of seal oil or eulachon grease. When I was young, the berries were jarred, canned or made into jams and jellies. Today most people freeze their berries or jar them for use through the winter.

Berry picking with my mother was serious business. She would take all of us picking—father, brothers and sisters—and unlike today, when we think we have a lot of berries when we have a coffee-can full, we did not quit picking until we had tons. I don't remember how many five-gallon buckets we picked each time, but it was a lot. My mother was precise about her berries and was really unhappy if we brought in leaves or sticks with our pick. We always cleaned them before we brought them back to be added to her big buckets.

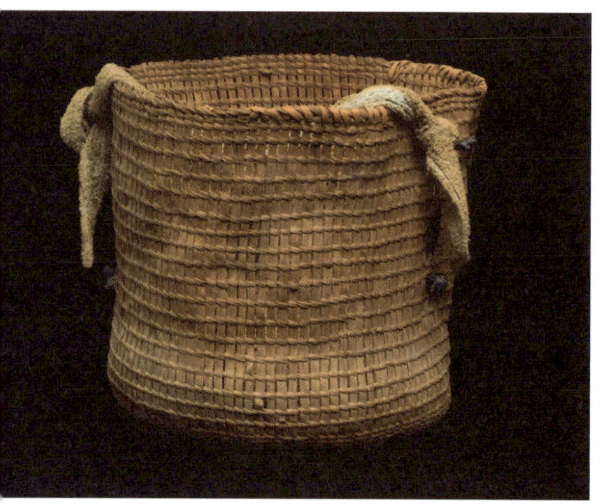

Small spruce root berry basket. *Canadian Museum of History*

In late May and into June, before we went to Langara, we picked elderberries in Massett. These were jarred up in medium syrup or made into a jelly. Elderberry seeds contain arsenic and need to be cooked to get rid of the poison.

In June, we picked strawberries south of the New Massett graveyard where the trees have since grown. Today the Massett people continue to pick wild strawberries where the Canadian military built its base, or at Rose Spit.

After the berries in Massett were picked, we moved on to the Inverness Cannery to work, located on the mainland of British Columbia. Our family picked salmonberries while we were there. One year we went to Oceanic, at the mouth of the Skeena, to pick salmonberries. Because they had not been picked in a number of years, there were oodles of berries. We did not even have to plough our way through the undergrowth to pick enough berries to satisfy my mother.

My mother would take us to Digby Island outside of Prince Rupert to pick berries from an old man's commercial raspberry, gooseberry and strawberry farm.

We got our blueberries and huckleberries around Inverness when they became ripe in July. Sometimes we walked all the way to Port Edward, picked our berries and walked back on the same day. Greyberries were picked in August before we returned to Massett. Some of us used a wide, shallow basket called a slapping berry basket. The picker would hold berry branches over the basket and slap the berries in. This basket was also used to clean these berries.

My mother was notorious for not wanting to quit picking sessions. One time, at Inverness, my brother Victor was fed up with picking berries and he started howling like a wolf. When my mother heard the howl she came back and said, "I guess we better go back now."

Soapberries don't grow on Haida Gwaii and my mother traded with the Nish'ga for this jarred berry that is frothed up with a little sugar as a special dessert. We ate this delectable treat from one bowl in the centre of the table. There is a real technique to eating the sour/sweet froth, where the foam is blown in and out of the mouth and seeds are removed. The berry harvest from Inverness had to be sent to Massett on a seine boat because cases and cases of jarred berries, jams and jellies had been put up.

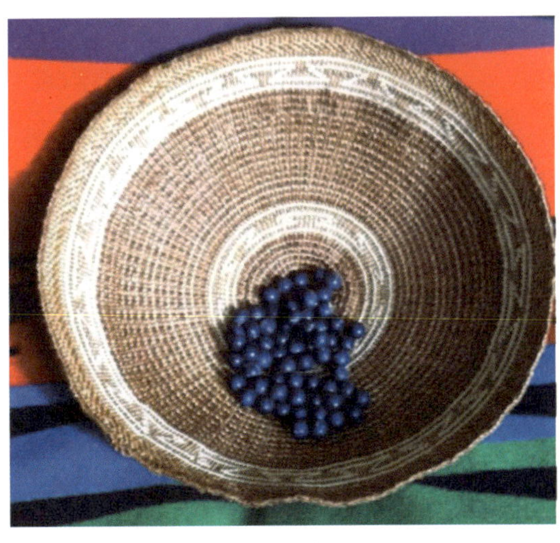

Holly Churchill's slapping berry basket. *Totem Heritage Center*

When we got home to Massett, it was time to pick salal berries. My mother called these laughing berries because when they are pinched at the stem, they unfold into what looks like laughing. This was about the same time my mother went up to the Aayan to harvest dog salmon and high-bush cranberries. I was in school during the fall harvests but I love high-bush cranberries, even though they have a pungent smell. Today I am so glad that my grandson Justin picks these for me.

In addition to dried dog salmon, salmon egg cheese, stink eggs and high-bush cranberries, my mother came back from Aayan with crabapples, muskeg cranberries, devil's club and root medicines.

The Haida potlatch ring berry basket is a common basket found in museums. Isabelle Rorick has an absolutely beautiful potlatch ring basket in the Haida Gwaii Museum in Skidegate that represents the largest-sized berry basket. Some have conjectured that the rings represent the number of potlatches a clan has had. I am more inclined to believe these are measuring lines.

Because the baskets were woven to harvest specific species and were not used for anything else, the baskets were dampened, folded flat, dried and then stored over the winter in a cool, dry place until next season.

Creating berry baskets for personal use is a great way to practice preparing material and improving weaving skills before tackling the more difficult or embellished baskets.

Gardening, Cedar Work Hats and Potato Baskets

The late Henry Geddis, a noted Massett Haida historian, would start his stories about my mother by saying, "That mother of yours sure was a hard worker. She rowed across the inlet to take care of her garden. She wove. She put up food. And she even raised her own cows and hunted and slaughtered cows and deer. She sure was a hard worker."

She was truly a hard worker. She rose early and worked steadily throughout the day well into the evening hours. She was a shrewd businessperson and travelled to the mainland with my father to trade and sell her weavings and harvests, including seaweed, dried halibut and potatoes.

There were gardens both in the village and across from Massett Inlet. Every family had a garden. Potatoes were a staple food for the Haida. My mother told me that the Haida potato was growing here before the Europeans arrived to the Haida Gwaii shores. These were an important trade item and were traded up and down the coast as far as Sitka, Alaska, at the same time that the canoes were being traded. Because the root vegetables take the full growing season to mature and will last through the winter if stored in a root cellar, these were the vegetables of choice when I was young.

Because the women prepared their gardens with seaweed and cow manure well in advance of seeding, the soil provided the food source for the plants throughout the growing season. The seaweed that was used for mulch kept weeds down and weeding was only needed when the potatoes were hilled every couple of weeks. On Haida Gwaii the moisture that was needed came abundantly. The low maintenance of root crops allowed the Haida to engage fully in the traditional harvest season.

My mother harvested and stored potatoes in large rectangular cedar plaited baskets. These are the easiest woven, and least embellished, utilitarian baskets. My mother used a wooden rectangular frame as a form for this style of basket.

She told me that the Haida were "gardening" before contact. Berry bushes and medicines were planted around the villages and food harvesting sites. Gardening was not limited to land. When I was a young girl, an old man who really liked chitons but was getting too old and stiff to walk from Massett to Yakun Point planted some chiton on the rock in front of Massett. This way he could just walk out his door to the beach to collect them when he was wishing for them.

My mother made plaited hats to protect us from the sun and rain. The cedar work hat is plaited and most often uses the "in-between" weaving technique. These were more functional than embellished. My mother also made these for sale and painted her own designs onto the hats with oil-based enamel paint. Today weavers are adding a wide variety of embellishments and some are incorporating a variety of weaving techniques and new materials. These beautiful hats are suitable as ceremonial hats.

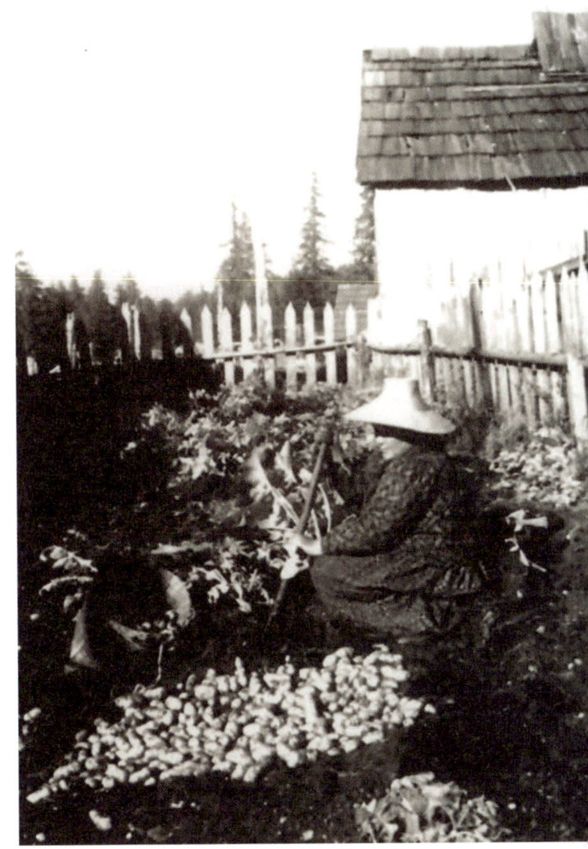

A Haida woman harvesting potatoes. *Alaska State Museum*

Trade and Sales

Trade has always been important to the Haida economy. Canoes were traded as far north as Sitka. Historically the Haida traded halibut, potatoes, furs, seaweed and other goods up and down the coast, including on the Eulachon Grease Trails that took trade into the interior of British Columbia. Early ship logs and journals verify that the Haida were shrewd traders.

The Haida, including my mother, continued this trade legacy. In addition to traditional trading with our neighbours, my mother entered into the new tourist trade, selling her weavings in Prince

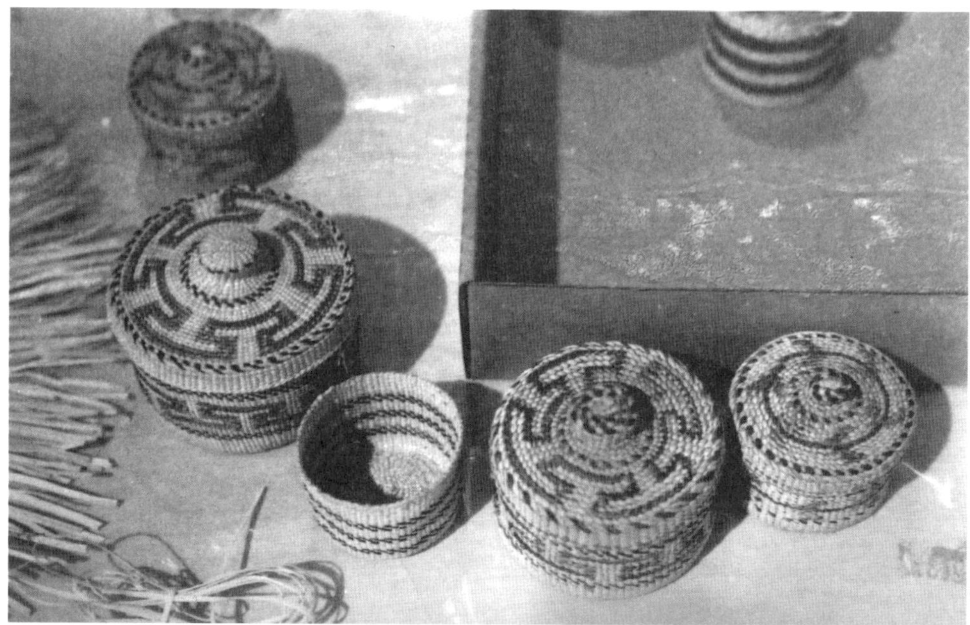

Collection of Selina's spruce rattle lid storage baskets.
Tony Pope

Rupert, Port Essington, Vancouver and Victoria. She continued these sales when she moved to Ketchikan. Through her classes and the relationships she built, she helped raise the prestige of Haida weaving from a craft to a recognized art form.

Early tourists preferred the more embellished weavings, which the woman's workbaskets and handbags offered. Hats were and still are high on the list of items that are in demand. When we went to Inverness to work at the cannery, my mother would stop in Prince Rupert to sell her weavings and shell art. When my father travelled for business and for the Native Brotherhood, he sold her weavings and the weavings of other village weavers.

The interest of museums in building collections of Indigenous artifacts contributed to weaving sales. For instance, my father sold seventy-five hats to the Canadian Museum of Civilization on behalf of village weavers in April 1929. Aside from the woven hats, my mother's most popular basket was the spruce rattle lid storage basket.

Spruce Root Hats

Arrival of Pestilence by Chris Hopkins is one of my favourite paintings. It is not a historical painting but depicts so well a Haida prophecy that predicted the arrival of ships to the Haida Gwaii shores. The large white sails of the prophecy had been described in terms of a supernatural being. Because of this prophecy our people expected the arrival of strange vessels and beings from the ocean.

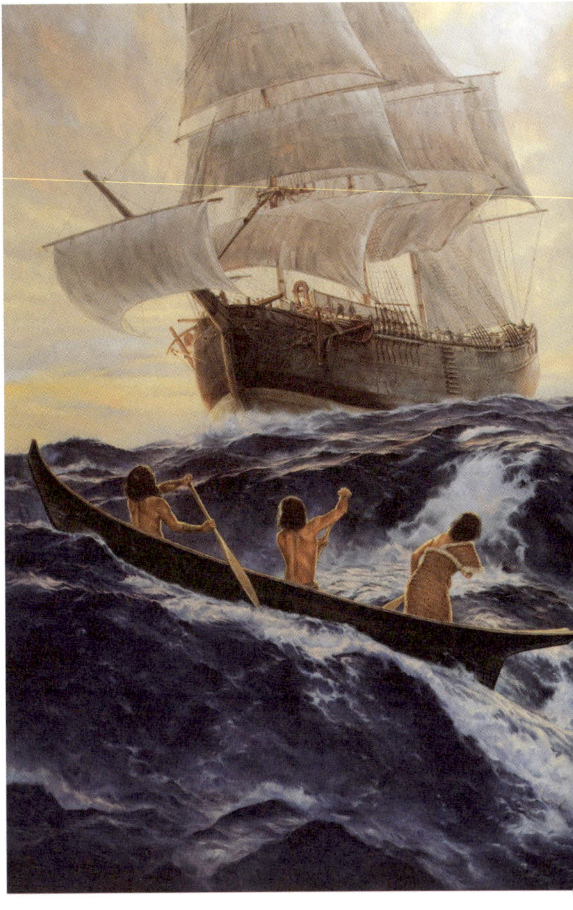

Arrival of Pestilence by Chris Hopkins—one of Delores's favourite paintings—depicts a Haida prophecy.

One of the earliest ships to visit Haida Gwaii was the Spanish *Santiago* captained by Juan Perez in 1774. We know from ship logs that Perez did not land on Haida Gwaii but was met by a party of canoes with the Haida ready to trade. Perez's journal describes trading with the Haida, but I had no idea that he had obtained a spruce root hat.

During my study in the Museo de América in Madrid, Spain, I was elated to discover a spruce root hat, which Perez had collected during his short time at Kiusta on the west side of Haida Gwaii. I was thrilled to find it woven in the same style and shape and carrying the same snail's trail design that my mother used on her hats. The hat is an affirmation that Haida spruce root weaving is an unbroken line of a traditional art form.

The hat Perez collected is a compact-twined conical shape that is truncated at the top. There are three distinct sections to the hat: the crown, the taper and the brim. These three sections are differentiated by the use of different twining techniques that are divided by a three-strand twined row, where the addition of warps occurs. The crown of this hat is woven using two-strand twine. The taper makes use of both

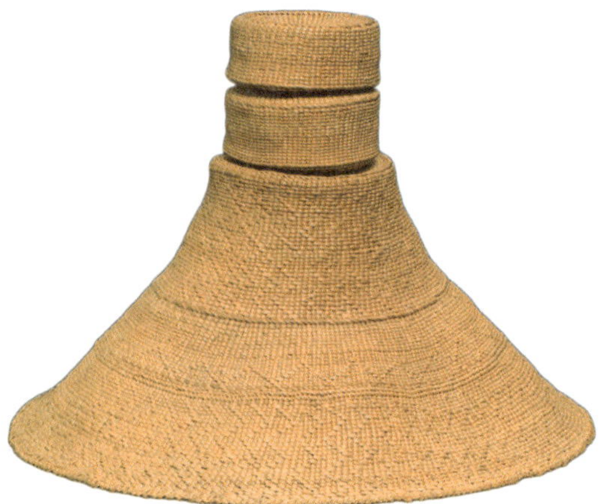

Potlatch ring hat by Selina Peratrovich. *Churchill family.*

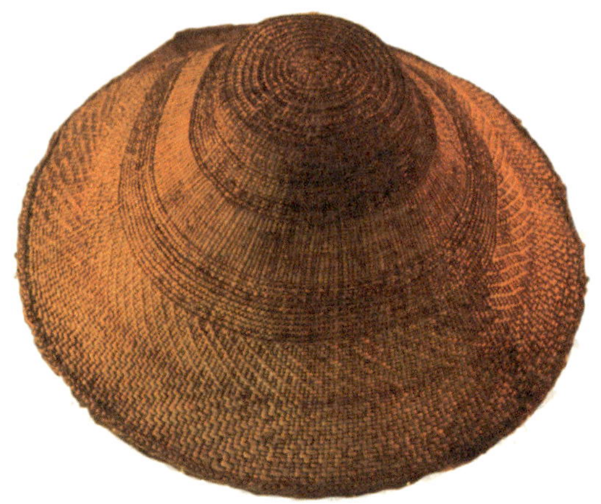

Spruce hat collected by Juan Perez in 1774. *Bill Holm, Museo de América.*

two-strand and three-strand twining, while the brim uses twill twining to execute the snail's trail design (see Chapter 5).

The shape of the hat collected by Perez is the same as that used by my mother to create her potlatch ring hats. The rings on the top of the hat indicate "the potlatches and feasts held by the clan." After each potlatch a ring is added. As my mother explained, the hats of the finest weave and design were used as ceremonial hats by the Chiefs and high-caste people, while those with little decoration were common work hats.

The potlatch ring hat that is represented here was woven by my mother and was used as a contract between the two of us. Her wish was that after her passing away, that two memorial feasts be held for her: one in her home village of Massett and the other in Ketchikan, where she is buried. After these were held, I was able to use the hat. When my daughters use this hat at feasts or potlatches that my sister Jane or I are unable to attend, they are representing our clan.

The shortest brimmed hats are in the style of the "canoe hats" or spruce root compact-twined work hats, which are designed to keep the sun out of the eyes while keeping the wind from flipping the hats off. My daughter Holly likes weaving this style of hat and has made one for each of her nieces, Carrie Anne Vanderhoop and Teresa Mae Varnell, as gifts for university graduation.

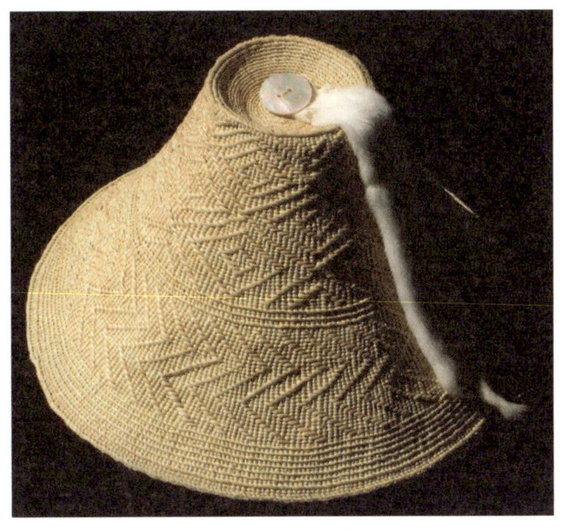

Spruce hat woven for Carrie Anne Vanderhoop by Holly Churchill. *Churchill family*

The spruce root hat of the Long Ago Man Found is in the style of a canoe hat with the shorter brim. During my study of this hat, it was difficult to determine the origin of the weaver because occasionally the Tlingit technique reverted to the Haida twining technique. In the end, I have concluded it is most likely to have been woven by a Tlingit.

The differentiation between the crown, the taper and the brim is evident. The crown is two-strand compact twined. The taper is three-strand compact twined for thirteen rows, followed by two-strand compact twining to the end of the taper. The brim starts with one row of false embroidery using spruce root as the embellishment. This is followed by one row of two-strand compact twine, followed by another row of false embroidery using spruce root. The rest of the brim is compact twined to the ending edge. The edge is the same six-strand technique that I had discovered at the British Museum in 1982.

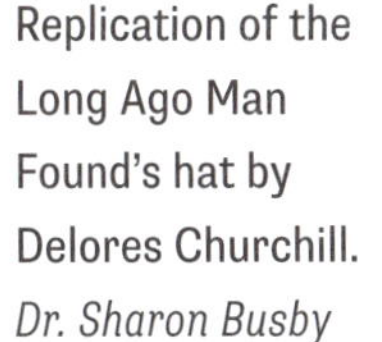

Replication of the Long Ago Man Found's hat by Delores Churchill. *Dr. Sharon Busby*

The traditional spruce hats are often embellished with the twill-twine technique. Hats are also embellished with crests that are painted by a design artist. Charles Edenshaw's beautiful designs are found on many older hats.

When my mother was helping me with my study at the British Museum, her information about the artifacts in the collection was immeasurable. We studied a hat whose brim was black. She explained that when people were in mourning, food and other taboos existed. The black brim informed others that they were in mourning.

From my studies of the ancient weavings of ancestors that are housed within museums, it appears that the Haida and Tlingit

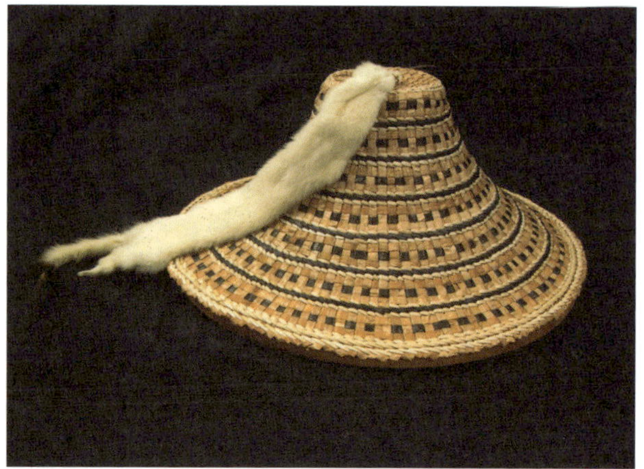

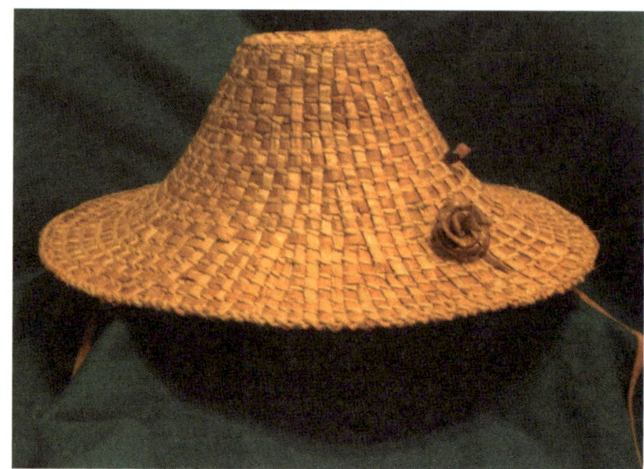

Red and yellow cedar work hats by Teresa Varnell. *Totem Heritage Center*

construction and shape for spruce root hats are similar, although woven using the unique techniques of each tribe.

The use of the hat form is relatively new to Haida weaving. My brother Victor was the first to make one of these forms for his wife, Primrose. The form is used to measure and dry the weaving as it progresses. If the weaving is done on the form, the left-hand index finger works between the form and the weaving wall. Prior to the forms, the hats and baskets were woven free form.

My recommendation is to become proficient at making cedar work hats, flared compact-twined baskets and a cedar compact-twined hat prior to attempting a spruce root hat. Spruce root harvest and preparation takes far too many hours and is too much work to use on a learning project of this size.

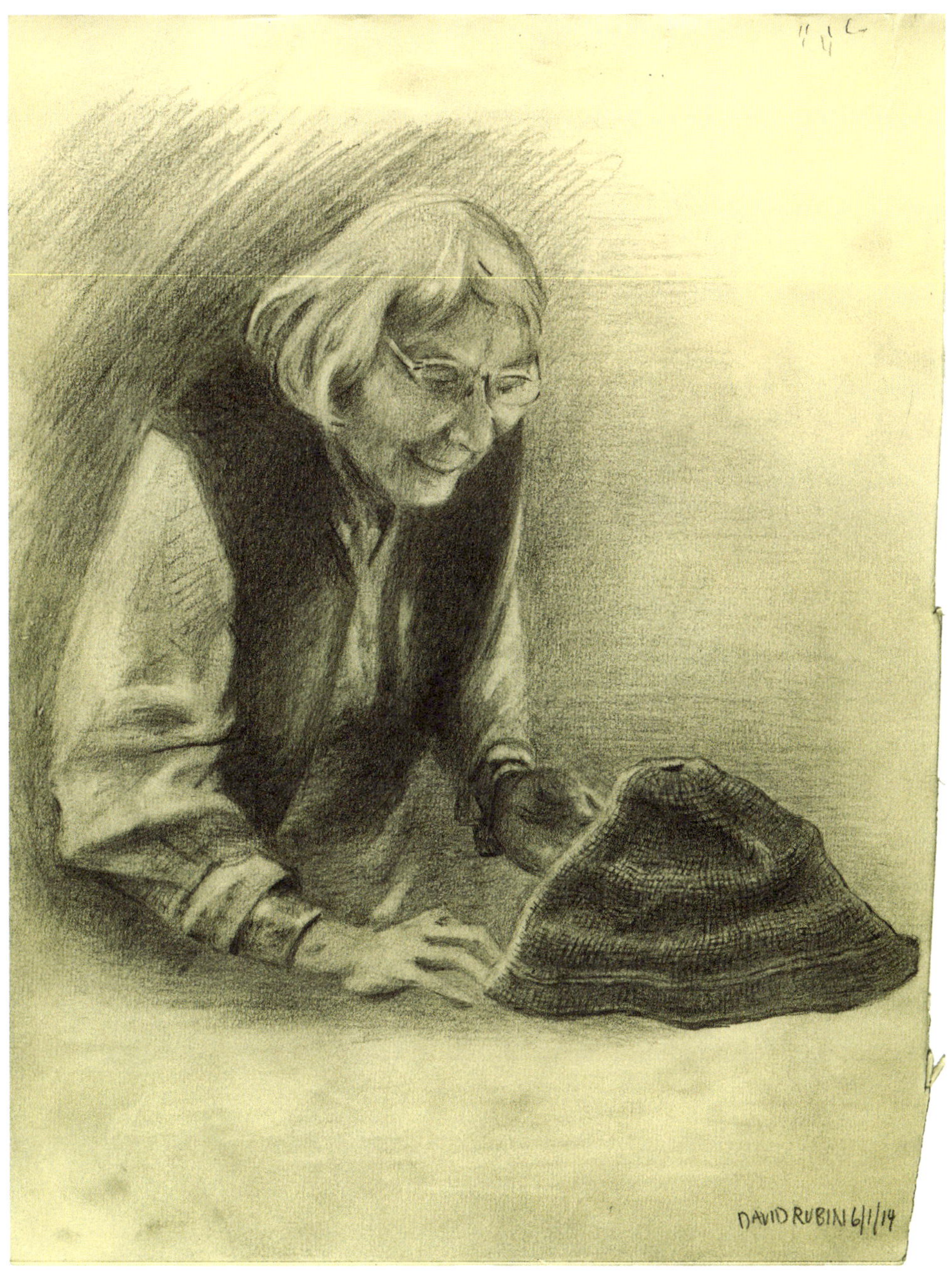

A drawing by Dave Rubin created for the documentary *Tracing Roots: A Weaver's Journey* by Ellen Frankenstein and Delores Churchill. *Ellen Frankenstein*

CHAPTER FOUR

The Weaving Harvest

> “The red cedar raises its head and boughs up to our creator in joyful praise for the gift of life, while the yellow cedar humbly bows its head and branches to our creator in reverence for the gift of life.”
>
> —DELORES CHURCHILL

Forest Yah’guudang

My mother, Selina, taught the old Haida way by modelling and then leaving the learner to imitate. When she came back to gauge the progress, if the learner was imitating properly, she’d nod her head, saying, “aang” (yes) and leave the learner to continue. If the learner was not able to imitate, she’d say, “King hlaa” (look) and she would again model.

She was careful not to let any of us harvest or move forward in harvest and preparation until we fully understood the processes, including the principles of yah’guudang in relationship to the trees and plants and the forest as a whole. She did not allow any of us to cut into the tree until after years of accompanying her. First we learned to

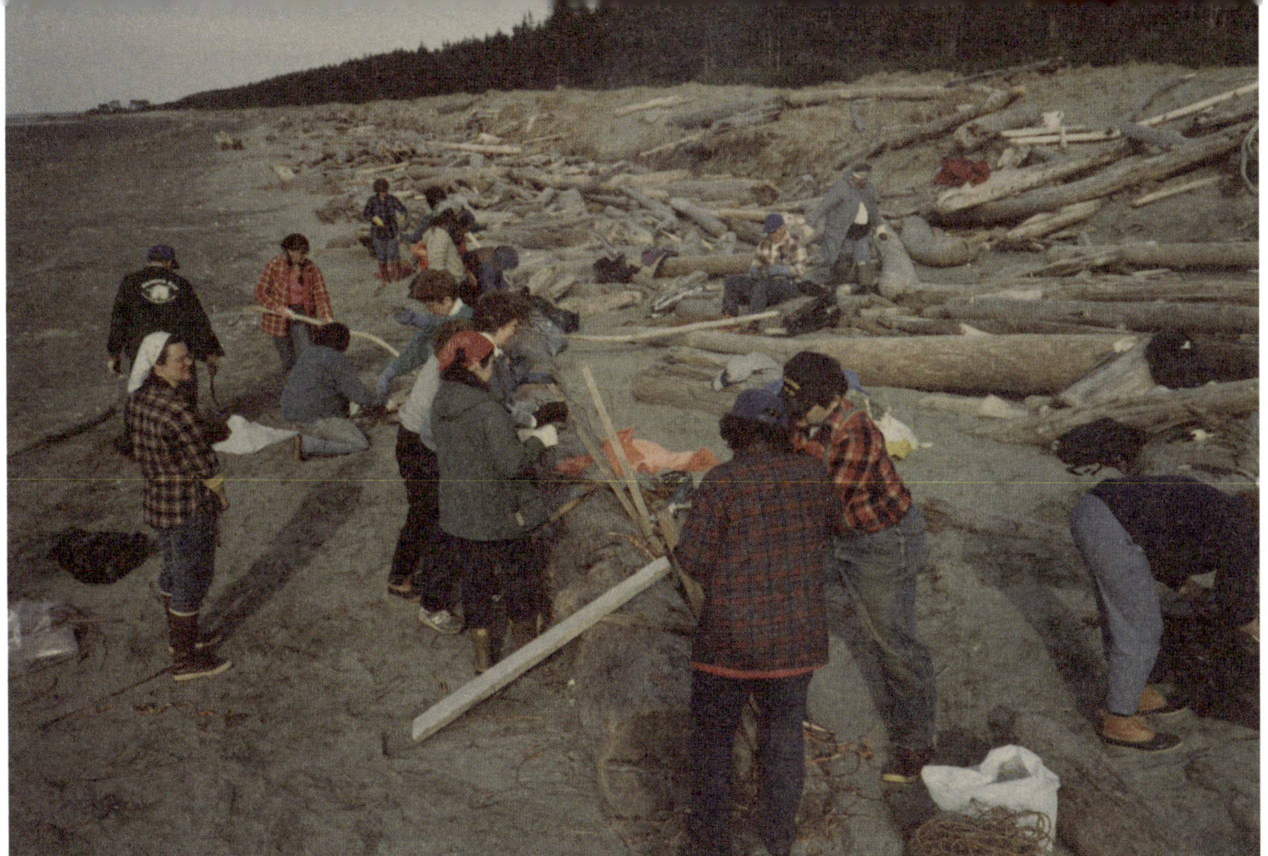

Students with Delores in 1988, harvesting yellow cedar in Masset. *Churchill family*

give our personal expressions of gratitude as we learned how a grove and a tree were selected. At last we were able to strip the bark from the tree and to take the outer bark off.

She did not allow others to do the final layering and thinning down of the material she would use for her personal weavings. We learned to prepare the material when we helped her prepare cedar bark weaving packages for her classes or worked on our own material.

She took this same care when she modelled harvesting spruce roots. She would select the area and trees and model the yah'guudang required for harvesting. We were then able to dig the roots and she periodically came back to check how it was going. We next learned to pull the cooked root through the debarking board and to bundle the cooked roots.

Over time we learned to cook the roots and could not move forward until we were not undercooking or burning them. She told us that the roots that burned or did not want to give up their bark were wanted by an ancestor on the other side. She showed us how to send these, and at least one very fine root, to the ancestors through the fire.

Layering and splitting were allowed early on, but only using roots that were crooked, discoloured or scorched by the fire. We then thinned and split them until we had the traditional technique mastered. My mother never allowed any of us to layer or split the material she would use for weaving.

An apprenticeship with my mother took years and through these repeated activities with her, her storytelling—and her occasional oral instruction, yah'guudang, as expressed when accepting the gifts from the forest—became ingrained. Haida stewardship laws express respect for the life and spirit of those things that gift us. They are based on common sense. These laws were applicable ten thousand years ago. They are applicable today. They will be applicable ten thousand years from now because they are founded in principles and values and not in the "letter of the law," which can be manipulated to one's own desires. The principles and values never change. Legislation, policy and regulations never stay the same.

The forest is not our home. It is the home of all that live in the forest, which means moss, lichen, insects, plants, trees, animals, fish, birds and even rocks. We announce ourselves to the bears before going into their home and let them know why we have returned. Just as we do when visiting the homes of our human relatives. We are not unnecessarily loud. We are attentive. We don't touch things unless offered or permission is given and we definitely do not destroy peoples' possessions or homes. We don't leave their houses dirty. We show respect for ourselves and others by behaving in highly respectful ways. These are all simple guidelines that apply while we are guests in the forest.

As well as a physical life, all things have a living spirit, which must be highly respected. The supernatural beings that make their homes in the forest must be respected. Loud noise is disruptive. Taking gifts without thanks is rude. Making fun of or wasting any gift from the forest will bring severe consequences. Those living items that give of themselves so we might live and thrive deserve to be treated respectfully. The spirit of the deer, fish and all living things, after giving their lives to us for food and our well-being, must be thanked and not wasted. Common sense and common etiquette while in the forest, the home of other beings, are very simple.

For the X̱aad Kíl learner, here is a song composed for children's use before leaving a cedar harvested tree. My Kyanuusalii cousin Phyllis Almquist, a X̱aad Kíl teacher, composed this for her language classes. (Sing three times. To end the song, after the last stanza, sing another "aa hii yaa haa.")

Haaw'aa ts'uu aa Haaw'aa ts'uu aa hee.
Thank you red cedar trees aa
Thank you red cedar trees aa hee
Giid dang wii ee giid dang wii aa hiiyaa haa
For bark strips ee
For bark strips aa hii yaa haa.

Cedar Bark Harvest and Preparation

My mother held onto the old-fashioned way of displaying regard for self and others through elegant dress. Even when harvesting she most often wore high-heeled shoes or boots, her gold and silver bracelets, and a dress, covered with an apron and work shirt. She finally gave in to wearing slacks after a pilot suggested that they would keep her warm. At first she wore them only in the woods and under her dress.

My mother would go out for bark every spring, a skill taught to her by her maternal grandmother, Edith George (Kujuuhl). Even before I had an interest in weaving, my children and I would accompany her into the cedar forests. No men would come with us. She did tell me that when she was a child, men helped the women harvest cedar bark.

My mother's harvesting ceremony started at the edge of the forest. Before entering, she shook a rattle—and on occasion let off firecrackers—as she called to the bears in X̱aad Kíl, "It is only me, your sister. I'm here for cedar bark. I won't take more than I need." She would promise that we would do no harm to the bears' home. As we hiked deeper into the forest she would occasionally stop to make these same announcements. She always recognized that when we were in the forest, we were guests.

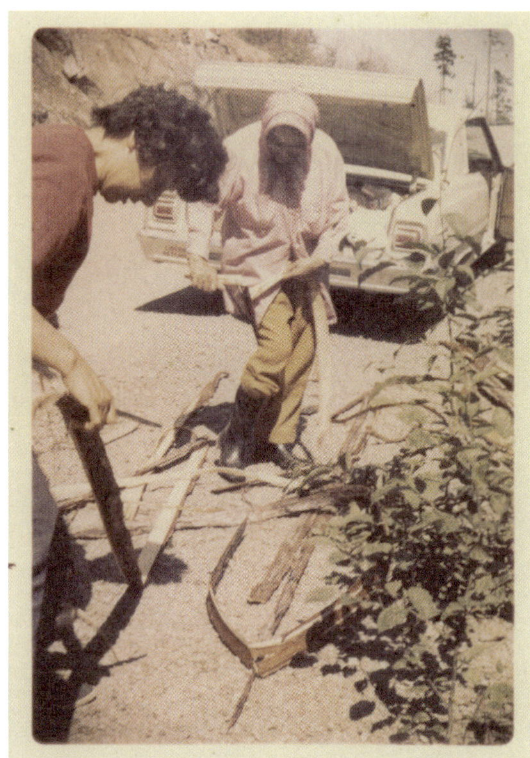

Delores and Selina cleaning bark in the 1980s. *Tongass Historical Society*

As we walked she would point out the trees that had been harvested in years past, nestled in a grove of untouched trees, saying quietly, "Look, the weavers left these trees for us."

There was no small talk or chatter once my mother's harvest began. The same undivided attention that she gave to guests was given to the tree. She paid close attention to how the material wanted to be handled. However, as she worked with the material she did speak to the tree, telling it that she would make beautiful baskets. She only took what she needed and could finish working on that day, as she had been taught.

Although she worked quietly on the bark, she made these outings fun during the breaks and lunch. She told us old stories and made us laugh with her funny observations. She laughed easily at herself and at the children's antics during our breaks.

When we were working and the children became loud or overly rambunctious, she would quietly and firmly remind them to play quietly. My children understood that when she made a sharp, rounded, clucking sound from deep in her throat (K'uu), it meant, "No good. No more," and they quickly adjusted their behaviour.

Some of the neighbourhood children and other grandchildren were also invited to help. However, any child who proved not to be quiet and respectful was not invited again. Her expectations were high. When she made a correction she expected self-correction would occur immediately. She had a low tolerance for the children who would not listen.

I would strip the bark from trees and take the outer bark off for her. My mother was quick at harvesting, and part of the children's tasks was to run my unpeeled bark over to her when she had finished her peeling.

Her expressions of appreciation when leaving the forest included thanking the ancestors and blessing the forest with a long and healthy life, with the hope that her children and grandchildren would be able to harvest in the same area.

The bark we got was her bark, and no pay was given or expected for helping her to harvest her material. One day early on in my apprenticeship after she and I had harvested, I picked up some material to prepare at my house. "What are you doing?" she quietly asked as I was heading out the door.

"I am going home to prepare my bark," I replied. "Where is your bark?" she asked. "You want bark, you go get your own." The next day I went out and got my own material.

The Haida know that what we give will be returned to us tenfold. My late cousin Steven Brown best described this concept, and I will paraphrase him here: "When I was younger, I wondered why my uncles did not pay me when I helped them to fish, trap, hunt or do anything. Now, I understand."

"Today, I am an old man, people bring me fish and food. People bring me chopped firewood. The things I need are coming to me. This is how I am paid back for what I did for the old people long ago."

Clan and personal esteem are built within the Haida society, in part, by hard work and a loving, giving and helpful spirit. At his passing to the other side, Steven was highly loved and esteemed by his Nation. He continued to give through his old age up until he died, by working each day making X̱aad Kil audio recordings so that the young Haida language learners would have learning materials after he was gone.

The ancient Haida law of reciprocity requires that learners do not receive pay. Instead, payment is made to the teacher. When my mother took my daughter April on as an apprentice she said, "I not charge you for teaching you. But I not want to wish for things when I am old."

In addition to harvesting material and medicines for my mother, April's payment to her included purchasing airline tickets. My mother would call April and say, "I'm wishing to visit your kids," and an airline ticket would be bought for her.

An apprenticeship is a lifetime commitment. The responsibilities of the learner or apprentice (as known today) include harvesting material for the teacher throughout their lifetimes. An apprentice does not step into the shoes of the teacher until the teacher is ready to step aside or passes from this world. I applied this law as my mother's apprentice. I did not move into her position as the teacher of Haida weaving until after her death. Up until that time, I served by harvesting material for her every season, helping to prepare her classroom materials and assisting in the classroom. My daughter Holly, a terrific teacher, gives me this same respect by asking me first if I'd like to take a teaching opportunity she is offered before she agrees to teach a class.

I continued the tradition of bringing children into the forest and teaching through modelling with my grandchildren after my mother passed away. However, my expectation was that my grandsons, even beyond their childhood years, help me harvest. My grandsons also learned to weave baskets, which is an adaptation and extension of the tradition.

In the long ago days, before her time, my mother said that weaving was women's work, except in the making of the fishing nets, traps, weirs, twine and rope. Women did not touch or even walk over the tools men used because the spirit of women was known to be powerful either for good or for bad. Women touching these things could bring very bad luck to hunting or fishing.

Cedar Trees

The cedar tree is known as the "Tree of Life." It provides for houses, shelter, transportation, tools, clothing, containers, diapers, ceremonial items, mats, baskets and other household and harvesting utensils. It is an important physical and spiritual medicine and considered the weaver's sisters.

The bark peeling done by our ancestors is evident throughout the forest. Today these are classified as Culturally Modified Trees (CMTs) and evidence of Haida use and occupancy from the coast into the interior of Haida territories. When I come upon one of these trees located deep within the mossy forest, I am overcome with emotional gratitude, knowing I am standing in a spiritual site of our people. At these times I always give thanks through silent prayer.

Red cedar (ts'uu) and yellow cedar (sG̱ahláan) are both used in Haida weaving. The western red cedar tree (*Thuja plicata*) and the yellow cedar (*Chamaecyparis nootkatensis*) are both coniferous trees that grow abundantly on the British Columbia coast up through southeast Alaska. The gigantic cedar of Haida Gwaii gave the Haida the ability to create the distinctive and immense canoes that were also a major trade item up and down the coast. I am told that some trees have grown as tall as ninety feet. The distinctive characteristics of red and yellow cedar make them easy to distinguish.

There is a danger to the trees and forest if the harvesting rules are not fully understood. Understanding and ingraining the harvesting stewardship laws into one's being comes about after years of harvesting with an experienced harvester. Each season, the modelling of the expert brings to light new knowledge and increases the depth of understanding and greater connection to the land and the trees.

My mother selected the area and trees for harvest. The areas are free of any signs of plant disease. The trees that are harvested are huggable (about thirty-five inches diameter or seventy inches circumference). The inner layer of the smaller diameter trees is too thin and those trees will have difficulty healing the wound. The inner layer of the larger diameter trees is usually too thick and can be brittle and pitchy.

My mother selected areas where the moss was thick and there was little debris, with lots of space for her grandchildren to swing around the tree on a bark strip and to land safely and softly, in the event she needed them to help remove a strip that had gotten stuck at the top of the tree.

The selected trees are perfectly straight, which is determined by observing whether or not the outer bark grain runs straight up and down or is swerving to one side or the other. If the bark does not run straight up and down it will be of little use. Stripping and thinning the bark down to weft and weavers will be difficult as the thinning requires fighting against the natural twisted grain. A lot of bark will be wasted, which is not respectful to the tree. Bark from these twisted trees produce short and substandard weft and warp that will break easily.

The side of the tree where the bark will be stripped has no branches and minimal knots that interfere with pulling the bark down. Knots and branches change the grain and can make the bark strip unsuitable for weaving.

Bark is not taken from the windward side of the tree, where whipping wind will tear at the bark-strip wound in the tree, making it harder for the tree to heal. The bark from the windward side tends to be brittle.

Trees that are growing on a slight incline against a gently sloped hillside more willingly give longer bark strips.

Because the yellow cedar primarily grows high up into the mountains where the wind whips and whirls, the appropriate trees will not be found on exposed mountaintops.

Bark (giidee)

Understanding the structure of the bark and the individual characteristics of red and yellow cedar bark makes preparation much easier.

The outer bark is separated from the inner layer while still in the forest. The outer bark is returned to the forest floor to provide nutrients. Care is taken not to cut into the sapwood. The tree will heal its wound if the proper moderation and stewardship laws of harvest are observed.

Red cedar inner layers may be used for both weft and warp. It shrinks little when it dries. It is stiffer, more brittle and is easily prepared because it stays true to its grain throughout the preparation.

The colour is naturally a deep honey and will hold this colour for many years if prepared while the natural moisture is still in the bark and exposure to water and light is limited.

Yellow cedar inner layers are used only as weft for twined weavings. The yellow cedar shrinks too much and leaves large gaps in the weaving if used as warp. Woven objects of yellow cedar are not used for food containers because the strong-tasting sap will transfer to the food.

Bark Harvest Yah'guudang

Harvesting times are dependent on the weather. The tree will only release its bark when the sap is moving up or down the trunk. A warm spring means early harvesting and a hot summer means a shorter harvest season. The bark will not come off the trees when the weather has been too hot. There is a short window of about two weeks in September when bark can be harvested but the bark will be pitchy.

Red cedar bark harvest generally begins at the end of April and usually goes through June and sometimes into July. Yellow cedar harvest at the higher elevations can go into the first of August. However, the earlier it is harvested the less pitch it will have.

It is much easier to get the outer bark off the red and yellow cedar trees in the spring. The lightest coloured bark, with very little pitch, is harvested early in the spring. The fall harvest may have crystallized pitch pockets in the inner layer and will be a darker colour.

Climate warming is changing harvesting times and the time changes are likely to increase. The time may be coming when yellow cedar can no longer grow in Haida Gwaii and southeast Alaska because it is too hot. Gauge the harvesting times by the warmth of the season. When nettles begin to push their heads out of the earth it is most likely that the bark is ready or nearly ready for harvesting.

The Haida weavers' demonstration of yah'guudang for the tree begins by first thanking the Creator and the spirit of the tree for the gift of bark and assuring that the gift will be used respectfully. Some say prayers of appreciation aloud. Some communicate their appreciation silently. Others gift the tree with a medicine. No weaver will leave the forest without thanking the trees and promising to use the material respectfully.

Even as an adult, my annual visits to Haida Gwaii have always excited me and I would want to get out on the land and begin harvesting everything I could because it is all so much fun, and my time on Haida Gwaii was always so short. My brother Victor, who knew of my enthusiasm and impatient character, would remind me of the ancient law as I headed out the door, "Delores, remember, harvest only one thing at a time and what you can finish working on today."

Respect for the life of the tree requires that care is taken when selecting the area for harvest, making certain that the trees show no sign of disease or distress. Sitting quietly with a clean mind and gentle spirit allows the tree of proper size and qualities to identify its willingness to share its bark.

The expression of respect includes connecting and being conscientiously with the forest, tree and material while harvesting, preparing and weaving. This mental and spiritual shift in approach produces weavings of spectacular beauty.

Today, new expressions of respect have been added that support the ancient responsibilities but address the conditions of today. In the days of old, permission to harvest cedar was needed from the Chief who was responsible for the area. Today permission may be needed from the Nation, tribal council, a fee-simple landowner, logging company or a governmental regulatory agency. Yah'guudang and proper stewardship in an area still requires getting permission before harvesting if the area is not a traditional harvest area for your people.

Long ago, everyone understood that harvesting bark in the proper way did not harm or kill the tree. Today, few in the broader society have this knowledge and may create unnecessary problems if they see a bark stripping. Yah'guudang requires respecting all people and not contributing to the creation of unnecessary concerns and problems, this includes making certain that bark stripping is not facing hiking trails or roads.

Bark stripping close to roads and car traffic exposes trees to those pollutants that trees cannot defend themselves against. It is the duty of the harvester to protect the forest and trees, which includes walking well into the forest and not bark stripping near roads and vehicle traffic.

A very clear memory and learning moment occurred at a picnic with my family when I was a child. In my excitement I had quickly laid out the picnic blanket and was running to get the food basket when Chief Wiah, my k`aagii Willie Matthews, stopped me and gently told me to lift up the blanket. Pointing at a small spruce sapling that had been under the blanket, he quietly said, "See the little tree under the blanket? It wants to live, too."

I moved the blanket and the lesson has never been forgotten. The trees, even the saplings, want to live and it is my duty to respect this universal desire to live.

A major rule of harvesting from a tree is moderation. Trees that have given bark in past years are not harvested a second time.

There are culturally modified trees whose bark strips are obviously wider than eight inches and some whose bark was taken in multiple years. I have no explanation other than it could have been that the tree was meant to come down or to be used to make boards at a future time. As it is with the unfinished canoes in construction that are found in the forest, those harvesters may not have been able to come back to finish the work because of the massive deaths from devastating diseases that decimated the Haida population.

My responsibility is to harvest as my teacher—my mother—taught me, just as it was her responsibility to teach me the way she had been taught.

It saddens me to see trees that will not likely live, or that are suffering because so little inner layer has been left to feed the tree, or trees that are harvested close to the roads, where pollutants will affect their health, or the youngest of trees that don't get a chance to live an undisrupted life. These things occur when harvesters do not spend adequate time harvesting with their teachers, or when someone decides that the bark is an economic commodity. Any time people see anything purely as a source of money, these things are greedily exploited and the supernaturals step in and take these precious things from us.

First Nations Harvesting Methods

Each First Nation has its own methods of harvest, which is guided by their environmental conditions, histories and their expressions of respect. I have described how I was trained by my Haida elders to harvest bark, and my personal preferences that were gained through many years of experience. However, because the old Tlingit and Tsimshian weavers trusted to teach me their ways, I have been privileged to learn about and to respect these differences.

The young weavers will learn a great deal more than the techniques of harvest and weaving when they spend time with their knowledgeable ones, and like the generations before, they will be able to pass the rich knowledge and unique history and traditions of their cultures to the next generations.

Weaving Harvest and Preparation Terminology

In the field, the terminology of harvesting is often used interchangeably. Because the teaching of harvesting is demonstrated, the terminology is easily understood. Written harvesting descriptions are at a loss without the actual material from which to demonstrate. For convenience and to avoid confusion, the following terminology will be used consistently throughout the harvesting pages.

Debark: taking the outer bark off of spruce roots by pulling cooked roots through a split stick

Debarking tool: a board or stick that is used to debark the spruce roots

Layer: cedar bark and spruce root fibres that have been thinned down from the thicker outer sheaths to a suitable thinness for weaving

Peel: taking the outer bark from cedar bark

Probe: a method of finding and digging up lead spruce roots through the moss or sand

Probing tool: a stick or other tool used to probe the moss and sand to find and dig roots

Splitting: separating spruce roots and cedar bark into weaving strands

Strands: cedar bark and spruce root layers that have been split down in width and thinness that are near or suitable to weaving

Strip (noun): cedar bark piece taken from the tree

Strip (verb): pulling cedar bark from the tree

Thinning: the thickness of material layers into a thinness that is suitable for weaving

Warp: the vertical strands that hang down; the structural foundation of the basket

Weft: the horizontal strands that actively enclose the warp through twining or plaiting techniques

How to Prepare Cedar Bark

Step 1: A horizontal cut that is about three- to four-inches wide is made through the outer bark and inner layer with a sharp hatchet at the base of a tree, just above the large roots. Care is taken not to cut the sapwood. Cutting at the very base of the tree provides leverage that is needed to whip the bark strip off the tree. If this first cut is made too high on the tree and the bark strip gets stuck against something at the top of the tree, there will be no leverage to whip the strip off and it may never come down.

Step 2: Along this horizontal cut, a large knife is slipped between the inner layer and sapwood and wedged along the length of the cut.

Step 3: The sharp butcher knife makes a vertical cut into the outer bark and through the inner layer to the sapwood at the corners of the first horizontal cut. These vertical cuts go up as high as can be reached. Sliding and wedging a knife or a meat cleaver down this vertical cut between the inner layer and the sap wood loosens the bark from the tree, which produces longer bark strips.

Step 4: The bark is grabbed with both hands at the base and pulled away from the sapwood. The bark is pulled off the tree with a slapping motion against the tree as the harvester moves out away from the tree. Care must be taken with red cedar not to let the bark get kinks or folds, which can cause the bark strip to break (at that crease point) when energetically whipping the bark strand against the tree.

Outer bark particles will fall off as the bark is pulled away. Care is taken not to look up while pulling the bark. The bark is heavy when it falls. The wise harvester is ready to move out of the way when the long strip falls away from the tree to the forest floor.

Repeat: After the first strip is down, the original horizontal cut at the base is extended another three to four inches and the bark stripping begins again. At all times the ability of the tree to heal is considered. No more than a six- to eight-inch-wide strip is harvested from a 35-inch diameter tree. This moderation in harvesting will give the tree a chance to heal itself.

Tip: Sometimes the bark strip will get hung up and the children are asked to swing on the strip until it breaks loose. Children's work also includes carrying tools and materials for adults. Older children learn to bundle the bark and to carefully carry the bundles out of the forest. When children demonstrate an understanding of the connection to the tree and the required respect, they begin to learn to help adults pull the bark from the tree.

Step 5: The inner layer is peeled from the hard outer bark starting at the top end (the pointed end). A slice is made across the width of the inner layer to a depth that brings the cut as close to the inside part of the outer bark as possible. The inner layer is held in the right hand, horizontal to the body. The inner layer is then rolled toward the body, away from the outer bark, with the strip hanging down, waiting to go through the rolling action.

Flora Mather, one of my Tsimshian teachers, peeled bark by putting it between her knees to steady the strip. This places the bark strip vertical to the body and both right and left hands peel the outer bark and inner layer apart. My mother used this style for the wider strips and I find that this method allows me greater control.

Step 6: The outer bark is peeled away from the inner layer the full length of the strip, taking care that as much of the inner layer is removed as possible. This may leave short thin strips of the outer bark remaining on the inner layer that are easily scraped away.

This outer bark is discarded in the forest, where it will feed the forest floor. This returning of the unused portion of harvested items to the place where it was harvested is a stewardship law observed for other harvesting. Clamshells go back to the beach. Entrails of river fish are returned to the river and those from the ocean go back to the ocean.

Step 7: The inner layer is bundled from the widest end and tied off using the tapered end. The bark bundles from each tree are tied together through the bundle loops. These bundles are placed into airtight bags as soon as possible so that the natural moisture is retained.

Some wrap the bark into circles. On occasion I use this method on shorter pieces. There is a danger of the bark moulding using this circular method if it is wrapped too tightly and not worked on immediately.

When the outer bark has been completely removed and left on the forest floor and the inner bark is bundled and put into garbage bags, the area is cleaned of any other sign of human presence, thanks is given to the trees, and the group of harvesters heads home to work on the bark.

My mother told me, “Only work on things when you are happy and thankful.” I need to keep my mind in a constant state of gratitude to keep this frame of mind when I am weaving.

The thinning down of the red cedar bark is completed on the same day as the harvest. The sooner the unprocessed bark is thinned into layers, the easier it is and the more golden and light coloured it remains.

If the work cannot be finished on the same day, the airtight bag of damp bark may be held in the refrigerator to be finished the next day. Cedar moulds quickly when damp and should be thinned and hung to dry as soon as possible. Also the bark will darken in colour the longer it waits to be prepared.

Some harvesters have begun to bundle and hang the thick, unprocessed bark to dry, planning to thin it down at a later date. This can be done, but there are drawbacks that include having to soak the dried-out raw bark for a long time before it is supple enough to thin down. The excessive soaking darkens the bark and it is more difficult to thin down without the natural moisture. As well, this kind of harvesting could encourage taking too much bark that is never thinned down and then lays in storage for years. My mother said, "Only take what you can finish on the same day."

If the thick, unprocessed bark is not dried thoroughly to its centre before storing, mould has an opportunity to establish itself, usually slimy and black moulds. These will spread when the bark is again exposed to moisture.

The unprocessed yellow cedar bark, if laid out loosely over a clothesline under a clean sheet and hung outdoors overnight, will be a lighter colour and the inside will be less pitchy when thinning down the next day.

My mother and Florence Davidson used this method of preparing the yellow cedar for thinning but it is not necessary. The drawback of not hanging the bark overnight is that the bark will be a darker colour and will be a little more difficult to thin down because of the overly pitchy inside layers. A rag with a bit of vegetable oil is used to clean pitch from hands and knives.

Thinning Bark

A raw bark strip right off the tree can usually be thinned into three layers. Thinning is started about a quarter of an inch from the widest end of the bark strip. Using a sharp butcher knife, a horizontal slice is made into the inner layer on the side that was against the sapwood. The cut depth is about one-third of the way through the thickness.

Step 8: The same technique of rolling the inner bark away from the outer bark, or peeling the bark from between the knees as described in Step 5, is used to thin the thick bark strips. Red cedar will be relatively easy to thin because it will follow the natural grain lines. Yellow cedar is more difficult because it will easily change thickness and has to be carefully guided to retain the same thickness down the length of the bark layer.

The first thinned bark layer is the one closest to the sapwood. The right hand informs as to whether the thinness of the bark layer remains the same down its length. The left hand provides the tension needed by the right hand to smoothly roll the bark apart.

If the bark in the right hand begins to thicken out, the right hand gently pulls away from the split until the layer returns to the proper thinness. If the bark in the right hand begins to thin too much then the left hand pulls more tension away from the bark split until the proper thinness returns.

Repeat Steps 5-9: Thin out the middle layer and the layer that was next to the outer bark.

The thinned bark layers are then wrapped in bundles as they were in the forest and again placed into garbage bags to retain the natural moisture for the next step of bringing the wide layers down to the desired width of warp and weft strands.

Grading, Drying and Storing

Each layer of bark has different colours and qualities. The bark closest to the sapwood is the darkest layer, the middle layer is the lightest and the piece next to the outer bark is best used as warp for compact twining.

There will often be pieces of the outer bark attached to the last layer. It is best to scrape these off with the knife at this time. However, I have waited until I am readying material for a weaving project with no ill effect.

Step 9: For weavings with the most consistent colour bark, layers that are closest to the sapwood are tied together, the middle layers together and the layer that was closest to the outer bark is tied together. These are each labelled with the date, the area it was collected and which layer it is.

It is at this point that the bark may be dried and stored for future preparation of weft and warp strands. My mother prepared her weft and warp before storing her winter weaving. However, she left the bark that she would use for classes in their wider bundles to be prepared when the project and the number of students had been identified.

Weft and Warp Strand Preparation

Step 10: The traditional technique for creating the proper width weft and warp was done with a needle and the thumbnail. This was the method of our ancestors, and my mother used this method throughout her life until we found the "Jerry's Stripper"—a leather lace maker—and developed the techniques needed to make proper cedar weft and warp strands. My mother and I saw tools in museums that were labelled "bark strippers" but she had never seen this tool used in her time.

The traditional technique provides the weaver with a wider range of weft and warp width because the blades on the Jerry's Stripper are limited to blade spacing of one-eighth inch, one-quarter inch, one-half inch and increases of one-eighth inch up to the widest spacing of three inches.

I introduced my students to the "Hallmark" ribbon cutter, which can be used to make strands of about one-sixteenth inch in width. It

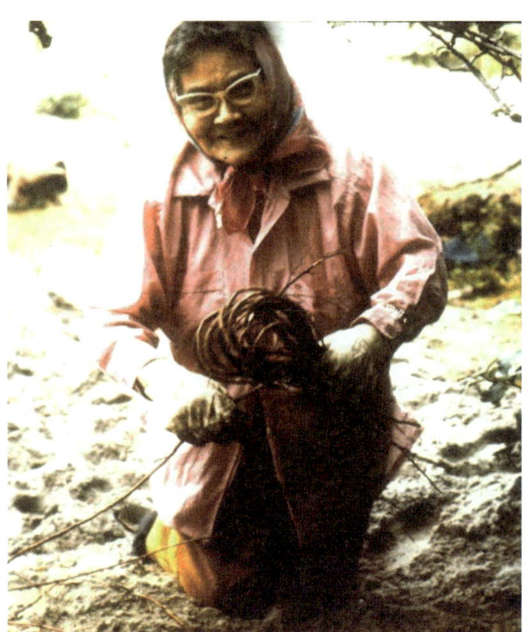

Selina bundling spruce roots out of the ground. *Dorica Jackson*

is cumbersome to use with long strips and the blades dull fairly quickly.

Before we found and taught ourselves how to use the Jerry's Stripper for bark strands, my mother and I made the strands using a needle and our thumbnails. It took us two months to prepare cedar bark material for two classes of ten students so that they could create three-inch diameter by three-inch tall compact twined baskets. With the Jerry's Stripper the same preparation for two classes takes four days.

The Jerry's Stripper has sped up the preparation time but must be used carefully. If the bark layer is not guided properly along its natural grain with the proper tension on both sides of the stripper, a lot of bark can be ruined by cutting cross grain to the strip.

After bringing the cedar layers down to the desirable width of weft and warps, the final work is making certain that all weft and warps are the same width and thinness down the full length of the weaving strands. This is done with a paring knife and a sharp tipped needle. This takes skill that is developed over time. The strand is run between index finger and thumb to identify whether or not the strand needs to be thinned further down or is so thin it needs to join the thinner graded strands for a different project.

Step 11: When the strand is found to be too thick down the full length, the strand is again thinned, making one of the two split-away strands the same thickness as those needed for the weaving piece. This is done by making a horizontal cut with a paring knife across the strand to the depth of the desired strand thinness. The thinning is done by gently rolling the two strands away from each other with equal tension. If one side begins to get thicker, more tension is applied to the opposite strand.

Step 12: To ensure that the full length of the strand is the same thinness, thicker sections are scraped with a sharp paring knife held at a 45-degree angle until the desired thinness is achieved. The point of a needle is used to sliver off any sections of the strand where the width is not consistent.

Final Grading, Drying and Storing

Bark may be woven right after harvesting. I have woven baskets with the material starting on the same day as I harvested the bark. My mother, however, was always harvesting about one year ahead of her weaving projects.

Each strand is tied in the weaver's Figure 8 and tied together according to width, thickness and colour. These are labelled and hung to thoroughly dry. Bark can be stored for years in a cool, dry, dark place. I store mine in pillowcases and cardboard boxes. Never store the bark in plastic or in a damp place.

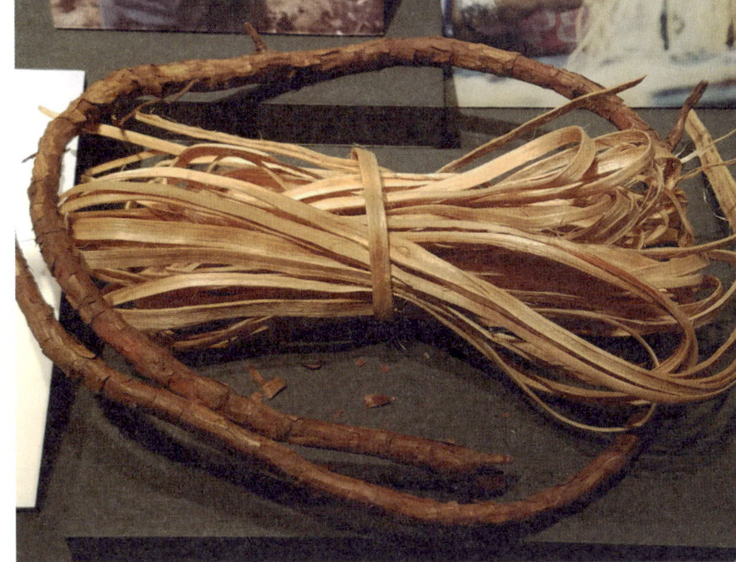

Spruce root bundle.
Stacey Williams

Spruce Root Harvest and Tree Recognition

Women worked in small groups harvesting roots from under the moss, just inside the edge of the spruce stand on the beach side. When the first group finished digging, they began to sing a song that let the others know that they were finished and were heading to the beach to build the fire. As each group finished digging, they sang the same song as they walked to the beach. Unfortunately, I do not remember the song.

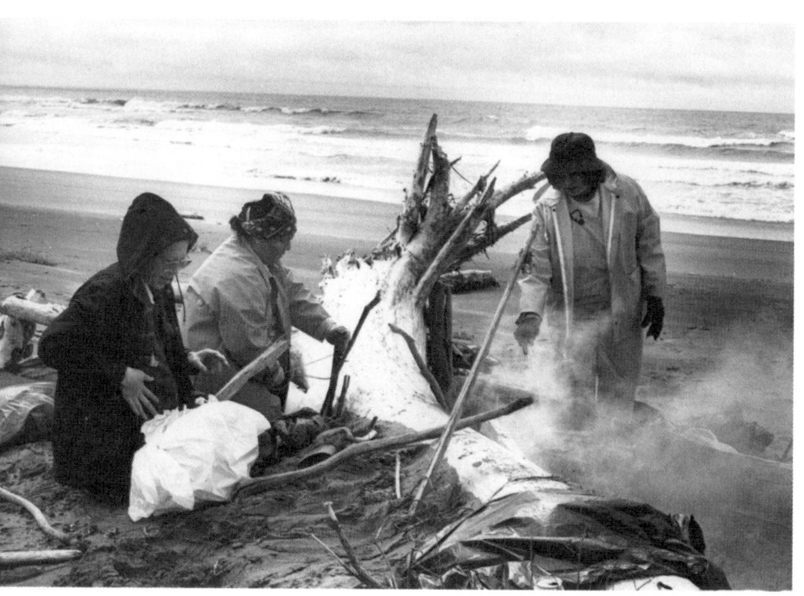

A spruce root gathering trip in 1995. *Churchill family*

As an adult, when I harvested with my mother she would stay in the woods for some time after we were finished digging and while I built the fire. I did not hear if she sang this song when she finally emerged.

When the spruce root gathering group arrived at the harvest area, the children first pulled up sea grass around the area the women were digging. After we had collected piles of firewood we were free to play on the beach. During the root cooking the women would occasionally call us from our play to replenish their woodpile.

While cooking and splitting the roots, the women worked quietly. However, during the breaks and at lunch there was a lot of storytelling, talking, joking and laughter. Everyone treated each other with so much respect and kindness in those days.

Once the fire was built, the roots were being cooked and the outer bark was being stripped away, the women would wind the warm, sticky outer bark of the roots into balls. While the women completed the work of preparing the roots we would play ball games with the root balls on the beach or play other children's games in the woods. The ballgames that we played included a game similar to golf. We dug holes in the sand and using a stick made from driftwood we would hit the root balls into the holes. Another game I really liked that parents today might not appreciate was a tag game where we flung the hard little ball at each other. We all ran really fast to stay away from the stinging root ball.

At this time children were still not subjected to harsh reprimand. Children were held to be precious, recognized as xants and consequently deserving of the respect given to the old ones. Stories of consequence for disrespectful behaviour were told over and over again. Through storytelling the need to exercise respect became ingrained into our being.

When in the woods we played quietly. All of the stories we were told as children reminded us that the places we went to harvest belonged to the living things that made their homes in these areas. It was just a natural part of our life to respect the animals, plant life and even the insects.

My memories of these harvesting times with the women are intertwined with laughter, fun and a warm sense of being loved, accepted and safe.

As children we were taught early in our lives to identify trees, plants and their uses. I've been an avid hiker throughout my life and my children were my hiking companions. They, too, had learned early to identify trees and plants. However, I was surprised when my granddaughter Dakota, at the age of five, stopped in front of a red alder tree as we walked through Ketchikan City Park. She gazed seriously at me as she told me, "Naanii Holly Dolly said that the red alder tree does not have a sign near it like the other trees because the people do not know that it is an important tree." Dakota went on to inform me very seriously that the wood is used to smoke fish, that the bark makes red and black dye for weaving, the wood is used to carve masks, bowls and spoons, and the tree adds food to the ground so other trees can be healthy. And so it is that our oral histories and knowledge continue moving from ancient days into the future through each generation.

Spruce Trees (K̲iit)

Sitka spruce (*Picea sitchensis*) grows throughout Haida Gwaii and along the coast of southeast Alaska. The tree requires rain during the summer months, abundantly provided in these areas. Spruce can be found in tree stands made up exclusively of spruce or in stands with other Pacific rainforest evergreens, including western hemlock

(*Tsuga heterophyllia*), western red cedar (*Thuja plicata*), yellow cedar (*Chamaecyparis nootkatensis*) and red alder (*Alnus rubra*). All of these are part of the Haida weaving traditions.

Although spruce trees abound throughout the Pacific rainforest, those that provide suitable weaving roots make their homes in sandy soil. The trees have good access to sunlight. A profusion of young spruce saplings growing just along the edge of a spruce stand is a strong indicator that the trees are willing to share their roots. Haida Gwaii provides ample root harvesting areas because of the extensive sandy beaches that are lined with spruce stands. This offers a continual supply of beautiful straight roots for Haida weavers.

The traditional harvest areas are just inside a high spruce canopy that is bordered by the ocean or other water way. The roots are harvested from under the thick moss. The mossy areas were my mother's preference for harvesting her roots.

The other area for harvest is along a sandy beach on the outside edges of a spruce tree stand. Roots are taken from under the sand and it is easy to get long roots. The primary drawback is when there has been a long spell of warm weather these roots may not have enough moisture to remove the root bark properly.

Roots (Hliin)

The weaving roots must be straight and growing in sandy soil. If there are interfering plant roots, rocks or debris, the roots will grow crookedly. Weaving with crooked roots guarantees a bumpy basket.

Roots are not dug where there is any appearance of tree disease. The most common disease symptoms to look for are trees with moulted bark covered with fungus or a profusion of branches whose needles have fallen off. For the health of the tree, roots from trees that are twisted are not taken. The twisting indicates that the tree has already undergone some form of stress and deserves to be left in peace.

The spruce tree roots grow out laterally and down in a tight network that keeps the tree anchored. The roots that are suitable for weaving are the lateral roots that grow out shallowly away from the tree. Roots are harvested in the spring as soon as the earth is no longer frozen and in the early fall before the first freeze. Roots picked during these times are a beautiful white colour. They are strong and the outer bark and inner pith are easily removed. Summer heat often produces pinkish roots that break easily, while winter roots are a dark caramel and the outer bark is stuck to the root. My mother harvested both in spring and fall.

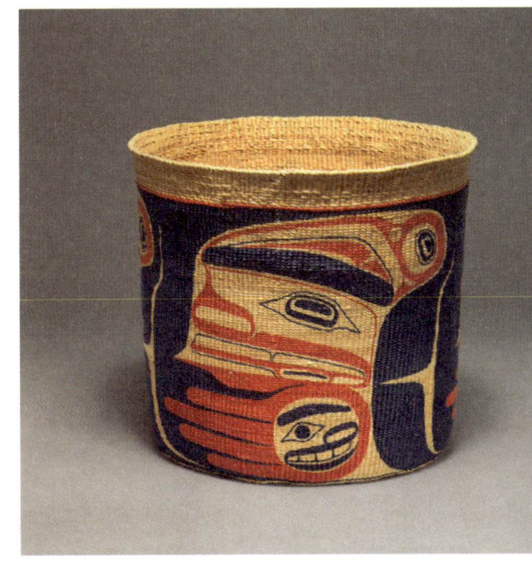

This basket, woven by April Churchill in 1983, was donated to the Met by the Ralph T. Coe Center for the Arts. *Metropolitan Museum of Art*

The roots at Kiusta, on the west northern end of Haida Gwaii, are about forty years old and are beautiful weaving roots because the Alaska tidal wave in 1964 knocked down trees and left wide spaces between the trees that remained standing. The late Grace Wilson-Dewitt, of the Raven Duugwaa Stl'ang clan, who had been married to my mother's uncle Augustus Wilson, was thrilled when we found the Kiusta roots. She created a spruce root hat from the roots we harvested there.

Each of the types of trees that provide suitable roots has its individual benefits and drawbacks. From years of experience and experiments, I have found that the two feet in diameter spruce trees with the reddish colour bark will provide strong roots with fewer "feeder roots," and are easiest to split, but their lateral root systems have grown into a tight maze, making it more difficult to follow the lead roots. It is easier to harvest these roots well away from the crown of the tree. I stand back and measure where I will begin by looking at the crown and following a 45-degree line down to the ground and begin there. A fall harvest of this size tree may include pitch pockets inside the roots.

A younger spruce tree about one foot in diameter will easily release strong roots of excellent colour and texture and has the softest and most pliable roots. The roots of the smaller trees are easy to harvest in mid-spring and in early fall when the ground is cool but not cold. The lateral root system of smaller roots is minimal. Harvesting these smaller tree roots outside of these times produces roots that are much weaker than the more mature tree roots.

Just as pruning trees produces more branches, harvesting of spruce roots produces new lateral roots and contributes to the health of the tree. After a root is cut, the tree quickly sends pitch to the wound to seal the wound and protects the tree from disease. The traditional application of yah'guudang, which dictates moderation when harvesting, and the fact that only surface and small-sized roots are harvested, ensure the continued stability of the tree.

Harvesting

The harvesting begins by centring oneself and connecting to the Earth, giving private expressions of gratitude to the trees, with a promise that the responsibility to care for the forest will continue to be upheld. Full attention is given to the roots as the work progresses. My mother was known for her great sense of humour and storytelling.

However, when she was digging, cooking, splitting and weaving roots she did not engage in casual conversation. Although she was very serious while she worked, my memories are also full of her humorous observations and stories, which she shared on our way to and from the harvesting grounds and during breaks and lunch.

> "Like the forests, the roots of our people are intertwined such that the greatest troubles cannot overcome us."
>
> **CONSTITUTION OF THE HAIDA NATION**

Root Harvesting

After the experienced harvester selects the area and the trees, the seeking out of suitable roots begins. Roots are dug carefully and the disturbed soil and moss are carefully set aside to be replaced when the digging is completed. If roots are left exposed the deer will over-prune and could cause the tree distress. When digging is completed, the area shows little to no signs of disturbance.

My mother probed for roots with a digging stick that was about two inches in diameter by about one foot long, with a dull pointed end. I prefer the garden hand rake or a fishing gill picker hook because of their stability and durability, and because they are easy to find on the ground.

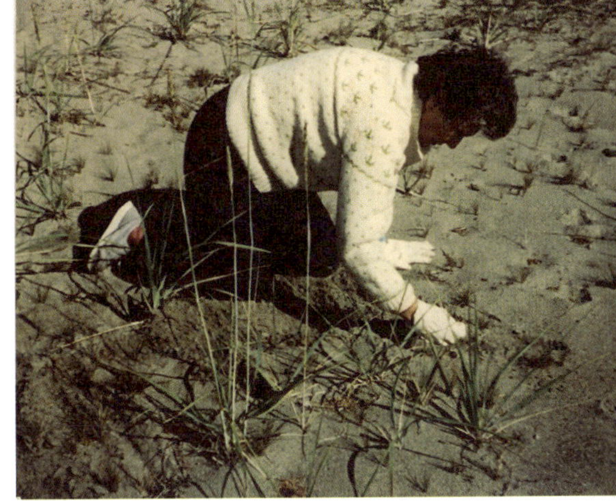

Delores digging for spruce roots in the sand on Haida Gwaii. *Churchill family*

The probing tool is drawn at a right angle to the tree, across the roots that are diverging from the tree until a lead root is found. If the lead root is larger than the diameter of the little finger, the large root is followed until coming to a side root that is no larger than the diameter of the little finger. Roots of suitable size are followed and dug up, others uncovered, and when each suitable root will no longer leave the soil, they are cut away and wrapped up individually in the weaver's Figure 8.

In the mossy areas, my mother, upon finding a lead root, would shallowly cut the surface moss over the root into a two-foot by two-foot square. She carefully removed this moss square to be replaced with the other moss and soil that had been removed as the digging progressed.

The roots are usually found no more than about five inches deep into the soil. Roots grow in layers with the smallest growing on the top layer. Roots get larger in circumference the deeper into the soil they grow. The circumference of the root that is sought is about the size of the little finger. However, roots of all sizes are taken as they are offered. The finger-sized roots provide both adequate weft and warp. Weavers that make jewellery and small projects may prefer smaller roots. The smaller roots are more difficult to keep from burning in the fire and do not provide the warp needed to complete a project. Larger circumference roots are useful for the larger and rougher utilitarian weavings.

Digging roots after a heavy rain is difficult because the soil becomes compact. Roots are easiest to pull up following a light rain or a very short dry cool spell. A long, hot, dry spell turns the roots pinkish and brittle. The dried out sandy soil makes it difficult to harvest.

Pulling a root that comes up easily through the sand or moss without crossing under other roots is exciting. However, the lead root will most often grow under other roots and needs to be gently probed and guided out as the harvester works at getting the longest roots possible. Root lengths are generally about four to six feet but I have seen roots as long as seventy feet.

When the root is dug up and cut away, it is next bundled using the weaver's Figure 8 bundling technique.

Because the roots dry out quickly, the bundle is immediately placed into the garbage bag so that the natural moisture is retained.

Another method for bundling that the old Tlingit weavers used was to simply coil the root into a circle and loosely wind the tail end around the circle. This method of coiling is best suited to the Tlingit method of cooking the root inside a bed of hot coals. My mother used the traditional Figure 8 bundling technique to cook her roots inside of hot flames.

Preparing Roots

One hour of digging becomes one hour of cooking the roots, followed by eight hours of splitting the roots in half, then removing the pith and, finally, many more hours thinning and scraping the roots down their length to create the warp and the weft that is ready to weave. The more splitting and thinning that can be done while the natural moisture is in the root, the less often the root has to be soaked in water. Excessive exposure to water will darken the colour.

Cooking, debarking, splitting in half and scraping the pith out is done at the fire. Working in groups of four gets the work done quickly: there is a cook, a debarker, a splitter and a grader. Fewer people working together can accomplish these tasks but it does take longer. Removing the pith can be done at home following the harvest but the longer the pith is in the root, the darker the root will become.

Working as a team, my mother and I were able to dig, cook, debark and split the roots in half at the fire. She would cook, I debarked and graded, and we both split the roots in half.

Cooking Styles

When the root digging is done and the area is restored, the next step is to go to the beach to build a large, hot, flaming fire to cook the roots.

My family members and I have done all forms of cooking experiments. We have found that cooking in coals takes a lot of time and it is difficult to evenly cook, with some parts of the root not being cooked enough and other parts burning through to the root's soft wood. This coal cooking is an ancient Tlingit style of preparing roots, which obviously produces high quality roots. The trick to this form of cooking is taking the time to understand how long any given circumference of root takes to properly cook inside the coals. I found that this form of cooking is best suited for my work when I am cooking very fine roots.

Boiling roots whose bark or pith has not been removed produces pinkish to caramel-coloured roots, while baking and microwaving will unevenly dry out the outer bark, making it nearly impossible to remove.

After all of our experiments we have all concluded that the Haida traditional method of cooking in a hot flame is the most desirable way for us to cook roots. When the weather has turned bad we have found that cooking at home in a sheltered area with a propane crab cooker or fire barrel cooks the roots efficiently. However, I find that it is not as much fun or fulfilling without the smell of the smoke, the crackle of the fire, the breeze on my face, the feeling of warm sand, the sound of the roaring ocean and the sense of our ancestors' presence.

Some of the late nineteenth century ethnologists were told that the roots are dug, hung to dry and the outer bark was later scraped off. This method was not a traditional Haida way of preparing roots. When my mother and I worked with Bell Deacon, an Athabascan weaver, she showed us how she used the drying then scraping process to prepare willow root. When my mother showed her our way of cooking the roots, Bell was surprised at how easily the outer root bark came off. This is a good example of how environment dictates process. On Haida Gwaii and the southeast Alaska coast, driftwood and dead wood abound. In Fort Yukon, where Bella Deacon lived, wood is scarce and building huge bonfires may not be practical.

Preparing to Cook

While some of the harvest party builds the fire, others make root cooking sticks (hotdog roasting style) from green tree limbs and others make a debarking tool for each team. While waiting for the fire to build up, the roots are readied for cooking by grading these according to circumference. The thicker roots are cooked first while the fire is large and very hot. The smallest roots are cooked last when the fire is smaller and less hot.

The cook of the team places a root bundle on the cooking stick through the two loops and holds it directly inside a high hot flame. Similar to cooking a hotdog, the root is turned periodically as the feeder roots burn down to a stub.

The root is ready to come out of the fire when the feeder roots have burned down and the root makes a quick "whooshy hissing" sound. Because of the crackling fire, this sound may not be heard. The root is removed when all the feeder roots have burned off and the bark looks dried out. If it becomes coal black it has been cooked too long. In our tradition, a burnt root indicates that one of our ancestors wants the root and we return it to the fire.

The Debarking Tool

My mother used a driftwood board about two to five feet long that she split with a hatchet, about six to eight inches down the centre from the top of the board. This board is pounded into the ground until it stands firmly on its own and will not become dislodged during the debarking. I use this method for the thicker roots but have found that the small handheld "debarking tool" that is part of my root harvest pack works well on roots up to a finger-sized thickness. This small handheld tool can be cumbersome to use when the root is exceptionally long. The Totem Heritage Center (Ketchikan) and some of my students have made their own style of debarking tool. The importance in the tool is that the split can accommodate a variety of root diameters and that the split is easily drawn together with one hand to exert the proper pressure needed to smoothly debark without damaging the surface of the root.

The debarker of the team takes the cooked root and immediately unwinds it by pulling the "tail" of the half bow knot. While the natural moisture of the root is still hot, the root is pulled through a debarking tool. If the moisture gets too cool the outer bark will stick to the root. Cooking the root again after it cools is not done because it burns. Instead, the root is sent to an ancestor by burning it in the fire.

The thickest end of the cooked root is laid into the split and is grasped with the right hand. The left hand squeezes the split together while drawing the root through the debarker as fast as possible. The outer bark will come off easily, leaving a beautiful white root.

Splitting and Thinning

Splitting and thinning the roots is easier when the structure of the root is understood. The root's diameter shape is more oval than round. The feeder roots grow opposite and parallel to each other down the length of the root, out from a small groove. After the outer bark and inner layer bark are removed, the root is then split in half lengthwise, following the natural groove line. If done properly the feeder root stubs will also split in half. The pith is the brown to caramel line that runs down the centre of the root.

Step 1: The team member serving as the splitter wipes away any residual charcoal with a damp, soft cloth. The cooked root will have a thin coating of slippery skin that if not immediately removed will stain the surface of the root an uneven caramel colour. This coating is gently scraped off by running the dull side of the paring knife down all sides of the root.

Step 2: A horizontal cut halfway through the diameter of the root (at its thickest end) is made with a sharp paring knife. This cut is then split down about three to four inches from the cut.

One side of the halved root is placed between the front teeth. The index finger and thumb on the right hand hold the right half of the root while the left-hand fingers hold the root side that is waiting to be split.

The teeth and hands hold the root taut. As the splitting progresses, each of these provides the pressure needed to keep the roots equal in thickness.

The head and right hand apply the right tension to each of the two sides. The index finger and thumb on the right hand gauge the thinness of the split root. The left-hand fingers push the root into the "Y" as the root is split. The splitting occurs because of the pressure put into the "Y" by the left hand and because of the gentle pulling away done by the right hand and head—this occurs just above the "Y."

The thumb and index finger of each hand will move down the root. When the "Y" is about five or six inches from the mouth, the split root on the left is moved up to the mouth and again placed between the teeth just above the "Y," and the process is repeated until completed.

When the index finger and thumb inform that the root piece is becoming thin on the right side, the head gently leans to the left until the root strand returns to the beginning thinness. However, if the finger and thumb inform that the piece being held by the teeth is getting thicker, then the right hand pulls to the right gently until the root returns to splitting equally on both sides.

If the unevenness becomes too difficult to correct, the root is cut at that spot and the process begins again. Also, if the root breaks, it is simply cut away and the splitting begins again. Those pieces that are split and cut are not thrown away. Every little piece will serve a purpose and is kept, except when they are too small in length to weave.

The best place for beginning weavers to start learning to split is with the smaller thin roots, which will become weft. The dull side of the paring knife is firmly but gently run down the length, along the sides where the feeder root stubs are sticking out. These will then generally separate easily along the groove line.

The two half pieces have a smooth, rounded, shiny side and a rough flat side. Any feeder root stubs left will be on the outside edges of these strands. The pith must be removed immediately if the intention is to retain the whiteness of the root.

Scraping the flat, rough side of the root strand with the sharp side of a paring knife until no sign of the pith is visible removes the pith of the smallest roots that will not be thinned a second time. Scraping the root is the same technique used to curl wrapping ribbon. Hold the paring knife at a 45-degree angle and draw the sharp side down the flat side of the root.

The thicker halved roots will be thinned one to three more times depending upon the diameter of the root. The same method of splitting the roots in half is used to thin the halved roots. This is more difficult because there is no natural groove to follow. The evenness of the thinning relies on the guidance of the right index finger and thumb, and on mastering the control over tension using the head and right hand (as described previously). Each of the thinned strips is scraped on the rough sides to make a very flexible strand and to remove the pith. There will be one internal strand that has the pith running down the centre.

Some basketry books state that the inner strip with the pith is discarded. I do not discard this piece. I scrape the pith off and bundle it with the other internal pieces for use as warp. The problem with saving this piece comes when the pith is not completely removed. If it is used as a warp strand, the sap in the pith discolours the outside weft roots as the weaving progresses.

After the roots are split to the proper thinness, the weft (those with the shiny rounded side) is wrapped using the weaver's Figure 8 bundling technique. The warp strands (those with two rough, flat sides) are loosely wound into a circle and tied off using the half-bow loop and leaving a tail. These two different bundling techniques make it easy to distinguish warp from weft when weaving begins.

These are then graded according to size and placed into clear plastic bags until all roots have been thinned down. Plastic bags are used to keep natural moisture in the roots, but are never used for storage as the risk of mould is too great.

The roots are then washed in rain or distilled water, tied together with a root strand or piece of string, keeping the same-sized warp and weft together in readiness for the final finishing steps of making warps and weft of the same width and thickness. This is best done while the natural moisture is still present. The use of tap water, which contains chemicals and metals, will alter the colour of the roots.

Before the fire is completely extinguished, all of the outer bark, scrapings and scraps are burned. Any spectacular roots that have been set aside to send to an ancestor are also burned at this time. As my mother did, I give a silent prayer of gratitude to the ancestors for the gift of weaving, to the trees for the gift of the roots and, in general, to the Creator for all that had been provided on that day.

Storing

When warp and weft are thoroughly dried they are stored in a cool, dark, dry place. Dry heat storage will make roots weak and brittle. I store my split and graded roots in paper bags, never plastic. Some of my students store the thoroughly dried roots in vacuum sealed bags in the freezer. My mother placed her prepared and dried roots into paper bags or pillowcases and stored them in her old-fashioned steamer trunks. It can take a number of harvesting trips to get enough prepared roots of the same size for the larger weaving creations. Label the year and place, and store together by colour and size.

On occasion in our fast-moving world, the work is interrupted and cannot be finished on the same day or there may be a physical limitation that interferes with completion on the same day. In these cases the roots that have been split in half may be put in the freezer in a plastic bag to hold until able to complete the work. This should not be done as a matter of habit and the work must be completed as soon as possible.

The longer the roots stay in the freezer the more often they go through a defrost cycle, which may create mould spots on the material that may not be evident at the time but will show up on the weaving later. I am told by some of my students that vacuum sealed bags retain the natural moisture.

Final Completion of Weaving Warp and Weft

When my mother finished harvesting for the season, her packages of basket materials were completely prepared, stacked and stored. The project materials were assembled, including dyed grasses that would be used for each basket. When she started a weaving project, the preparation had already been done and she simply started weaving.

It takes years to learn to prepare the roots for weaving with the larger roots. My mother's warp strands were as thin as typing paper.

I reserve the final preparation until just before I begin to weave a project. Because the natural moisture is no longer present, the dried roots are soaked in distilled water or rainwater for a couple of hours before the warp and weft are made exactly the same width and thickness, with all the crooked pieces cut out, the feeder root stubs slivered off and the weft ends thinned for splicing. All of this takes a sharp paring knife and a lot of time and patience. This step is an art form in itself. In fact, I firmly believe that weavers cannot claim a piece to be theirs exclusively if they have not done the preparation. At least 90 per cent of the basket is harvesting and preparing. The spirit of yah'guudang guides us to acknowledge publicly the person who may have prepared our material.

The end results of properly prepared materials can be seen in the works of the true masters, our ancestors. The beauty of what can be achieved when this is done with loving attention can be seen in the work of those who are meticulous in the preparation.

Design Material Harvest and Preparation

Sun-dried natural grass and maidenhair fern are weaving embellishment materials that do not lose their natural colour with time. Tsimshian weavers used these exclusively in their false embroidery design fields on baskets. Tlingit and Haida also use these materials in their natural state. Maidenhair fern is difficult to weave because it is naturally brittle and the edges are sharp, resulting in many "paper cuts" during the weaving. The pain is well worth the results that can be achieved with this material.

Maidenhair fern and grass are best harvested from areas that are protected from the wind because if wind checked, they will break apart easily.

Maidenhair fern grows on rocky mountain and hill faces that have water running down the rocks and where the fern roots have good drainage. The ferns are harvested in late spring or early summer when the stalk diameter is at its largest and before the stalk becomes too brittle. The maidenhair fern stalk is mahogany in colour, running close to black on one side and dark chocolate to a light root beer colour on the other.

On the same day of harvesting, while the natural moisture is still in the stalk, the maidenhair fern is prepared by gliding the handle side of a paring knife down the stalk to flatten it. Care is taken to make certain that the two colours are separated evenly.

Next, the inside green pith is pulled down to split the stalk open while separating the black and chocolate sides. The inside green pulp that is attached to the inside walls of the stalk is scraped out.

The stalk is then blanched for a few minutes and laid out to dry. When it is completely dried, it is stored in a paper bag in a cool, dark place.

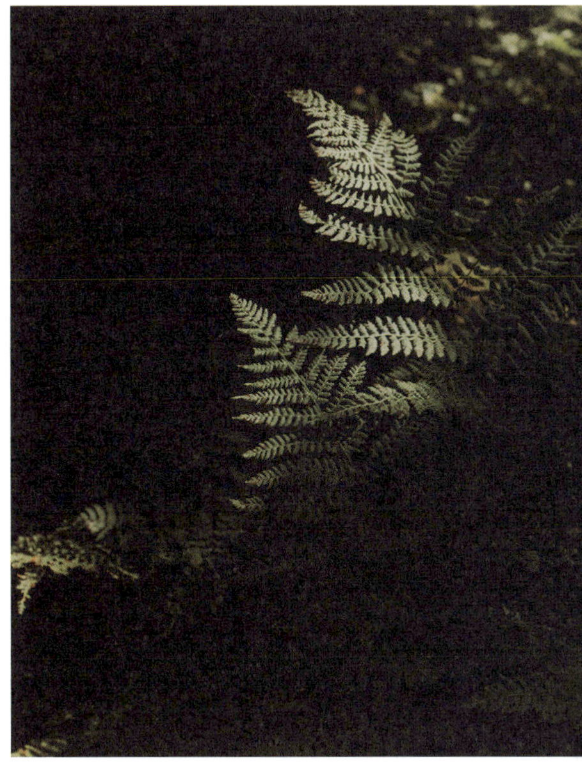

Maidenhair fern.
Mathilde Langevin

When it is time to use the fern, the stalk is thinned down to the same width as the weaving's weft by splitting with a needle and the thumbnail. Flattening the stalk is done by rolling the piece over the index finger.

Tip: After harvesting the fern stalk, it may be placed into a plastic bag and stored in the freezer for a couple of days before preparing. However, because the diameter is so small the fern can dry out and become brittle and not useful if left too long.

A more uniform colour of black (hlahl) can be achieved around the full circumference of the stalk by placing the fern stalk into an iron oxide bath for a few days. However, if it is left in too long it becomes brittle.

Reed canary grass is easily accessible because it grows along roadsides. It is picked the last week of June into the first week of July, just as the seed head is forming. The stalk of the grass grows with joints between each section. The section of the grass that is used for weaving is the third section down from the seed head. The first and second sections may be too thin in diameter to be useful and those below the third are too brittle. The stalk taken is cut above both the third and fourth joint. The seed stalk, the two top sections and the grass blades are left at the site of harvesting. Sometimes, if I harvest grass soon enough, the first joint and third joint are also taken. This is a judgment call based upon the quality of the stalks at the time.

That same day, the grass stalks are blanched in boiling water until they bleach out to a pale green-yellow colour, at which time they are removed from the boiling water using tongs.

When the stalks have cooled and drained, they are strung together with a needle and thread through the top joint and hung in a sunny window to complete the bleaching process. They are ready for storage when there is no longer any colour in the stalk and they are a beautiful pale straw colour. These can now be stored in a paper bag in a cool, dark place until needed (either for dyeing or for use in their natural state).

Thinning the grass strips into the same width as the weaving's weft is done with the same needle and thumbnail technique that is used to prepare maidenhair fern.

Tip: Through experimentation I have found that the stalks will fade faster by putting the grass stalks into the freezer for a few days before blanching them.

After bleaching and draining, the stalks may be placed into a clear jar in a window rather than strung together and hung. They will have to be rotated periodically and the bottom of the jar must be kept clear of any water to avoid mould.

Design Colour

At one time I was consumed with learning to dye with natural materials. Harvesting, drying, crushing and steeping to create beautiful shades from natural materials is exciting but takes a great deal of time. Because there are so many well-researched books about the art of natural dyeing I will not go into detail here other than to provide an overview, some dyeing tips and a few of my own recipes to start the journey of natural dyes.

1. Natural Colour

Sun-bleached grass produces the straw colour that is found in the design technique called false embroidery. The darker colour—a shiny black to a rich chocolate brown—within these beautiful false embroidery designs is from the natural stalks of the dainty maidenhair fern, as described in the previous section. Occasionally a dull black material is found in the old Tlingit design fields of baskets, which I was told are the roots of the prehistoric plant horsetail, which I have never used.

From my studies in museums, the old Tsimshian weavings that contain false embroidery design seem to use bleached grass and maidenhair fern exclusively and do not include dyed material.

The Tlingit, on the other hand, are known for their intricate and ornamental baskets that are decorated with natural grass, maidenhair fern and coloured grasses.

The Haida also use the false embroidery technique in basket design fields, but not to the extent of the Tlingit. Rather, Haida basketry designs are most usually created through self-weave design techniques, the distinctive black bands, alternating coloured weft and painted crest designs.

TRADITIONAL DYES

In the days of old, the ammonia in children's urine was used as the "mordant" (the fixative to hold dyes). Today, natural dyes are stabilized with vinegar, salt, ammonia, alum, cream of tartar and the highly toxic copper oxide.

Varying shades of red (sg̲id) and orange are made in an alder bark bath. Black is achieved in an alder bark and/or hemlock bark bath that includes a piece of iron such as a galvanized nail. Green (k'anhlahl) can be produced with fish gall, which I have never tried because when these are popped they are really stinky.

Onion skins make beautiful shades from honey colours to light browns. Octopus ink and squid juice produce black but some species, I've been told, contain a highly poisonous element—so much so that the poison is absorbed through the skin. I have not researched this myself and I have never used octopus dye.

Shades of yellow (k'inhlahl) can be achieved with wolf moss. Berry dyes are the least stable of all the natural dyes. Brilliant shades of aquamarine can be achieved with salmon eggs and copper oxide. Fireweed creates a beautiful light shade of pink.

Colours and shades of colour are determined by the material that is to be dyed, how much coloured material is used to make the dye, the age and colour of the dye material, the season when the material is collected, the area where the material is gathered, the length of time the material soaks or simmers in the bath and the mordant that is used to set the colour.

Making natural dyes is an art form unto itself. It takes patience and impeccable record keeping. For those who would like to further explore the world of natural dyes, I recommend beginning this journey referencing *Earth Dyes/Nuunam Qaralirkai: Dyes for Grass Made from Natural Materials,* by the late Rita Pitka Blumenstein. Rita was a Yupik/Athabascan weaver and a traditional healer with whom my mother and I had the great privilege and joy of working. She was one of the International Council of Thirteen Indigenous Grandmothers.

Other fine books about natural dyes, including those for fibre weaving, are easily available.

After a year of experimenting with plant dyes, I found that if the dyed material is kept away from light, the natural dyes will maintain colour but are highly light sensitive and fugitive. A bottle that I wove about twenty years ago using the red alder dye has bleached down from a red to a pink-caramel colour. The bottle had been displayed in a very sunlit room. For this reason, and because it is easier to get a consistent colour, commercial dyes are now used by most weavers.

2. Commercial Dyes

My mother told me that when coloured cloth became available, it was boiled to draw out the colour for use as a weaving dye. Even carbon paper dye was made. When the commercial dyes became available the weavers began to experiment with these new colours.

Although more stable than the natural dyes, over time the commercial dyes will also give up some colour to excessive light. Direct sunlight is an enemy to colour and baskets should not be stored near an area that receives sunlight. Even those baskets that have been stored in the dark museum collections have lost colour. The outside of the basket usually has muted shades of dyed material while the inside may still bear evidence of the brilliance of the original colour. This is true for wool weavings as well. The outside of the robe is usually dull in colour while the inside has often kept the original dyed colour.

Over-the-counter, hot-water fabric dyes will hold colour but still need to be protected from the light. I prefer to use powdered reed and wood dyes. Cold-water fabric dye holds colour very well with little bleeding. Follow the directions on the packaging and take the same precautions.

Dyeing is often dangerous. Do at your own risk. Keep dye equipment separate from food preparation equipment as some of the dyes are poison.

3. How to Dye Material

DYEING TOOLS AND EQUIPMENT

- Sharp butcher knife and paring knife for harvesting and shredding dye bark
- Garbage bags to collect material
- Blender or processor to shred dye materials
- Paper bags to store dried natural materials
- Large glass bowl to soak materials before putting into the dye bath
- Long-handled, stainless-steel spoon to stir dye baths
- Stainless-steel tongs to lift dyed material
- Stainless-steel strainer large enough to drain and rinse dyed material
- Large coffee can for oxidizations
- Rubber gloves
- Facemask when using commercial dyes and mordants
- Protective eyeglasses
- Measuring spoons and measuring cups
- Hot pads to handle hot pot
- Plastic table covers and rags to protect counters and stovetop, and to clean up
- Stove or camp stove (don't use the camp stove in the house)
- Shallow enamel, glass or stainless-steel pot that is large enough to hold material and dye bath
- Sink with running water
- Quart jars with lids and clear labels to store dye mixtures and dried dye materials
- Paper bags to store dyed weaving materials

GENERAL DYEING TIPS

Natural dyeing and commercial dyeing have some common needs:

- Always use rubber gloves, eye protection and face mask when using mordants or commercial dyes.
- Protect counter tops with plastic table clothes. Wood and reed dyes are particularly difficult to remove from laminate.
- Store mordants and commercial dyes in well-labelled, tightly-covered containers in dark areas that are not accessible to children.
- The weft material to be dyed must be ready for weaving. The spruce and cedar bark weft must be the proper width and thickness. Because the dye often does not penetrate the full thickness of the material, any thinning or slivering off of material after it is dyed will show up on the weaving.
- Grass is better dyed in the whole before thinning to the width needed for the weaving project.
- Before placing material into a dye bath, thoroughly soak it in water.
- For dyes requiring heat, slowly raise the heat to the simmering point and maintain the simmer for about 30–45 minutes, while stirring the material in the dye bath.
- Keep the dye bath covered to avoid inhaling fumes.
- Allow the pan to cool with the material before removing from the heat.
- Once the colour is achieved, the dyed material is drained and rinsed until no colour is evident in the rinse water.
- Although rinsed well, residual dye can still be present in the material. To avoid dye transferring to the walls of the basket, soak the dyed material then scrape both sides with the dull side of a paring knife to extract the excess water and any residual dye.

- Wipe the dyed material with a soft cloth and keep the weaving material slightly damp but not wet while weaving.
- Dye baths can be stored for additional use in tightly closed glass jars in a cool, dark area, although each time the same dye mixture is used the colour will be lighter. Strain the used dye mixture and pour into the jar. Use within a few weeks. Periodically remove the lid for a time to avoid mould developing.

4. Plant Dyes

I have learned natural dyeing from a variety of people and everyone has their own methods, even when the dye material is the same. Each tribe and person have developed individual processes and recipe preferences.

Natural dye materials take a lot of time to harvest and prepare. The amount of material dyed can only be the amount that can be held in the dye pan. Each time the dye is reused it will produce a different shade, so all of the material needed to complete a weaving piece must be dyed in the same dye bath.

All dye materials can be dried or frozen for future use. When using hemlock or alder bark care must be taken to make certain that not too much is taken from any individual tree. Trees depend on the bark to live. Taking this bark from trees that are fallen in the spring for firewood or other uses is the best way to collect this tree bark.

5. Natural Dye Recipes

A few natural dye recipes are offered here to help start the adventure of natural dyeing. Colours can be mixed to create new colours. *Disclaimer: Some of these ingredients are toxic and dyers should use them at their own risk.*

ALDER BARK: REDDISH ORANGE TO ORANGE

- 3 cups of shredded alder bark cambium layer (chunks equalling about 4 inches by 20 inches, in rectangular strips)
- 6 cups water
- 1–3 teaspoons of ammonia

Step 1: Shred the alder bark pulp in a blender with about 1 cup of alder bark. Soak the material to be dyed in water for about 30 minutes or until fully wet. In an enamel or stainless steel bowl cover the yellow cedar bark, spruce root or grass with enough dye to cover the material. Add a teaspoon of ammonia and let sit for 20 minutes to make a light orange. If a darker shade is desired add another teaspoon of ammonia and let sit at least half an hour. The material will get darker as the oxygen further treats the dyed material.

Step 2: Soak the material to be dyed in water for about 30 seconds or until fully wet.

Step 3: In an enamel or stainless steel bowl, cover the yellow cedar bark, spruce root or grass with enough dye to cover the material.

Step 4: Add a teaspoon of ammonia and let sit for 20 minutes to make a light orange. If a darker shade is desired add another teaspoon of ammonia and let sit at least half an hour. The material will get darker as the oxygen further treats the dyed material.

Note: Using the outer bark of the alder will result in an orange-brown colour.

BLUEBERRY: BURGUNDY

(*More blueberries and the use of vinegar as the mordant will create blue.*)

- 2 cups fresh blueberries
- 4 cups water
- 1 teaspoon alum
- (For darker colour, add ½ teaspoon ammonia)

Blend the berries and 1 cup of water in the blender. Simmer the above ingredients with yellow cedar, spruce roots or grass for 20 minutes. A darker shade of burgundy is achieved by adding ½ teaspoon of ammonia to a cup of water and adding this to your mixture.

Tip: The blueberries that are picked after the leaves have fallen off will create a darker blue.

Blueberry Variations:

- For slightly different burgundy hue use vinegar in place of alum
- For lighter colour use just 1 cup of berries
- To darken material that is pre-dyed with blueberries place in 1 cup of water with ½ teaspoon ammonia

OXIDIZATION: BLACK OR GRAY

- Coffee can
- Rusty nails
- 6 cups of chopped outer bark of alder or hemlock
- 6 cups of water

Place nails, chopped outer bark and water into the coffee can, cover, and let stand for two days. When the water begins to get black, add weaving material to the dye mixture. Leave in the bath until the desired result is achieved. Leaving the bath overnight will produce a deep black colour.

ELDERBERRY: PALE PINK

- ½ bucket elderberries
- 2 cups water
- ¼ cup vinegar

Boil the elderberries and water together for 20 minutes. Reduce heat to a simmer and add ¼ cup vinegar. Turn off the heat. Add the weaving material and soak material in the bath for at least 12 hours.

BEETS: DARK ROSE

- 4 fresh beets, diced
- 2 quarts of water

Boil beets with two quarts water until well cooked (about 15 minutes). Reduce heat and simmer for 15 minutes. Blend the mixture to a pulp. Strain the mixture through cheesecloth as is done to make jelly. Discard the pulp and place the liquid into the dye bath pan. Add ¼ cup of vinegar and the material to be dyed to the pan. Simmer for about 20 minutes. Turn down the heat and soak in the mixture for about 20 minutes or until the desired colour is achieved.

SALMON EGGS: AQUAMARINE TO TURQUOISE

- 2 skeins salmon eggs
- 2 tablespoons ammonia

Blend two skeins salmon eggs in blender. Add a little water before blending. Add 2 tablespoons ammonia. Add copper oxide. (Caution: Copper oxide is poisonous.) Let this sit for a couple of weeks.

ALDER DYE WITHOUT MORDANT: VARIETIES OF ORANGES AND REDS

Varieties of orange and red can be achieved by sitting and continually mixing and aerating alder bark that is soaked in water. The longer it is aerated, the darker it becomes.

CHAPTER FIVE

Weaving Instruction

Basketry Terminology

My mother used the traditional style of teaching, which is to "watch, try and undo; and again watch, try and undo," until the skill was mastered. Very little oral instruction was provided. When I assisted her with classes, I would provide translation for her when it was needed to express an instruction or description. The Haida style of teaching and learning requires little use of terminology.

The basketry classes are usually no more than thirty hours long and require extensive oral instruction along with the Haida style of watch and try. The written text that is needed to provide weaving instruction demands consistent terminology to avoid confusion. This section allows the use of the same language throughout instruction.

Although there are multiple names used for the weaving components and techniques by different people (at times even by myself in different situations), the terminology presented here are the terms that will be used throughout the written instructions. Some may call the weft a weaver or a woof. But as they say, "A rose by any other name..."

Writings about Tlingit weaving by Emmons (1903), Shotridge (1921), Paul (1944) and Gunther (1984) used overlapping terms but

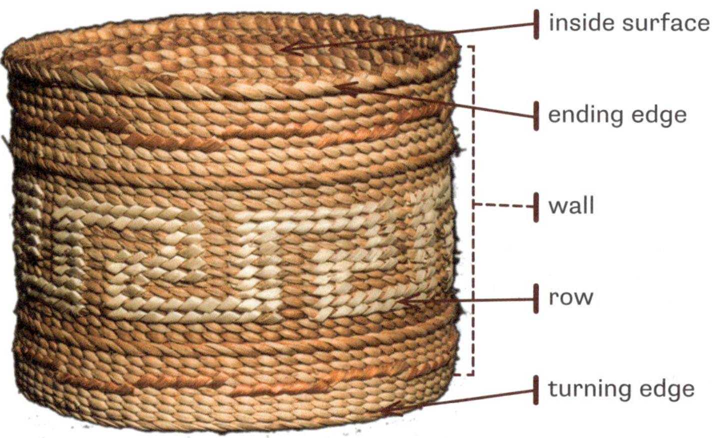

Cedar compact cylindrical open basket by Holly Churchill. *Jack Littrel*

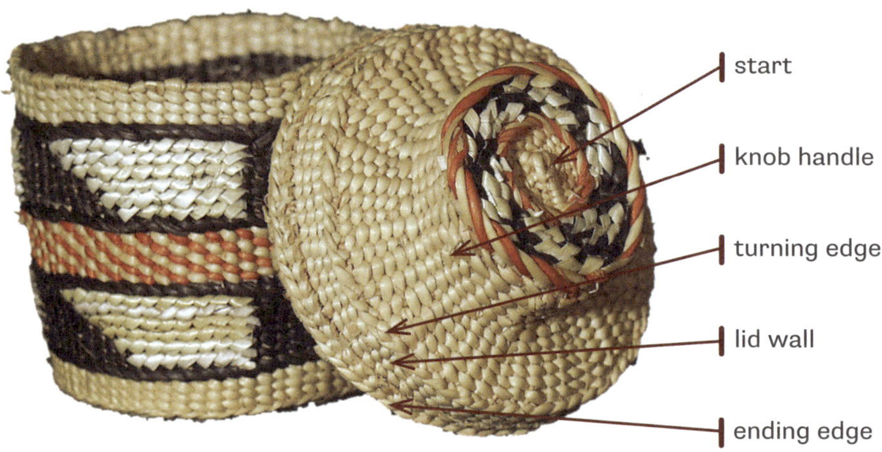

Trophy Bear Lodge story basket by Delores Churchill. *Jack Littrel*

each used different terms for the same thing. In March of 1988, an Alaska State Museum publication, *Concepts,* featured "A Proposed Glossary of Spruce Root Basketry Terms" by Peter Corey, who was, at that time, the Sheldon Jackson Museum Curator of Collections. His research reviewed and unified the best of the terms put forward by spruce root-weaving researchers. His research and the 1988 paper started teachers, students and weavers on the road to refining the language of weaving and has been an invaluable tool for me.

The terminology put forward here is an expansion and, in some cases, adaptation of Peter's early work. The differences between his proposed glossary and my terminology used in this book have evolved

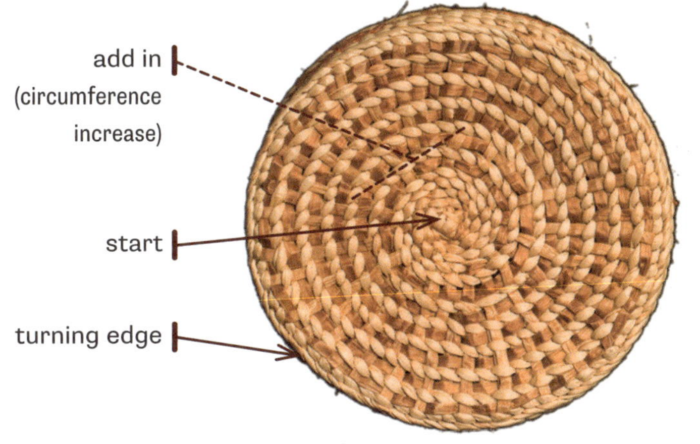

Base of cedar compact cylindrical open basket by Holly Churchill. *Jack Littrel*

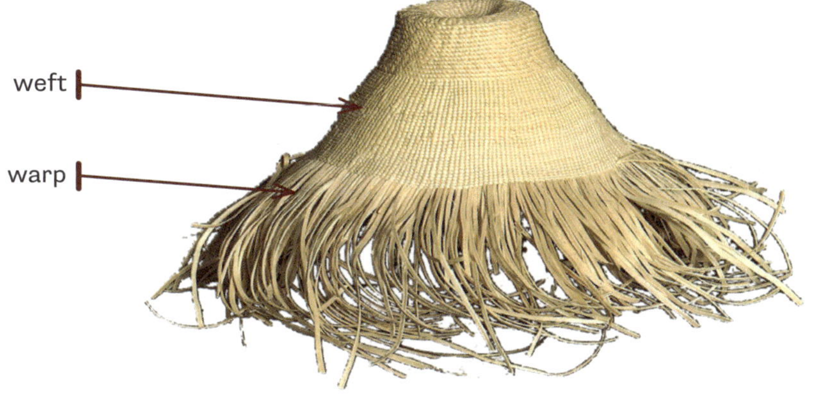

Long Ago Man's Hat replication by Delores Churchill, in progress. *Jack Littrel*

over the years of teaching, lecturing and working with other weavers. As with all things, there are exceptions to the rule.

Add In: Adding warp strands to expand the circumference or to strengthen or lengthen warps.

Compact Twine: Technique of wrapping horizontal weft strands around vertical warp strands. The succeeding weft rows enclose the same warp strands. The adjoining rows are spaced tightly together.

Compact Twine Lid: The compact twined cover of a compact twined basket. The walls of the lid overlap the basket wall.

Design Field: The total area of the basket wall or cover, which contains "Designs" and "Design Bands" (see Chapter 6, Design).

Ending Edge or Finishing Edge: The row(s) that bind off the weft strands to end the weaving piece.

Inside Surface: The internal cavity of a basket or lid.

Knob: The projections from the top surface of the lid. They may have a rattle chamber that contains rocks or shells as sound makers or they can be concaved or domed from the underside of the lid without a rattle chamber. The size can range from a small button or be large and flat. They may be below, even with, or—as shown on previous page—above the surface of the lid.

Row: A single complete circuit of the basket in any weave that is horizontal to the base.

Start: The point where the initial weft is inserted to start twining around the warp.

Turning Edge: The row that changes the warp from horizontal to vertical and starts the wall.

Wall: Vertical sides that start at the turning edge and end at the finishing or ending edge.

Warp Strand: These form the "bones" of the basket that hang down vertically in Haida weaving and that are held upright in Tlingit and Tsimshian weaving. These primarily passive strands are wrapped by the active weft strands.

Weft Strand: These form the "skin" of the basket. In twined basketry these are the active horizontal strands that enclose the warp strands through twining techniques.

Basketry Shapes

Cylindrical: A form of relatively consistent diameter from the turning edge to the ending edge.

Flared: The basket wall flares gradually, but markedly outward from the turning edge, giving an increasing diameter to the ending edge.

Oval: The add in technique produces an oval rather than a round base, which usually results in walls that are consistent in diameter but may flare.

Basketry Handles

Bail handle: The semi-circular handle that spans the opening of the basket, similar to a pail or kettle handle. Usually plaited spruce root sewn into the basket's wall.

Loop handle: Usually short, made of plaited spruce root that is sewn onto the lid.

Tab handle: Sewn to opposite sides of the basket walls, either to the inside or outside. The tab can be woven, or made of leather or a cloth strip. I've seen many on berry baskets.

Twining Terminology

Compact Twine: Twined rows that touch each other and produce a closed wall.

Jog: area of weaving that shows the direction of the spiral weaving rows, right over left.

S- and Z-twist: These are the indicators of Nation origin and are not indicative of whether the weaver was right- or left-handed. In the S-twist twining method of the Tsimshian, the stitches slant from the left up to the right. In the Z-twist twining method of the Haida and Tlingit, the stitches slant from the left down to the right.

Warp Bundle: Warps within one twining stitch. The number of warps wrapped within one twined stitch may be one warp strand or two warp strands in each stitch.

Working Edge: The part of the unfinished perimeter where the weaving is occurring. The working edge is kept directly in front of, and parallel to, the weaver's chest.

Working Surface: The surface which faces the weaver, most usually the outside finished side of the weaving.

Working Weft: The active weft that is working to achieve a twined stitch. The weft strand to the left becomes the working weft when the sequence of twining begins.

Two-Strand Twining Instructions

The Haida twining technique is a "spiral" weave with the warps hanging down as weaving progresses. The weft moves from left to right using a Z-twist. When the basket is sitting upright, the jog of the rim and the design fields are located to the right. The use of the spiral weaving requires periodically measuring the wall and making adjustments with the awl to ensure that the height of the wall remains the same around the basket.

Keeping the warp and weft the same width and thickness, and ensuring that the warps are laid together closely, results in little pearl-like stitches. Too few warps produce elongated stitches. Too many warps result in bumpy, wavy baskets. Letting the weaving material become too dry creates funny looking square stitches. Care is taken not to twist the weft. The same surface of the weft is always facing up. At the end of each row of compact twine, use the awl to push the row up against the previous row.

Recommended Practice Materials For Each Technique

- 3″ × 4″ craft foam that has 16 ¼″ × 2 ½″ vertical strips cut vertically (warps)
- ¼″ × 12″ ribbon (weft)
- Awl or butter knife

Step 1: Loop the weft under the first warp and fold weft strand (A) to the left.

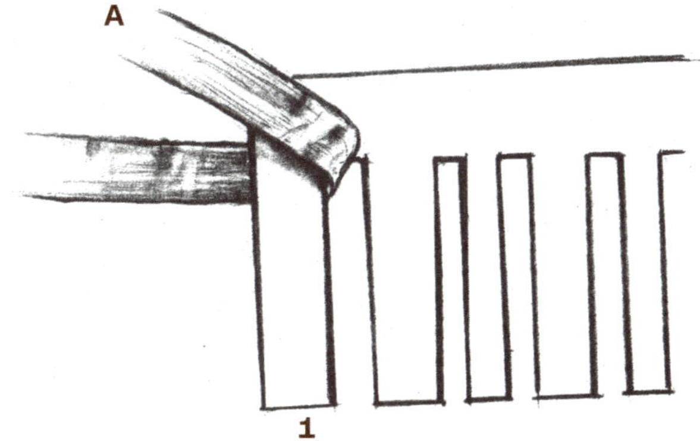

Step 2: Weft strand (B) is laid over warp (1) and under warp (2) then folded to the left.

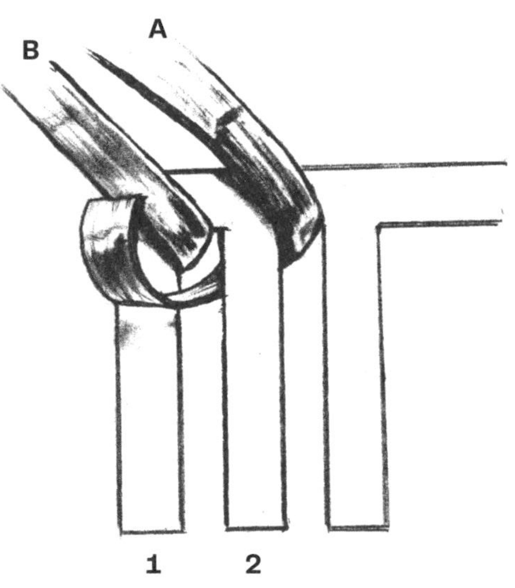

Step 3: Weft strand (A) is laid over warp (2) and under warp (3) then folded to the left.

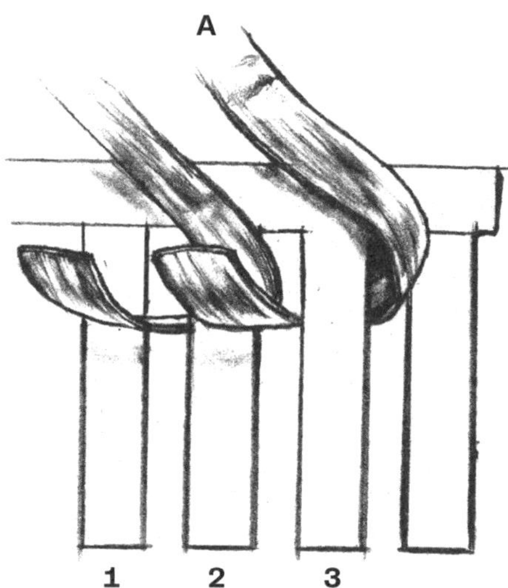

Step 4: Repeat steps 2–3 to complete the row of two-strand twining.

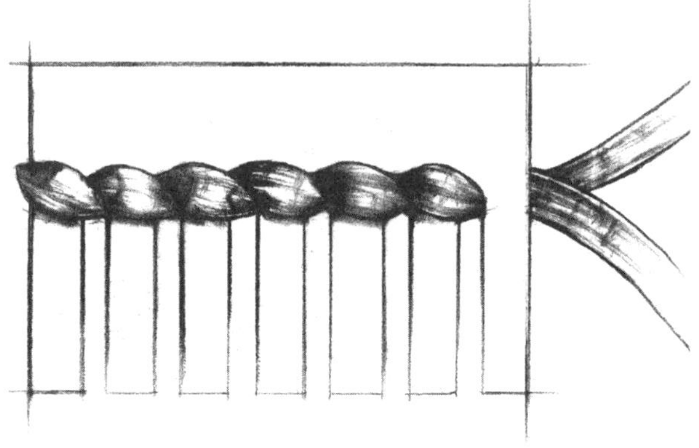

Repeat **Steps 2-4** for as many rows as needed. Using the awl, push each row up against the previous row. Spiral twining pulls the warp to the left. To keep the vertical lines of the weaving perpendicular, pull the warps back into place from left to right.

Z-Twist, Three-Strand Twining

The Z-twist, three-strand-twining technique is most often used at the turning edge as an ending edge or as a secondary design that borders a primary design. The crown of compact-twined hats is often three-strand twining.

Z-twist, three-strand twining is similar to two-strand, with the addition of a third weft and, instead of going over one warp and under one warp, the working weft goes over two warps and under one warp.

Practice Materials: Prepare a craft foam sheet and two ribbons as described for the two-strand-twining instructions.

Step 1: Loop a weft on warp 1. Add in a weft (C) under warp (2) as illustrated.

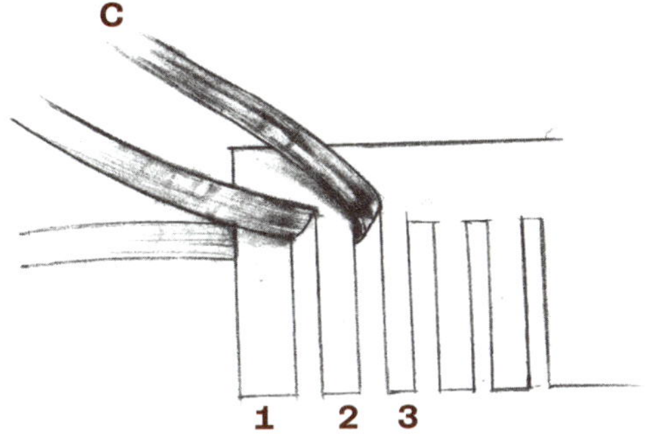

Step 2: Bring the weft farthest to the left (A) over warp (1) and (2) and under warp (3). Pull weft (A) up and fold to the left.

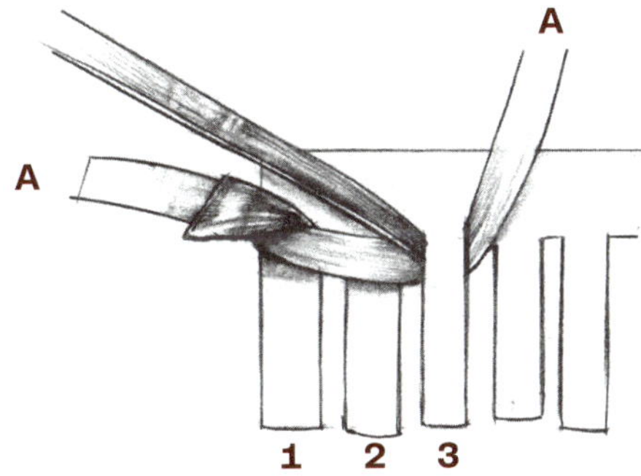

Step 3: Repeat the pattern "over-two warp; under one warp; pull up and fold to the left" with the working weft until the desired number of rows are completed.

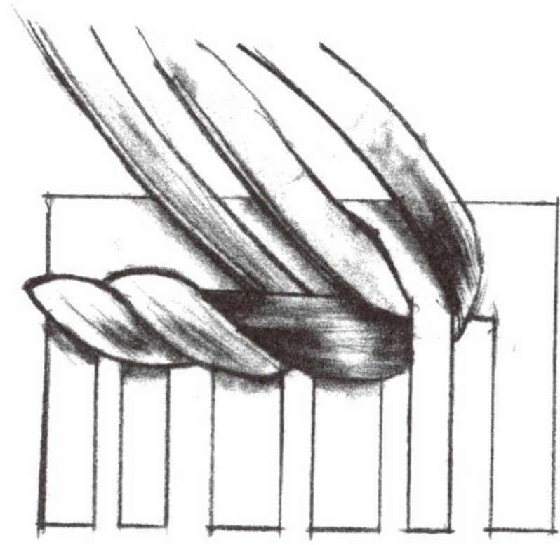

Variations

The following are common Haida techniques. Other twining techniques are located in the "Ending Edges" section and may also be used as decorative additions to weavings.

SPACED WEAVE ("SIEVE") INSTRUCTIONS

The seaweed harvesting basket uses the sieve technique. Any harvesting basket that requires draining liquid could use this technique. Often the sieve and fisheye techniques are found on bottles to better gauge the amount of liquid still in the bottle.

Step 1: Gradually twine each warp to the desired space height between rows.

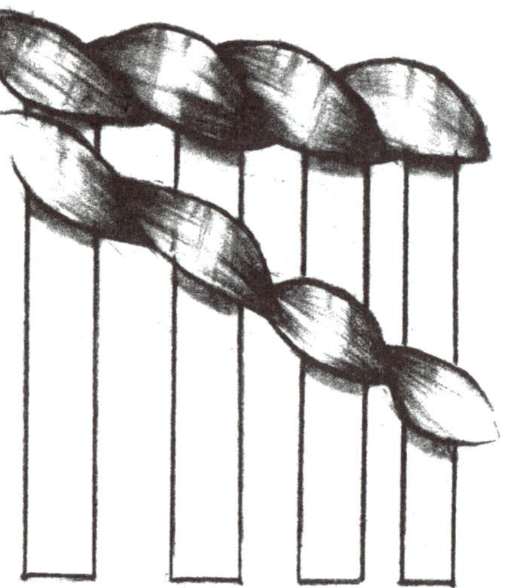

Step 2: Twine a row leaving a space between each twined row.

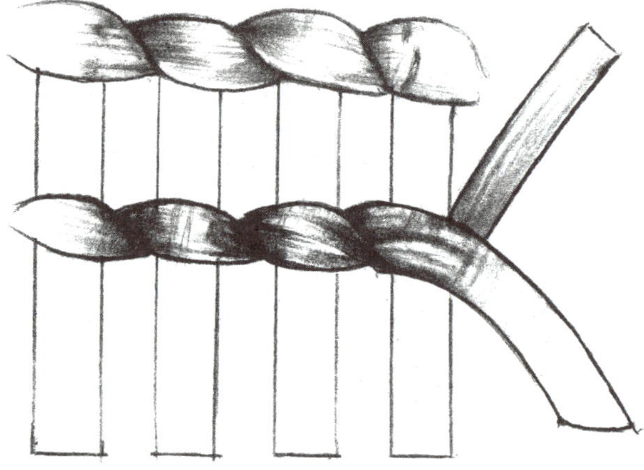

Repeat **Steps 1 and 2** for each row. Remember the weaving is on a spiral and it is important to use the awl to ensure that the wall is the same height around the circumference.

FISHEYE TWINING INSTRUCTIONS

The fisheye is used to make fish, clam, mussel, bird egg and spoon baskets. It may also be used as a design element. Two-strand twine is the stitch most often used to twine the warp. An even number of warp is needed for this technique.

Step 1: Cross the right warp (A) over the left warp (B) and twine it in place. Twine warp (B). Warp (A) and (B) Form an "X."

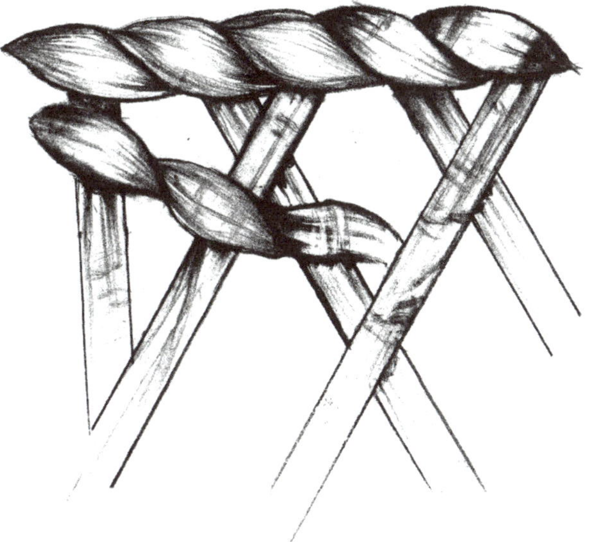

Step 2: Continue making the "X" always crossing the right warps over the left warps.

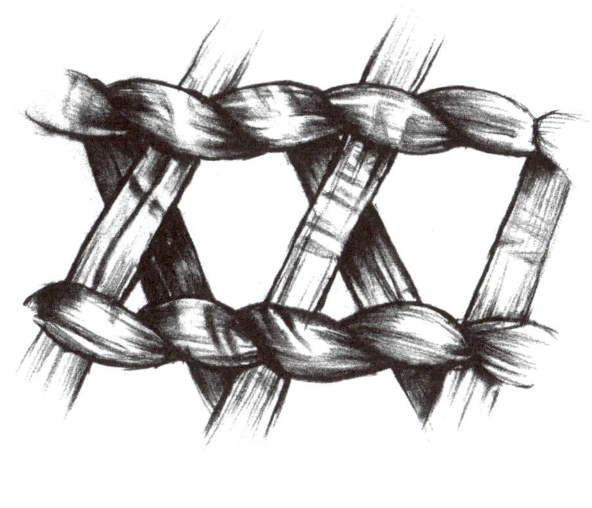

Plaiting

Haida plaiting is done with red cedar bark and in some cases with spruce roots. Yellow cedar is not used because it shrinks too much and creates large gaps between plaited stitches.

1. Checkerboard Plaiting

When I was growing up, many checkerboard-plaited mats, work hats and baskets were still in use. The women in the village carried checkerboard-plaited missionary book handbags to church and to the Anglican Church Women meetings. Larger bags were used as shopping bags, suitcases and for storage. The featured potato harvest basket and the missionary book handbag include the checkerboard-plaiting technique.

Checkerboard plaiting is accomplished with an "over one strand and under one strand" movement with the running strand. This type of plaiting is usually taught in kindergarten but don't let that fool you. To do this right for Haida weaving, paying meticulous attention to stitches is required. The strands lay closely to each other forming square stitches where the vertical and horizontal strands intersect. Rectangular shaped stitches indicate that the strands are too far apart and the shape of the weaving will be off kilter.

If the weaving is to include walls that will be checkerboard, an uneven number of warp is needed around the last row of the start.

There are a number of ways to start a plaited piece. My students find it is easiest to maintain square plaited stitches by starting from the centre on the small- to medium-sized baskets. Plaiting in from the left and working to the right is used for large projects and mats.

Step 1: Lay one strand down vertically. Lay a second strand horizontally over the vertical strand.

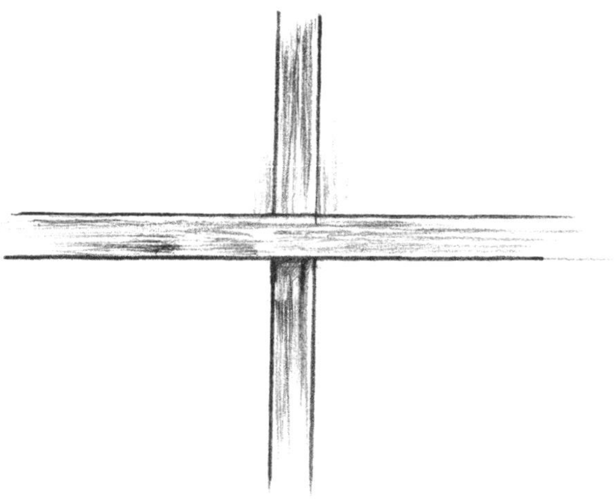

Step 2: To the right and left of the first vertical strand add strands under the horizontal strand.

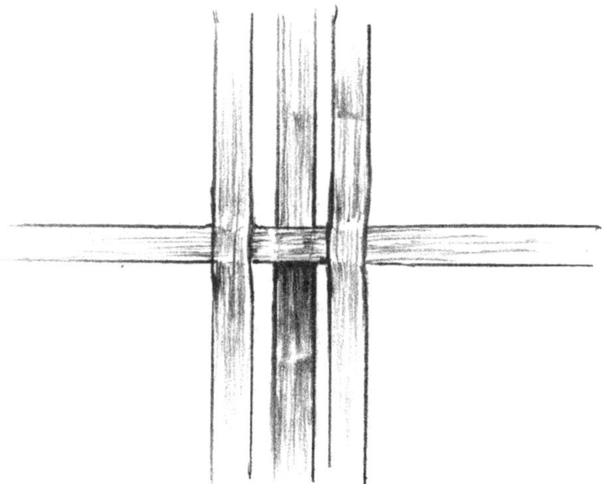

Step 3: Add a fifth strand by going under the vertical strand on the left, over the one in the middle, and under the one on the right.

Step 4: Add fifth and sixth horizontal strands by going under the vertical strand on the right and over the one on the left. Continue inserting strands horizontally and vertically by drawing the running strand "over one warp and under one warp" to create a checkerboard base comprised of seven vertical strands and eight horizontal strands.

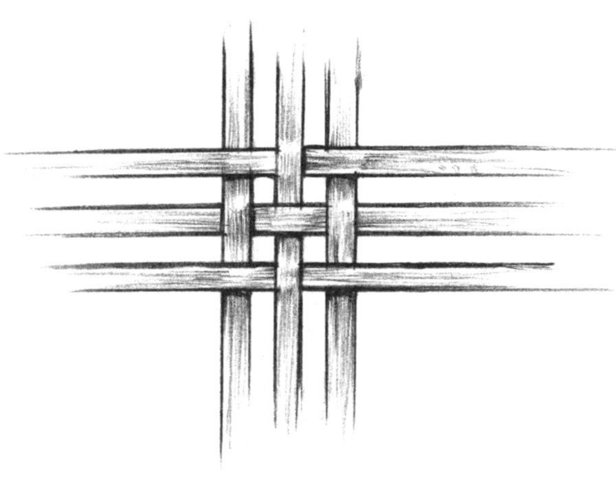

2. Twill Plaiting

There are many resources that explain twill plaiting techniques, which I recommend for greater exploration into these techniques. I am including the basic twill-plaiting technique that the Haida use to create the "Box-Within-A Box" design.

Twill plaiting is found in old mats and utilitarian baskets. It is a great way to decorate any plaited item. Twilling is the action of a running strand going over and/or under two or more strands.

Box-Within-a-Box

The use of black dyed plaiting strands is a Haida technique as demonstrated in museum collections. Many mats and baskets can be found that use twill weaving with two or more colours to add decorative touches to utilitarian baskets.

The late Brenda White, from New Metlakatla, Alaska, taught me the Tsimshian style of plaiting. I was giving a class on the Haida style mat weaving on a loom when Brenda said, "Too hard. Put it on the floor." She then showed me how the Tsimshian weave their mats and how to apply the Tsimshian design called "Seagulls Coming Home." My mind's eye saw the black negative space and said, "How about we call the design 'Raven's Coming Home?'"

"How come a Haida is trying to tell me the name of a Tsimshian design?" She pointed out that the positive design was the light part of the design, as she firmly and emphatically said with a twinkle in her eye, "The design is 'Seagulls Coming Home.'" She was so funny, in the old- fashioned tongue-in-cheek way that I remember from my own elders.

I really enjoy weaving the Box-Within-a-Box and have made small napkin holders and small storage baskets for family and friends using this technique.

Step 1: Place a black stand horizontally over the top of a vertical black strand to form a cross.

Step 2: Place a natural strand over the vertical black strand on working edges (C) and (A). Remember that the working edge is that which is currently being woven.

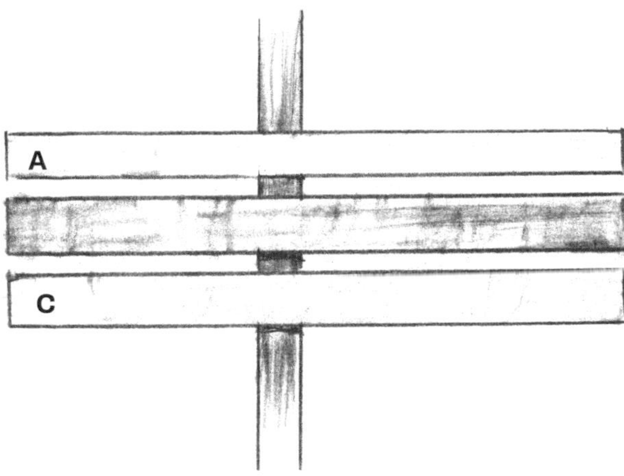

Step 3: Lay natural strands over top of the three vertical strands to form working edges (B) and (D).

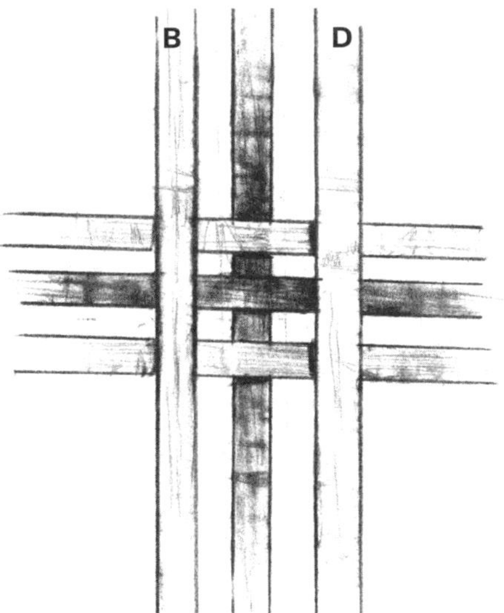

Step 4: Checkerboard plait black strands on working edges (A) and (C), going over the natural strands and under the black strands.

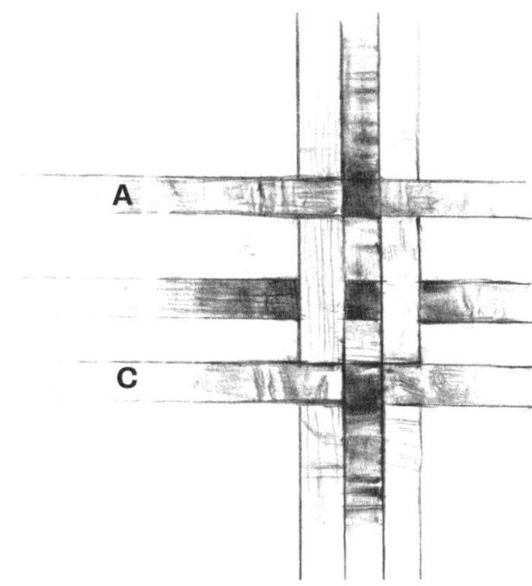

a. On the working edge, moving from left to right, lay a black strand over the black and the natural vertical strands (twill stitch).
b. Plait the black running strand under the central vertical black strand.
c. Twill over the last two vertical strands.
d. Repeat the twill, plait, twill pattern on working side.

Step 5: Checkerboard plait a natural strand on working edges (D) and (B), going over the black strands and under the natural strands.

a. On working edge (C), moving from left to right, lay a natural strand over the natural and the black vertical strands (twill stitch).

b. Plait the natural running strand under the next vertical natural strand, over the central vertical black strand, under the next natural vertical strand, ending with a twill stitch over the next vertical black and natural strands.

Step 6: Checkerboard plait black strands on working edges (D) and (B), going under the black strands and over the natural strands.

a. On working edge (C), moving from left to right, lay a black strand over the black and the natural vertical strands (twill stitch).
b. Plait the black running strand under the next vertical black strand, over next vertical natural strand, under the central vertical black strand, over the next natural vertical strand, over the next natural strand, ending with a twill stitch over the next vertical black and natural strands.

Repeat the pattern of plaiting the vertical strands and twilling the corners of working edges for the number of boxes you want to create.

Secure with a twined, an ending edge or turn up to make the walls of the weaving.

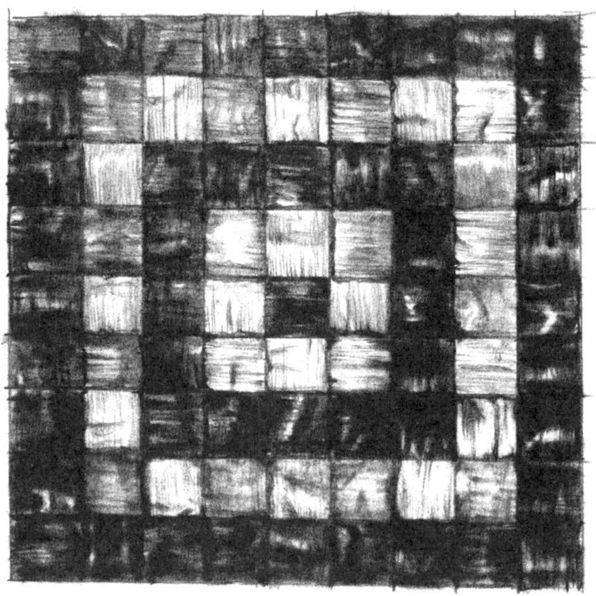

Twill plaiting is versatile. I love this particular plaiting technique because there are so many mathematical options.

CHAPTER SIX

Basketry Designs

Like Haida art, there are traditional rules for weaving and like Haida art, there are exceptions to the rules and the ability to stretch the boundaries. Knowing the basic rules of design will assist in developing innovative designs that retain the unique Haida indicators. When a rule is broken to achieve personal expression, it is important to know the rule and why it needs to be broken or stretched.

Traditional basketry designs are geometric representations of the things around us. Although Haida, Tlingit and Tsimshian weavers use many of the same geometrical designs, each Nation may use a design to represent a different object. Many Haida and Tlingit geometric designs represent the same item.

Some design fields tell a story or document an event. This spruce root rattle lid basket is my documentation of the day that my daughters and I went to harvest roots at Tlell, on the east coast of Graham Island, Haida Gwaii. We used the trail that has been commonly used by everyone to get to the beach. The property adjacent to the trail had been purchased by a trophy bear-hunting lodge and the owner came out to tell us that we were trespassing. My daughter April firmly and in no uncertain terms informed him that the Haida Gwaii was Haida territory and purchasing the property did not give him the right to close off the trail to a traditional root harvesting area.

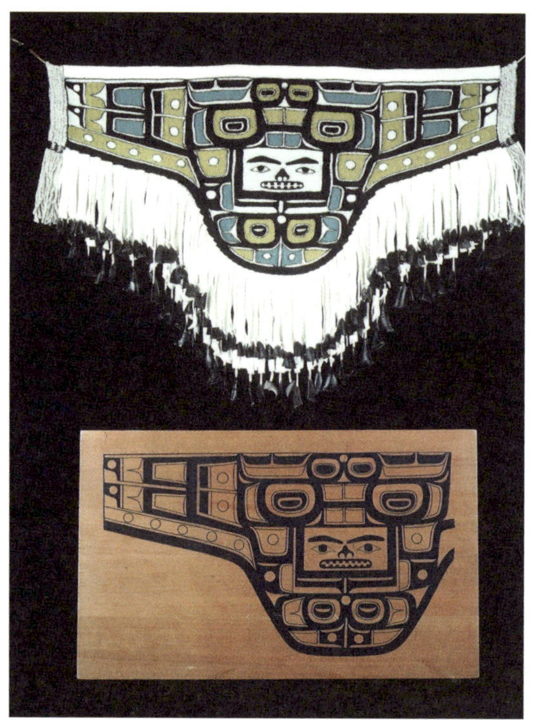

Naaxiin dance apron based on a design board by John Livingston. *Ward Serrill*

He attempted to inform her about his legal rights, explaining that he would have to call the authorities if we stayed. April said, "Call them, because I am staying to harvest roots."

She went on to reprimand him for killing our sisters, the bears, just for the fun of killing. She abruptly turned and walked into the root gathering area. The authorities did not come and after April calmed down and centred herself, we harvested a few roots among the strawberry plants.

The brown and straw-colour false embroidery design that is made with natural grass and dyed spruce root is the bear track design and represents the bears—our sisters—that were being killed. The centre red self-weave alternating coloured design is called "strawberry" and represents the strawberry plants that surrounded us. The lid, instead of repeating the design on the walls as is most usually done, represents the swirl of confusion that we live in because of two cultures clashing, as well as the confusion of laws that make us criminals in our homeland when we are only doing those things we have done for thousands of years.

Other basketry designs can represent the social status of the owner or can be expressions of appreciation to the life that will be harvested using the basket.

In days long ago, harvest baskets were woven for specific species. For instance, a berry basket woven to pick strawberries would not be used for anything except strawberries. A blueberry basket was woven specifically for picking blueberries. This is one of the ways the Haida express high respect for the gifts from the spirits of living items.

Traditionally, women did not weave the crest designs into baskets. Women did weave crest designs into the Naaxiin (Chilkat) wool weavings, but only because the men had created the design on a design board. The weaving by women of crest and realistic animals and birds did not occur until after European contact and basketry became commercialized. Until that time the crest designs were exclusively carved and painted by men.

Geometric Basketry Design Layout

The geometric designs are believed to have the same power as the object that it represents. This power needs to be contained and to be protected. This is done by enclosing the primary design with secondary designs. This balance between the primary and secondary designs provides the tension and balance that reveal the life held within the weavings.

Design Terminology

There are many terms used by weavers for the same elements or techniques. For ease of instruction these terms will be used throughout the instructional pages when applicable. The terms are an adaptation of *A Proposed Glossary of Spruce Root Basketry Terms* by Peter Corey.

Parts of Design

Design: This photo demonstrates a single geometric motif of a design which may or may not be repeated horizontally in a band on the wall of a basket. In this basket, the designs are made using the false embroidery designs of a variation of tying together (orange) in the centre of the top and bottom design bands, and of the cresting wave (straw colour) in the centre of the middle design band.

Design Band: A horizontal band around the wall of a basket or on the top surface of a lid. It may be solid in colour or contain repeated single-design motifs. In this case the top and bottom design bands consist of a top and bottom three-strand secondary design that borders the variation of the Racks in Smokehouse, and the middle design band of cresting wave, whose secondary design is the top and bottom design bands.

Design Field: The total area of the basket wall or surface of a lid that contains designs and design bands. In this case the design field consists of a top design band, a middle design band and a bottom design band. The bottom turning edge and top ending edge rows of three-strand twine serve as the secondary design for the complete design field. The design field is usually a combination of one, two or three design bands. When a combination of design bands is used together, the tension of symmetry is retained. For instance, when using three design bands, the two bordering the middle design band will most usually be the same design motif. When this is done, the middle design field would become the secondary design.

Primary Design Band: This is the predominant design and is bordered by a secondary design. These can be found in the centre of a basket. In the example, the primary design band is the repetition of the cresting wave design.

Secondary Design: Because the life that is represented in the geometric design of the primary design has a powerful spirit, each of the design bands are usually enclosed with a secondary design on the bottom and top of the element. This contains and protects the spirit represented by the geometric design. The bordering of a primary design band with a secondary design provides a tension and the symmetry within the design field.

The secondary design can be a simple three-string twine row, one of the more common secondary self-weave or false embroidery designs, or a more complex design, so long as it does not distract from the primary design.

Design Techniques

Twining: Twines of coloured weft strands to produce a design.

Solid Band: Achieved by twining the same colour weft strands. On this example, the solid bands are serving as the secondary design for the false embroidery primary design, cresting wave.

Cockleshell: The parallel, vertical, black solid lines are achieved by twining two different coloured weft strands over an even number of warp strands.

Strawberry: The checkerboard is achieved by twining two different coloured weft strands over an uneven number of warp strands.

Twill: Twill is achieved by twining two or more wefts together to create a design that is raised out of the surface of the basket. The top design band on this basket uses this technique and is called Fish Flake.

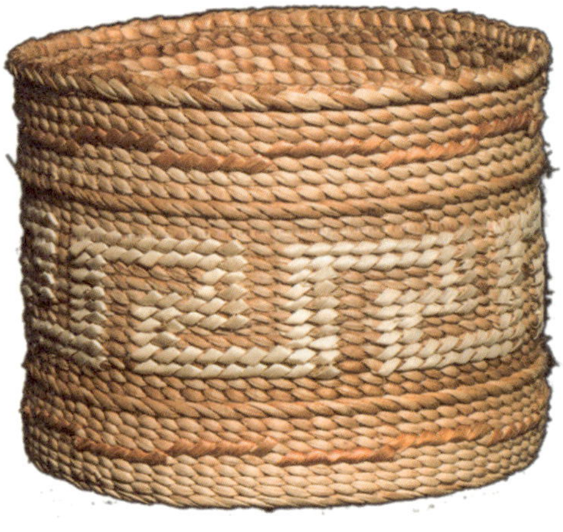

A basket with the well-known Haida "Cresting Wave" pattern, created using false embroidered technique.
Holly Churchill

A weaving story that is often represented on Haida baskets and hats that my mother passed to me tells of a snail that was overcome with the beauty of a dew-laden spider's web that had caught the morning sunlight and was radiating rainbows into the forest. The spider looked smugly down at the snail, thinking, "Poor thing, he has no talent."

The snail slowly and sadly turned around and started back down the way he came. Suddenly, he noticed coloured rays flickering up

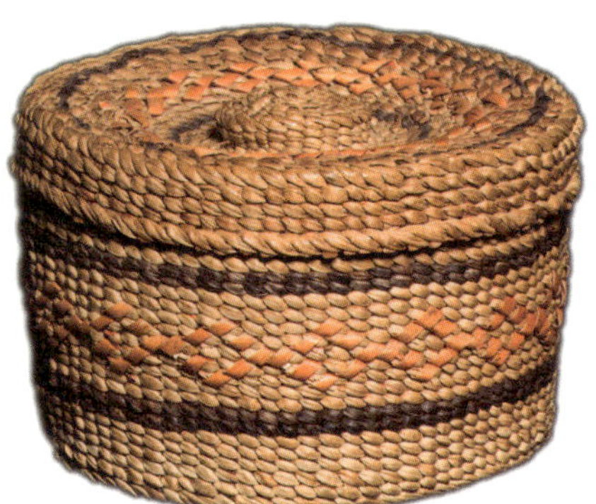

Round, red cedar basket used to store small jewellery objects. *Churchill family*

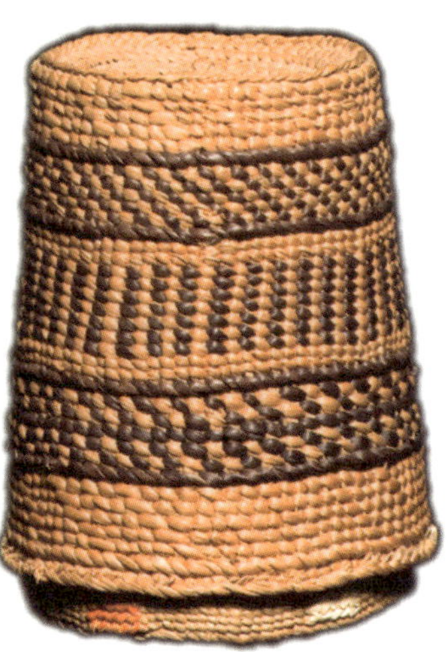

Spruce root Shaman's drinking cup with cover. *Churchill family*

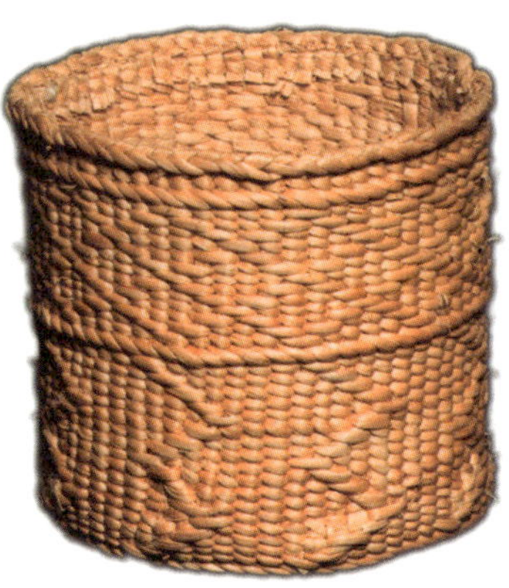

Small spruce root basket with spider web and snail trail design done with skip stitch twining technique, creating the uplifted design. *Churchill family*

from the ground into the forest branches. When the tiny snail saw that the sun beams were bouncing off of the slime trail that he had left behind, he proclaimed with amazement, "I can make something beautiful as well." The spider looked down at the beauty created by the snail and humbly realized that even the humble snail can create beauty. One of the lessons of the story is that all things of this world are able to bring beauty to the world. We just need to look for beauty and allow our beauty to shine and to share our beauty with the world.

Graphing the Design

My mother did not use graph paper to layout her basket designs. She would say, "Just see what you want to do and do it." I use graph paper to layout my basket designs.

Count the basket warps. Find the common denominator for the number of warps. If there are no common denominators, splice in a warp or combine two warps. For instance, if there are 91 warps, combining two warps will provide 90 warps and 2, 3, 5, 6, 9, 10 or 18 are the common denominators.

Determine which common denominator will provide the most balanced design. For example, using the Hudson Bay Blanket design we find that ten warps per design will provide nine design motifs around the circumference.

Number each column on the graph paper. Begin with "90" then continue from one to ten for nine motifs.

Mark each graph square to represent a false embroidery stitch (1–8). Leave the spaces blank where there is no false embroidery (9–10). Continue until there are nine motifs.

The design count includes both the false embroidery stitches and the blank spaces. For this pattern there are eight false embroidery stitches and two blank spaces, which equal ten stitches for each design motif.

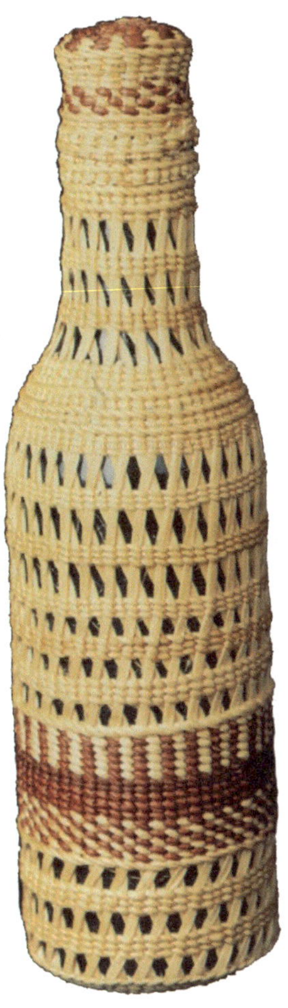

Haida weavers began covering imported bottles with spruce root open weave to protect the glass and make them easier to carry. *Churchill family*

Step 1: The first strip of grass, reed or stalk is laid on top of warp 90. Eight stitches of false embroidery are made, followed by two standard twined stitches (no false embroidery) for a total of ten stitches.

Step 2: The long tail of the grass strip is cut off, leaving about one-sixteenth inch below the stitch line. This is laid on top of the next warp and Step 1 is repeated, adding new embellishment material until nine motifs have been laid out.

Step 3: After each row, push the stitches up tightly, making certain that the weaving remains the same height.

Step 4: Continue weaving in the grass, reed or stalk following the graph paper pattern.

Step 5: The little grass stubbles sticking out from the outer surface of the wall are snipped off after the basket is dry.

False Embroidery Design Examples

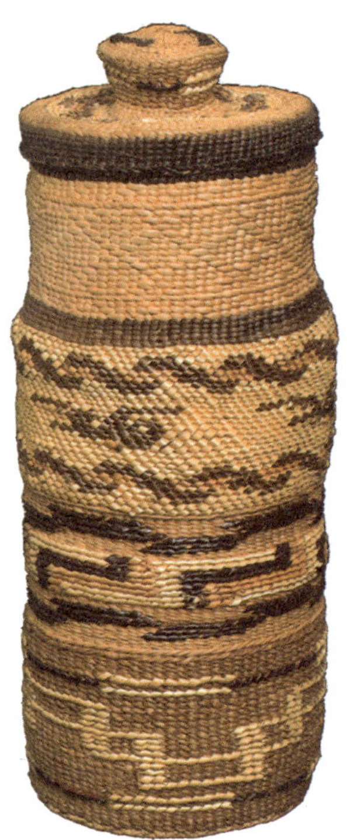

Basket woven in Tsimshian, Tlingit, Nuu-chah-nulth and Haida styles.
Churchill family

Spruce Root Basketry of the Alaska Tlingit by Francis Paul and *Design Units on Tlingit Baskets* by Erna Gunther provide many examples of designs. The Haida may use different names for the same designs. Because these books are so clear and well done I am providing only a few examples of false embroidery designs commonly used by Haida.

Primary Design Examples

Because I wanted an example in the classroom that showed the different styles and materials of coastal weaving, I wove this cylindrical basket with a lid that includes Tsimshian, Tlingit, Nuu-chah-nulth and Haida styles of weaving.

The Tsimshian band on the bottom is red cedar and represents their distinctive lightning design. The next band is woven Tlingit-style and contains the Shaman and what they call the Fish Wier Sticks.

The next is in the Nuu-chah-nulth style and represents a seabird and beach rocks. The top design band is woven in the Haida style and uses the Haida solid band as the secondary design to the primary design, the Spider Web.

After weaving this basket sampler, I have never woven Nuu-chah-nulth style again. These people continued to weave from centuries ago and continue to weave absolutely beautiful weavings in their ancient and unique style.

As soon as our people obtained bottles, they began weaving over them. These weavings most often use the fisheye weaving technique so that the level of water can easily be seen.

There is no limit when creating designs for basketry, and when the spiritual law is respected and balance is applied, the designs come alive.

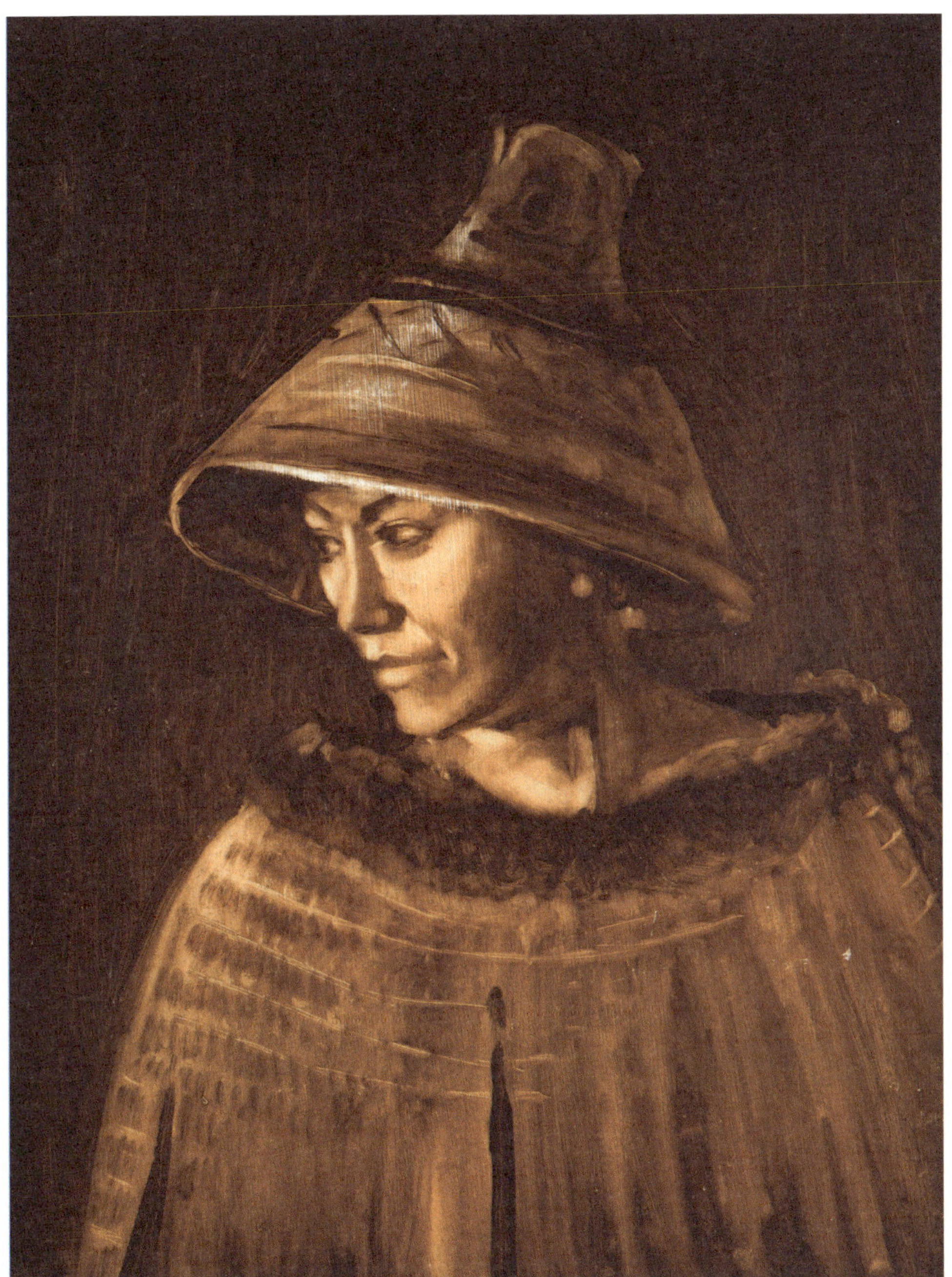

Painting of Family Spruce Root Hat, woven by Delores and Holly Churchill. The roots were gathered by Selina before her passing, and Delores's children and grandchildren contributed gathering and additional weaving. Rain cape by Holly Churchill. Painting by Dave Rubin. *Dave Rubin*

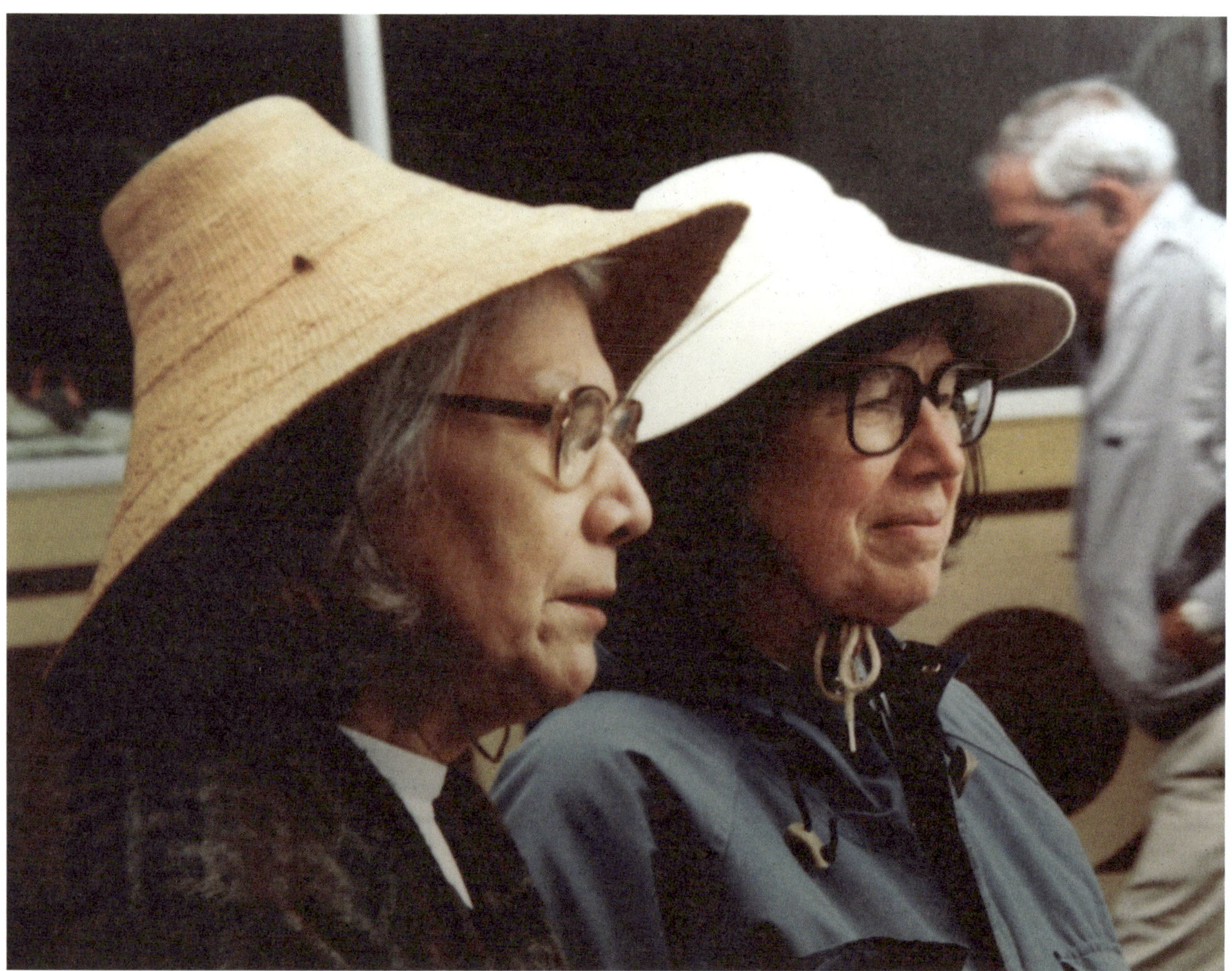

Delores, wearing Primrose Adams's spruce root hat, and Mary Lou King.
Churchill family

CHAPTER SEVEN

Weaving Terms and Haida Endings

Two-Weft Ending to the Inside

Step 1: Lay weft (1) up to the left and the right weft (2) down to the right.

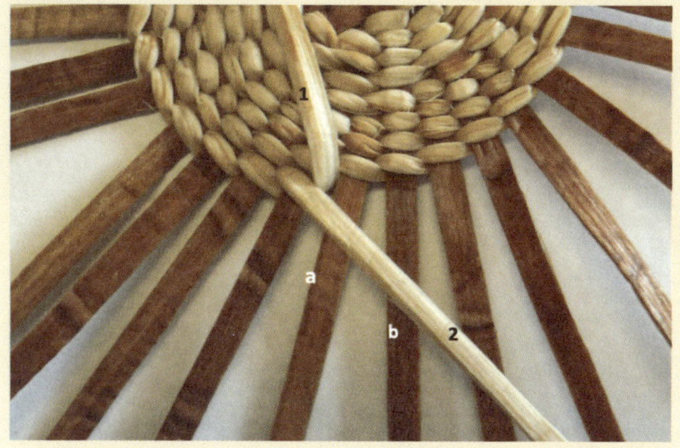

Step 2: Bring weft (2) down under warp (b), leaving enough room to fold warp (a) up above weft (2) and between warps (b) and (c).

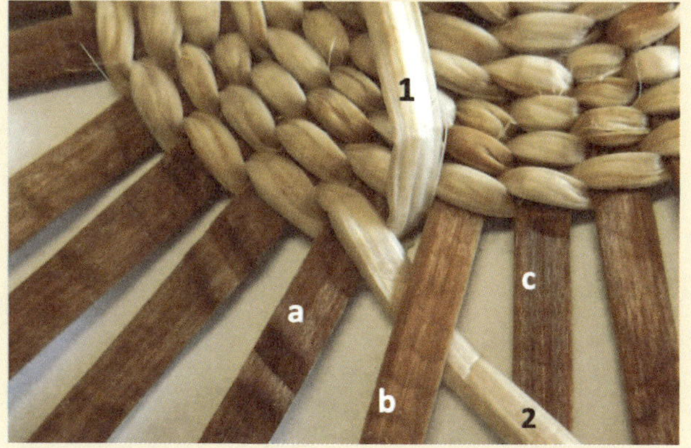

Step 3: Fold warp (a) over (b) and behind warp (c) to the inside of the basket. *See step 6.*

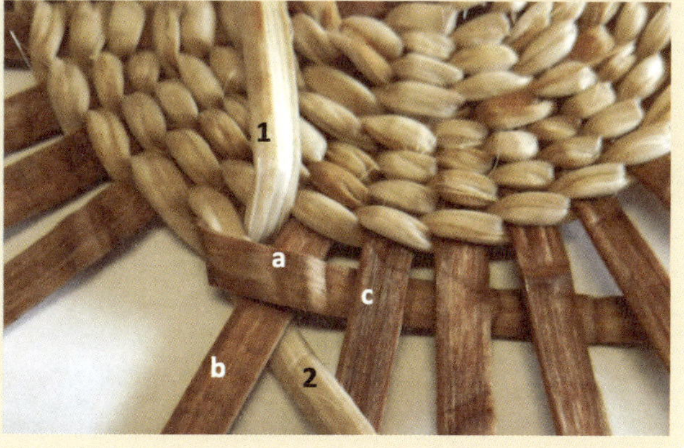

Step 4: Bring weft (2) up, pulling warp (a) snugly against the weaving and to the inside or back of the weaving.

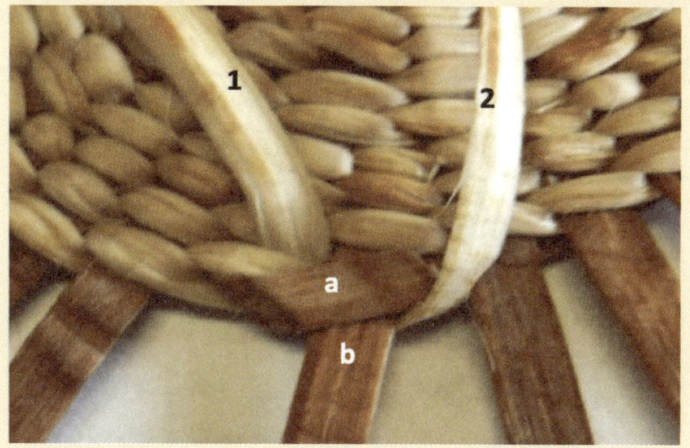

Step 5: Continue to weave following steps 1 through 4. Leave the last warp for finishing your weaving.

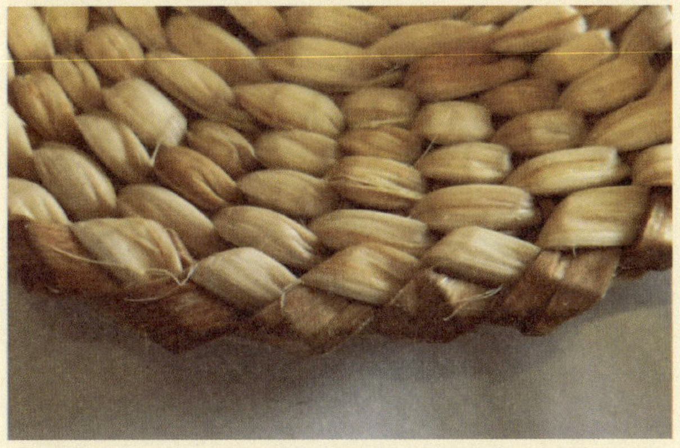

Step 6: Picture showing warps to the back or inside.

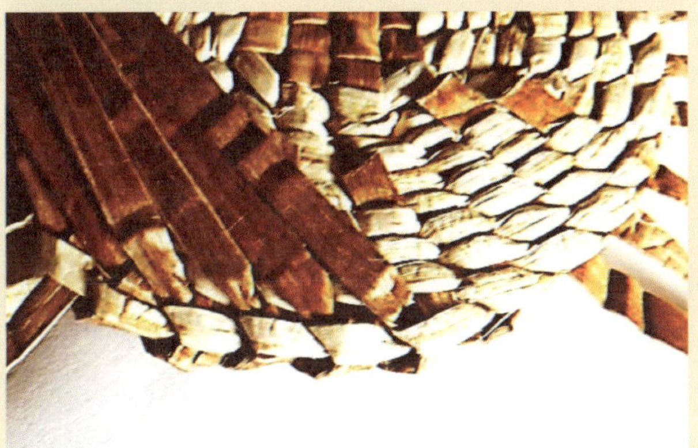

Step 7: Using a large needle with a blunt end and a large eye, thread the two wefts up under two or three rows of weaving on the back or inside of the weaving.

Step 8: Final step to finish the basket: Carefully pull on each warp to tighten just enough to make the top of the weaving even. After warps are dry or nearly dry, trim ends evenly (close to the weaving but not so close that they will pop out).

Two-Weft Ending to the Outside

Step 1: Lay the weaver (1) up and to the left, and the right weaver (2) under warp (b).

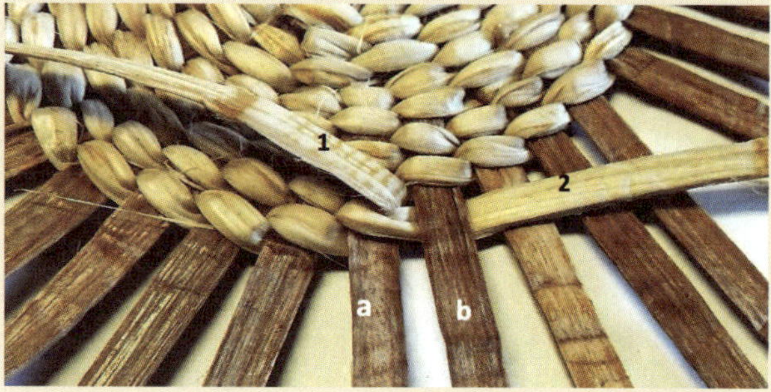

Step 2: Fold warp (a) over warp (b) and up to the outside.

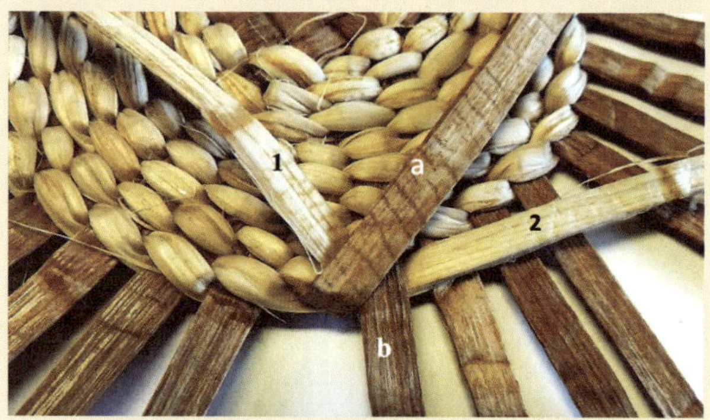

Step 3: Bring weaver (1) down across the top of the folded warp (a).

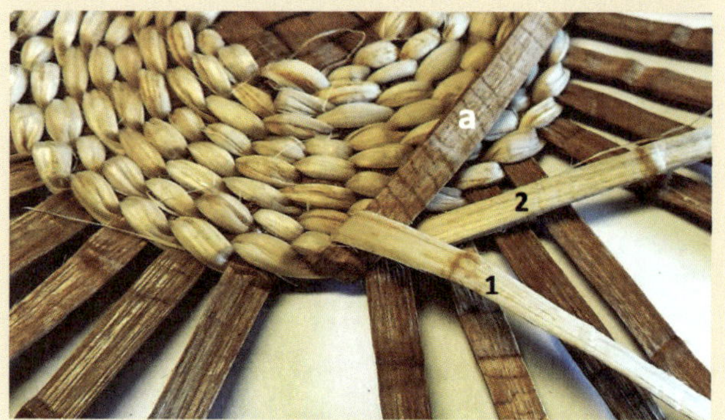

Step 4: Bring weaver (2) up and back to the left, then weave (1) under the next warp (c).

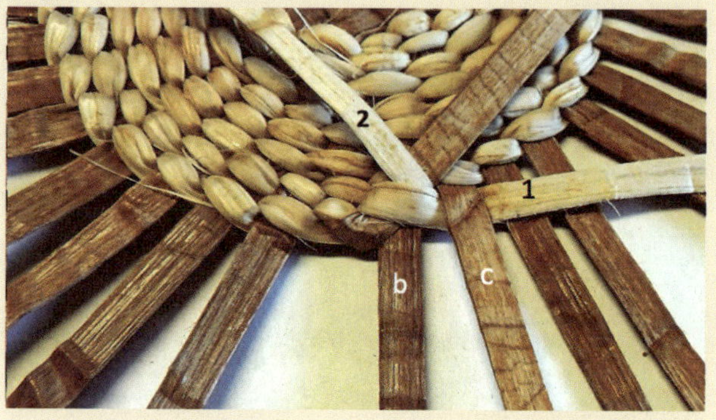

Step 5: Continue all the way around the basket, following steps 2, 3 and 4 until just one warp and the two weavers remain.

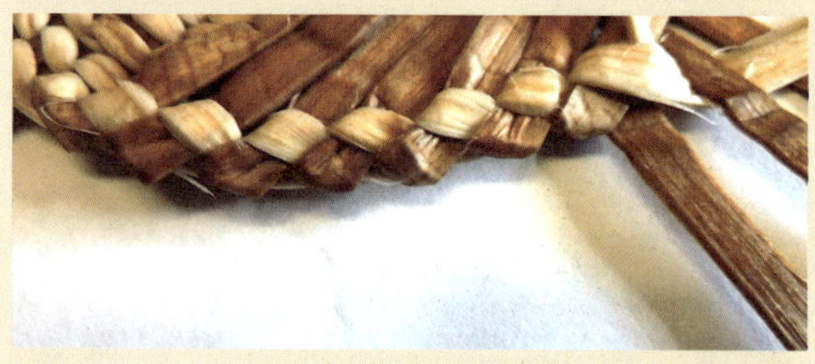

Step 6: To finish the ending, fold warp (a) up and bring weaver (1) over folded warp (a). Using a large needle with a blunt end and a large eye, thread weaver (1) up through the weaving on warp (c). Next, thread weaver (2) up through the weaving on warp (b). Trim all the long ends, but not so short that they pop out.

Two-Weft Ending to the Inside With Folded Warps

Begin this weaving by having long enough warps to fold them to the back or inside of the weaving, with enough space to weave the ending on the folded warp.

Step 1: Fold the warps to the back of the weaving with a single row of weaving to hold them in place. It is easier to do this if you fold just a few at a time and then weave over them with the one row of weaving.

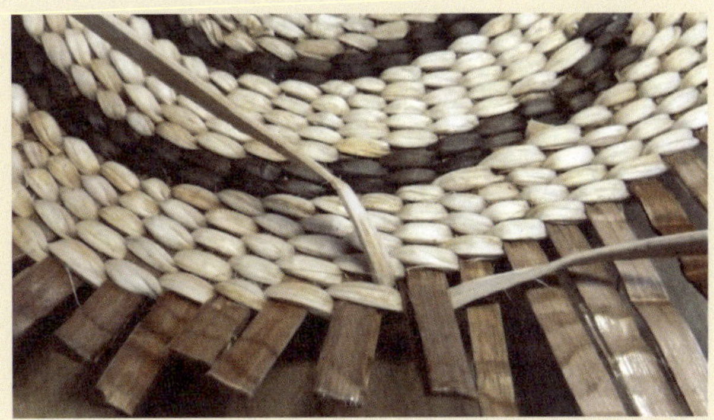

Step 2: When all of the folded warps have been woven over, use a large needle with a blunt end and a large eye to secure the two weavers. First, thread weaver (1) on the needle and pull the needle and weaver (1) up through two or three rows of weaving. Next, thread weaver (2) on the needle, then move weaver (2) over the last folded warp. Pull weaver (2) up through two or three rows of the weaving.

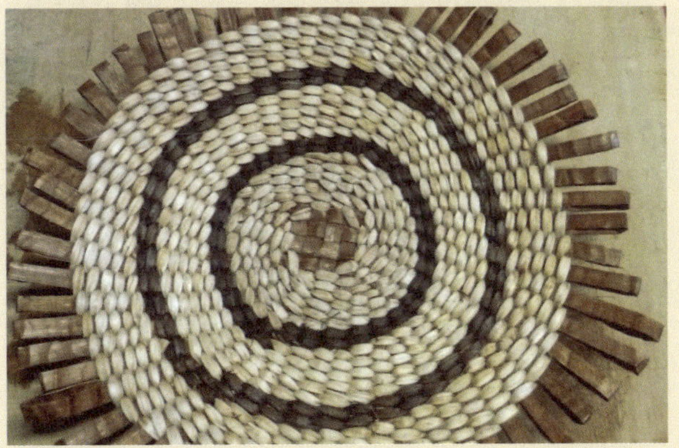

Front or outside view.

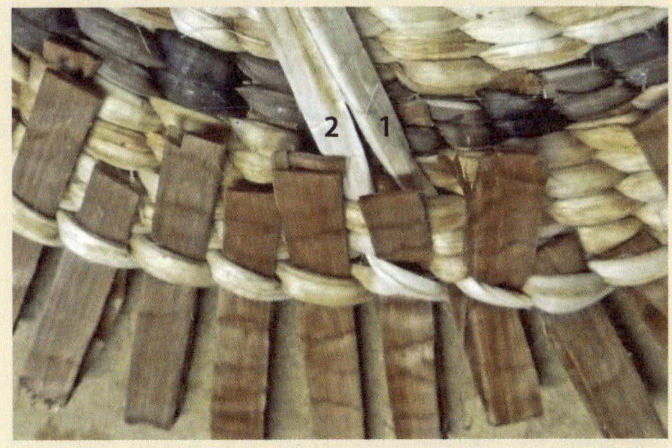

Back or inside view.

Continues on next page

Step 3: Thread very strong material, such as dental floss or very strong thin string, on a needle and thread it between the two layers of the warp. It will need to be down right next to the weaving. It is easier to tighten dental floss right next to the weaving if you pull it tight a few at a time as you go around. Pinch the back floss end with your fingers so you don't pull it out as you tighten. Tie the two ends of the tightened material together when you have gone all the way around.

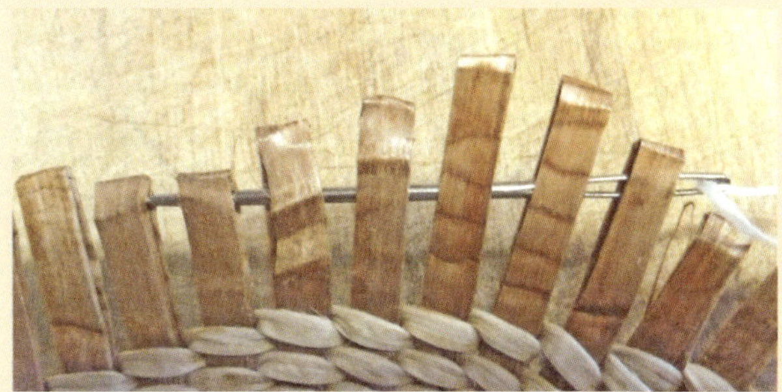

Step 4: With your hand or pliers, turn the weaving to the back and pull each end of the warps down evenly and snugly to the weaving.

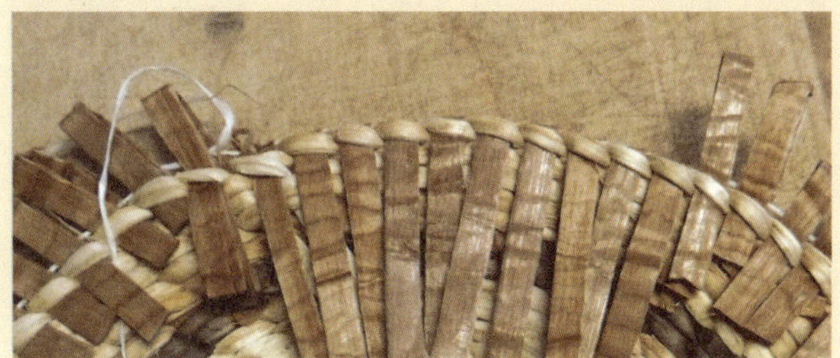

Step 5: Trim the warp ends, but not so close that they will pop out of the weaving.

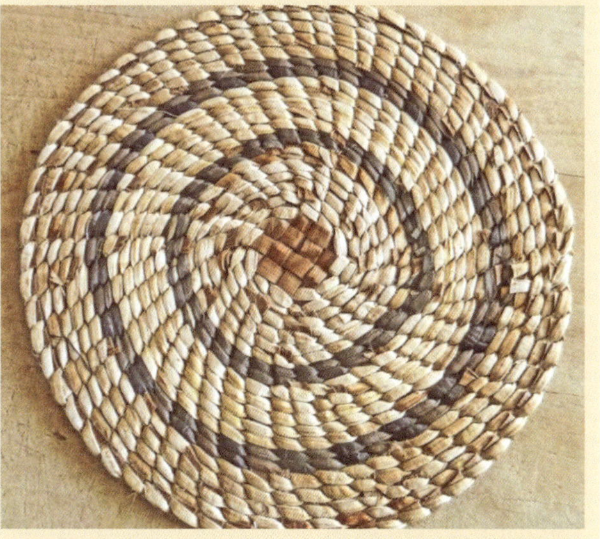

Back or inside of weaving.

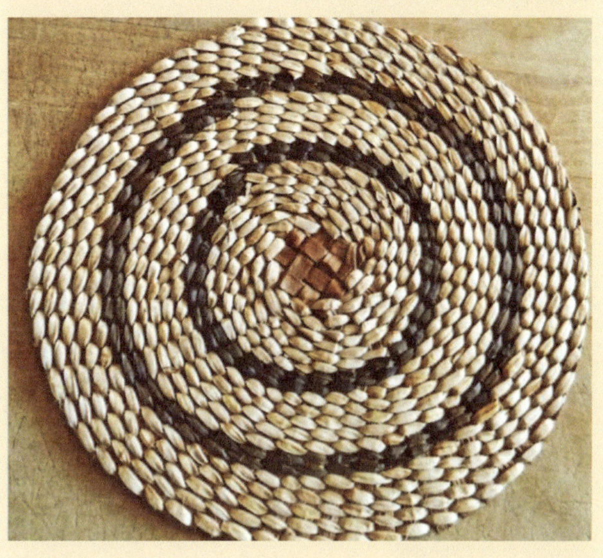

Outside of weaving.

Two-Weft Ending to the Outside With Folded Warps

Step 1: This is a very strong ending. Start by folding all of the warps to the outside, weaving over them as you go around.

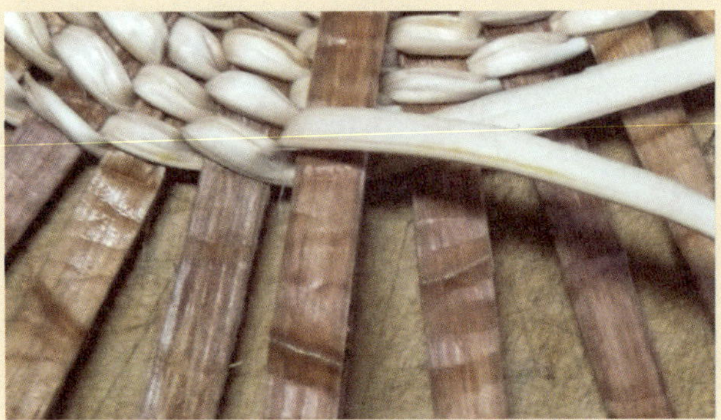

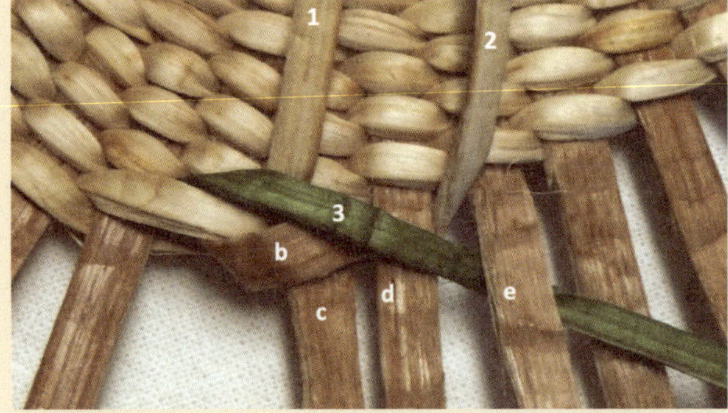

Step 2: Add a new folded weft to the first folded up warp's end (a).

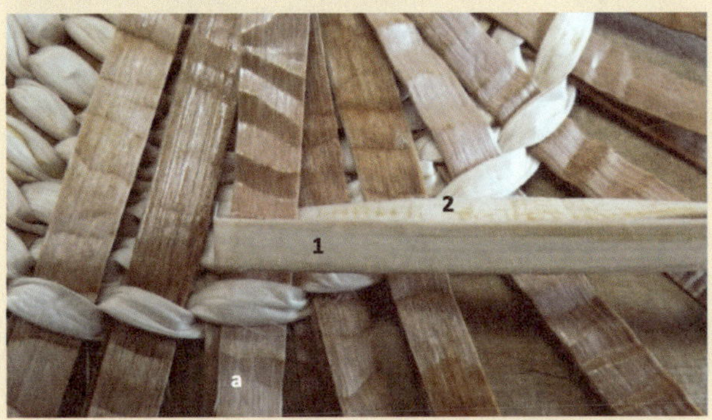

Step 3: Weave weft (1) that is over warp (a) under warp (b), leaving weaver (2) up and back.

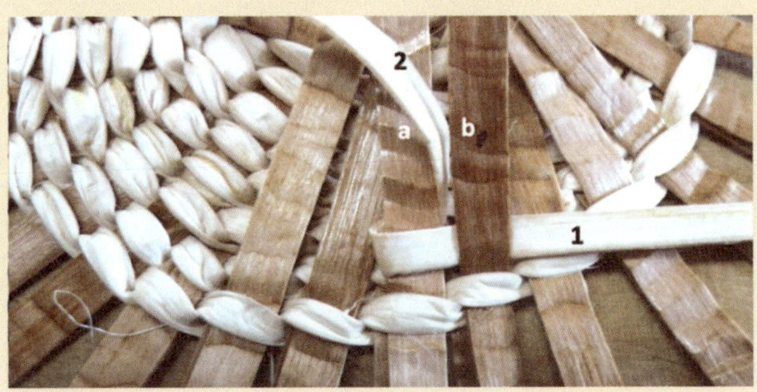

Step 4: Bring weft (2) down over warp (b) and weft (1) up.

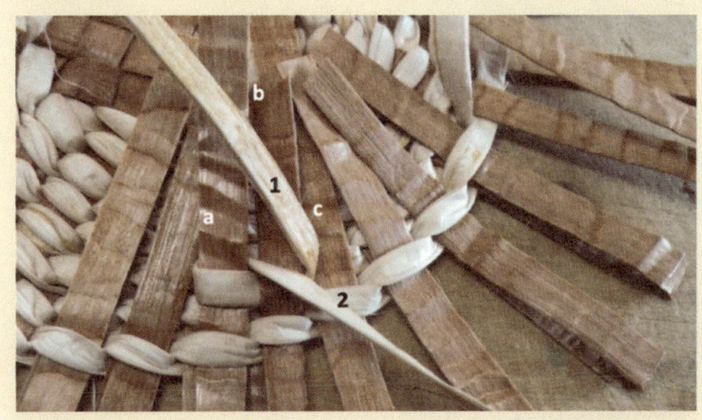

Step 5: Weave weft (2) under warp (c). Continue weaving around to the beginning of the ending.

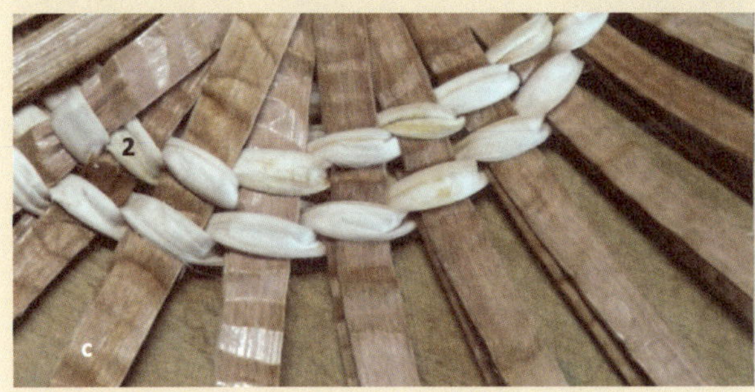

Continues on next page

Step 6: Thread a weft in a large needle and pull the weft through the folded warps.

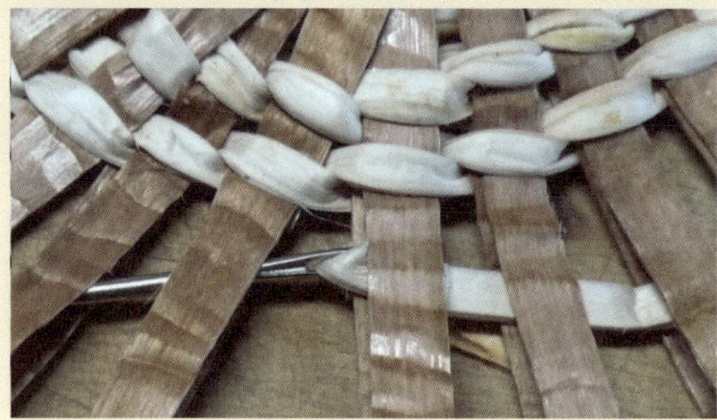

Step 7: Pull the warps up one at a time. They should be evenly pulled against the weaving, but not pulled so far up that the weaving could come out. Using a tool, push the top row of weaving down one at a time so there is no gap between the two rows.

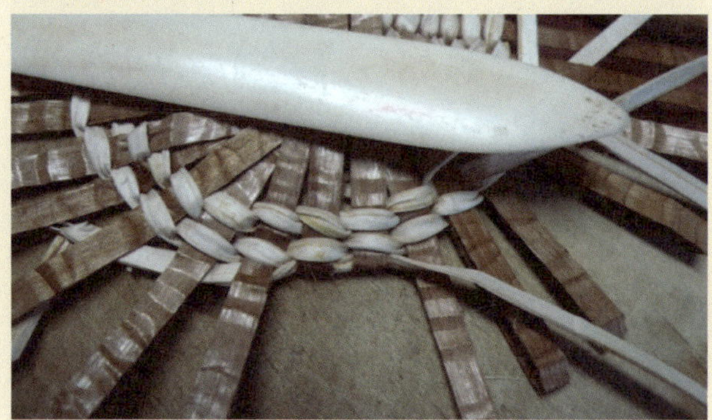

Step 8: When all of the warps have been pulled up and tightened, pull the weavers to the back or inside. Thread them on a large needle and pull these wefts up through two or three rows of weaving. The last step for finishing is to trim the warp ends off close to the weaving, but not so close they could pop out.

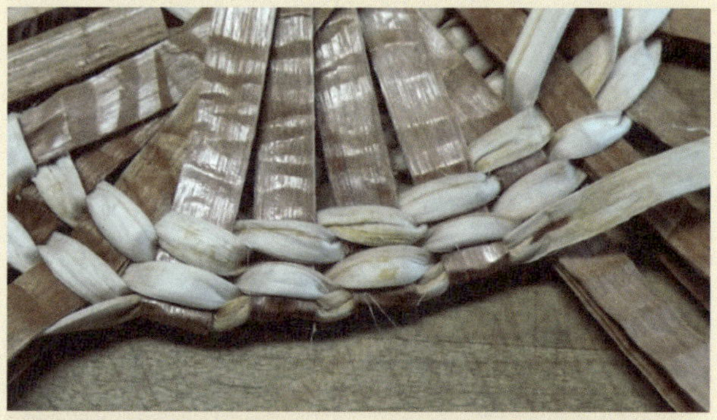

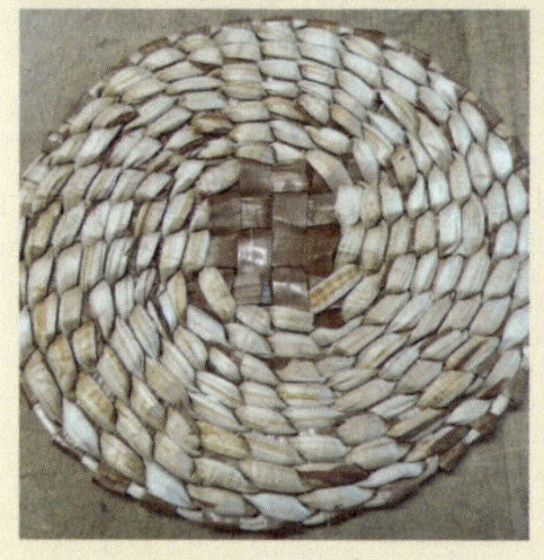

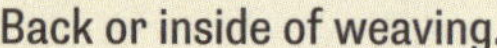

Back or inside of weaving.

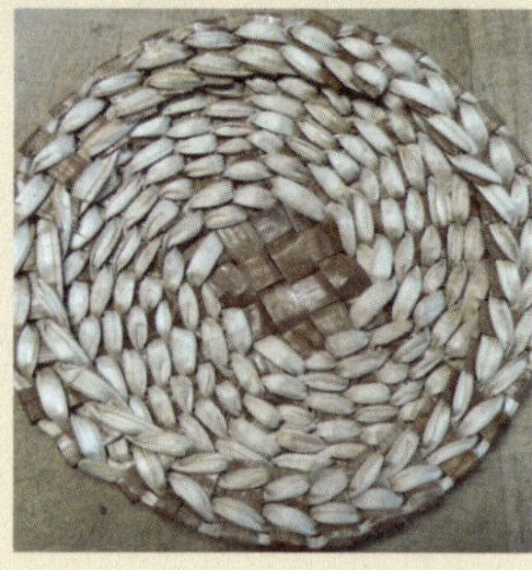

Front of weaving.

Three-Weft Ending to the Inside With Folded Warps

Note: For these instructions the added weft material is coloured to make it easier to understand the actions.

Step 1: Insert a green weft (3) between the first two warps (a) and (b) and between wefts (1) and (2).

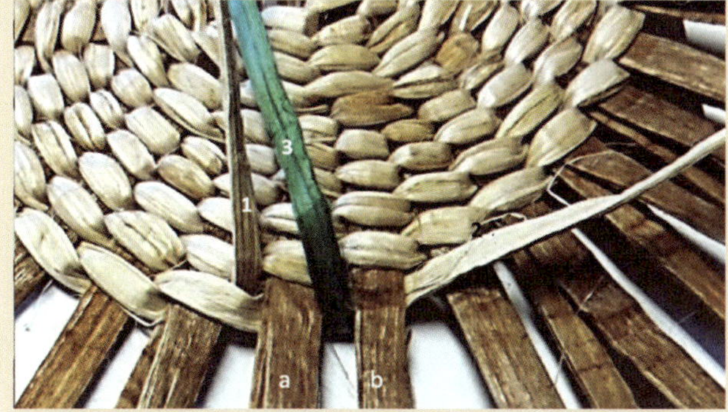

Step 2: Weave the weft (1) over warps (a) and (b) under warp (c) and up.

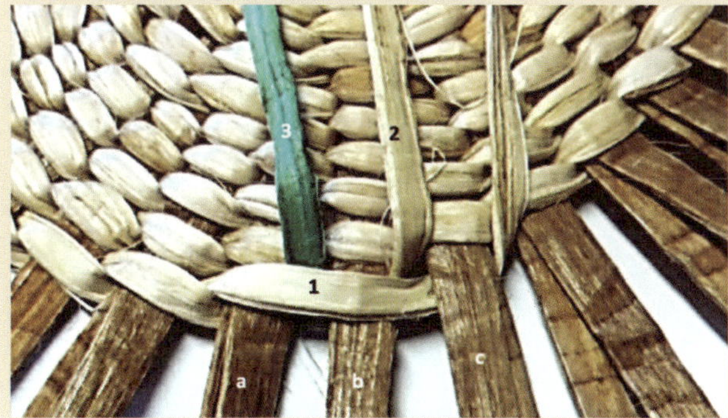

Step 3: Weave weft (3) over warps (b) and (c) under warp (d) and up.

Step 4: Weave weft (2) over weft (3), warps (c) and (d) then under warp (c) and up. Continue to weave this ending around to the end of the basket ending.

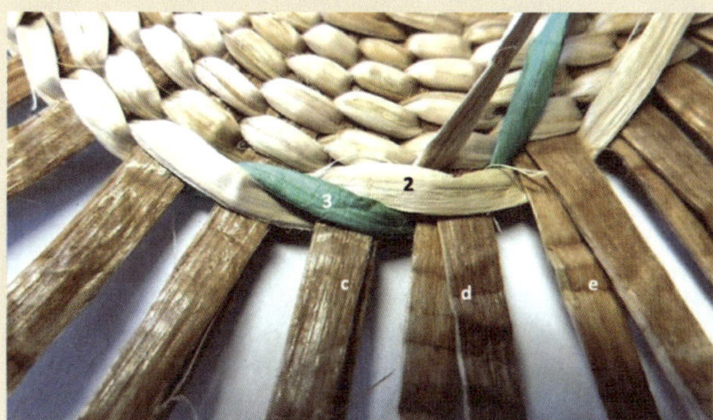

Folded-Warp Start

Begin the folded-warp ending by folding the first warp to the back, leaving enough space on the folded warp to weave the ending rows. Weave over folded warp (a).

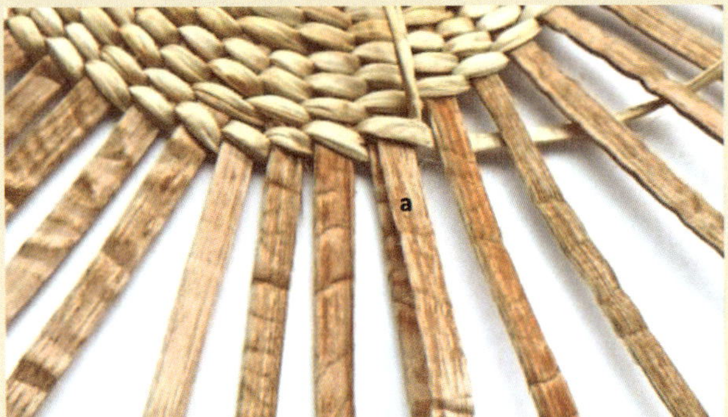

After all of the folded warps have been woven over, continue by weaving one of the Haida Basketry Endings.

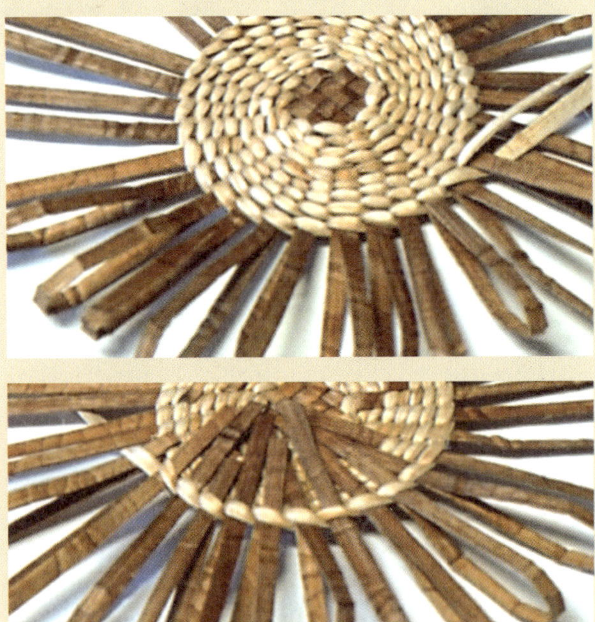

Folded-Warp Ending Start

Begin the folded-warp ending by folding the first warp to the back, leaving enough space on the folded warp to weave the ending rows. Weave over folded warp (1).

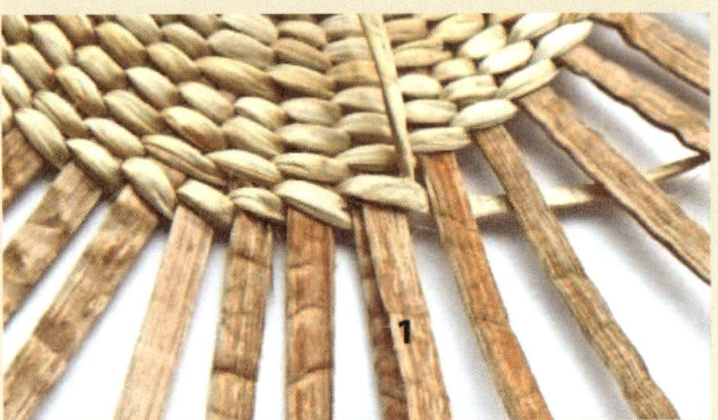

After all of the folded warps have been woven over, continue by weaving one of the Haida Basketry Endings.

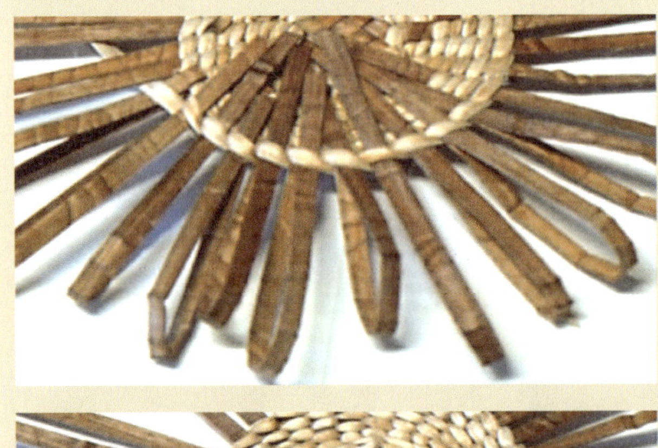

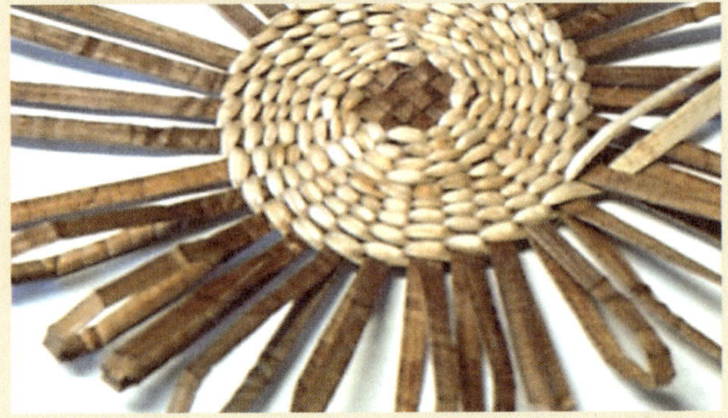

Folded-Warp Ending Finish

To finish a folded-warp ending, first secure the wefts by using a large needle with a blunt end and a large eye. Pull each weft up through two or three rows of weaving on the back. Each weft should come out on a different warp.

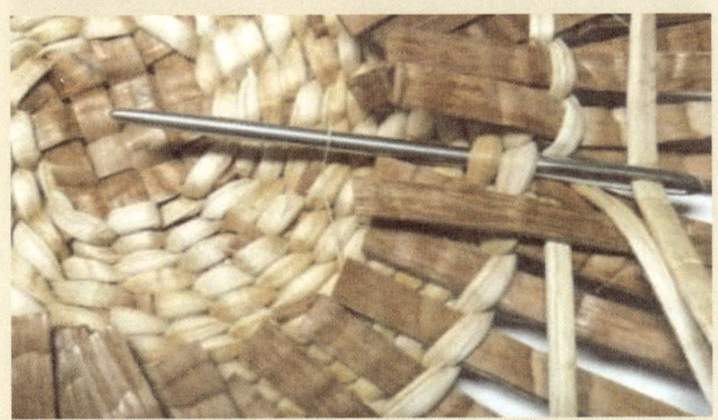

Thread a very strong material, such as dental floss or small string, on a needle and thread it between the folded warps right next to the weaving. It is easier to tighten the dental floss right next to the weaving if you pull it tight a few at a time as you go around.

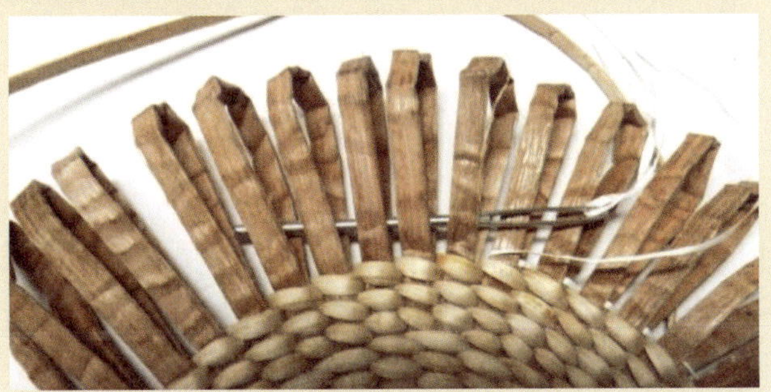

Pull the two ends of the floss really tight up against the weaving and tie a knot.

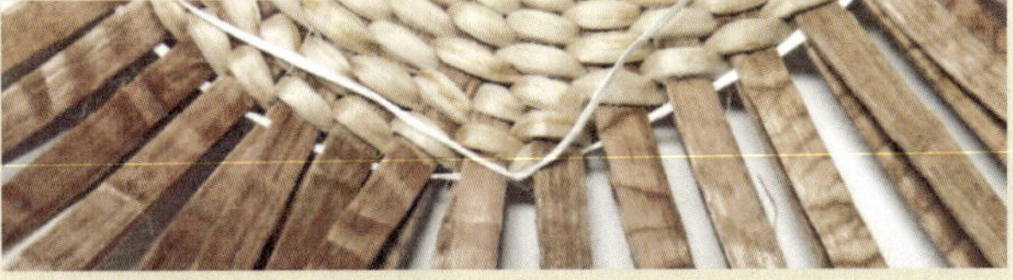

Turn the weaving to the back. With your hands or pliers, pull each warp end toward the centre of the weaving very evenly and snugly. Trim the warp ends but not so close that they will pop out of the weaving (at arrow).

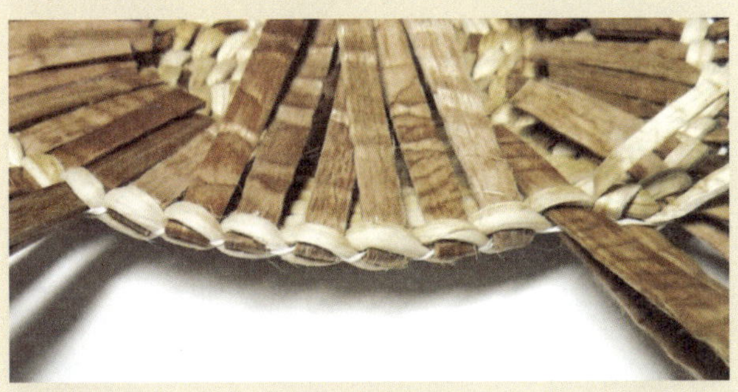

Three-Weft Ending With a Vertical Weft

Step 1: Weave weft (1) over warp (a), under weft (2), and under warp (b). Insert a vertical weft (3) between warps (a) and (b).

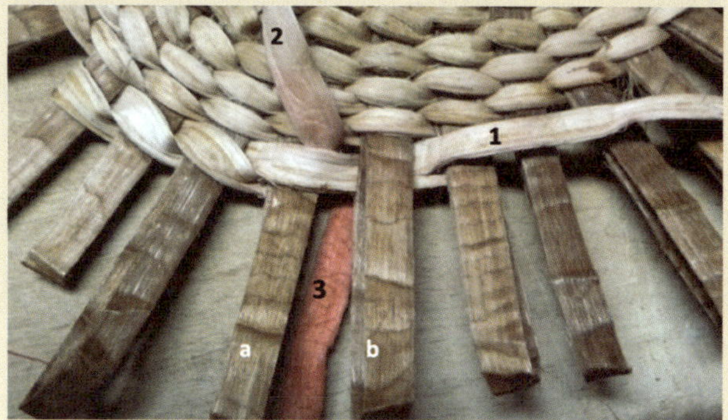

Step 2: Bring vertical weft (3) up over warp (b) and between wefts (1) and (2).

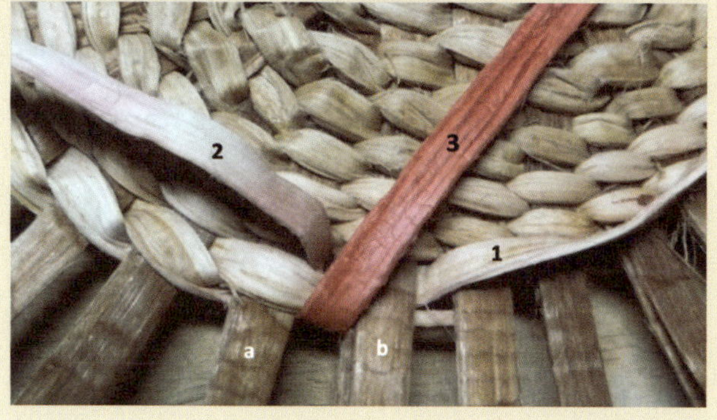

Step 3: Weave weft (2) over weft (1) and warp (b) and under warp (c). Bring weft (1) back to the left and above weft (3).

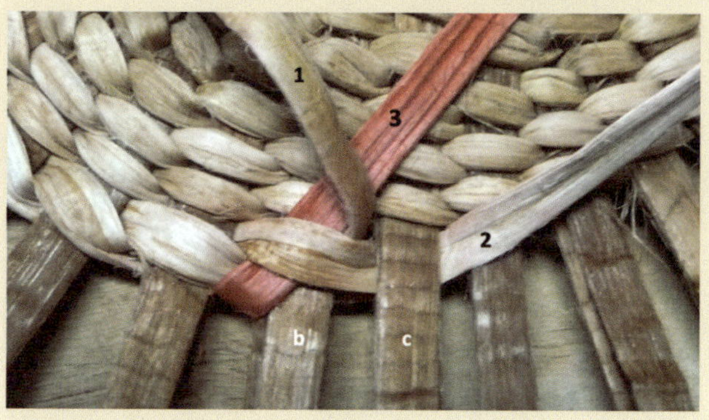

Step 4: Bring weft (3) above weft (1) and down over warp (c).

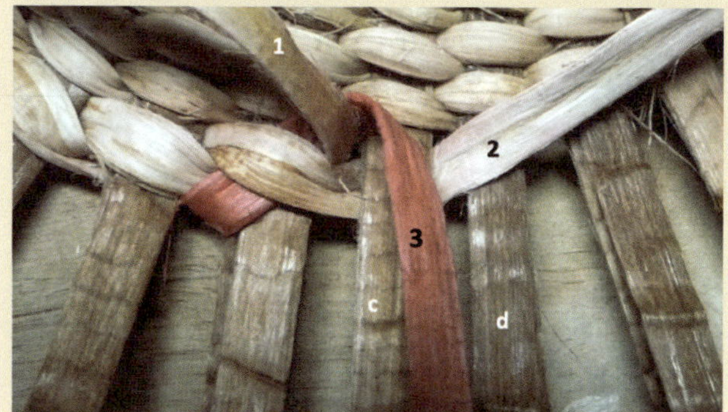

Step 5: Weave weft (1) over weft (3) and warp (c), then under warp (4).

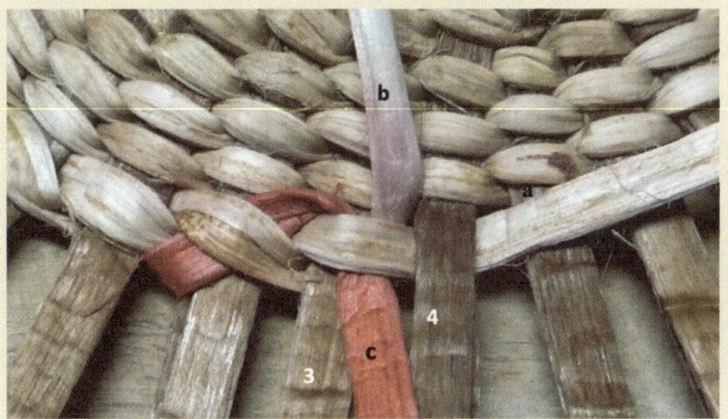

Step 6: Bring weft (3) up over warp (e) and between weft (1) and weft (2).

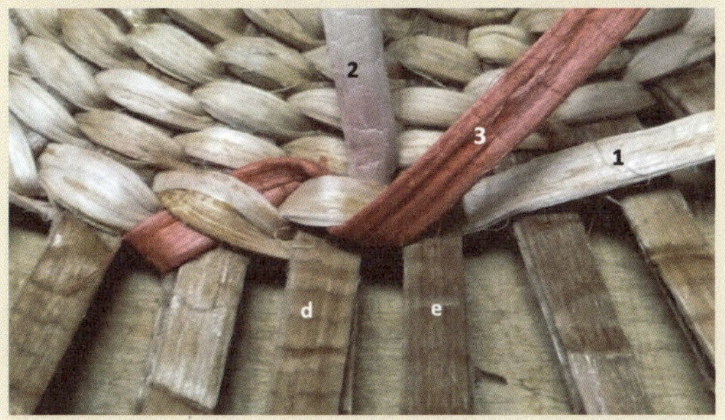

Step 7: Weft (2) comes down over weft (3) and warp (d). Weft (1) comes back to the left above weft (3).

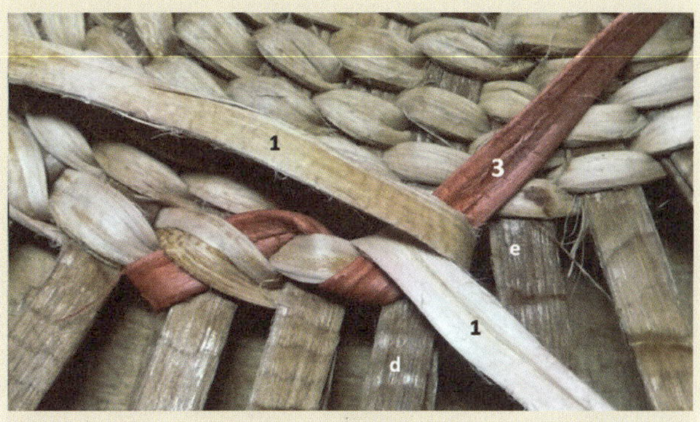

Step 8: Weft (2) goes under warp (b). Continue weaving around to the start of the ending.

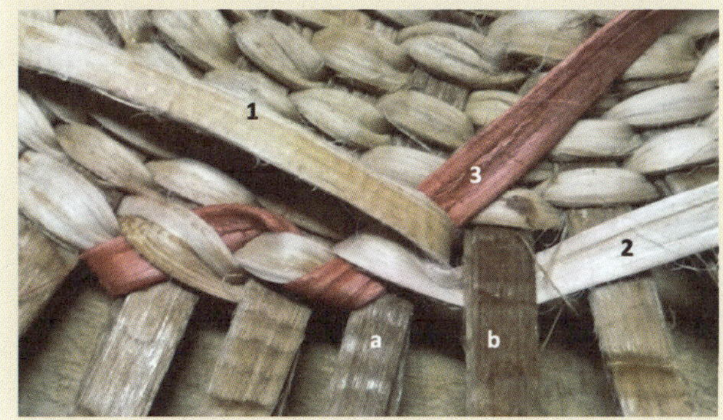

Three-Weft Ending With Warps to the Inside

Step 1: Start the ending by weaving weft (1) under warps (a) and (b) as shown on the back of the weaving. Next tie a knot in the beginning end of weft (3). Place the knotted end in the back of the weaving, then pull the weft to the front of the weaving between warps (a) and (b) and up.

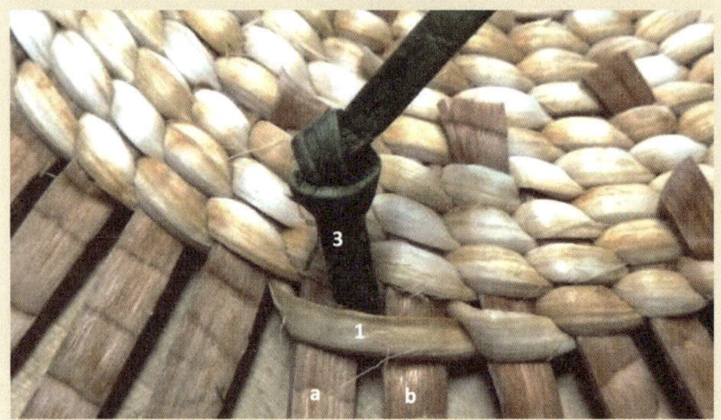

Step 2: Weave weft (2) down over warp (a), below weft (3), over warp (b), below weft (1), down halfway under warp (c).

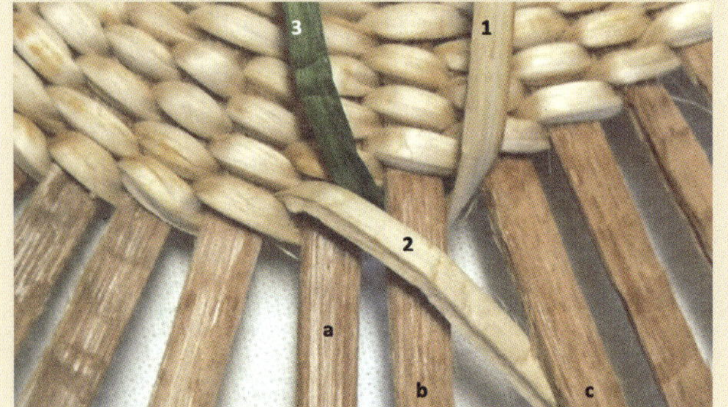

Step 3: Fold warp (a) up over warp (b), under warp (c) and above weft (2) (that is down from the instructions in step 2) and to the back.

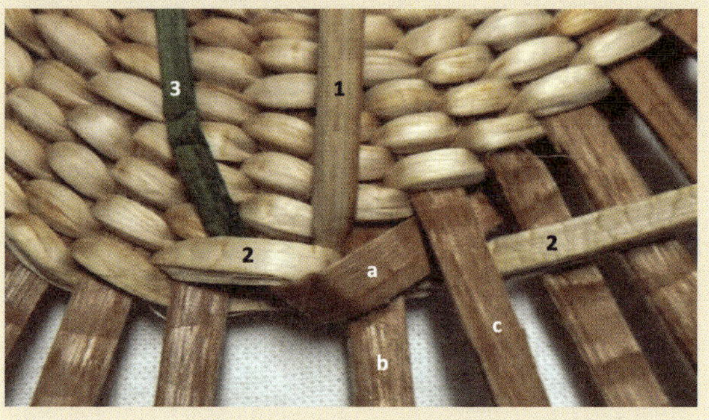

Step 4: Using weft (2), pull warp (a) up tight against the weaving. Leave weft (2) up in the front of the weaving.

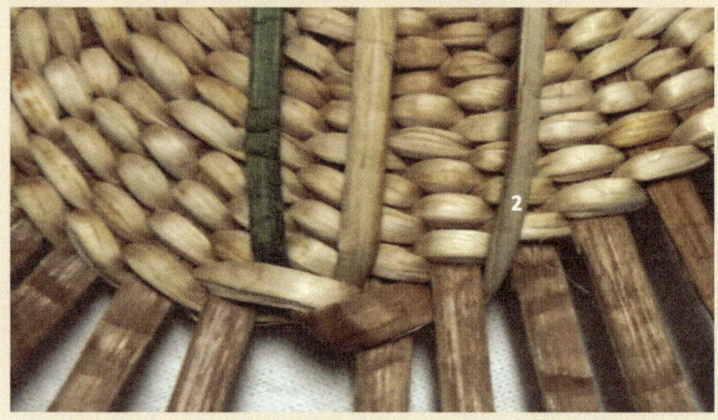

Step 5: Bring weft (3) down below weft (1), over warps (b), (c) and (d), and down halfway under warp (e).

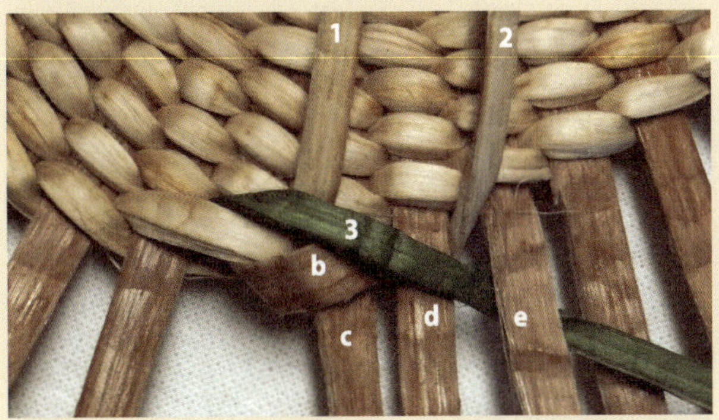

Step 6: Fold warp (c) over warp (d), weft (3), and under all the warps to the right. Using the end of weft (3), pull warp (c) up tight to the back or inside of the basket.

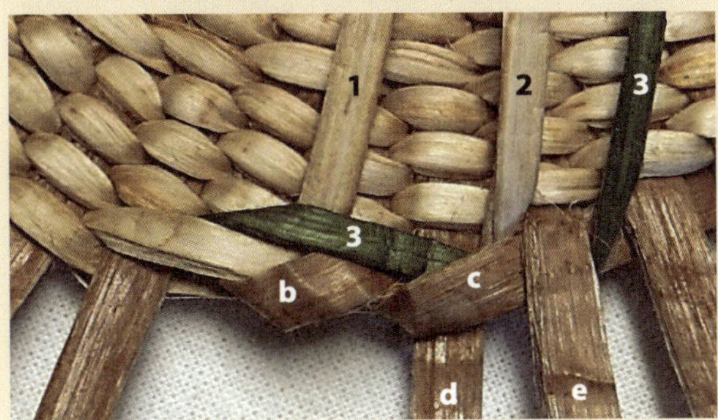

Step 7: Continue around to the beginning of this, ending following steps 3 and 4.

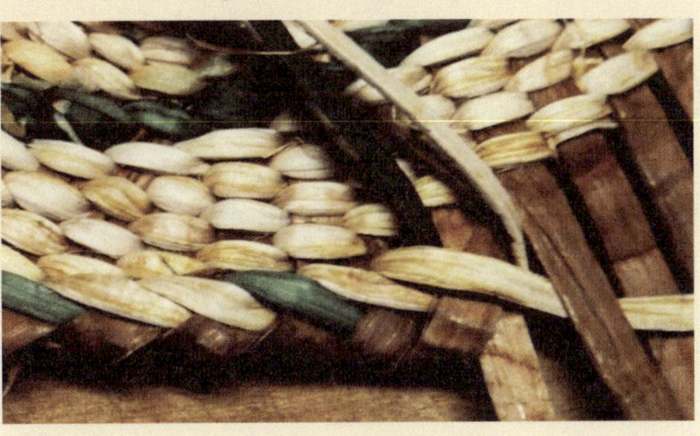

Step 8: Final finishing: Fold warp (a) up over warp (b), under warp (c), above weft (2), and to the back. Pull weft (3) down.

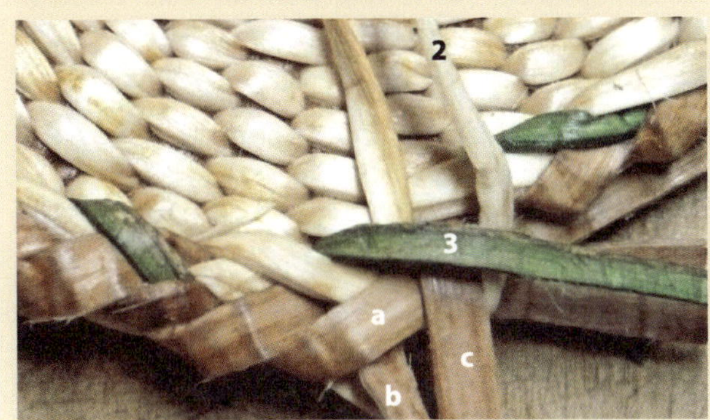

Continues on next page

Step 9: Pull weft (3) tight under warp (a) and up to the back.

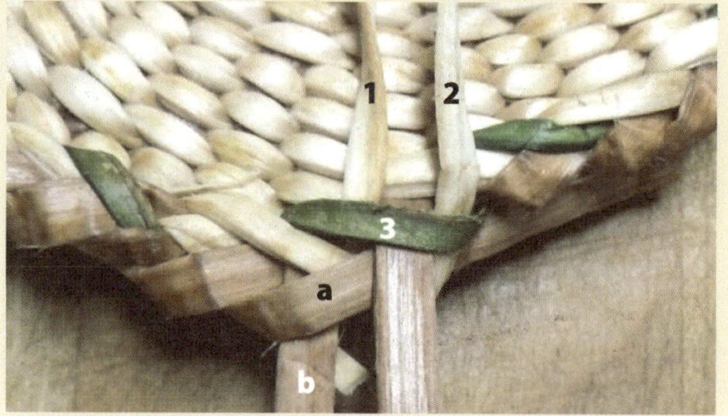

Step 10: Pull weft (1) down, then pull warp (b) up over warp (c), weft (1), and to the back. Next pull weft (1) up and to the back, tightening warp (b), leaving the weft up. Pull weft (2) down, then pull warp (c) up over warp (b) and to the back. Pull weft (1) to the back over warp (c) and up.

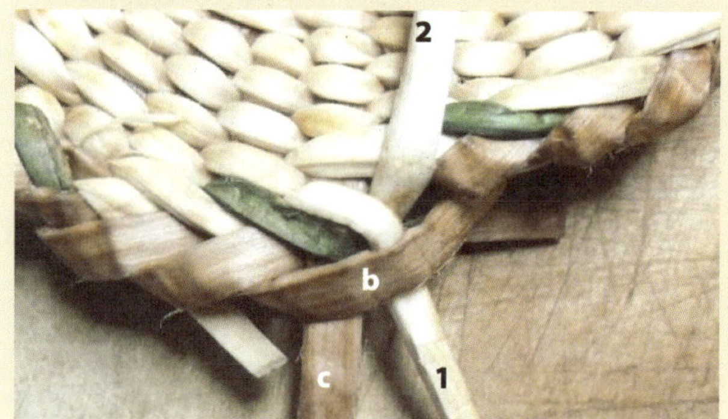

Step 11: On the back or inside of the weaving, using a very large needle, pull the three wefts up through at least two rows of weaving. Even the edge by pulling on the warp ends that need it. Trim all of the long ends on the inside but not so close that they might pop out.

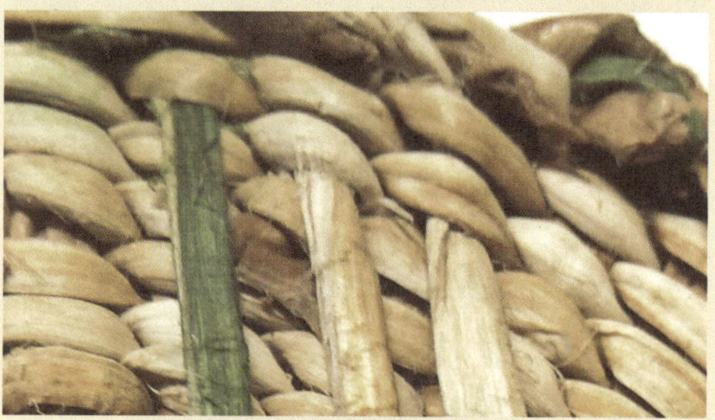

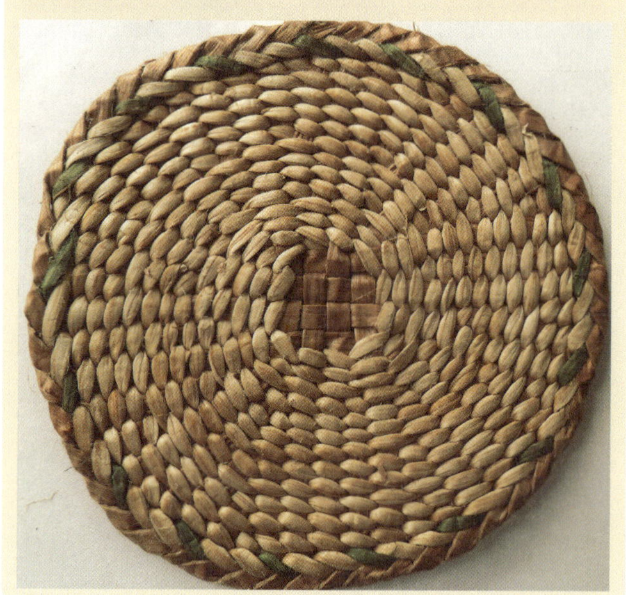

Three-Weft Ending to the Outside

Step 1: Weave weft (1) under warps (a) and (b) and up.

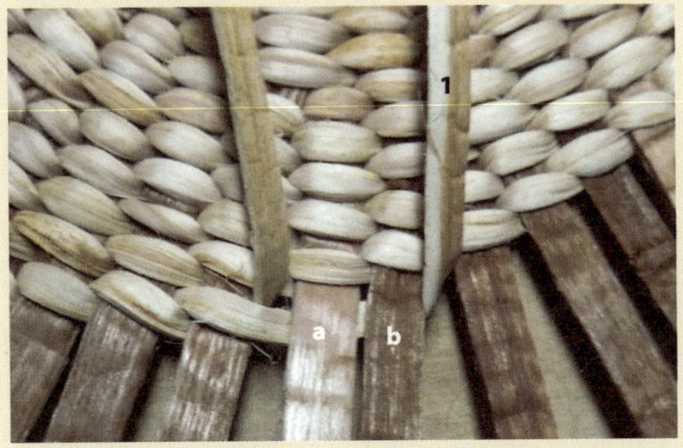

Step 2: On the back of the weaving, tie a knot on the beginning end of weft (3), then pull it to the front between warps (a) and (b) and up.

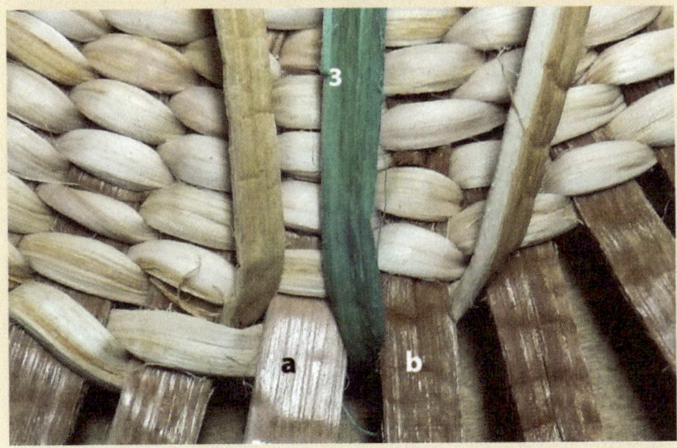

Step 3: Weave weft (2) over warp (a) below weft (3), over warp (b) below weft (1), then under warp (c) and up.

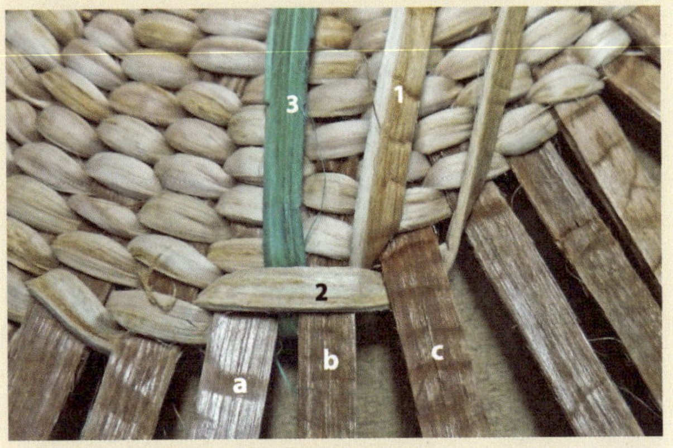

Step 4: Fold warp (b) up over warp (c) and over weft (2), then pull weft (2) up over warp (b).

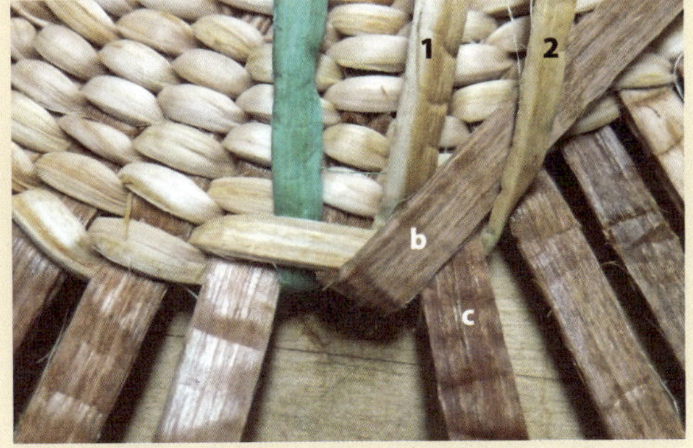

Continues on next page

Step 5: Weave weft (3) over folded warp (b) and not folded warp (c) and under warp (d). Leave weft (3) laying off to the right. Fold warp (c) up over warp (d) then pull weft (3) up over warp (c).

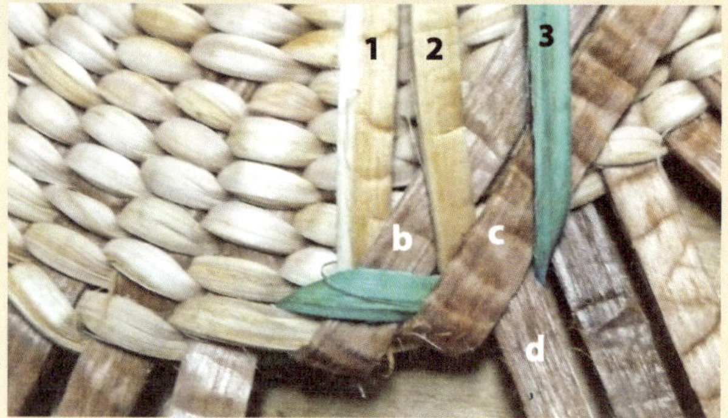

Step 6: Weave weft (1) over folded warps (a) and (b) and not folded warp (c) and up. Fold warp (c) up over warp (d) and under weft (1). Weave weft (2) over folded warps (b) and (c) and not folded (d) and under warp (e) and up. Fold warp (d) up over warp (e) and under weft (2).

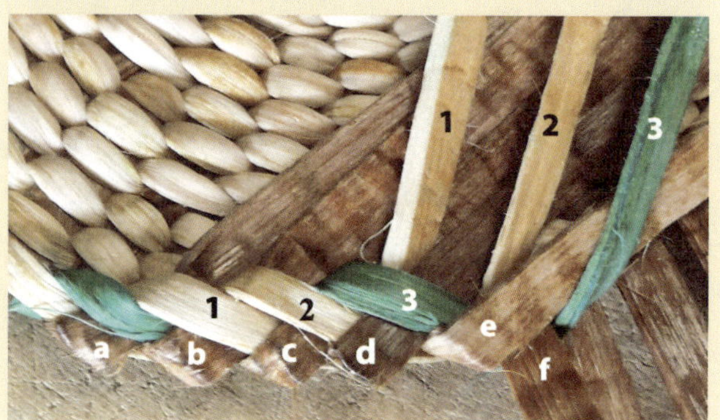

Step 7: Weave weft (3) over folded warps (c) and (d) and not yet folded (e). Next fold warp (e) up over warp (f) and under weft (3). Continue weaving on around the basket to three warps before the beginning of the ending.

Step 8: On the third warp before the beginning of the ending, as each of the three wefts finish their last pull them to the back, thread them on a needle and pull them up through two or three weaves.

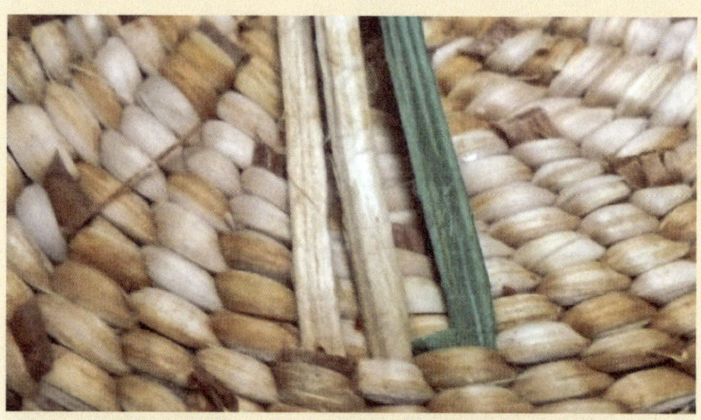

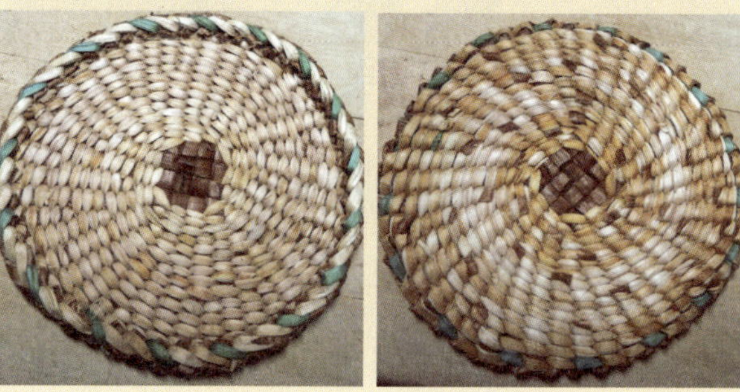

Three-Weft Turning Edge

This can be used on a hat after the circle at the top of the hat is completed to make the turn, and start weaving down the hat or on a basket before weaving the sides.

Step 1: To add a third weft to the weaving, tie a knot on one end of a long weft and thread it on a big needle. On the back of the weaving pull the weft through two rows of weaving between two existing warps.

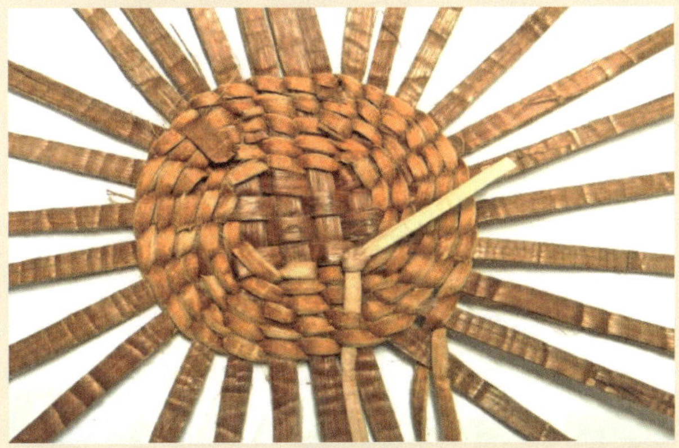

Step 2: Turn weaving to the front and pull the inserted weft (3) to the front.

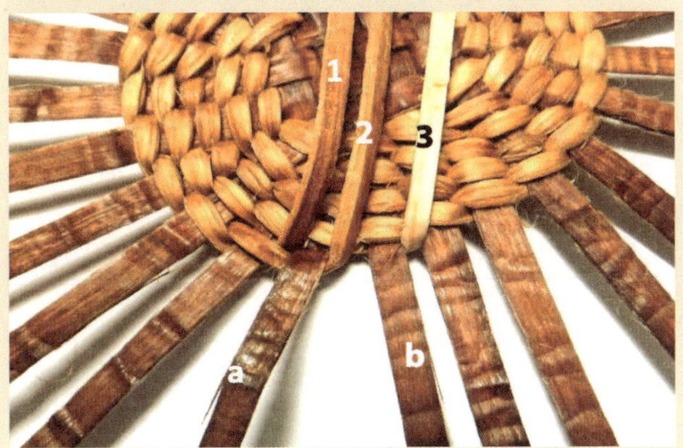

Step 3: To start a three-weft weaving, bring the middle weft (2) down, weave the left weft (1) over warp (a), the middle weft (2) and warp (b), then under warp (c) and up.

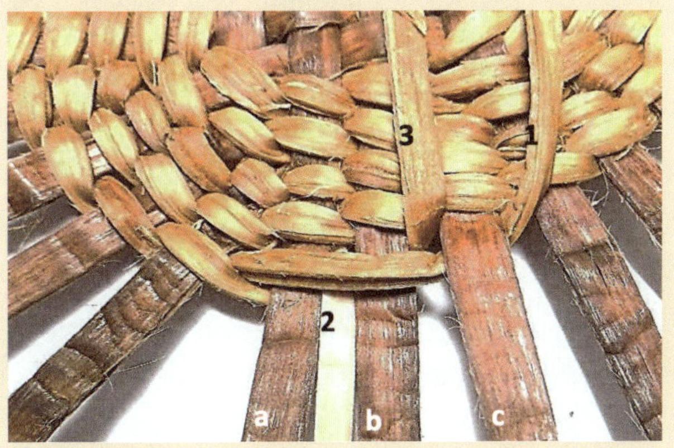

Step 4: Bring the middle weft (3) down, then weave weft (2) over warp (a), weft (3), and warp (b), below weft (1), under warp (c) and up.

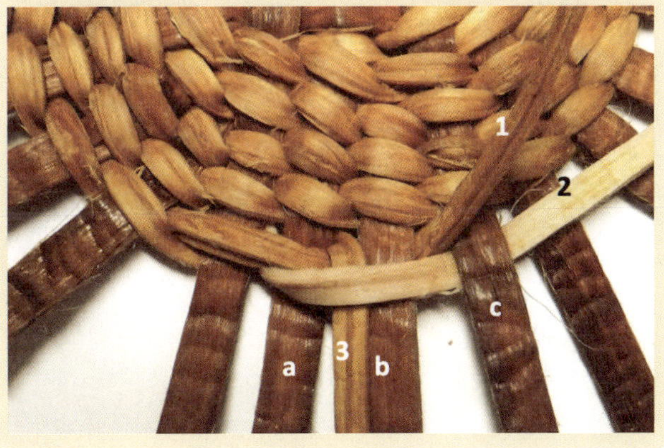

Continues on next page

Step 5: Continue the pattern all the way around: middle weft down, left weft over warp (a), the middle weft, and warp (b), then under warp (c) and up.

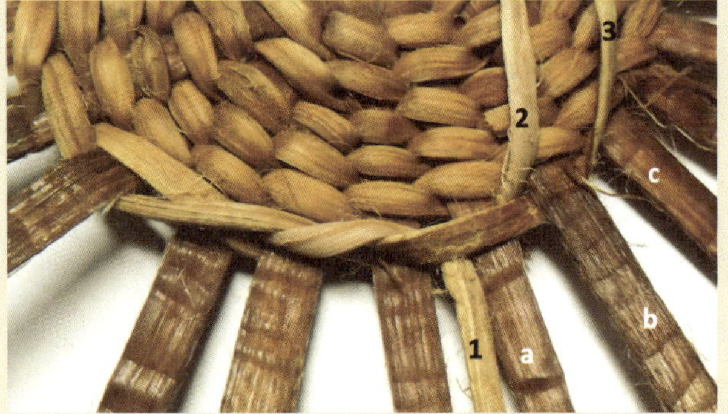

Step 6: Weave around to two warps before the beginning of the three-weft row. Bring weft (2) down, then weave weft (1) over warp (a), weft (2), and warp (b), then bring it to the back of the weaving. Next bring weft (3) down, weave weft (2) over warp (b), weft (3), and warp (c), then bring it to the back of the weaving.

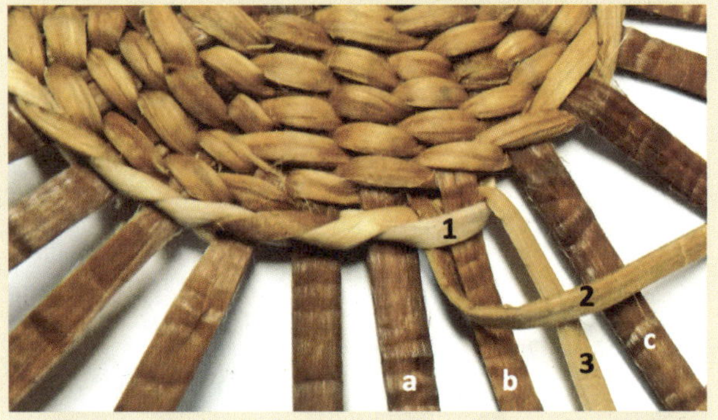

Step 7: Thread a large needle on weft (3) and pull the weft up, over and down through the beginning of the three-weft row, and then pull it to the back.

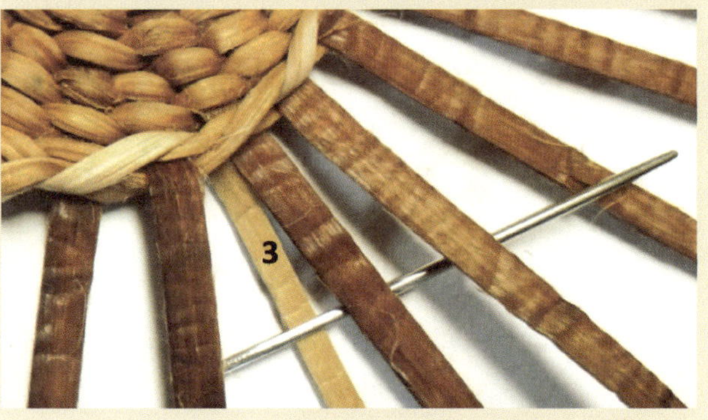

Step 8: Finally, using the large needle, pull wefts (1), (2) and (3) up through two rows of weaving on the back. Trim all of the weft ends.

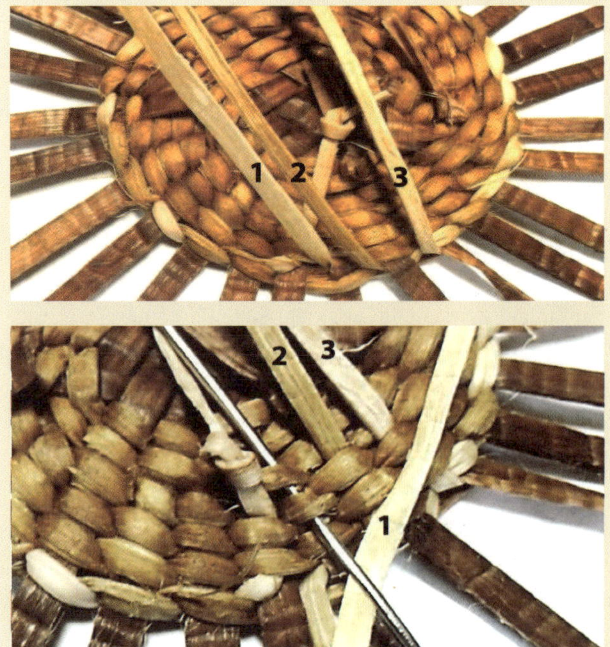

Step 9: The completed turned edge should look like the photo below, left. The warps can now be turned down to continue weaving a hat or basket with a new weft.

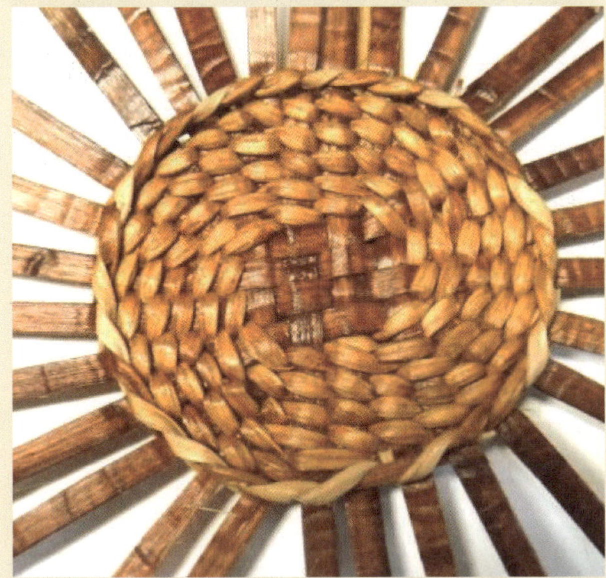

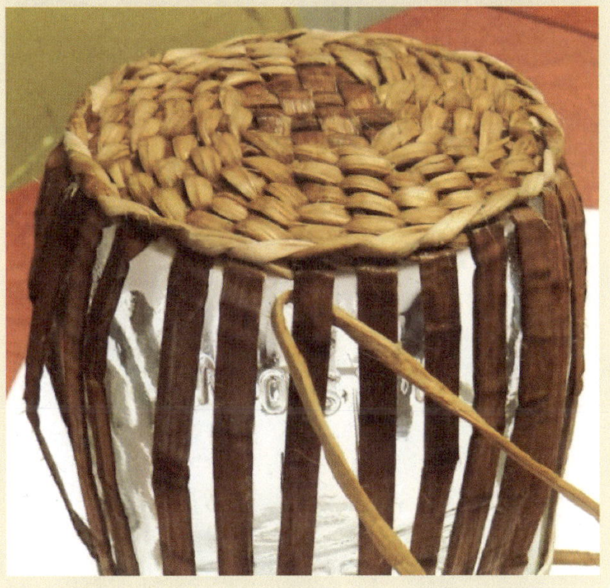

Four-Weft Ending With Folded Warps

Step 1: With weft (a), go over warp (1), then under warps (2) and (3) and up, leaving weft (b) up. Insert new weft (blue) under warps (3) and (4) and pull up.

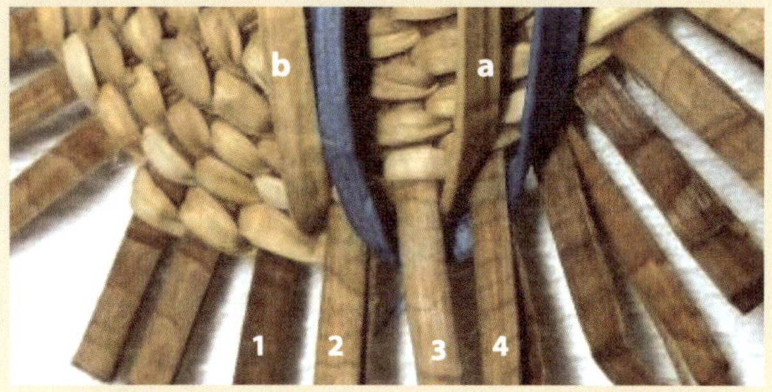

Step 2: Bring left weft (b) below the other three wefts, over warps (2), (3) and (4), then under warp (5) and up.

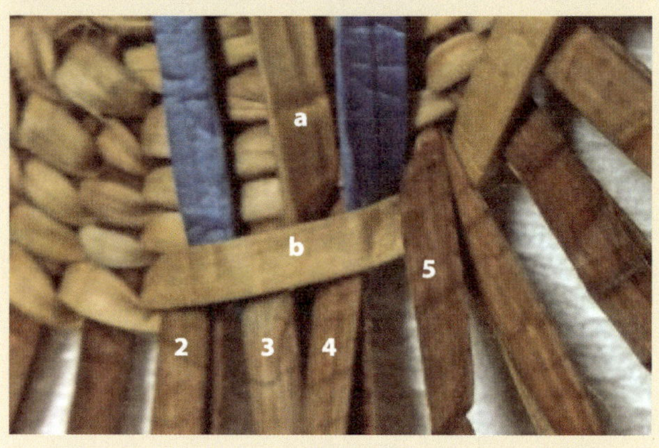

Step 3: Repeat by bringing left blue weft below the other three wefts and over the three warps below, then under warp (6) and up.

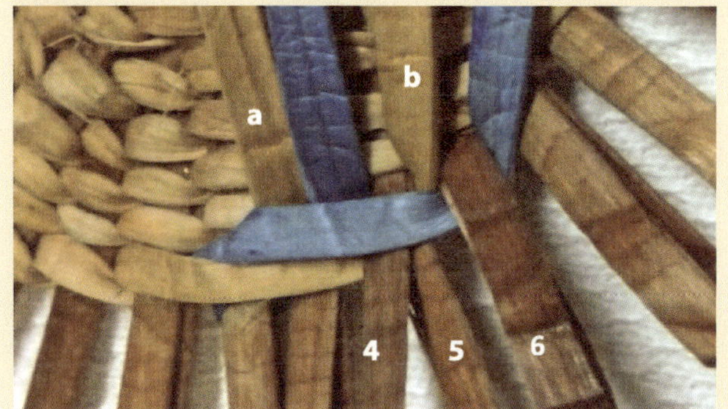

Step 4: Continue around to the start of the four-strand weaving.

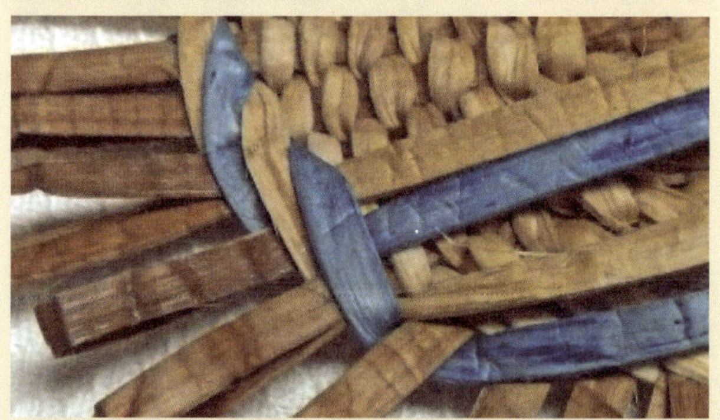

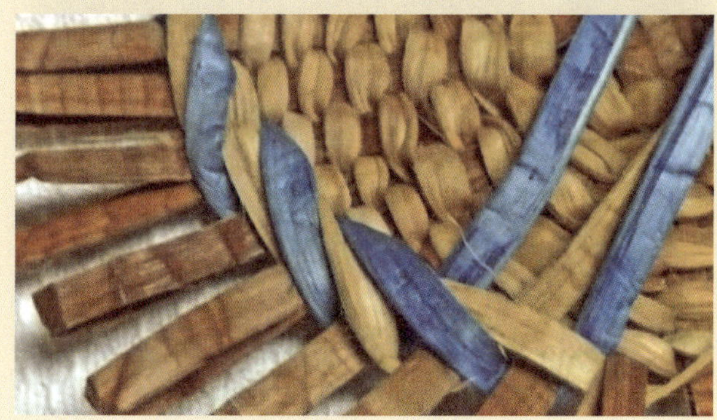

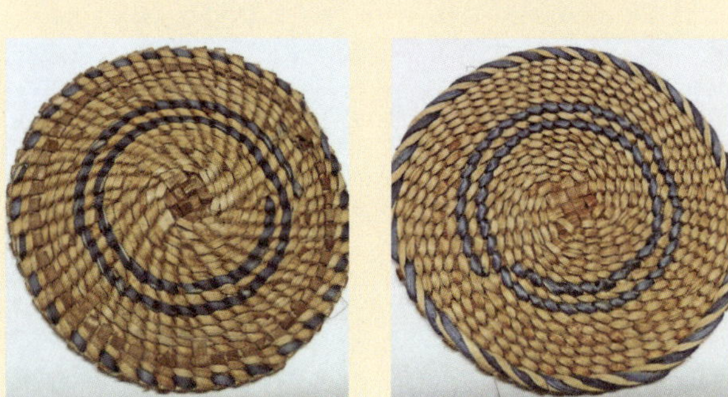

Four-Weft Ending to the Inside

Begin the ending by folding the warps to the inside. Leave enough space on the folded warp to weave the finishing rows. Weave one row to hold the folded warps in place. It is easier to fold just a few warps, weave over them and then fold a few more to weave over them. *For these instructions, some of the weft material is coloured to make it easier to understand the actions.*

Step 1: Lay a green weft over warp (1) and between weavers (a) and (b).

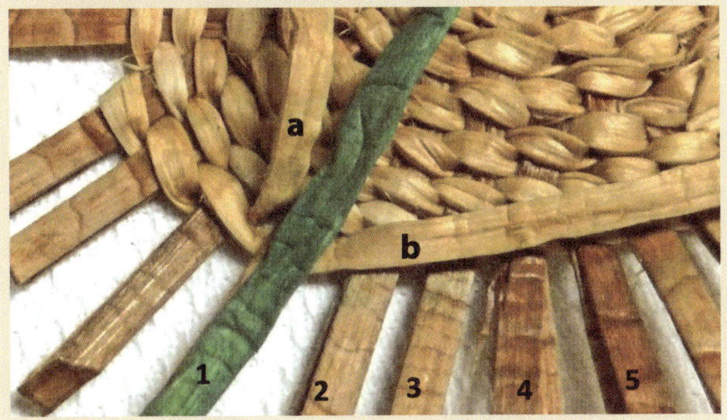

Step 2: Bring weaver (a) down over the green weft and warp (1) then below weaver (b and under warp (2). Move weaver (b) up to the left.

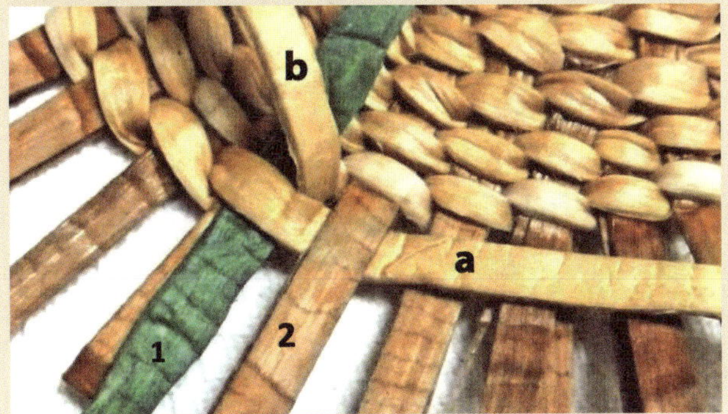

Step 3: Move weaver (a) up then bring the bottom of the green weft up over warp (2) and below weaver (a) and weaver (b). Next bring weaver (a) up and to the left and weaver (b) over the green weft and below weaver (a) and under warp (3).

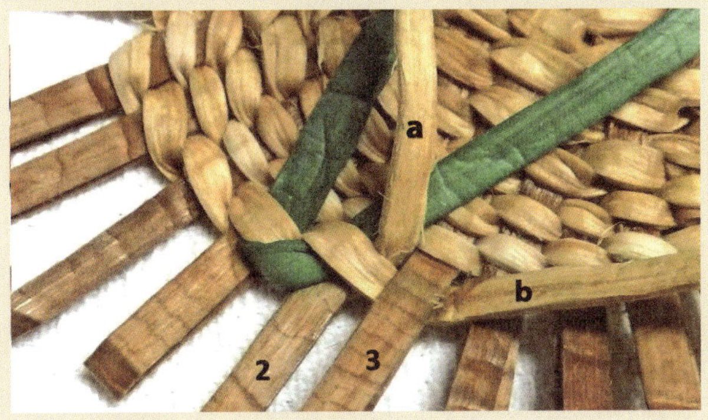

Continues on next page

Step 4: Bring weaver (a) down and to the left, then move the left green weft behind the right green weft and down over warp (3) between weavers (a) and (b).

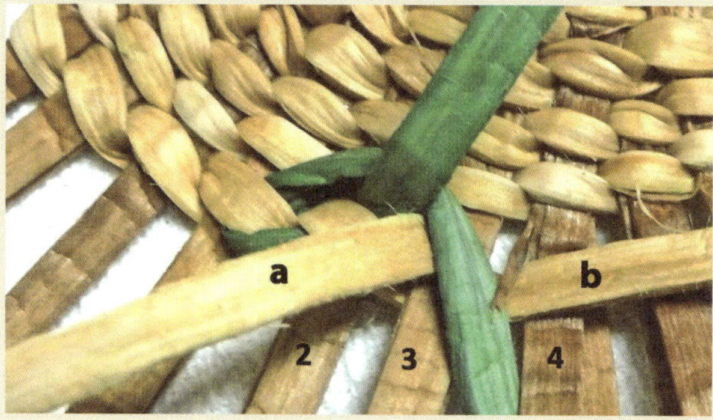

Step 5: Next, bring (b) up and (a) over the green weft and under warp (4) and up.

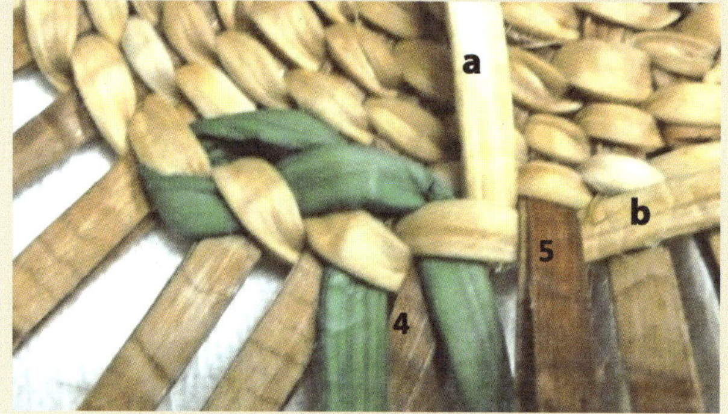

Step 6: Bring weaver (b) down and to the left, and the upper green weft down over warp (4) and weave (b) over the green weft and under warp (5).

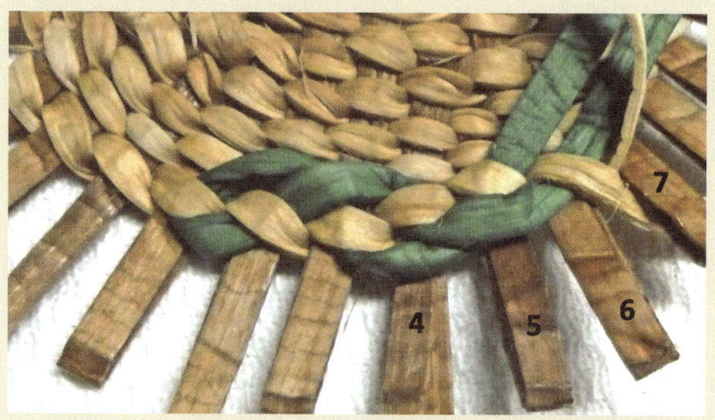

Step 7: Now bring the left green weft up over warp (4), under the right green weft and over warp (5) and up. Weave over it and under warp six. Then bring the lower green weft over the left green weft and warp (6) and up. Then weave over it and under warp (7).

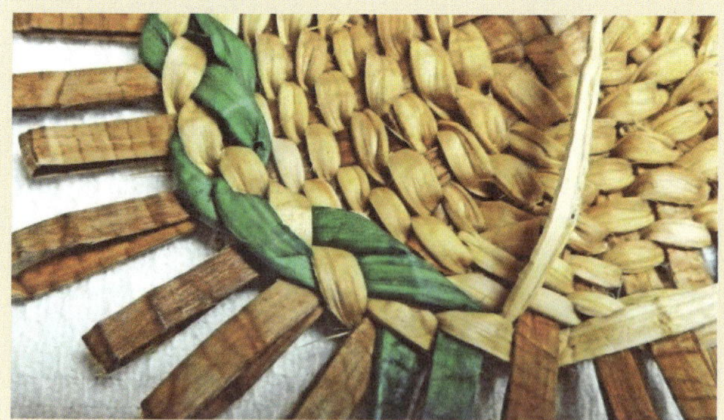

Step 8: Continue with Steps (4), (5) and (6) to the beginning of this four-weft ending.

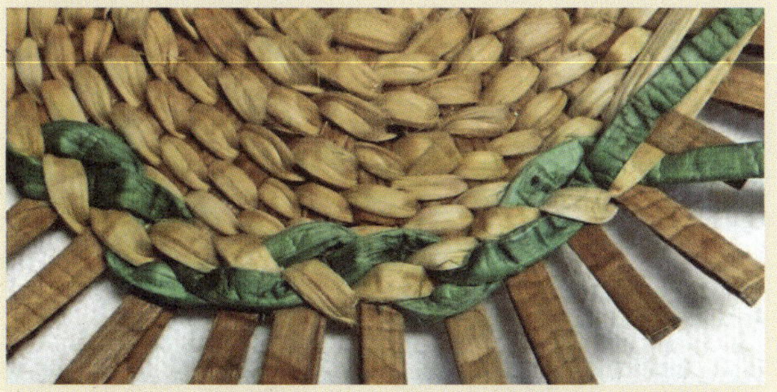

Step 9: Finish the ending: Bring wefts one at a time to the back of the weaving and thread a weft in the large eye of a needle and sew it under two or three of the weaving stitches in the weaving. Thread a needle with dental floss or very small tough string and run the needle through the folded warps. Pull the thread tight and push it tight against the weaving. Turn the weaving to the back and with your fingers or a needle nose plier, pull the ends until the loops are tight against the string and the weaving and then trim the warps next to the weaving.

Four-Weft Rolled Ending to Inside

Step 1: Begin the ending by folding the warps to the inside. Leave enough space on the folded warp to weave the finishing rows. Weave one row to hold the folded warps in place. It is easier to fold just a few warps, weave over them and then fold a few more to weave over.

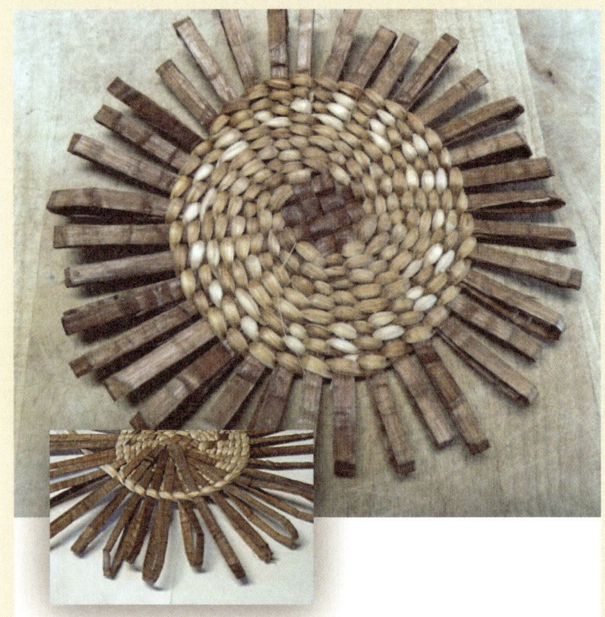

Step 2: Begin the weaving of this ending by doubling a blue and white weft.

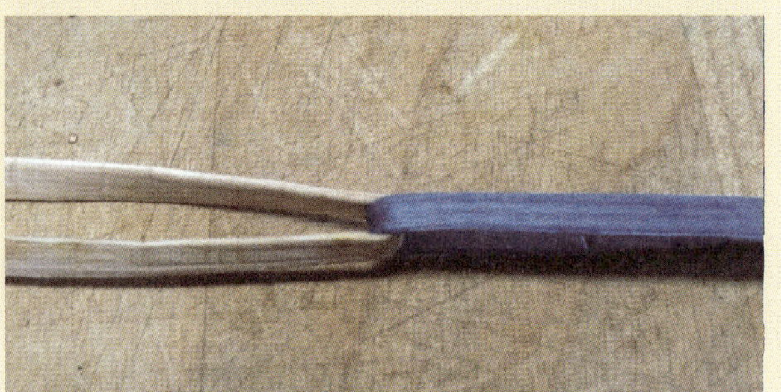

Step 3: Insert the doubled wefts under warp (1) with weavers (a) and (b) out to the left and the blue weavers (c) and (d) to the right with (c) up and (d) down.

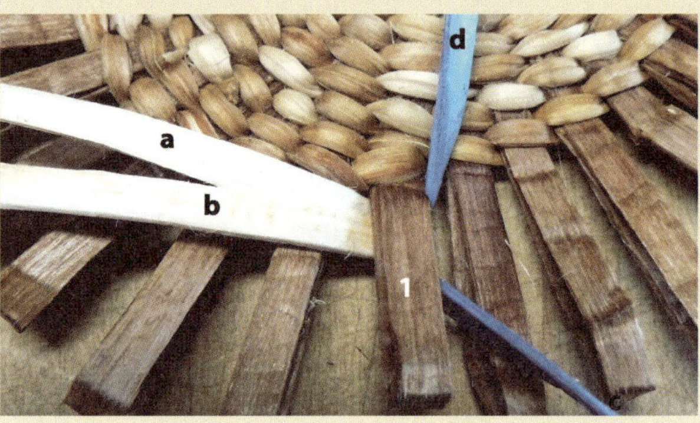

Step 4: Weave (a) above (b) and (c) and warp (1), then under warp (2) and up.

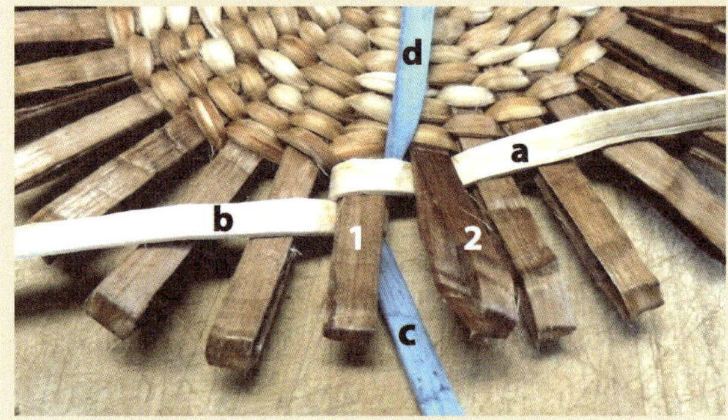

Step 5: Bring blue weft (d) down then weave weft (b) over warp (1), weft (c) and (d) and warp (2) and under warp (3) and up, so it is out of the way.

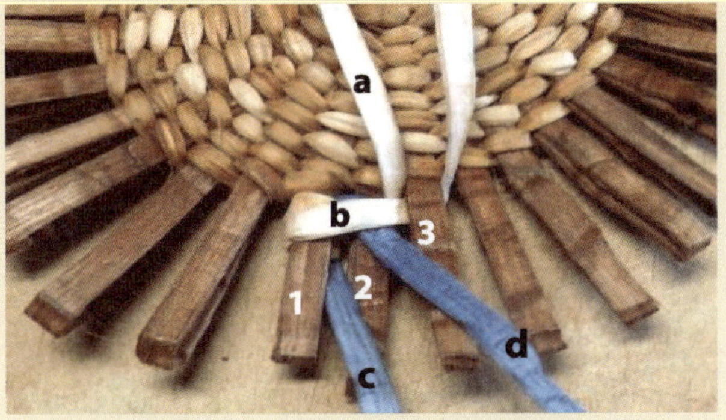

Step 6: Bring weaver (a) down, then weave (c) over (d) and (a), plus warps (2) and (3), then below (b) and under warp (4) and up.

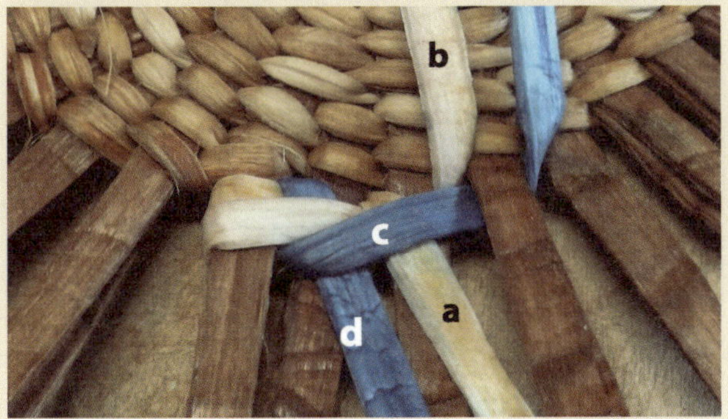

Step 7: Bring weaver (b) down.

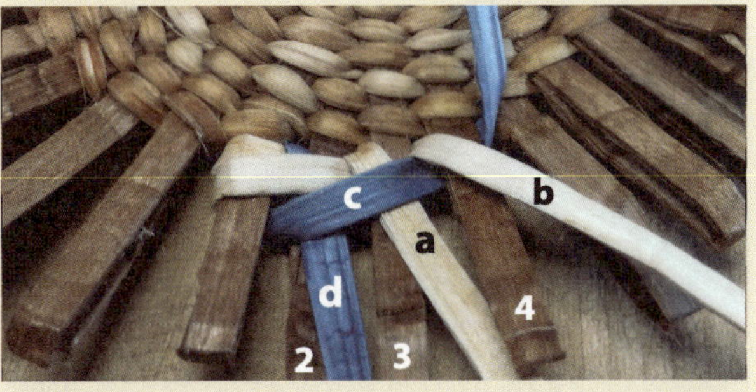

Step 8: Weave (d) over (a) and (b) and warps (3) and (4) and below (c) and under warp (5).

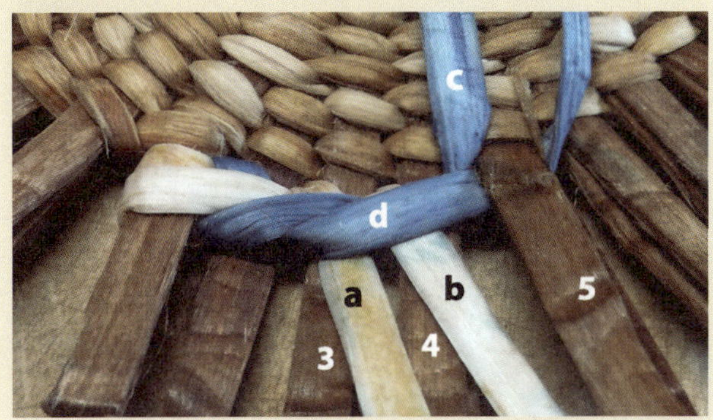

Continues on next page

Step 9: Weave (a) over (b) and (c) and warps (4) and (5) below (d) and under warp (6) and up.

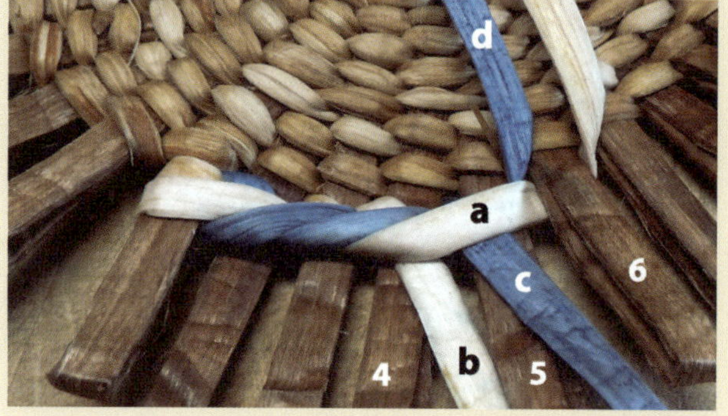

Step 10: Weave (b) over (c) and (d) warps (5) and (6) and under warp (7) and up.

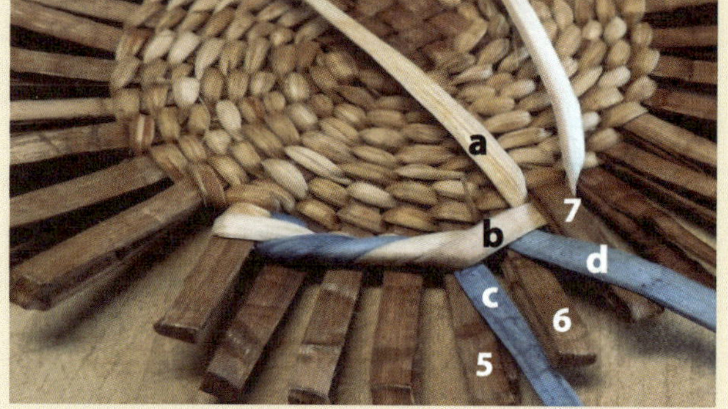

Step 11: Continue weaving to the beginning of the ending. To secure the wefts, bring them one by one to the back of the weaving.

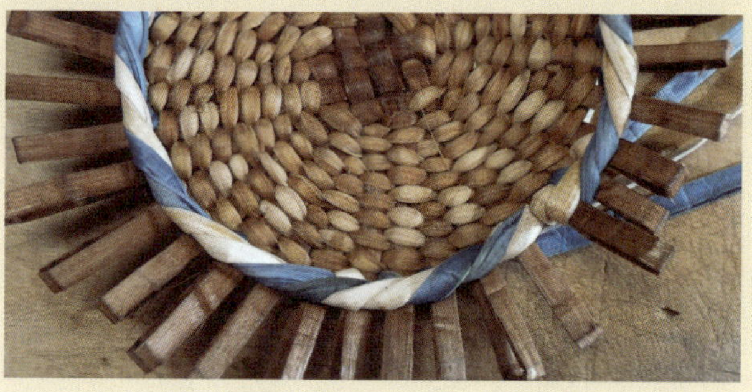

Step 12: Thread the wefts one by one on a needle and pull them down through two or three rows of weaving.

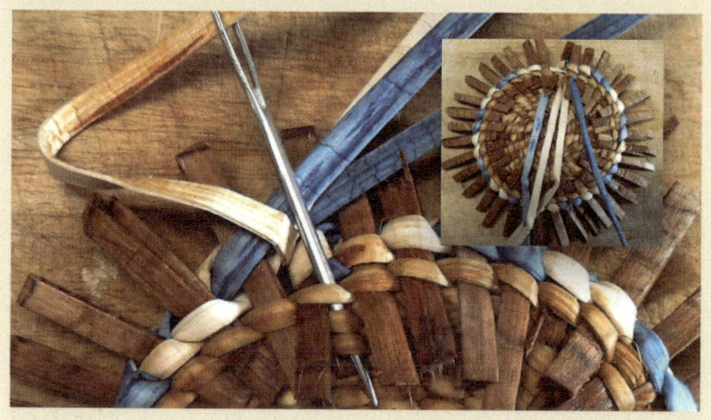

Step 13: Thread a needle with either very strong string, dental floss or a weft. Then pull it through the folded warps pulling it snugly up against the weaving as you move through the warps.

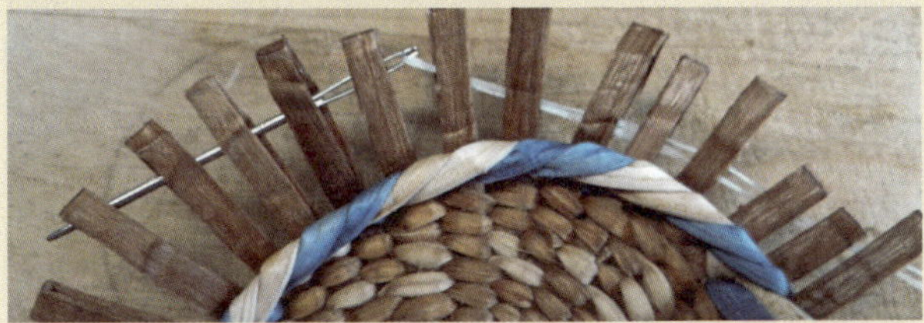

Step 14: Pull the two ends really tight up against the weaving and tie a knot.

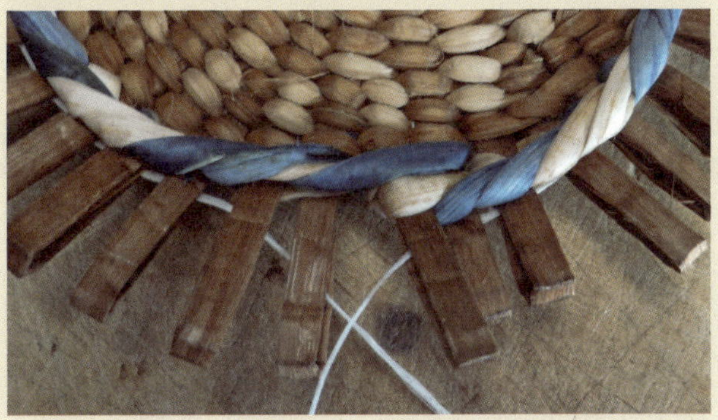

Step 15: Next, turn to the back of the weaving and with your fingers or pliers, pull the warps down against the floss, but not too far.

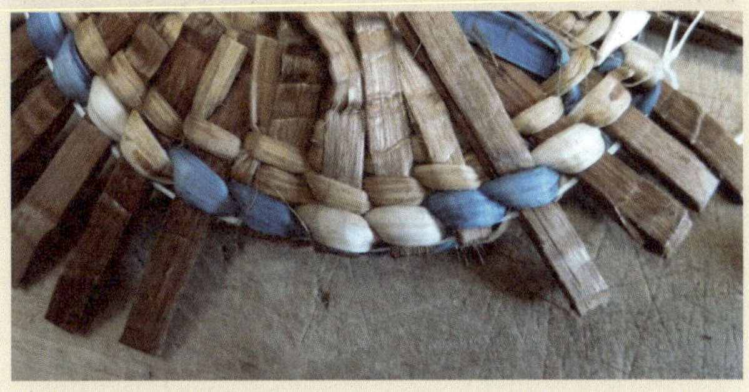

Step 16: The last step is to even the warps all the way around and then, on the back or inside of the weaving, trim all of the endings.

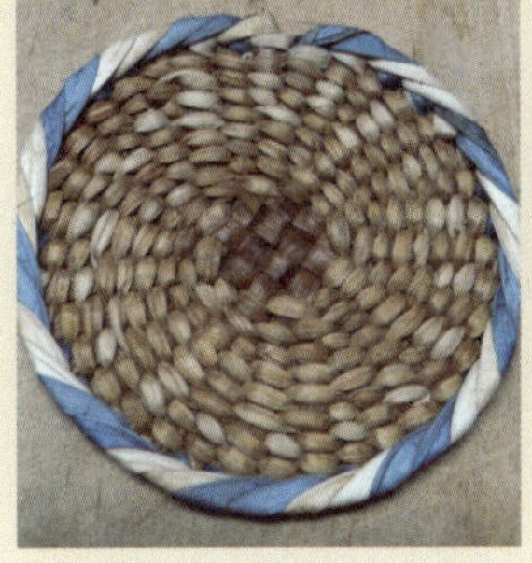

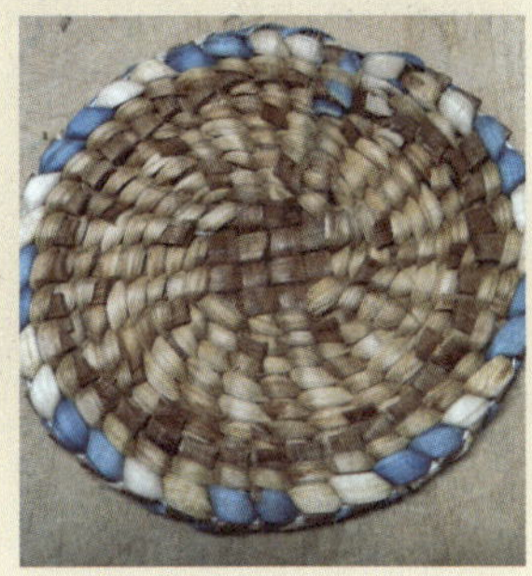

Four-Weft Braided Hat Ending

Step 1: Place blue weft (c) and (d) under warps (2) and (3) and up.

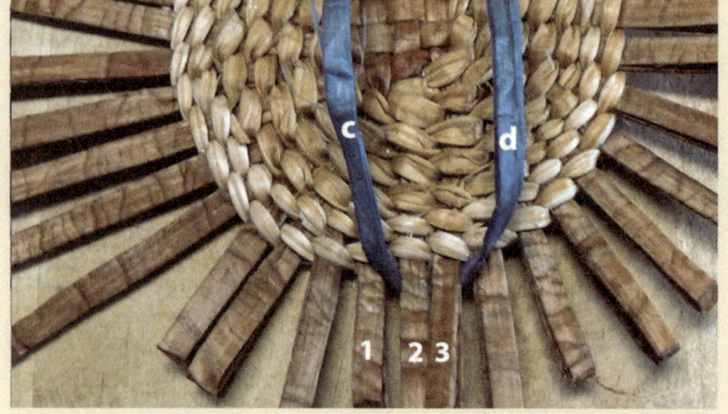

Step 2: Place the ends of wefts (a) and (b) under warps (1) and (2) and up.

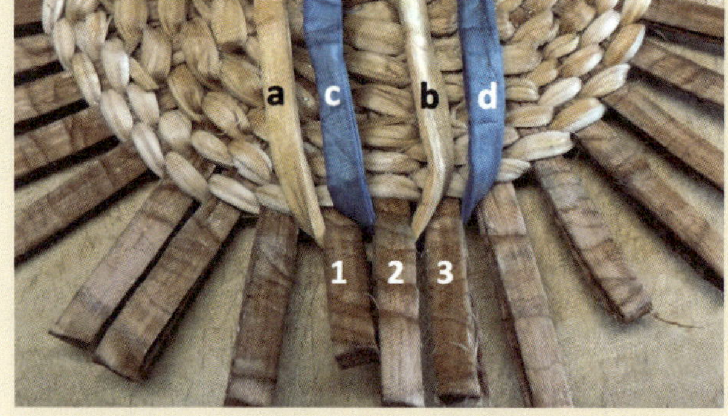

Step 3: Weave weft (a) over the blue (c), warps (2) and (3), below (d), then under (4) and up. Bring (d) down.

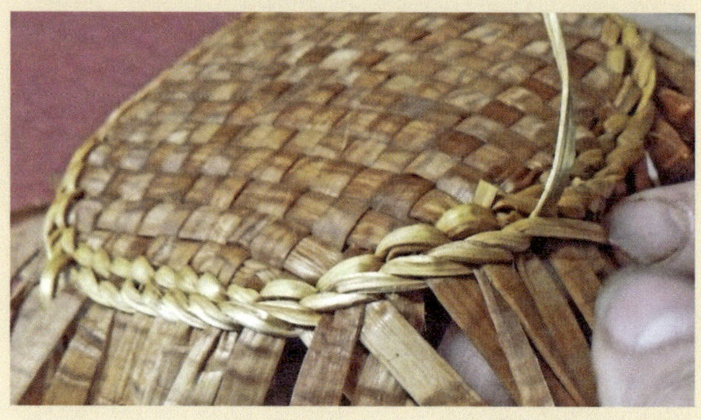

Step 4: Weave blue (c) over weft (b), warps (3) and (4), below (a), and then under warp (5).

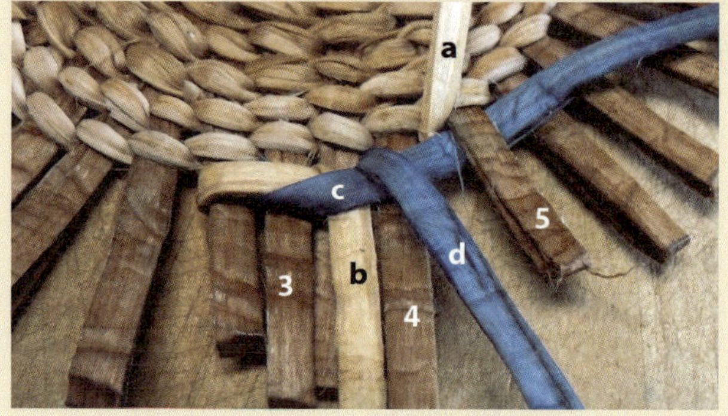

Step 5: Bring (c) up. Weave (b) over (d), under (a), and then bring (a) down. Continue by weaving (b) over warps (4) and (5), below (c), then under warp (6) and up. Bring (a) down.

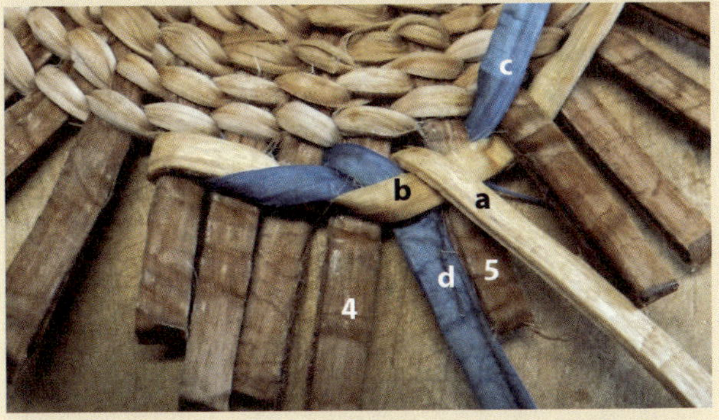

Step 6: Weave (d) over (a), warps (5) and (6), below (b), under warp (7) and up. Bring (c) down.

Step 7: Continue weaving to the start of this ending.

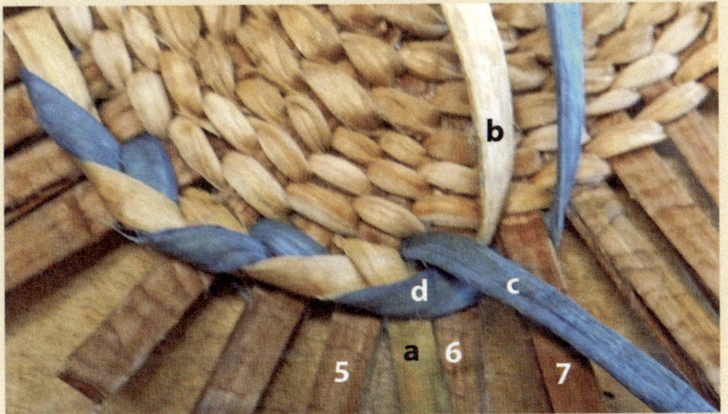

Four-Weft Herringbone Ending to the Inside

Step 1: Weave with weft (a) under the beginning warp (1).

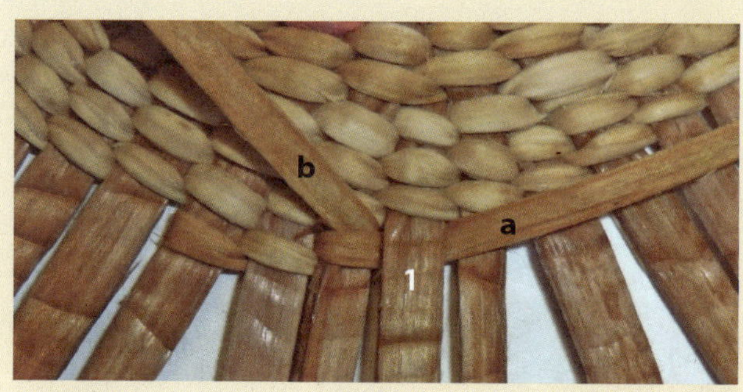

Step 2: Fold weft (b) over warp (1). Next add a doubled pink weft over wefts (b) and (a) and between warps (1) and (2). Then weave weft (c) under warp (2) and up, and weft (d) under warp (2) and down.

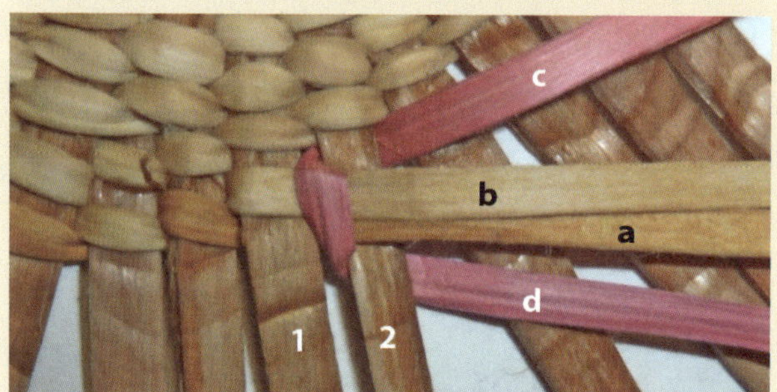

Step 3: Move weft (b) up and weft (a) down. Move wefts (c) and (d) together between (a) and (b), then fold them to the left. Bring (b) and (a) under warp (3).

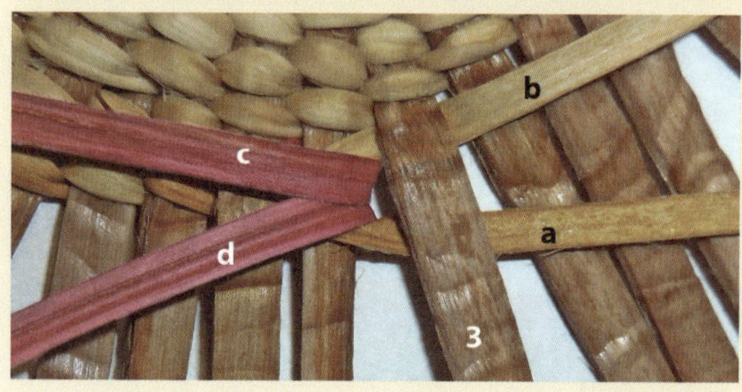

Step 4: Move (a) and (b) together. Fold wefts (a) and (b) back to the left between wefts (c) and (d), over warp (3), and then move (c) and (d) under warp (4).

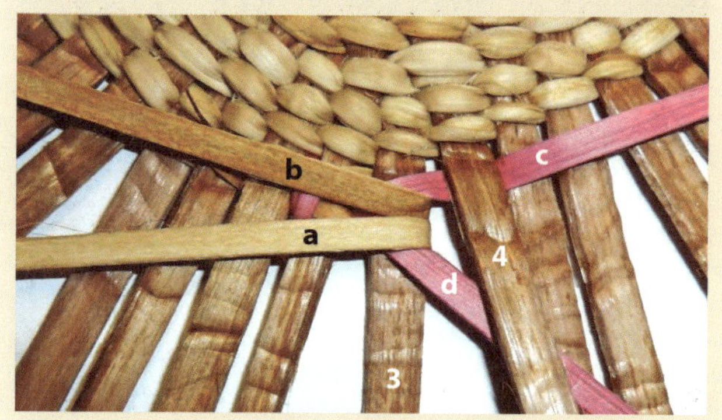

Step 5: Continue around the basket to the start of the basket ending.

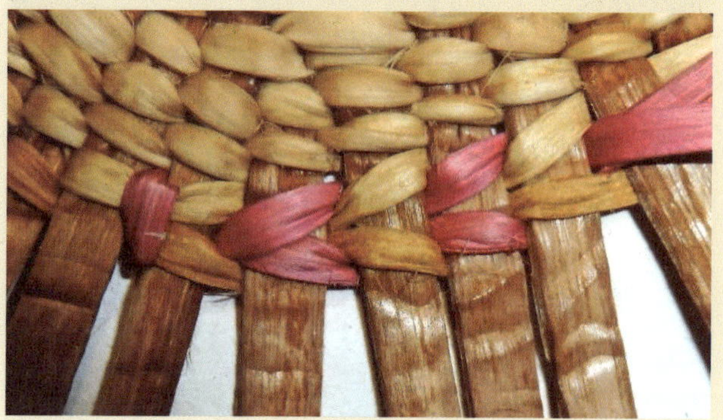

Four-Weft Ending With a Z-Twist

Fold the two working wefts to the back and needle them up before beginning the steps below.

Step 1: Begin this ending by inserting a weft under warp (1).

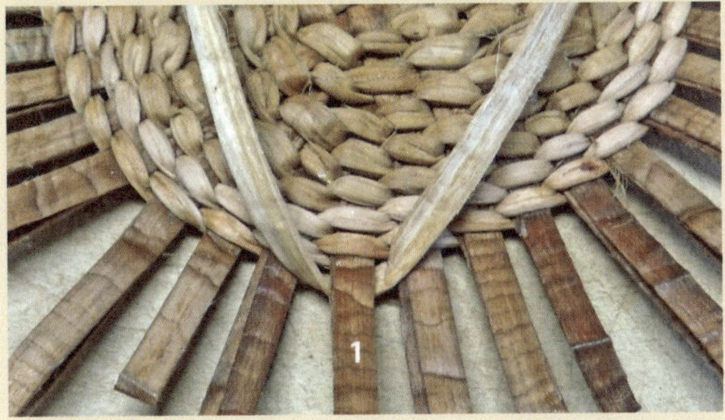

Step 2: Place another weft (red) over warp (1) and between weavers (a) and (b).

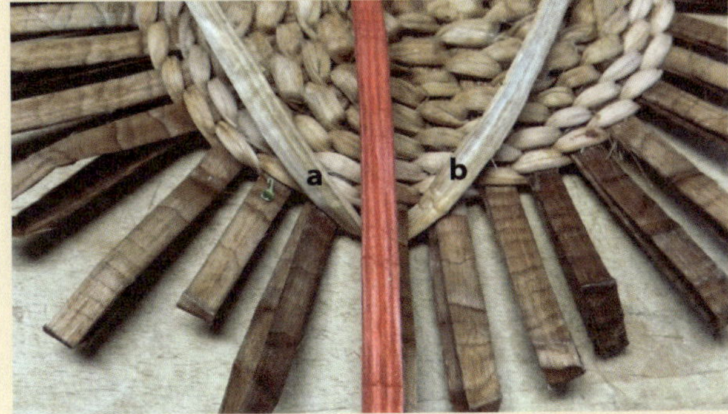

Step 3: Weave weft (a) over the red weft (c-d) and warp (1), under warp (2). Weft (b) should be up and to the left.

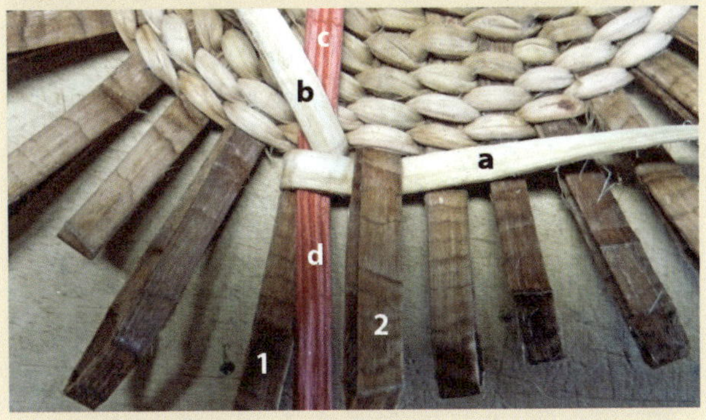

Step 4: Bring red weft (c) down to the right of weft (b), over warp (2) and weft (a).

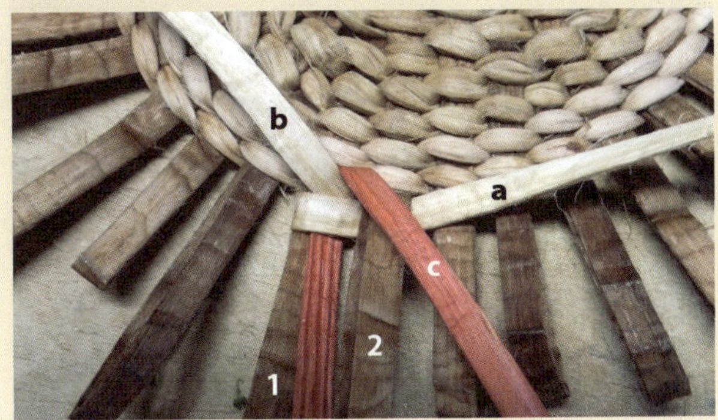

Continues on next page

Step 5: Bring red (d) up over red (c), making an X with the two red wefts on top of (a) and warp (2).

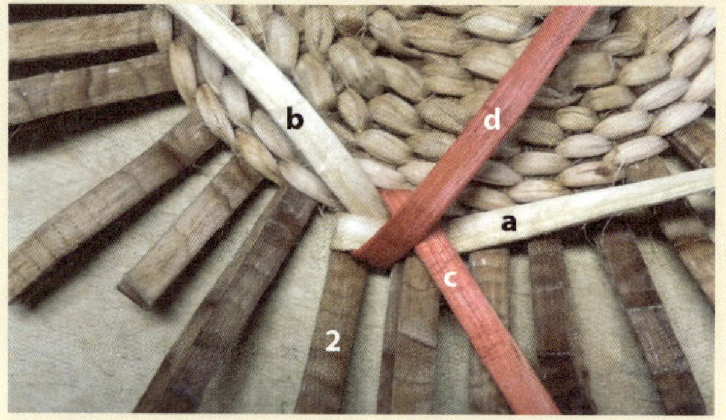

Step 6: Weave weft (b) over the red X and then under warp (3), keeping both the weaving and the red wefts to the centre. Move weft (a) up and back to the left above red (d).

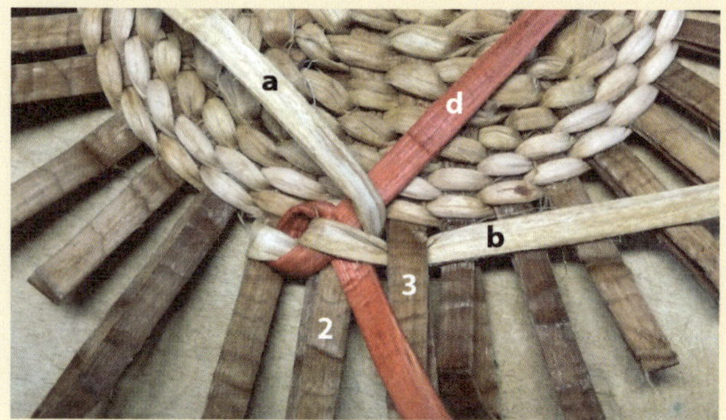

Step 7: Bring red (d) down, behind and to the right of (a), and over warp (3) and weft (b).

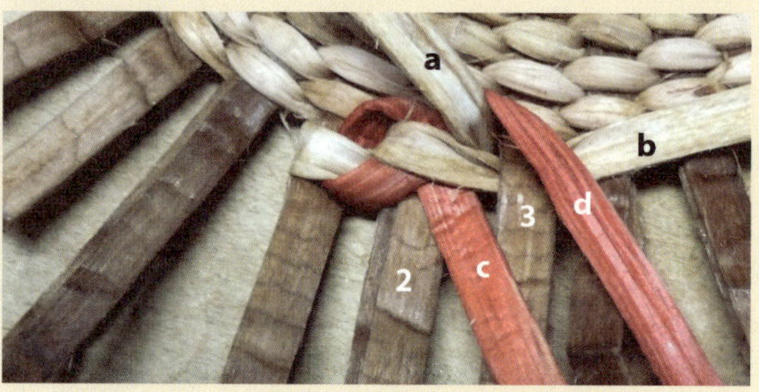

Step 8: Bring red (c) up over red (d), making an X.

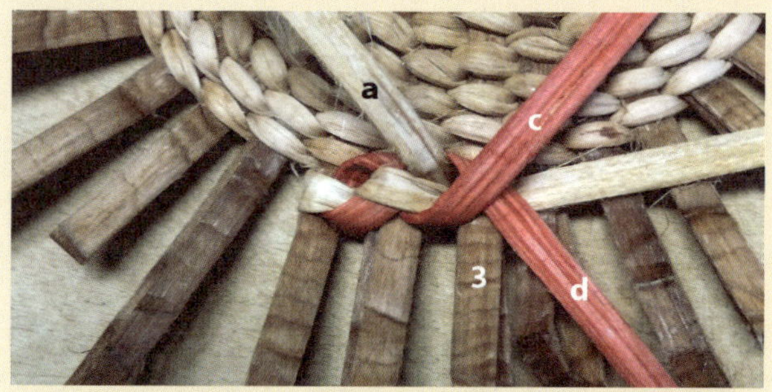

Step 9: Then weave (a) over the middle of the red X, under warp (4). Bring weaver (b) up and back to the left over red (c).

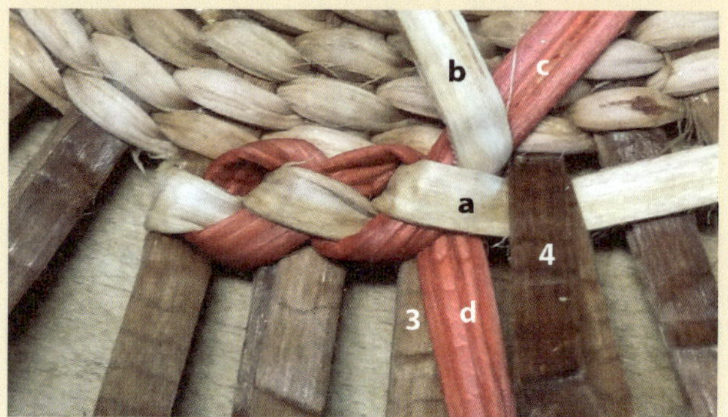

Step 10: Continue until you have gone all the way around.

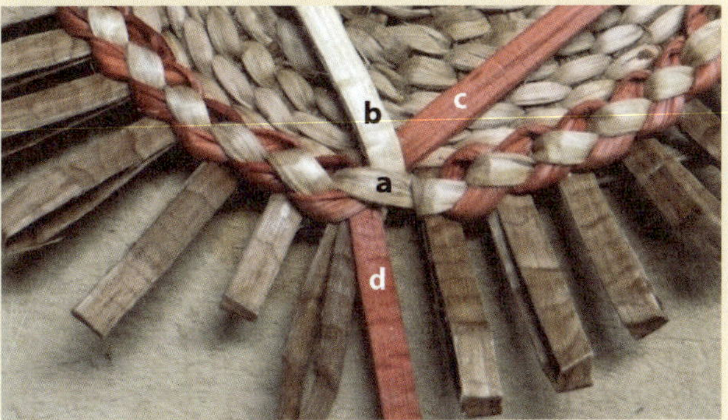

Step 11: When you have reached the end, tuck weaver (a) to the back.

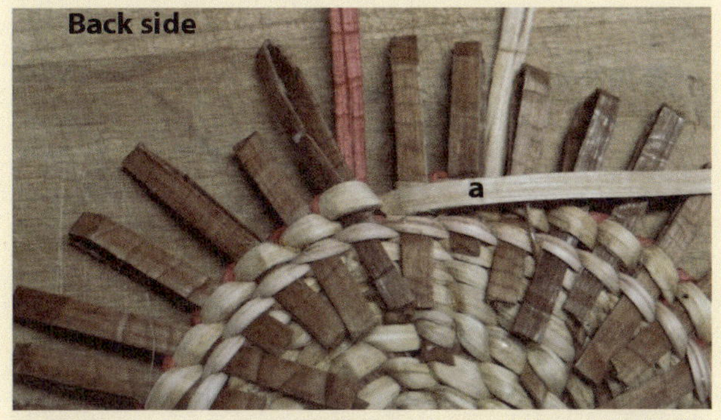

Step 12: Bring red (c) down and (d) up to make an X.

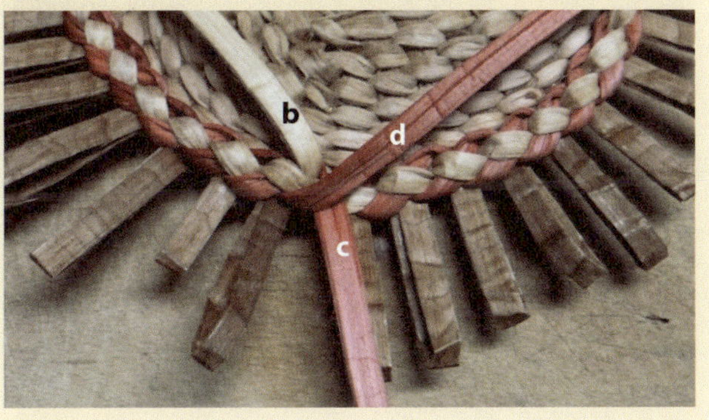

Step 13: Weave weft (b) over the X and leave to the back.

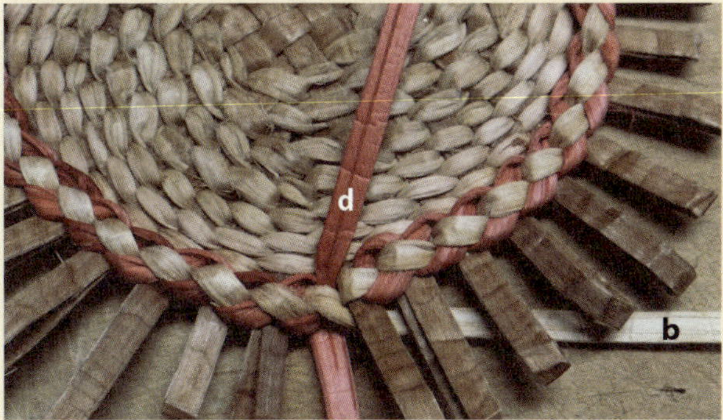

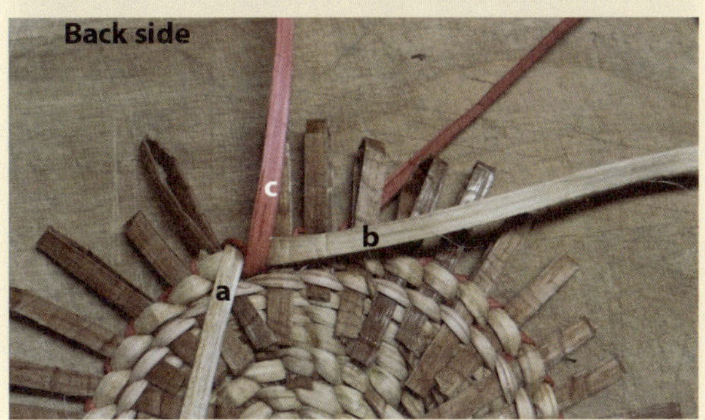

Five-Weft Vertical Ending With Folded Warps to Inside

Step 1: Start by tying a knot in a red weft (5), place it on the back between warps (a) and (b), then bring it to the front through (a) and (b).

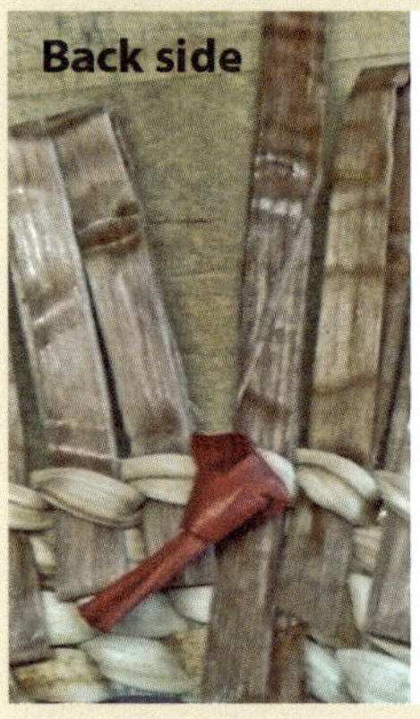

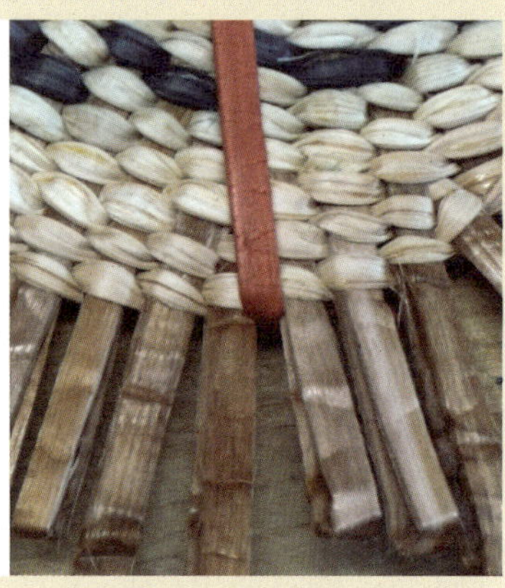

Step 2: Place a blue weft (3/4) over warp (a) just to the left of the weft (5).

If needed, add a doubled weft (1) and (2) around the warp to the left of warp (a). If using wefts (1) and (2) from the weaving above, continue with Step 3.

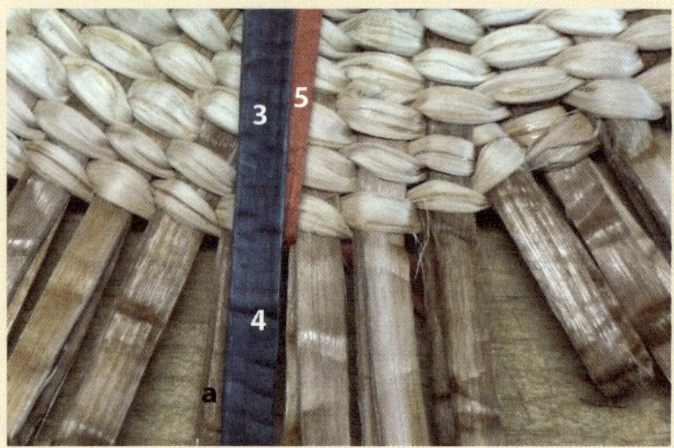

Step 3: Weave weft (2) under warp (a) and weft (3/4), then up to the left above weft (3/4) and (5). Weave weft (1) over weft (3/4) warp (a) and under warp (b).

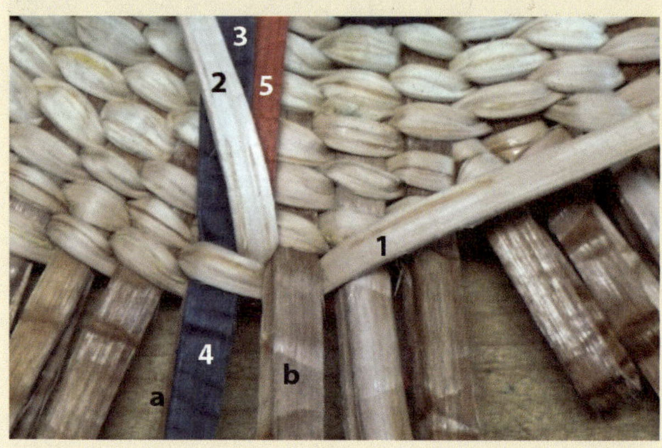

Step 4: Bring weft (3) down to the right of warp (b) and over weft (1) that is under warp (b).

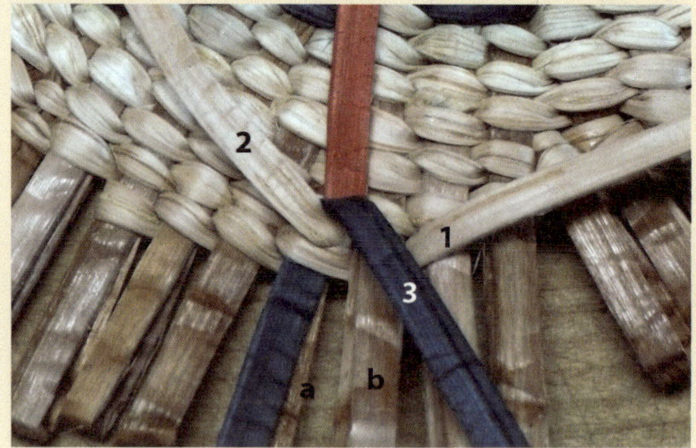

Step 5: Bring weft (4) up and over weft (3) and to the right of weft (5), making an X.

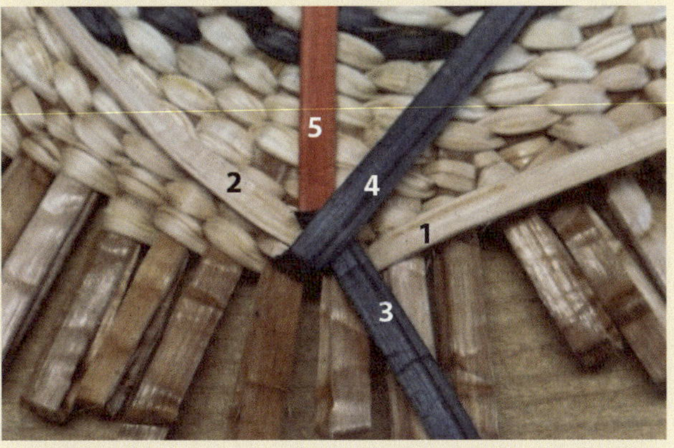

Step 6: Bring weft (1) back to the left above weft (3) then weave weft (2) over the blue X, under warp (c) and to the right.

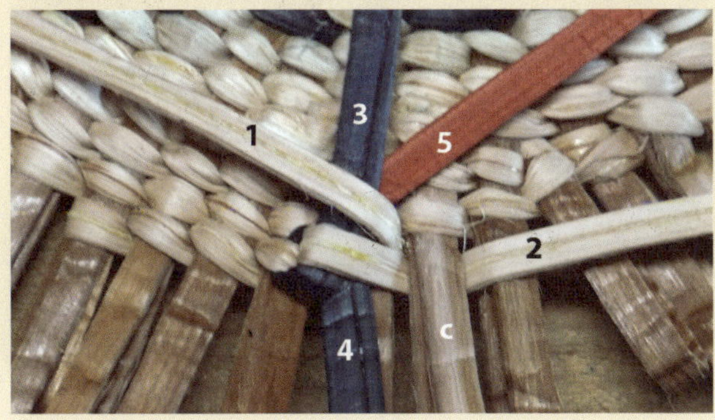

Step 7: Bring red weft (5) down behind blue weft (3), over warp (c) and weft (2).

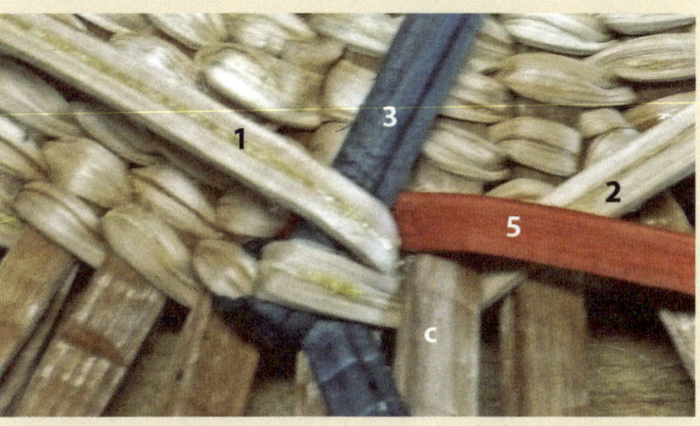

Step 8: Bring blue weft (3) up over red weft (5), making an X that is on top of warp (c) and weft (2).

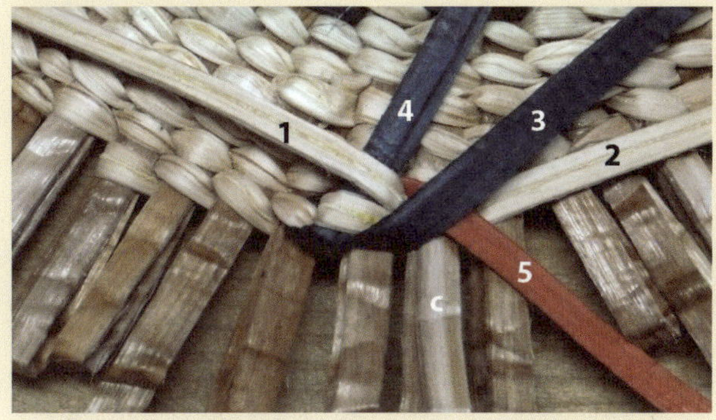

Continues on next page

Step 9: Weave weft (1) over the blue weft (3) and red weft (5) X, then under warp (d). Fold weft (2) up and back to the left above wefts (3) and (4).

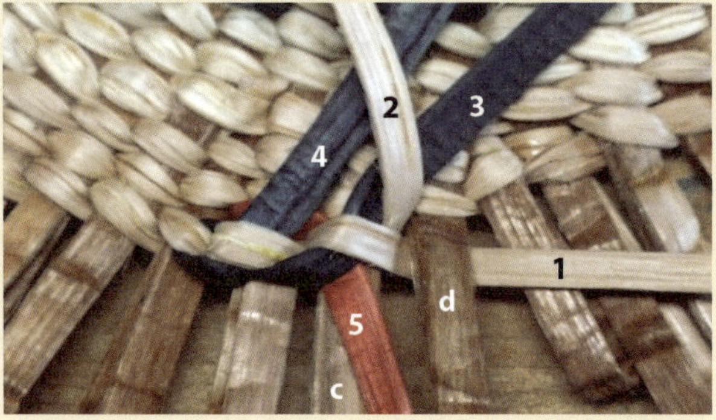

Step 10: Bring blue weft (4) down behind blue weft (3) and weft (2), then over warp (d) and weft (1).

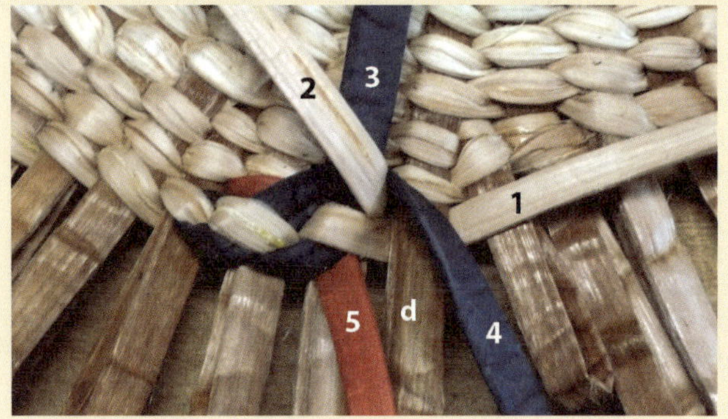

Step 11: Bring red weft (5) up over blue weft (4) and warp (d), making an X.

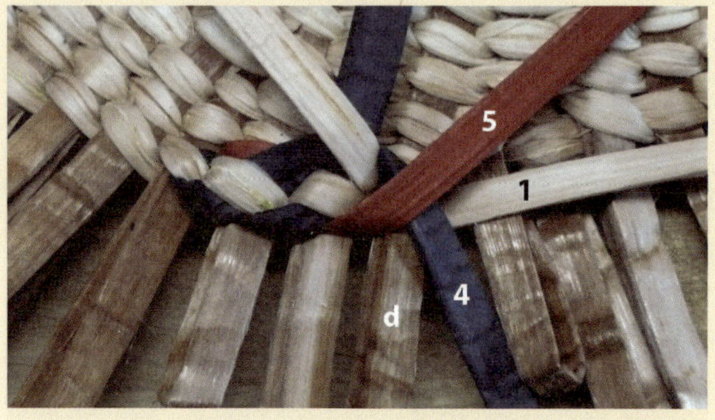

Step 12: Weave weft (2) over red weft (5) and blue weft (4) X and continue all the way around to the start of the ending.

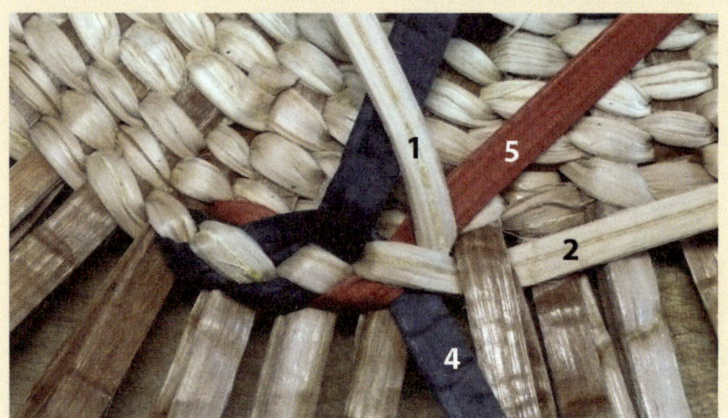

Step 13: To finish the ending, weave weft (1) over blue weft (4) and red weft (5) X then under warp (a). Bring weft (2) up and back over blue weft (4) and blue weft (3).

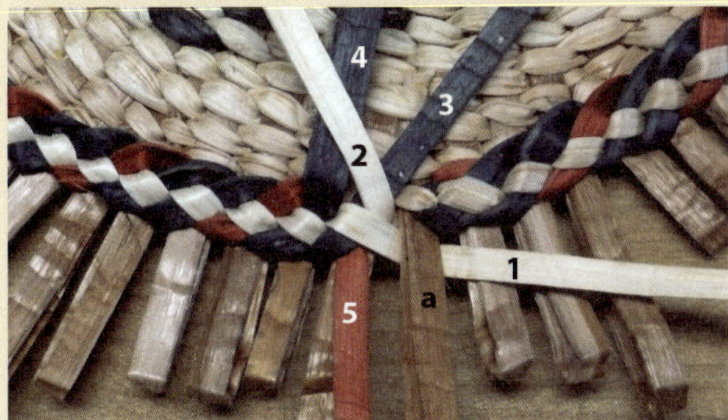

Step 14: Bring blue weft (3) down behind weft (2) and down. Fold red weft (5) up over blue weft (3), making an X.

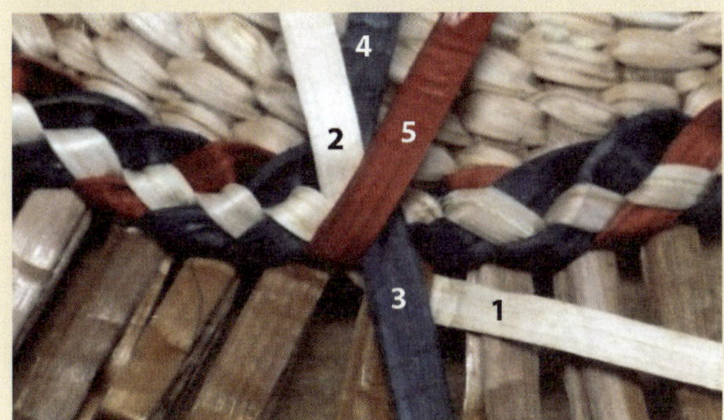

Step 15: Bring weft (1) to the back of the weaving, then thread it on a needle and secure it by pulling it through two or three rows of weaving. Next, weave weft (2) over (red weft (5) and blue weft (3), then bring it to the back of the weaving. Thread it on a needle and pull it through two or three rows of weaving to secure it.

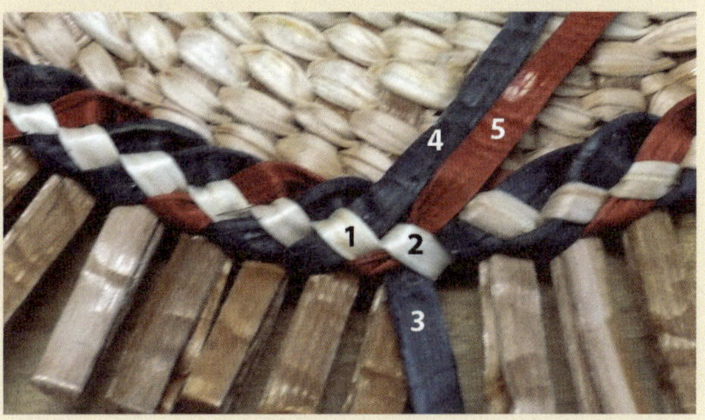

Step 16: Fold red weft (5) down. Using a needle, pull blue weft (4) down between the first two weavings and then to the back. Thread it through two or three rows of weaving on back of the weaving to secure the blue weft (4).

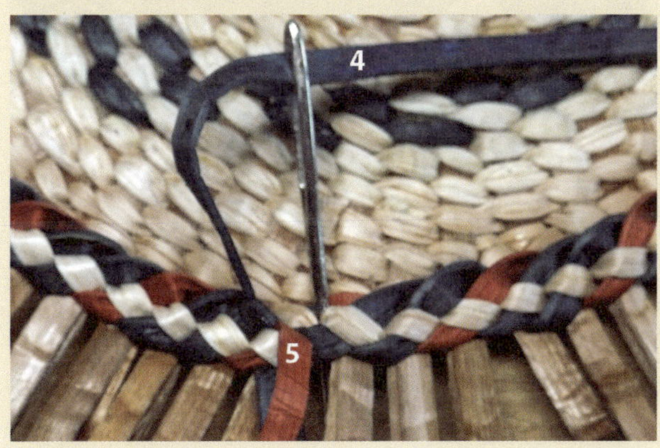

Continues on next page

Step 17: Fold red weft (5) back up over the weaving.

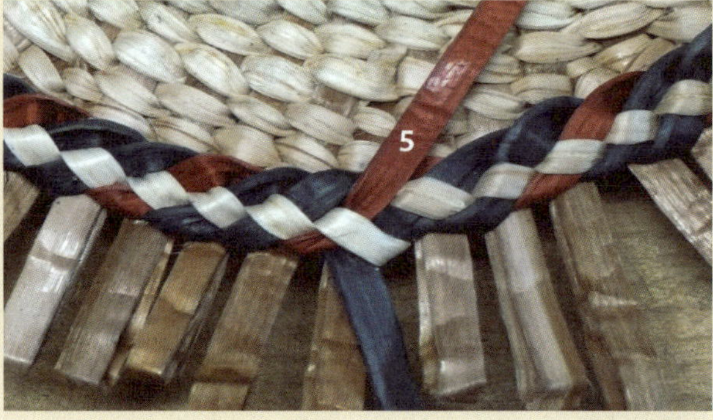

Step 18: Thread red weft (5) on a needle and pull it down so it is between the first two warps of the start. Then on the back, pull the red up through two or three rows of weaving to secure it.

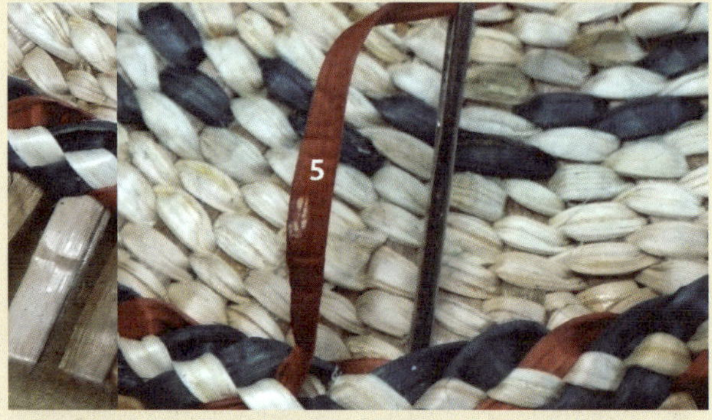

Step 19: Thread the last blue weft (3) under the first weave of white weft (1), so it lays on top of the blue weaver (4).

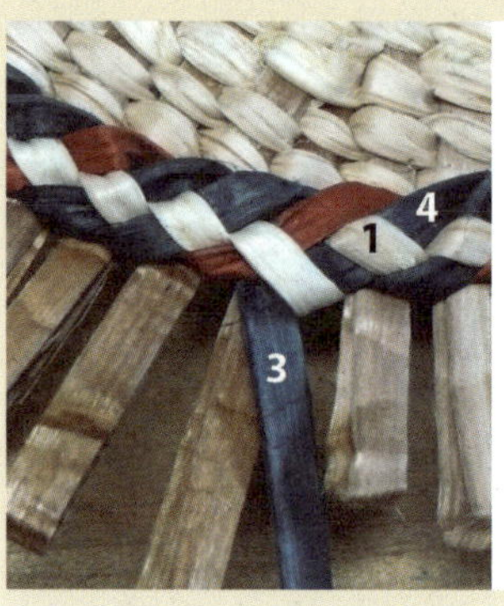

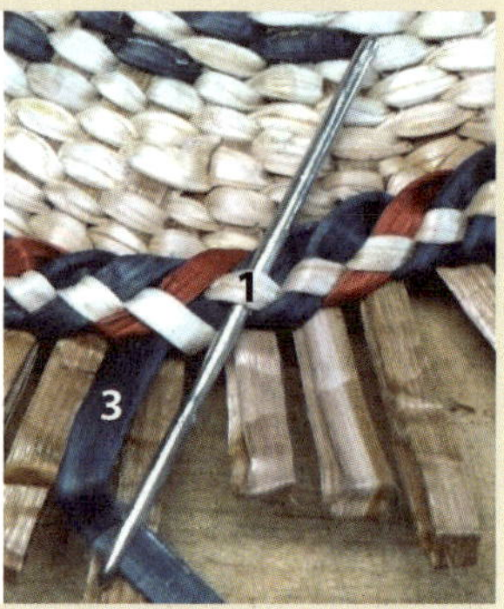

Step 20: Using a needle, pull blue weft (3) over the top of blue weft (4), to the back of the weaving. Then on the back pull the blue up through two or three rows of weaving to secure it.

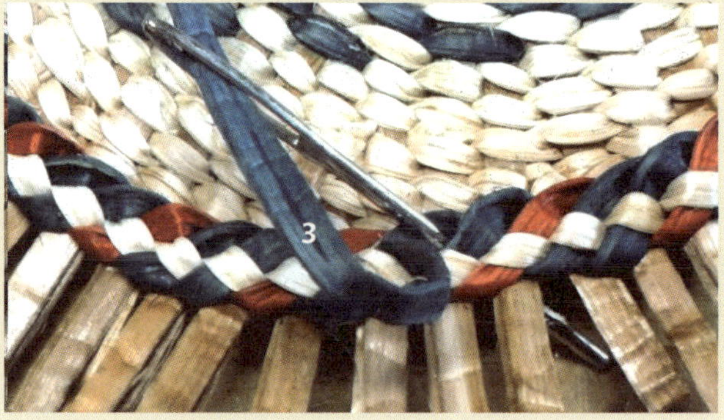

Five-Weft Vertical Twining Ending With Warps to Outside

Step 1: Place a red weft on top of warp (1). Tie a knot on the end of what will be this single weft, then place it behind the weaving and to the front slightly to the right of warp (1) and up. Place a long blue weft (1) on top of the red. Bring weft (b) up and to the left. Next move weft (a) over warp (1) and the blue weft, below the red weft and under warp (2). The coloured wefts will not go under the warps in this ending.

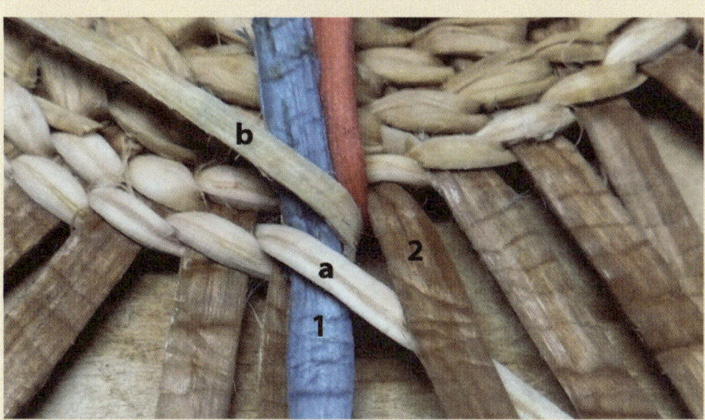

Step 2: Bring the top blue weft in front of the red weft and down. Bring the bottom blue weft up over the top blue weft, making an X.

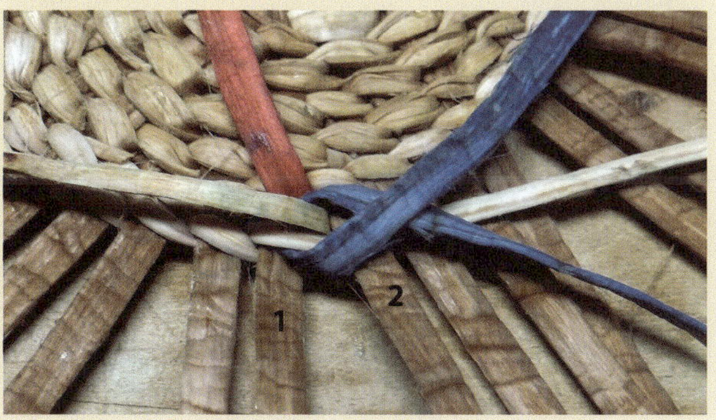

Step 3: Bring weft (a) up and back to the left, then weave (b) over the blue X and under warp (3). Fold warp (2) up and over warp 3 and weft (b).

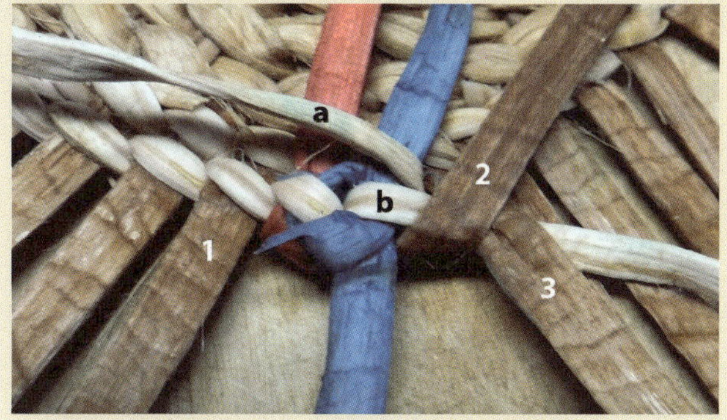

Step 4: Next bring the red weft down over warps (2) and (3) and weft (b). Then bring the blue weft up over the red weft, making an X.

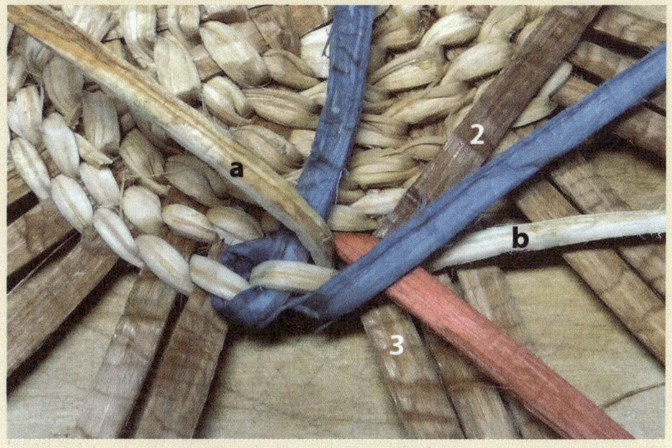

Continues on next page

Step 5: Bring weft (b) back to the left above the two blue wefts. Weave weft (a) over the red and blue X and under warp (4). Bring warp (3) up and over warp (4) and weft (a).

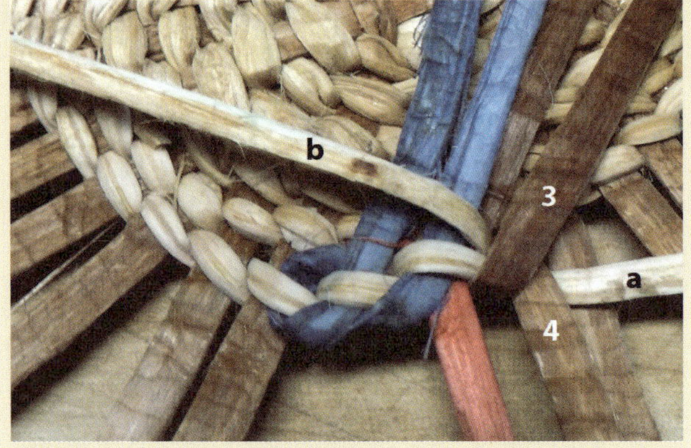

Step 6: Next bring the top left blue weft behind the right blue weft, then down and over the folded warps (2) and (3) and warp (4) with weft (a) underneath. Bring the red weft up, making a blue and red X. Then continue as before, weaving over the red and blue X and under warp (5).

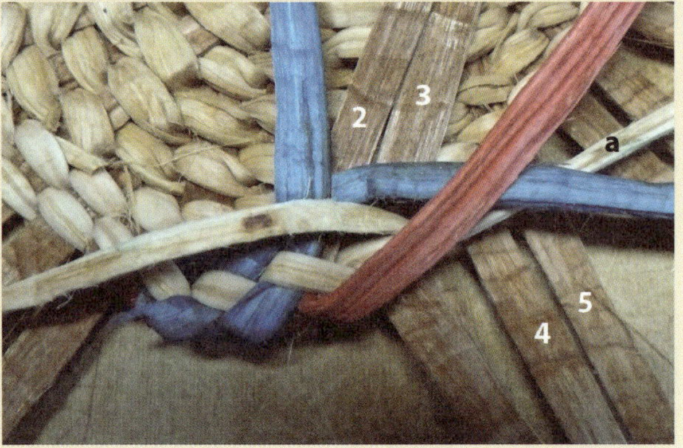

Step 7: Continue around to the start of the ending.

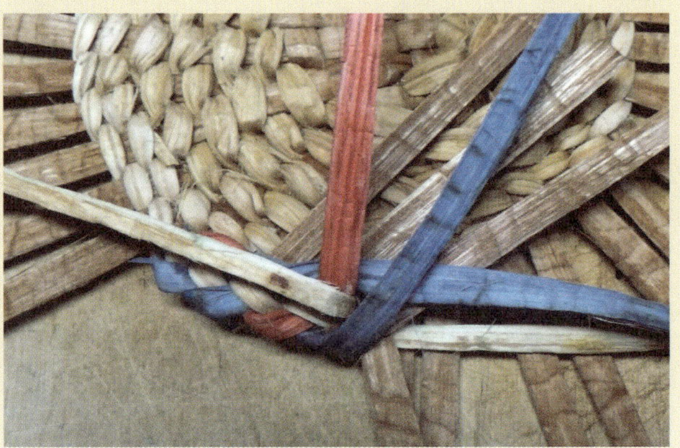

Five-Weft Vertical Twining Ending With Warps to Inside

Step 1: Place a red weft (coloured to make it easier to see on these instructions) on top of warp (1). Tie a knot on the end of what will be this single weft, then place it behind the weaving and to the front, slightly to the right of the first warp and up. Place a long blue weft over the first warp (see photo of FIVE-WEFT VERTICAL ENDING WITH FOLDED WARPS TO INSIDE on page 222). Weave over the first warp and blue weft, below the red weft and under the warp (2), with the red weft left up.

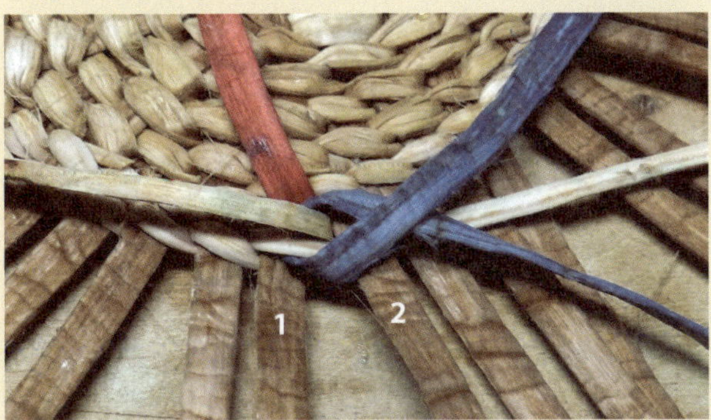

Step 2: Bring the top blue weft in front of the red weft and down. Bring the bottom blue weft up over the top blue weft, making an X.

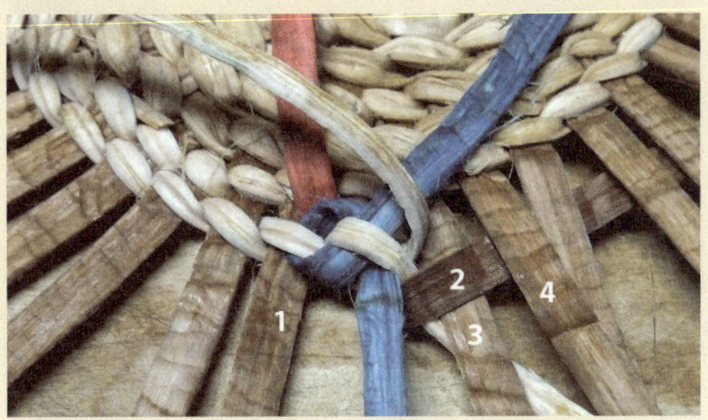

Step 3: Weave over the blue X, under warp (3), leaving the weaver down halfway. Bring warp (2) under the blue weft, over warp (3) and under all the warps to the right.

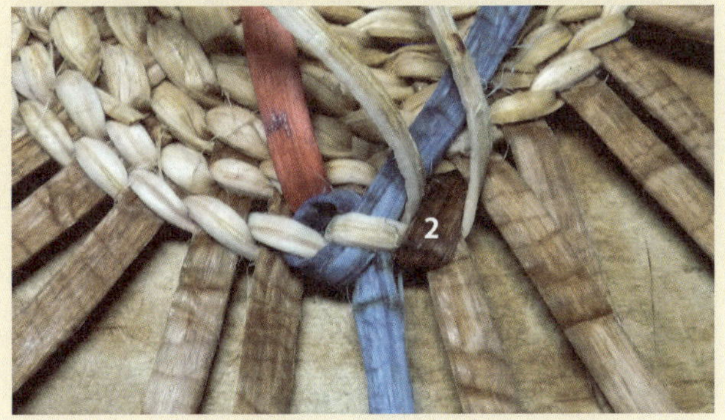

Continues on next page

Step 4: Using the right-most weft and your hand, pull warp (2) up snug against the weaving.

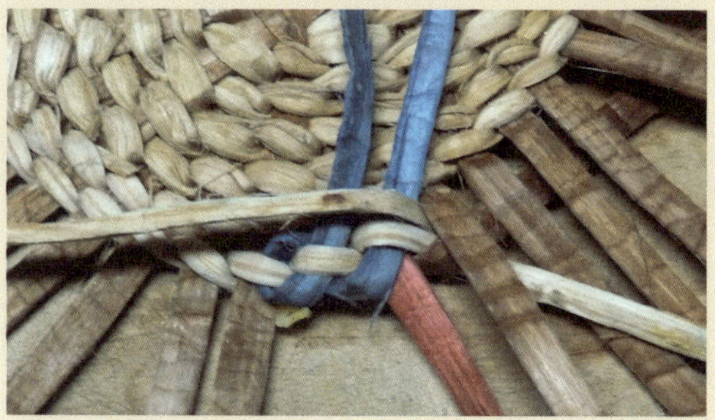

Step 5: Bring the red weft under the blue, then weave over the X.

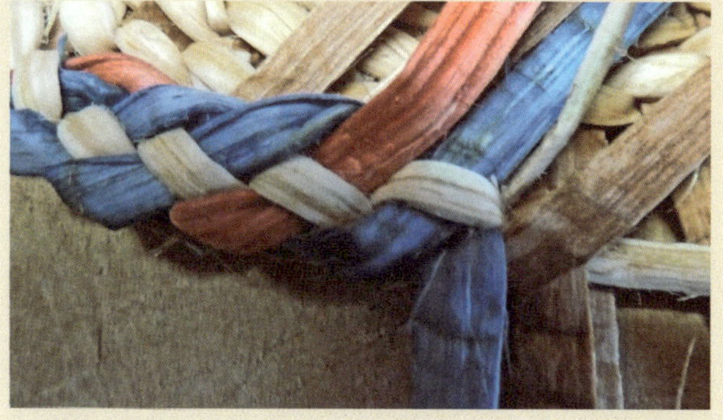

Step 6: Continue to the start of the ending.

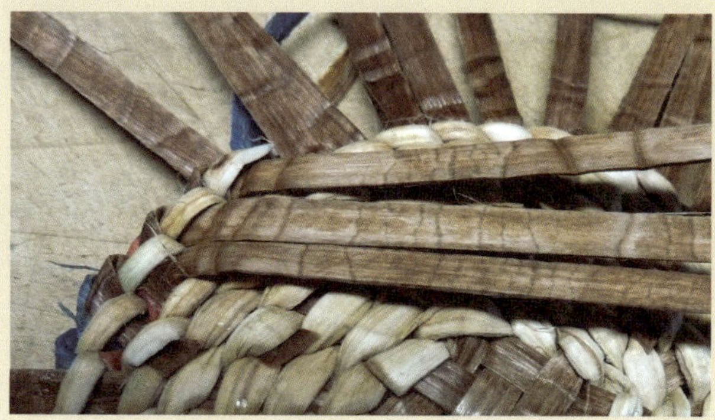

Six-Weft Ending to the Inside

Turn the weaving so that you are working on the top side.

Step 1: Place the blue vertical weft (a/b) on top of warp (1) and the red weft (c/d) on top of warp (2). Weave with weft (1) and (2) over warp (1) and the blue weft. Then weave over warp (2) with the red weft. Bring weft (2) under warp (3) and out to the right, and weft (1) up and to the left above the top red and blue wefts.

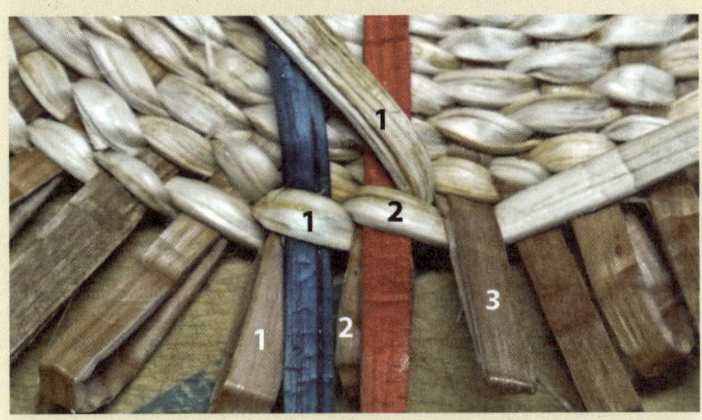

Step 2: Move the top blue vertical weft (a) to the right, under the red vertical weft and weft (1). Move the bottom vertical weft (b) under the red vertical weft and to the right above the warps.

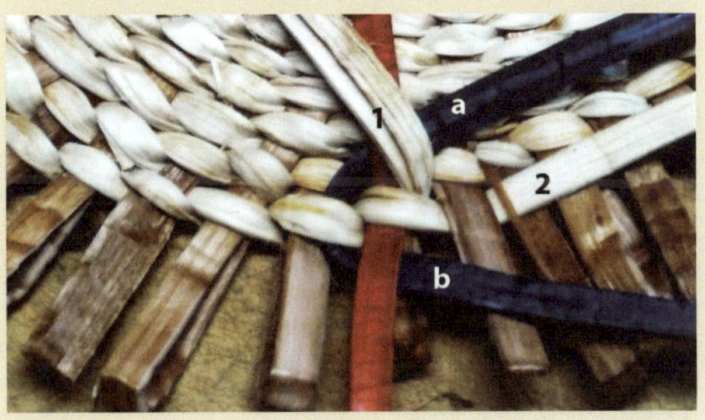

Step 3: Bring top blue (a) to the right under the top red and weft (1), then down. Move the bottom blue weft (b) under the lower red and up, making an X over weft (2).

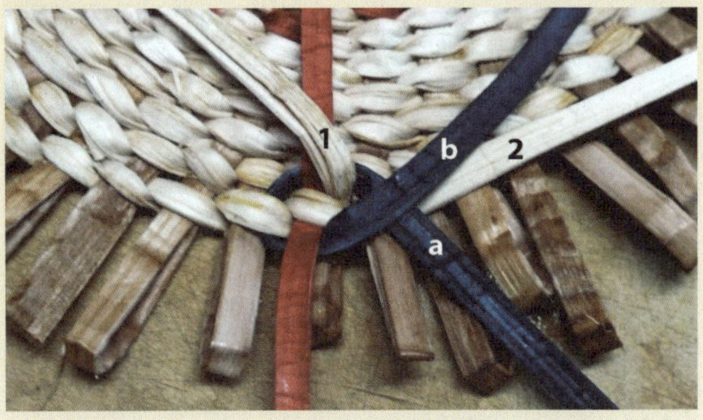

Step 4: Weave over the blue X with weft (1) and under warp (4) to the right. Bring weft (2) up and to the left.

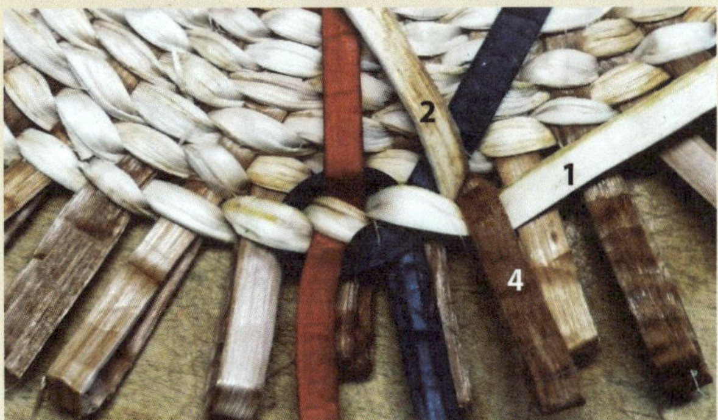

Continues on next page

Step 5: Move red (c) under blue (b) and weft (2). Move red (d) under blue (a) and to the right above the warps.

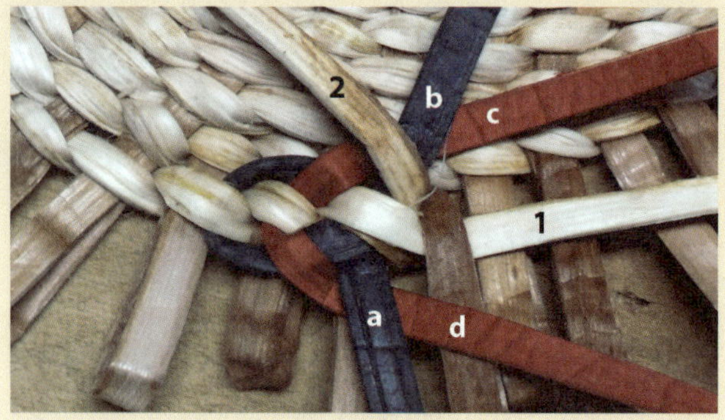

Step 6: Bring red (c) down over weft (1), then move red (d) over red (c) and up, making an X.

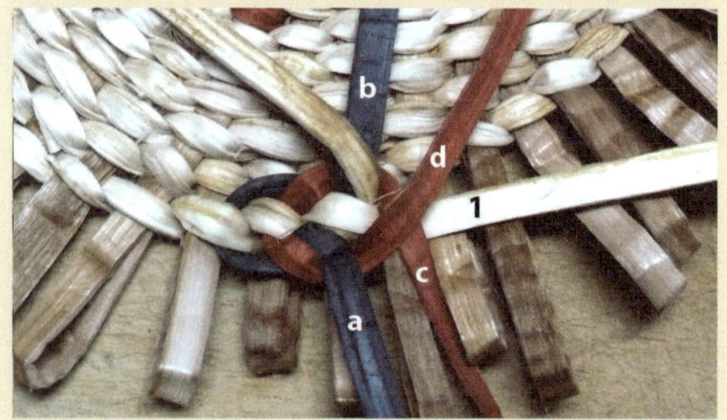

Step 7: Weave over the red X with weft (2) and under the next warp. Bring weft (1) up and back. Continue until you reach the start of the ending.

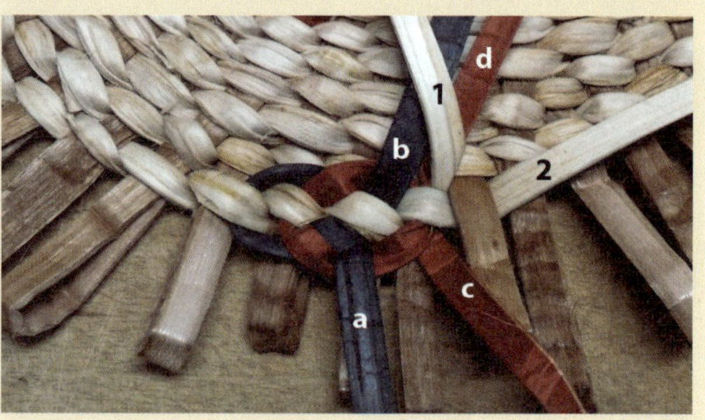

Step 8: To finish the ending, after weaving the last warp, leave weft (1) in the back and use a big needle to thread it through a few rows of weaving and trim.

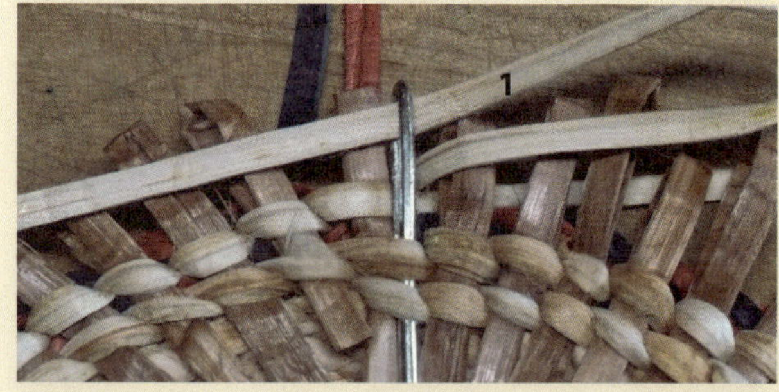

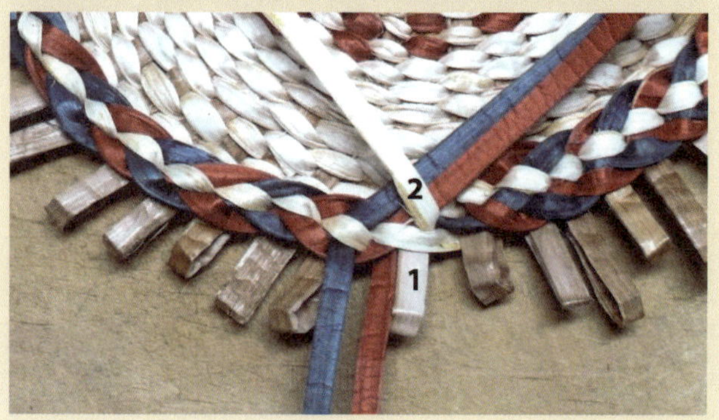

Step 9: Take weft (2) and bring it to the back, and use a big needle to thread it through a few rows of weaving and trim.

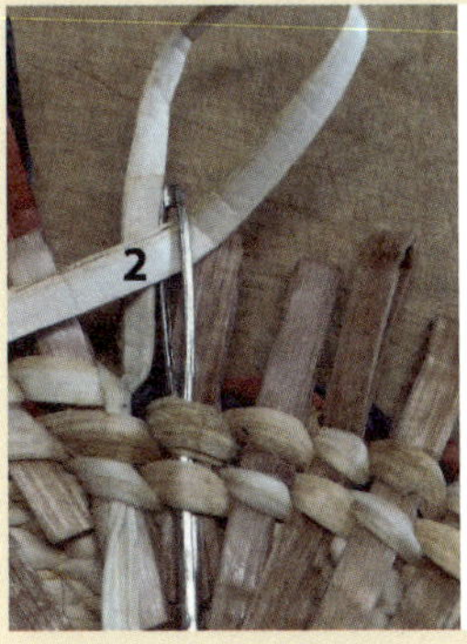

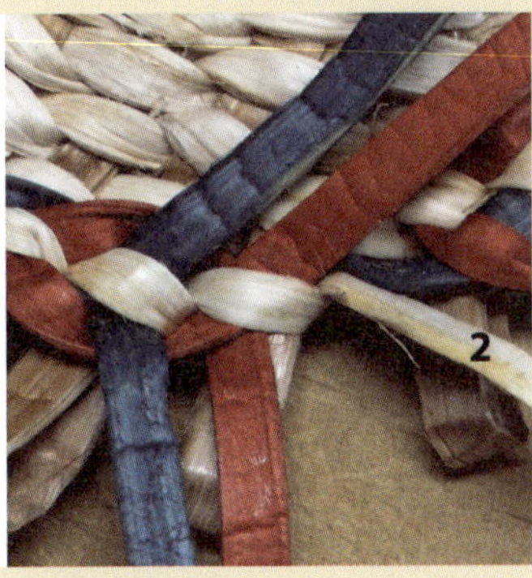

Step 10: Move blue weft (a) under red weft (c) and to the right. Then move blue (b) under red (d) and to the right.

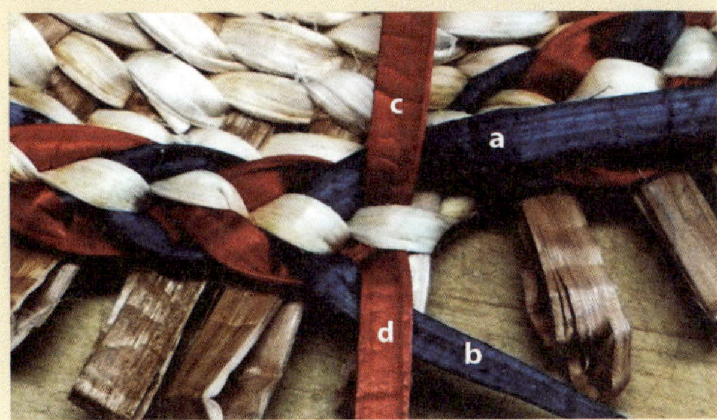

Step 11: Thread blue weft (b) on large needle, bring to the back, and thread through a few rows of weaving and trim.

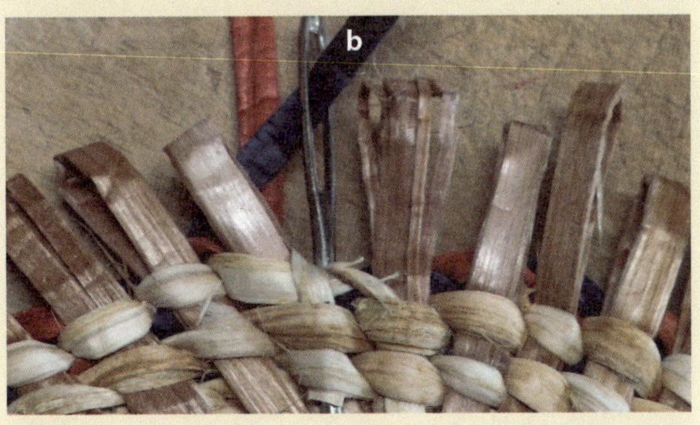

Step 12: Take blue weft (a), bring around to back and thread through a few rows of weaving and trim.

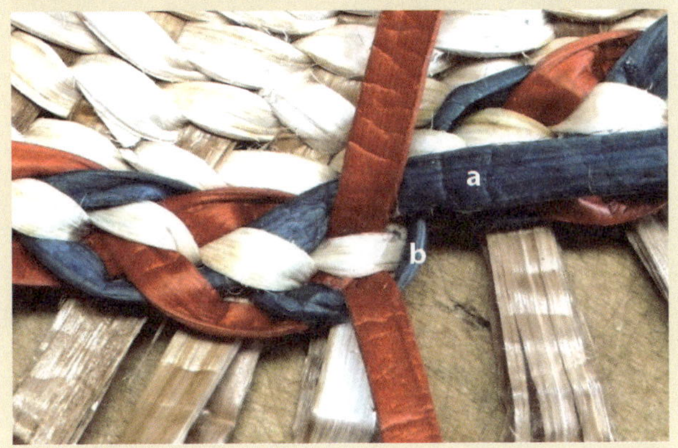

Continues on next page

Step 13: Using the large needle, thread red weft (c) through the weaving at the base of the first blue weave made at the beginning, so it looks like a continuous weave, and pull through to the back. Thread through a few rows of weaving and trim.

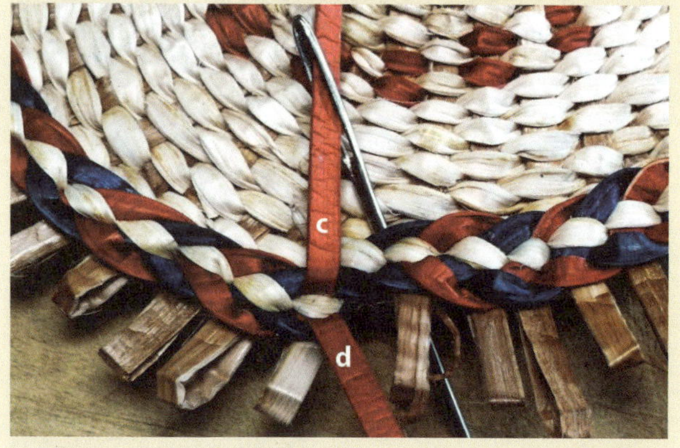

Step 14: Do the same thing with red weft (d) on the opposite side of weaving, so it looks like the weaving continues. Once the red is in the back, thread through a few rows of weaving and trim.

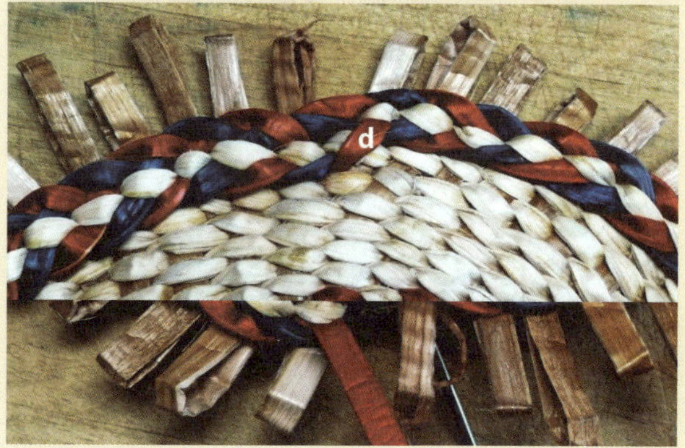

Haida Hat Top Plaited Square Beginning to Round

Step 1: Weave a temporary row with wefts along one side to hold the plaited warps in place while starting the permanent weaving.

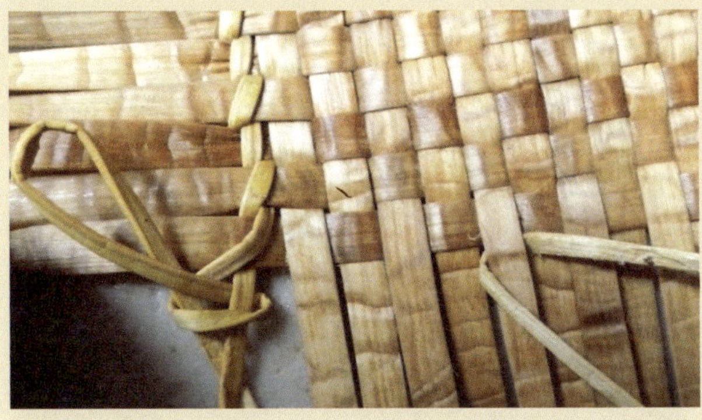

Step 2: Fold in half a long yellow cedar weft (a/b) and place it under the fifth warp on one side, then weave along snugly next to the warps.

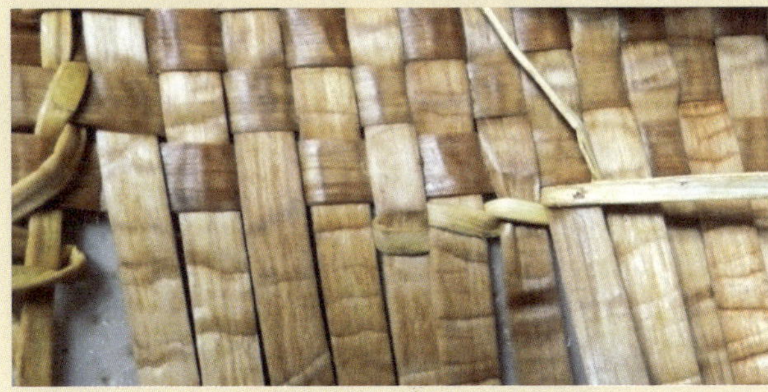

Step 3: To begin turning the corner, weave weft (a) under warp (4) and (1a) and then pull up.

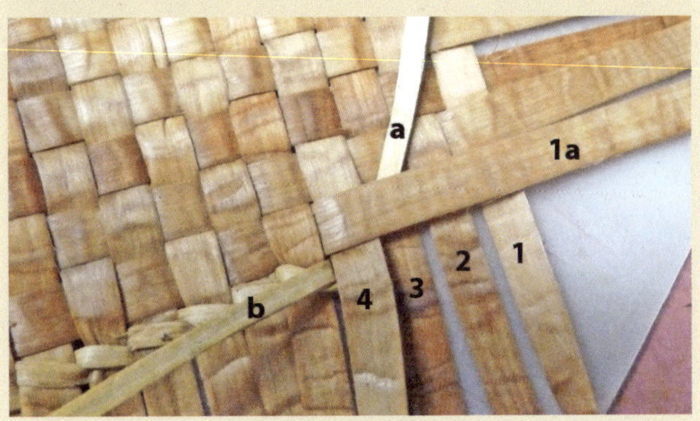

Step 4: Weave weft (b) over warps (4) and (1a), then under warp (2a) and (3) and pull up.

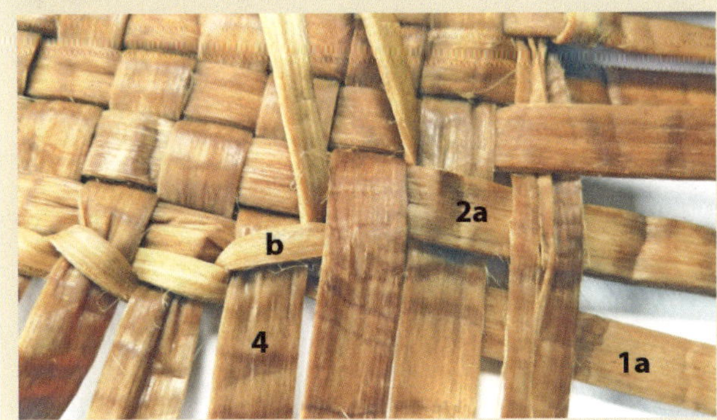

Continues on next page

Step 5: Weave weft (a) over warps (3) and (2a) and under warps (3a) and (2) and up.

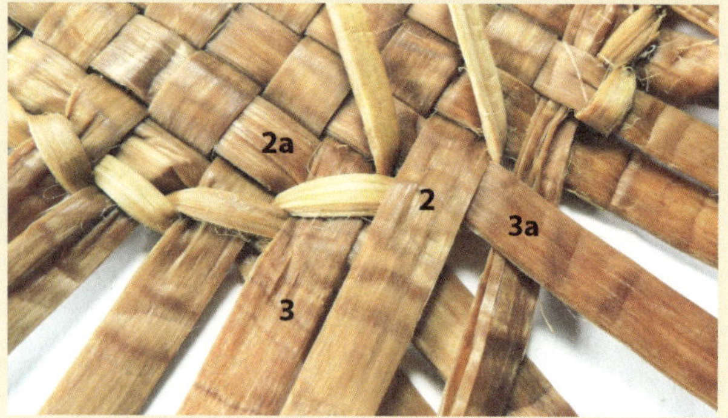

Step 6: Weave weft (b) over warps (2) and (3a) and under warps (4a) and (1) and up.

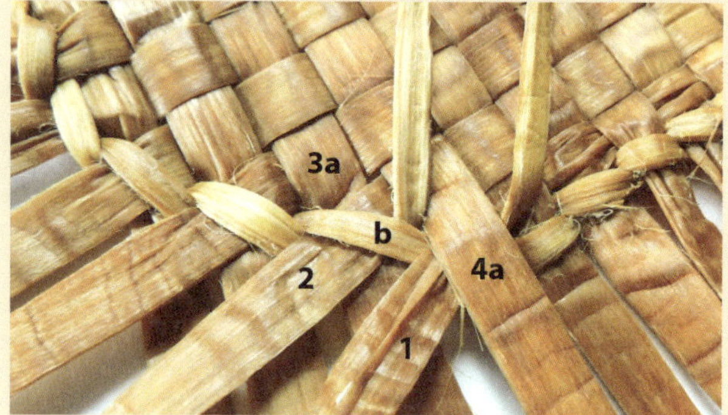

Step 7: Repeat this process at the remaining three corners until you reach the starting point.

Add a third warp to tighten the hat top circle and create a turning row.

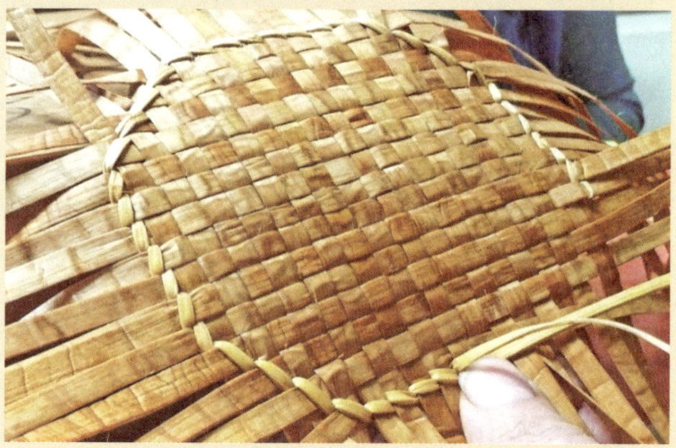

Step 8: Insert a third weft (c) under warp (3). Leave a 2- or 3-inch end sticking out to the right.

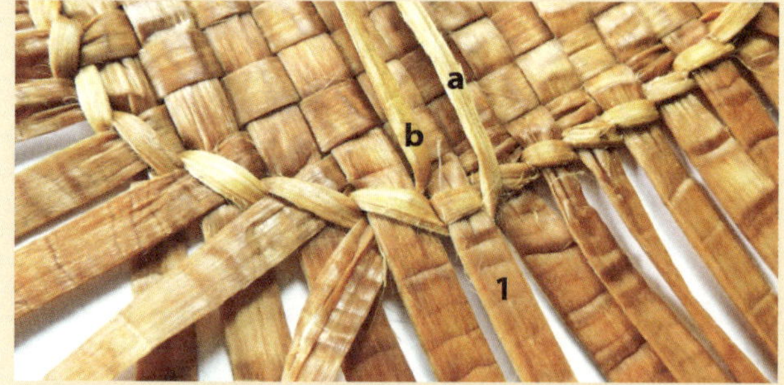

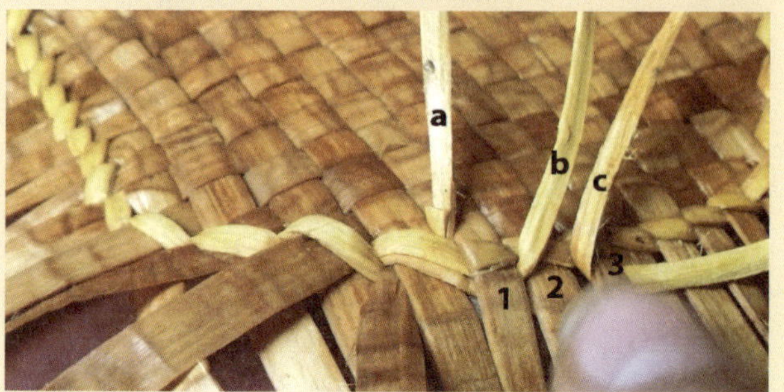

Step 9: Weave weft (a) below wefts (b) and (c) and over warps (1) and 2), then under warp (3). Warp (3) has the short-ended weft under it. The short end can be dropped to the inside after weaving over two more warps. Continue by weaving weft (b) below wefts (c) and (a), over warps (2) and (3), under warp (4), and up.

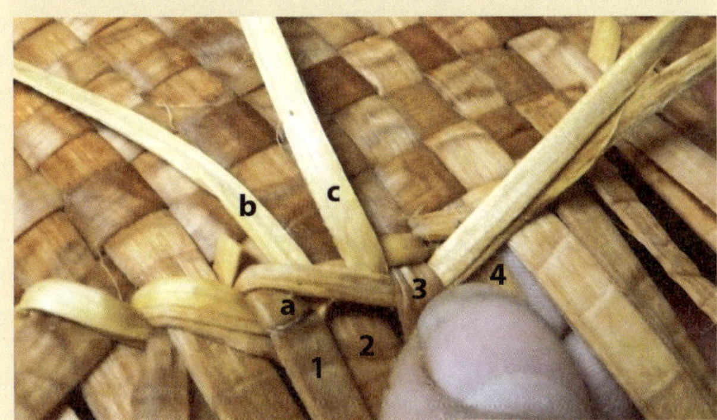

Step 10: Weave the three warps around the circle, separating one of the doubled woven warps in each corner.

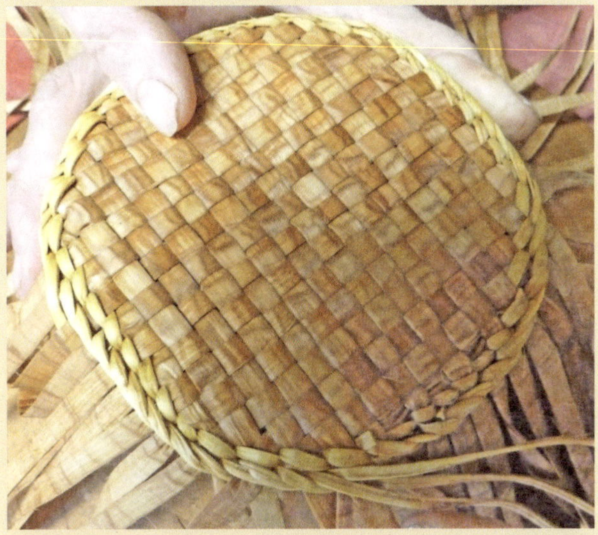

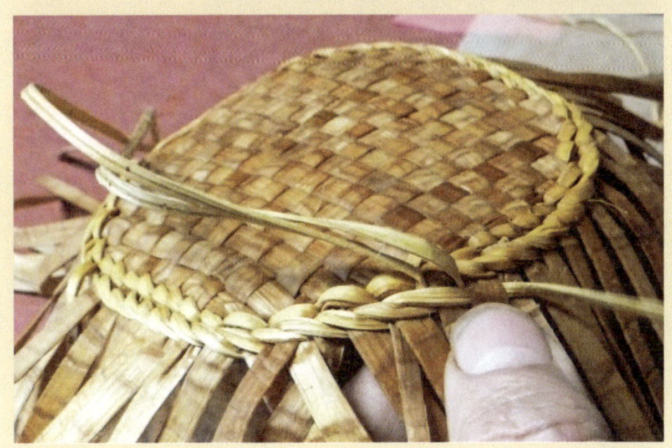

Continues on next page

Step 11: Use your hands to tighten the three wefts as you weave.

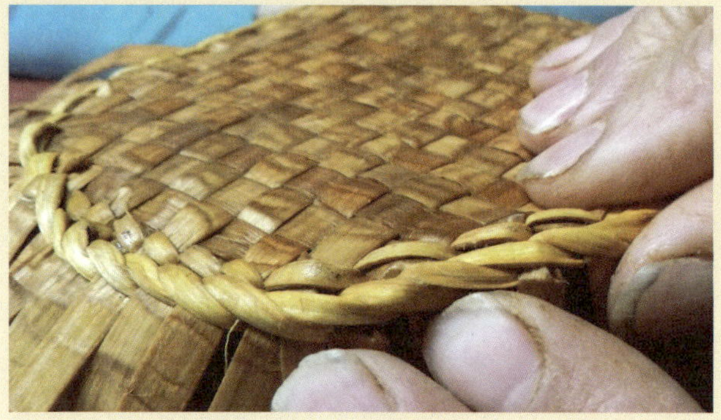

Step 12: Complete the three-weft weaving row, then pull weft (3) to the centre. Continue regular weaving with the remaining two wefts.

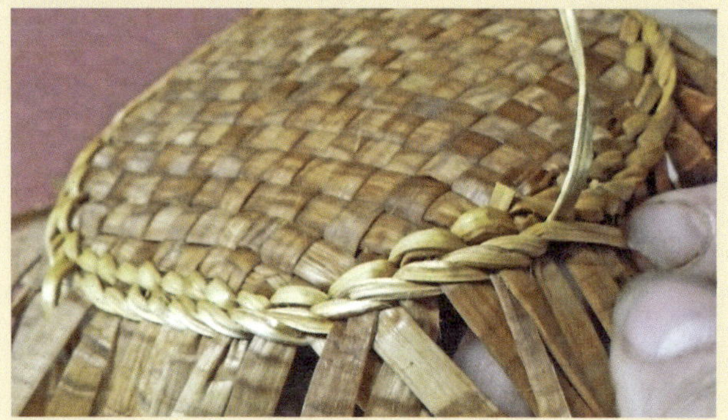

Step 13: Choose one of the endings to finish the hat brim. This picture shows a typical Haida hat.

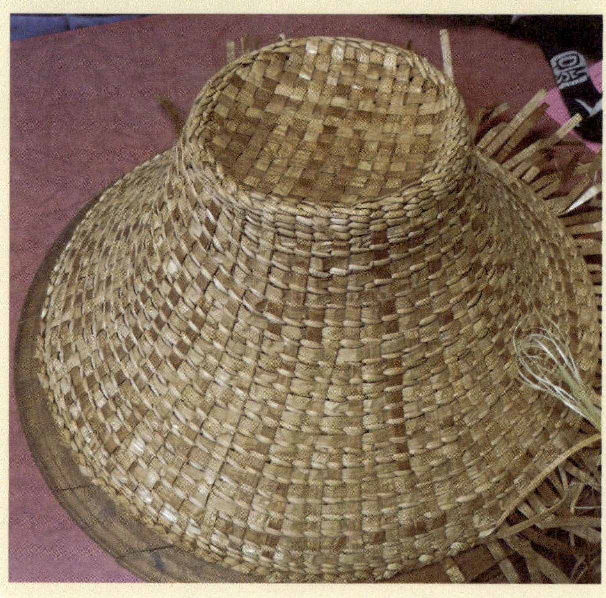

Full Circle

Quality weaving requires carefully prepared material and executed technique that follows the rule of balance and tension. But more importantly, understanding the context of the weaving pieces and developing relationships with land, sea and all things that live, is the breath that brings the weavings to life.

This book is intended to contribute to the greater understanding about weaving and to assist the Haida weaving instructors and their students. The techniques in Haida weaving are also used by other cultures. It is the way that these techniques are applied and the weaving materials used that make Haida weavings unique to the world.

The Haida have come from square to circle while keeping our culture alive through times of rapid change and great loss. As our young people acquire greater cultural knowledge and skills, it is more important than ever that our intellectual properties are protected. Those that have knowledge of these matters can help with this protection. Collectors and galleries can make certain that they purchase and sell authentic work from Indigenous artisans and encourage others to direct their artistic talents to the creation of other types of art and weaving.

Weavers are encouraged to enjoy creating weavings for personal use but please leave sales of Indigenous weaving styles to the weavers from those cultures. Instead of replicating Indigenous art and weavings, make use of unexpected materials and combinations of design and technique to creating new works of art. Jan Hopkins, an acclaimed weaver, expands the use of unexpected materials to create beautiful weavings from materials such as seaweed and fruit peelings.

Exploring the weaving traditions of personal origin will reveal the richness of that culture. Weaving belongs to all of us. Each of our cultures of origin includes the weaving arts. It is the strand that binds us together as Earth's family and connects us to the land, the past and the future. I am fortunate to be one of many throughout the world who have had this art form teach and guide me through my life.

APPENDIX

Selected Reading

The Spirit Wraps Around You; Northern Northwest Native Textiles, by Steve Henrikson, Lani Hotch, Marie Oldfield and Evelyn Vanderhoop. Alaska State Museum, 2021.

Weaving Stories of Art, pp. 217–220, Delores Churchill, Edited by Lynda Jessup and Shannon Bagg, Canadian Museum of Civilization, 2002.

Mythic Beings: Spirit Art of the Northwest Coast by Gary Wyatt.

Delores Churchill, Weaver, Basketmaker, *The Southeaster,* 1991, Vol. I, No. I.

Collector's Eye, Southwest Art, November 1990.

Siberia to Alaska, Crossroads of the Continents (exhibit catalog), Smithsonian Institution, 1989.

A Treasured Heritage, Institute of Alaska Native Arts and University of Alaska-Fairbanks Museum.

Curriculum Guide, *Women in Alaska History,* January 1988.

Master Basketworks, University of Alaska Magazine, January 1986.

Basketry, Alaska Native Arts and Crafts, Alaska Geographic, 1985 Vol. 12, No. 3.

Interwoven Expressions, Institute of Alaska Native Arts and UAF Museum, 1985.

Interview: Selina Peratrovich and Delores Churchill. The Newsletter of Alaska Native Arts, Institute of Alaska Native Arts, 1983.

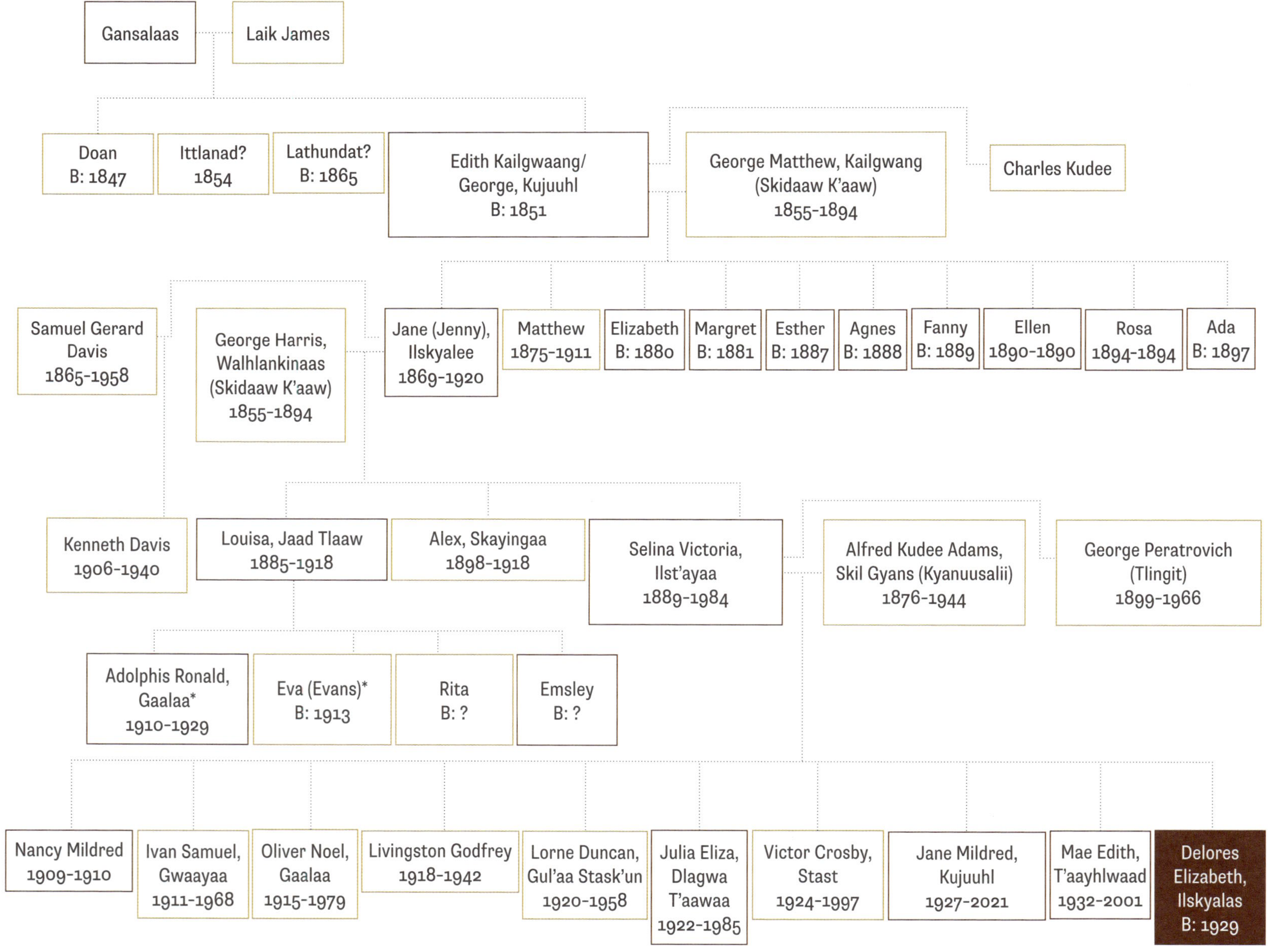

*Legally adopted by Selina Ilst'ayaa when Louisa died.

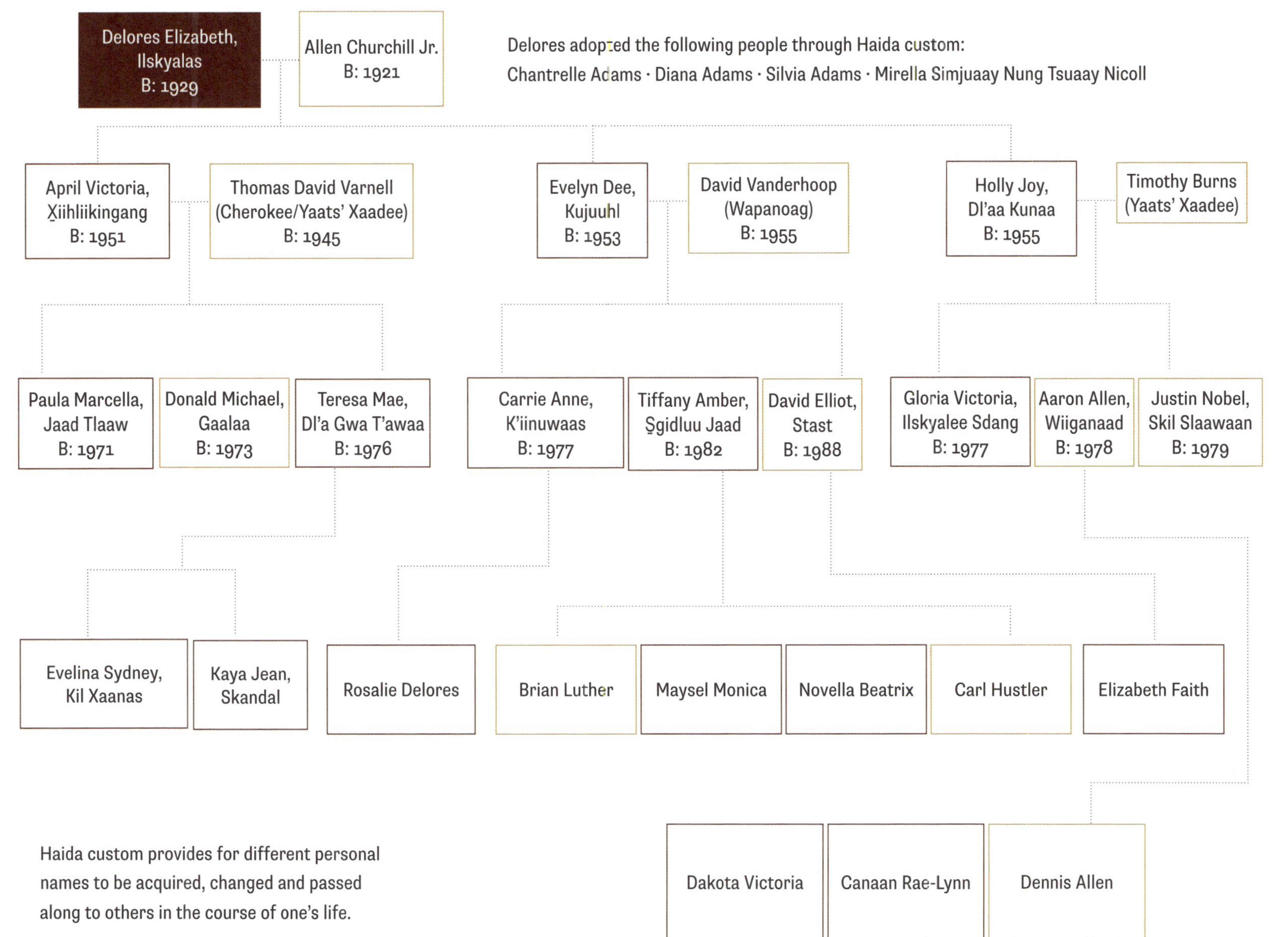
Delores Elizabeth, Ilskyalas B: 1929
Allen Churchill Jr. B: 1921
Delores adopted the following people through Haida custom:
Chantrelle Adams · Diana Adams · Silvia Adams · Mirella Simjuaay Nung Tsuaay Nicoll
April Victoria, X̱iihliikingang B: 1951
Thomas David Varnell (Cherokee/Yaats' Xaadee) B: 1945
Evelyn Dee, Kujuuhl B: 1953
David Vanderhoop (Wapanoag) B: 1955
Holly Joy, Dl'aa Kunaa B: 1955
Timothy Burns (Yaats' Xaadee)
Paula Marcella, Jaad Tlaaw B: 1971
Donald Michael, Gaalaa B: 1973
Teresa Mae, Dl'a Gwa T'awaa B: 1976
Carrie Anne, K'iinuwaas B: 1977
Tiffany Amber, S̱gidluu Jaad B: 1982
David Elliot, Stast B: 1988
Gloria Victoria, Ilskyalee Sdang B: 1977
Aaron Allen, Wiiganaad B: 1978
Justin Nobel, Skil Slaawaan B: 1979
Evelina Sydney, Kil Xaanas
Kaya Jean, Skandal
Rosalie Delores
Brian Luther
Maysel Monica
Novella Beatrix
Carl Hustler
Elizabeth Faith
Dakota Victoria
Canaan Rae-Lynn
Dennis Allen
Haida custom provides for different personal names to be acquired, changed and passed along to others in the course of one's life.